CECIL COUNTY PUBLIC LIBRARY
ELKTON, MARYLAND 21921

Muffled Drums and Mustard Spoons

Cecil County, Maryland 1860–1865

Jerre Garrett

 Burd Street Press

Copyright 1996 Jerre Garrett

ALL RIGHTS RESERVED - No part of this book may be reproduced in any form without permission in writing from the publisher, except by a reviewer who wishes to quote brief passages in connection with a review.

This Burd Street Press publication
was printed by
Beidel Printing House, Inc.
63 West Burd Street
Shippensburg, PA 17257 USA

In respect for the scholarship contained herein, the acid-free paper used in this book meets the guidelines for permanence and durability of the Committee on Production Guidelines for Book Longevity of the Council on Library Resources.

For a complete list of available publications
please write:
Burd Street Press
Division of White Mane Publishing Company, Inc.
P.O. Box 152
Shippensburg, PA 17257 USA

Library of Congress Cataloging-in-Publication Data

Garrett, Jerre.
    Muffled drums and mustard spoons : Cecil County, Maryland, 1860–1865 / Jerre Garrett.
       p.   cm.
    Includes bibliographical references and index.
    ISBN 1-57249-043-8 (acid-free paper)
    1. Cecil County (Md.)—History. 2. Maryland—History—Civil War, 1861–1865. 3. Cecil County (Md.)—Biography. 4. Soldiers--Maryland—Cecil County—Registers. I. Title.
F187.C3G37   1997   96-42018
975.2'38—dc20   CIP

PRINTED IN THE UNITED STATES OF AMERICA

With love to my children
Geraldine Mary Garrett Pierce
Monique Marie
Shivaun Maureen
Richard Taylor
John Francis
Patrick Seamus
and
Michael Kevin Garrett

In gratitude to my mother
Helen C. Taylor

In memory of my father
Richard T. Taylor

In appreciation of friends
in Cecil County

Contents

Foreword VII

Chapter 1
    Cecil County Late 1850s–1860 1

Chapter 2
    Cecil County 1861 28

Chapter 3
    Cecil County 1862 86

Chapter 4
    Cecil County 1863 166

Chapter 5
    Cecil County 1864 212

Chapter 6
    Cecil County 1865 250

Appendix A
    Letters
        Ben and Lottie Ricketts 280
        Miscellaneous 293

Appendix B
    Cecil Confederates 299

Appendix C
    Military and Pension Records of
    other Cecil County Soldiers 306

Appendix D
    "Cheap" John Rowbotham 325

Bibliography 329

Index 330

Foreword

George Johnston wrote a history of Cecil County, but oddly, or not so oddly, he skipped over the Civil War as though it never happened. Evidently, the memories were still too painful to deal with even at the end of the 19th century. Members of the Historical Society of Cecil County, therefore, suggested that I fill in the gaps of county history. Local history was never a particularly strong suit of mine, but I liked the people in the Society and had enjoyed many happy hours in their facility on Main Street in Elkton. Knowing full well that each person in there had forgotten more history than I'll ever know, I began the project by looking over the Civil War files.

A few names came to the fore immediately: the Ricketts—Ben, Lottie and Palmer—the Torberts, and Ewings, among others. Then, in the course of working on unrelated assignments, I heard from his family the exploits of blockade runner, Gustavus Henderson. Finally, I read the pages of the *Cecil Whig* and *Cecil Democrat* and added other names to the list. "Cheap John" Rowbotham, Big Elk, Dr. Charles Manley Ellis, William and Sophia Jeffries, and Stephen Cameron.

Despite the intervening years, one can easily identify with Lottie Ricketts as she wrote from her log cabin in Drummondtown, Virginia, to ask those at home to send her one touch of the elegance she was used to: her mustard spoon. Then there was the account of the graveside services for Private Andrew McGuire. Muffled drums sounded in Elkton, but few recognized their import.

It's well nigh impossible to read the 19th-century weeklies without elbowing the unfortunate person in the next chair and directing his or her attention to an intriguing ad or a revealing article. Imagine that you are sitting in an otherwise comfortable place, reading a book of your choice while a Civil War nut—for in short order that is what I became—is persistently tapping your arm and urging you to read the latest find.

That's what this book is: a collection of all the things that grabbed my attention as I read the papers and searched the files. The difference is that here you may read in peace without my jabbing and poking you at ever whipstitch. For that you should be profoundly grateful.

JTG

1

Cecil County

Late 1850s–1860

Beginning at its western extremity, Cecil County's northern boundary shoots in a straight line along Pennsylvania's southern edge for about 20 miles due east before it makes a 90-degree turn south. Skirting Delaware's western limits for roughly another 30 miles, it reaches the east-to-west course of the Sassafras, which separates Cecil from Kent County, Maryland. The Sassafras empties into the Chesapeake Bay at Grove Point. From here to the arbitrary northwest starting point, Cecil is bounded by water—the Bohemia, Elk and North East Rivers carving deep indentations, the mighty Susquehanna rolling majestically to the Bay.

In 1858, when Simon Martenet completed a map of the county, there were nine districts, each named for the principal town within its limits: Cecilton, No. 1; Chesapeake City, No. 2; Elkton, No. 3; Fair Hill, No. 4; North East, No. 5; Rising Sun, No. 6; Port Deposit, No. 7; Mt. Pleasant, No. 8; Brick Meeting House, No. 9.

The Philadelphia, Wilmington and Baltimore Railroad crossed Cecil, connecting Elkton, North East, Charlestown and Perryville with points beyond. Another railroad, the Philadelphia and Baltimore Central, reached Oxford, Pennsylvania, via Chadds Ford, Kennett Square, and Avondale in 1860. But it did not advance to Rising Sun until 1865.

The population of Cecil County in 1860 was 23,862 (19,994 white; 2,918 free blacks; and 950 slaves). 1,528 people occupied Elkton, the county seat. Not a single Civil War battle was fought on Cecil soil, but from the 352 square miles on Maryland's northeasternmost edge came 1,500 men who served in the Union forces. Twelve of them were surgeons. Others, whose numbers are difficult to estimate, joined the Confederacy. Whatever their political persuasion or occupation, they left behind anxious relatives who simultaneously clamored for news and dreaded its arrival.

At the end of the 1850s, a letter in the *Philadelphia Bulletin* painted a picture of Elkton, which, while not flattering, was certainly intriguing.

> For one characteristic, however, it [Elkton] is remarkable. It is a spasmodic town—a little place in which everything is done by fits and starts. Sometimes a great religious or temperance revival springs up. Then it dies out and is followed by a season of hard swearing or whiskey drinking. Sometimes balls, parties, and all manner of gaiety and dissipation are the rage. Then comes a stagnation—a perfect dead calm in the social world. Sometimes we get up a fair for the benefit of the church, and at other times a fight for the benefit of the fire company. In a word, the Elktonions are always on the alert for some new excitement, and if the ghosts of all our defunct Lyceums, Temperance Societies, Fire Companies, and other "sensation" Associations that have lived through a brief but bright existence, were to come up from their unhonored grave, like Pharaoh's frogs, they would cover the land....

The paper overlooked a requirement in the Land Records Book. Since 1789, every parent was to give neighbors a "Punch Drinking" within one month of the birth of a child. It would seem then, that instead of being ridiculed for indulging in a season of whiskey drinking, Cecil Countians should have been lauded for observing the letter [and especially the spirit] of the law.

However fitfully Elkton roused from provincial dormancy through the 1850s, it changed irrevocably in the 1860s. Winds of change ushered in welcomed technological advances such as gaslights for the town. But at gale force they also rent families asunder as sons and fathers joined one side or the other of a bloody Civil War.

Residents got their news from the papers that arrived daily via the Philadelphia, Wilmington and Baltimore Railroad, whose route passed through town just a couple of blocks beyond Main Street. These papers received their information from the telegraph, which already linked major cities.

The Cecil Whig and *The Cecil Democrat*, both published weekly, kept Countians caught up on area events. Local papers summarized events on the battlefields, but this information was stale news, merely a recap of what readers had already gleaned from the dailies.

Elkton's 19th-century weeklies did not run the banner headlines that characterize later papers. The front page featured a poem or two, short stories, and articles of general interest. Excerpts from

---

ELKTON
MARBLE WORKS

THE subscriber has opened a MARBLE YARD in Elkton, and will keep on hand, and prepare to order, all kinds of work such as

Monuments, Head and Foot Stones, Tombs, Mantles, Table and Bureau Tops, Door Sills, Window Sills STEPS, &c., &c.

☞Cemetery Lots enclosed, and all kinds of IRON WORK done at the shortest notice.

☞Tomb Stones cleaned and re-lettered. Italian and American Marble constantly on hand. All to be sold at the lowest possible Prices. EDWARD CARR.

other papers were included. Although the camera was in use, photographs did not yet accompany the text. Articles ran in long columns and did not continue onto another page.

Local news appeared inside with the editorials. There was no strict demarcation between news and editorials, though. An editor, for example, did not hesitate to call the alleged perpetrator of a crime "a suspicious looking character."

Often, to the frustration of researchers, first names were omitted. A subject was designated simply as Mrs. Smith, Lieutenant Jones, or Mrs. Brown. Also, in obituaries, the deceased was identified as the son of *Mr.* White. The mother's name was given only occasionally.

Medical diagnoses as reported in the local press employed terminology somewhat less exact than the modern reader is used to. We read, for example, that people died of "softening of the brain."

The last two pages carried advertisements for just about everything: medicines, stores, schools, real estate, farm machinery, and ice boxes for corpses. These ads told a great deal about what products were available and what businesses were in operation in the county and beyond. The following "cards" appeared during the decade of the 1860s in the *Whig* and *Democrat*.

John D. Michener of West Nottingham advised farmers that he sold Wheeler, Melick and Company's patent single and double horsepower and combined thrasher and winnower. "Its capacity, under ordinary circumstances, has been from 125 to 175 bushels of wheat and from 200 to 300 bushels of oats per day. It works all other kinds of grain equally well, and also thrashes and cleans rice and timothy seed."

James Cantwell sold the "Buckeye Reaper Mower for 1864." Grove and Baker's ad for their New Shuttle Sewing Machine promised to ease the lot of homemakers everywhere, while the saponifier made by Salt Manufacturing Co. of Philadelphia changed kitchen grease into good soap.

Jacob B. Ash obtained a patent for a grubber, a device that he claimed was "unequalled by any other machine, as a stone-gatherer, gully filler, and road scraper. At prices from Twenty-five to Fifty Dollars."

In Elkton, Samuel King advertised his brick and draining tile yard; Edward Carr solicited patrons for his marble works, a firm that specialized in monuments, mantles, table and bureau tops, and door and window sills; and John V. Reardon offered new or used carriages.

**ELKTON
Brick and Draining Tile Yard.**

The subscriber having commenced, in connection with his

Old Established Brick Business,

the manufacture of

DRAINING TILE,

begs leave to call the attention of his former customers, (to whom he is thankful for past favors,) to the fact that he is prepared to furnish

BRICK AND TILE

AT THE LOWEST CASH PRICES, and respectfully solicits a continuance of public favor in his line of business.
All orders promptly attended to.
The subscriber will also attend to laying Tile in the best manner, where it may be desired: SAMUEL KING.

In his gallery in the *Cecil Democrat* building, C. E. Cook took pictures on clear or cloudy days. He did ambrotypes, photographs, melaneotypes, and crayontypes. Down in the Hollow, Morris Cummings baked fresh crackers daily. He sold cakes, too, "with particular attention paid to cakes for parties."

There were plenty of accommodations for travelers. Visitors stayed on North Street at the Bull's Head, a hotel under the management of R. M. Walmsley, or at the Railroad Hotel on North and High Streets, whose proprietor was James R. Smith. Taylor's Hotel occupied a corner of Gay and Bow, while the Howard House, under the management of James E. Oldham, was located on Main and North Streets.

The *Democrat* editor recalled that there was once a fan manufactory in town. He saw no reason why a machine shop should not do very well now. It could be operated, he suggested, in conjunction with the foundry already in place.

Those who traveled to Philadelphia could purchase military clothing for officers of the Army and Navy at J. T. Wills, 52 Arch Street. The firm featured "cloths, Cassimers, beavers and superfine Kerseys."

Cheap John Rowbotham

Probably the most eye-catching ads were Cheap John's. He merited the notice of the *Delaware Republican* on Christmas morning, 1860, when he gave away a thousand loaves of bread to Wilmington's poor: "Men, women and children presented themselves and none were sent empty away. One old Colored man in receiving his loaf exclaimed: 'God bless you, massa!' 'He has done that already,' replied John, 'or I should not have been able to make you happy today.'" John's Elkton store was located in the Hollow. Some of his ads are printed in Appendix D.

On January 17, 1863, the *Whig* reported that a new firm was coming to Elkton in the grocery and dry goods business. Robert C. Levis and Thomas Merritt opened a store on Main Street now in possession of Mr. Rowbotham, alias Cheap John, who consolidated his Elkton and Wilmington stores in the latter city. The *Whig* predicted that the new enterprise would be successful if the firm continued to sell at Cheap John's reasonable prices.

The Pure Food and Drug Act of 1906 was a half-century in the future. Patent medicines crowded the market, each making exorbitant claims and few listing their ingredients truthfully.

For weeks the ad for D. Mott's Chalybeate Restorative Pills of Iron ran in the *Whig* under the Medicinal column. Note its wide range of application in the following:

An aperient [mild laxative] and Stomach preparation of IRON purified of Oxygen and Carbon by combustion in Hydrogen. Sanctioned by the highest Medical Authorities, both in Europe and the United States and prescribed in their practice.

The experience of thousands daily proves that no preparation of Iron can be compared with it. Impurities of the blood, depression of vital energy, pale and otherwise sickly complexions indicate its necessity in almost every conceivable case.

Innoxious in all maladies in which it has been tried. It has proved absolutely curative in each of the following complaints, viz:

In Debility, Nervous Affections, Emaciation, Dyspepsia, Constipation, Diarrhoea, Dysentery, Incipient Consumption, Scrofulous Tuberculosis, Salt Rheum, Mismenstruation, Whites, Chlorosis [greensickness, an iron-deficiency anemia chiefly affecting girls at puberty and characterized by greenish skin color], Liver Complaints, Chronic Headaches, Rheumatism, Intermittent Fevers, Pimples on the Face.

The Foutz Company distributed its Celebrated Horse and Cattle Powders, but Foutz's Mixture was somewhat more comprehensive in its application; it claimed to be "the best liniment for man or beast."

Shriner's Balsamic Cough Syrup ads appeared often. But if a person suffered from "putrid sore throat," the *Democrat* recommended that "good fresh yeast, taken internally, will give instant relief."

Another popular item was Duryea's Maizena, a forerunner of modern cake mixes. Sold in one-pound packages, it was used for cakes, custards, blanc mange, ice cream, and as a thickening agent, "with few or no eggs and without isinglass."

The ads extolled various brands of bitters, too. These preparations cured at least as many diseases as the Chalybeate pills, but they usually contained a high percentage of alcohol. That was the manufacturer's secret. Thus, people could claim to be teetotalers, while consuming prodigious amounts of alcohol under the guise of medication. Most did not know what they were drinking, but they invariably felt better for a time. So what if their condition deteriorated in an hour? They just took more medicine.

Those who were a little more up front about their imbibing, but who still needed a plausible reason for the habit, responded to the ad for Bininger's Old London Dock Gin, a "delicious tonic stimulant" and a "remedial agent." In fact, it was "especially designed for the use of the medical profession." D. S. Barnes and Company, 13 Park Row, New York, stated: "Our long experience

---

HARNESS! HARNESS!!

The undersigned, nearly opposite the Court House in Elkton, respectfully informs the public that he keeps constantly on hand, or is prepared on the shortest notice to furnish, HARNESS of all kinds; SADDLES at various prices to suit everybody; Carriage, Wagon and Riding BRIDLES; a large assortment of WHIPS at all prices; COLLARS of best make; Chamois Skins; Curry Combs; Sponges; Brushes; Mane Combs; Spurs; Halter Chains for cattle and horses; Whip Sockets; Girths, Surcingles, and in short every article usually found in a well regulated Harness Establishment.

☞ Particular attention is called to a large and cheap lot of HORSE COVERS to suit all tastes and pockets.

JOHN PERKINS, JR.

and familiarity with the requirements of DRUGGISTS, and our superior business facilities, enable us to furnish them with choice liquors for medicinal and family use."

Even these medications were not proof [no pun intended] against disasters to one's home and possessions. People worried—sporadically, of course—about fires. *After* big ones occurred, everybody wanted to start a fire company.

Usually when fire erupted, bucket brigades formed from the water source to the burning site. Sometimes men and boys passed the filled buckets toward the fire, while women and children returned the empties to the source. Everyone dreaded fires in winter, when creeks and cisterns could freeze solid. Not too many years before, Elkton Academy was destroyed in just such a blaze.

The old hydraulion, in use since 1827, was a hand pumper. Bucket brigades supplied it with water, and men operated hand pumps on either side to force a jet of water where it was needed. Occasionally, they took time to argue about who would direct the water [not a bad job] and who would man the pumper [an invitation to apoplexy].

The Vigilance Fire Company formed in 1859. At their March meeting, members elected the following: president, John Andrew Jackson Creswell; vice presidents, John B. Rowan and Palmer C. Strickland; secretary, James B. Grooms; treasurer, William H. Eder; chief engineer, Arthur W. Mitchell; 1st assistant, Adam Meisel; 2nd assistant, R. Morris Cummings; 3rd assistant, W. Francis A. Torbert. The board of directors included J. E. Brown, J. V. Reardon, Joseph Wells, T. H. Benton Hollingsworth, Andrew J. Smith, Willis Ruther, and John McCauley.

The next month Captain Ford brought a suction engine from Baltimore via his schooner *Iglehart*. The new engine, the *Arrow*, drew water from a stream or cistern. But could it outspray the faithful hydraulion? One day at the end of April, somebody decided to settle the question.

> The new "squirt" was rid up in gallant style on Monday last amid applause from the crowd and stentorian vociferation from the fire company. It looked very black in some places and very brassy in others and, again, the handles were dingy white. "Vigilant" was painted on it in two places and "John Rodgers" in one; which made most people think it was the "Vigilant John Rodgers" in one;— certainly a very appropriate name perpetuated by it. The company paraded it out and around town and afterward gave a specimen of its power at the Court House. The old engine was, however, too much for it, and after a thundering deal of cheering on both sides, loud talk, and talk about blows, this opinion seemed to prevail. Nevertheless the new engine is a regular suction which will drain water out of Elk Creek and throw it over any house in town. The members paid $450 for it. The

company is well organized and we all ought to rest satisfactory in our beds at night if we ain't.

But scarcely a month passed before the *Whig* complained when boys pulled the engines around town, filled them with water and deluged the Court House: "'Tother day they ran wild with the Vigilant, the new engine for which the citizens paid some $500—broke the tongue, bent the lever, and we shall probably soon hear of it being as disabled as to be useless in case of fire. There ought to be some better authority exercised in regard to this matter."

A fire company was not really functional until the formation of Singerly Fire Company in 1892. However, members of the Vigilance Company of 1860 could not be charged with indifference. Surely, their attention was almost totally absorbed by the calamitous events unfolding on the national scene. Many of their names figured prominently in Cecil County's role in the Civil War.

As if worrying about relatives in battle was not enough to contend with, the papers occasionally warned readers about bands of gypsies. They were "traveling vagabonds... notorious thieves who should not be allowed to pitch their encampments near a town."

Finding entertainment in a small town was difficult at best, but just when something interesting turned up, the authorities stepped in and ruined the fun. In the fall of 1856, H. A. Jones brought a 1,950-pound California grizzly to Chesapeake City for a show. Officer Colmery arrested Jones under an 1841 law that forbade exhibiting bears without a license, and Justice Owens fined him $20 and costs.

Denied the joys of watching a grizzly perform, people sought entertainment where it might be found. Members of a select group attended the annual meeting of the Fellowship Persistive Horse Company in Nottingham; in fact, if they did not attend, they were charged 25 cents for the oversight. Furthermore, "members neglecting to attend and not paying their fines will not be under the protection of the company," said secretary W. Waring. Active members were credited in 1858 with tracking down and recovering a stolen horse from thieves.

On a hot summer evening in 1854, the *Democrat* was pleased when a group of about 15 young ladies and gentlemen took an evening horseback ride on E. Main Street. The intense heat caused them to turn back, but the editor hoped they would ride again in more agreeable weather, for they made such a pleasing sight.

That summer, too, there was an "Indian exhibition," in which several Native Americans explained the culture of their ancestors.

ELKTON LEATHER STORE,
OPPOSITE THE HOWARD HOUSE,

JAMES HASSON offers an assortment of Leather at the lowest prices for cash. Spanish and Slaughter Sole; Morocco—smooth and grain; ditto Madras and Tampico; French and American Calf; Wax and Buff Uppers; Harness and Skirting; Bridle, fair black; French and American Lining; Tops and Bindings; Kips and Findings.
☞The highest prices paid in cash for green Hides and Skins.

The Fourth of July highlighted summer events. Well in advance, restaurant owners took orders for as much as 50 gallons of ice cream. In 1854, a crowd gathered at the store of Joseph P. Krauss, for he sent a huge balloon aloft. Everyone watched until it was lost to view.

Those who turned to overindulgence to break the monotony were periodically warned by the papers of the evils of association with John Barleycorn. The *Whig* outdid its righteous self: "John Dick, having a jug of whiskey with him at the time, was run over by the cars one and a half miles below Elkton, on Monday night, cut to pieces and killed. So much for whiskey."

Charles M. Ellis was secretary of the Elkton Juvenile Temperance Society. Regarding soft drinks, the *Democrat* reported in May 1854, that bottlers Mahan and Company sold 550 dozen bottles of sarsaparilla in one week.

The use of drugs was not frequently mentioned in the papers. However, the *Democrat* reported in December 1855 that Eliza Evans, 20, daughter of George Evans, and an employee of Lord's Mills, bought laudanum at Brinton's store and later died from an overdose. Her body was found on the rocks of a quarry, and she was buried in the cemetery at Cherry Hill Methodist Church.

People did depend on a little change of pace every March 25, for that was Moving [or "Flitting"] Day in the county. Everybody who wanted to move for whatever reason made arrangements to do so. Wagons loaded with household items crossed the county as people labored from early morning to late at night vacating their old houses and settling into new ones. The papers took a dull view of the custom, saying that participants falsely assumed that a change in geography would solve all their problems. George Green, who moved to Indiana, wrote back to express serious reservations.

> **A Great Victory**
>
> The public having met at the Central Stove Store have decided that there is the place to get one of the best Cook or Parlor Stoves in the country. All of which we are retailing at Philadelphia prices.   WM. M. EDER.

Morgantown, Indiana, April 27, 1854

MR. RICKETTS—*Dear Sir.*—I wish to inform yourself and my old friends of Cecil county that we have arrived safely in the Hoosier State. If I had known I would have had so much trouble and expense moving with such a large family nothing could have induced me to leave Old Cecil; and if I don't feel in better spirits you will see me back by the 25th of next March. Stock here is very high. I paid $310 for three horses, and they would not bring much more in Cecil, cows sell for from $30 to $35; wheat is $1.00 per bushel, and corn 35 cents and potatoes 50 cents. Land in this [Morgan] county brings $15 to $40 per acre; it is very rich, and I believe the county is one of the healthiest in the state.

If ever any of my old friends come to Indiana, I wish them to come and see me; they will find the "string of the latch always on the outside of the door."

The *Democrat* ran the following to demonstrate the cost of living in Elkton in November 1854. "Barrel of flour, $10; corn, 87.5 cents per bushel; lard, 14 cents per pound; potatoes $1.00 per bushel; dried apples, $2.00 per bushel; dried peaches, $3.00 per bushel; mackerel 12.5 cents per pound; coal $7.50 per short ton; butter 25 to 31 cents per pound."

10,000 Chestnut Rails, for Sale.

When necessary they will be delivered at any landing within twenty miles. Inquire of the subscriber in Elk Neck, or by letter to the North East P. O., Cecil county, Md. ISAAC Z. COLLINS

Those who qualified could apply for Bounty Land. An Act of Congress in 1855 stipulated that all who served 14 days or more in the Revolution or in any other war engaged in by the United States were entitled to 160 acres. Anyone who participated in any battle, even though he served for only one day, widows [or if no widows, children under 21], teamsters, wagonmasters, mariners, and sailors were also eligible. "Having peculiar advantages for obtaining the warrants, and from extensive travel through the West, for advantageously locating the same, persons entitled to Land should apply personally, or by letter to Wm. Pinkney Ewing."

Mill owner Daniel Lord was praised in July 1853 when his operation at Elk Mills went on the 10-hour system.

The earliest settlers in Cecil County built mills on the banks of the Big and Little Elk Creeks. By the 1850s some had already disappeared, and the *Whig*, in the interest of preserving history, asked an old-timer for whatever information he could recall about the mills of his boyhood.

THE MILLS AND MANUFACTORIES OF CECIL COUNTY HALF A CENTURY AGO.—We have from Mr. Jeremiah L. Leslie, a native of this county, but for the last half century a citizen of Ohio, an intriguing letter, part of it in answer to certain inquiries about the mills and manufactories on the streams of this county.

Mr. Leslie, who is upwards of 80 years of age, still writes an excellent letter in a bold hand but slightly tremulous with age. He is a cousin of Miss Leslie, the well known writer, and of the eminent painter C. R. Leslie, now of England, and has still many relatives in this county.

His recollections in relations to the mills of the county will, doubtless, be interesting to many of our readers, and we print that part of his letter. He says:

"One of the first occupants of a mill on Big Elk was Moses Foreman, who a time went by the name of *Ready-money Mosey*, but it afterwards got to be *Mosey-in-bran-and-shorts*, or *Mosey-out-of-the-mill*. There was also a mill owned by a Ricketts—perhaps Wm., and another by Levy Tyson, both on Big Elk, this last was above May's forge, which afterwards became Stephen Hayes'. Capt. John Evans owned the next waterworks and then came the rolling mill and nail factory of Ellis Passmore. If my memory does not deceive me Doct. Wallace owned a mill near the Rock Meeting House. These are the mills and factories I can call to mind on the Big Elk. On second thought Wallace's mill must have been on the Little Elk.

On Little Elk was Jonathan and Ebenezer Booth's mill, then Henry Hollingsworth's mill and saw mill afterwards a nail factory and tilt forge carried on by myself, and since converted into an Iron Works by Stephen Hayes. Immediately above was a woolen factory, built, if my memory serves me, by a company, and occupied while I lived at Marley, by an Englishman named John Wilson. A little farther up was John Anderson's saw mill and I recollect no other waterworks on Little Elk unless Wallace's was there.

As far as my recollection and knowledge extend, the following is a list of the other waterworks in the county at that time. Thomas Maffit's mill at the mouth of the creek below the juncture of Big and Little North East. Russell's two Iron Works were immediately above; the lower forge embraced the water of both streams—the upper that of Big North East alone. On the little branch, in ascending, Andrew Reed's mill was the first, Wm. Miller's the next, then Robert Cloud's sawmill and if my memory does not deceive me, Thos. Rogers owned a mill on this stream. In ascending Big North East the first above Russell's new forge was a saw mill built by Robert Leslie who sold it to Charles Johnson, who moved it farther down and built a woolen factory. The next in my day was Gilpin's Falls; the next Thomas Underhill's mill; the next, if I am correct, was Joseph Reynold's mill, then Levi Kirk's mill, besides which I recollect no other. On recollection, I think there was a fulling mill on Big North East, owned by Roger Kirk. There was a small stream which emptied into the head of North East river, called Stony Run, on which in olden time there was a saw mill owned by a man named Crookshanks, and above this a short distance was a mill built by John Hall.

Near the mouth of a small stream called *Principii,* between Charlestown and the Lower Ferry was a furnace and mill. This closes my recollection of water works in Cecil county."

If the old gentleman could visit his native county again, he would be astonished at the changes wrought since the time of which he writes.

As familiar scenes fade into history, the *Whig* mourned the passing of the Frenchtown Railroad.

An advertisement of certain road Examiners, in another column, recites that they are commissioned to consider the laying out of a county road on the track of the Frenchtown Railroad, *which has been abandoned.* Frenchtown, for many a day was a prominent point with the traveling public of this county. First packets, propelled by sails, shortened the land travel on the great northern and southern route, by carrying passengers between Baltimore and Frenchtown. Across to New Castle, the proprietors of the line made a turnpike, which remains, a public road, some places but little used. Then, when steam locomotion was invented, a railroad, [among the first in the country,] was laid down between Frenchtown and New Castle, and for years it was crossed with travel. The Citizens' Union Line had excellent steamboats on both the Chesapeake and Delaware ends of the line. Subsequently the owners of the Phil., Wil. & Balt. R.R. Com. became proprietors of that line, and finding the through railroad competent to carry all the passengers, and cheaper, they have "abandoned" the Frenchtown track, taken up the rails, and now it is about to become [part of it at least] a common neighborhood road. Frenchtown will remain a name, but its glory hath departed. No gallant steamers longer come teeming up to its wharf, driving the narrow river into a cauldron of waves, no whistling engines, or rumbling cars fly along the old embankment with their load of human freight; no carriage loads from the country around crowd down to its shore to take the boats or cars. It dwindles down to a plain country hotel; a boarding house for people who seek a quiet retreat, away from the noise and dust of busy life. So change the thoroughfares, the habitations and the affairs of men.

The roadbed did not go to waste entirely because occasionally horse races were held there.

1859 bowed out with an eerie occurrence on the P. W. & B. Railroad. During a late December storm, a light appeared on the tracks as the 8 o'clock train approached the depot. Bystanders panicked when they believed it to be an oncoming train; but the light mysteriously disappeared, giving rise to even more talk and unrest. The *Whig* patiently explained that the glow was undoubtedly an *Ignis Fatuus*, also called Jack with the Lantern. The flame was produced when spontaneous combustion occurred in marshy areas. Since the light of science had illuminated the dark recesses of the human mind, people no longer followed the fire into ponds or other dangerous places, under the delusion that they were led by departed relatives or friends.

GUANO:—
PERUVIAN, A..
MEXICAN, A. A.
AND COLUMBIAN.
For sale by   JOHN PARTRIDGE

Holly Hall, a landmark familiar to 20th-century travelers along Route 40 in the vicinity of Big Elk Mall, was sold at a trustees' sale on March 6, 1860, on the Court House steps. The estate comprised 205 acres.

> The brick mansion is commodious, and was built by the late General Sewell, at great expense, for the use of himself and the family. The main building is sixty feet square, and three stories high. The back building is large and convenient; and the whole establishment is fitted up with every regard to comfort and elegance. The Grounds are extensive, and well shaded with Trees, both Fruit and Ornamental. The Fencing is neat and substantial.

The Out-Houses and Farm Buildings are constructed of the best material and are ample for all the requirements of domestic and farming purposes.

The society of the neighborhood cannot be excelled. The Elkton Station of the Philadelphia, Wilmington and Baltimore Railroad is about a half a mile distant from the Mansion House above described. Churches and Schools convenient. The property is in every way desirable.

TERMS OF SALE

As prescribed by the Decree: The whole of the purchase money to be paid in Cash to Trustees on the day of sale.

February 4, 1860   George Earle
                          John A. J. Creswell, Trustees

The *Democrat* announced on March 17 the sale of Holly Hall to James E. Barroll, Esq., for the sum of $18,000.

Following the death of editor Palmer C. Ricketts, 42, on March 8, J. S. Crawford took over the *Whig* on May 12.

April brought articles about conventions as politicians geared up for the November election. The Young Men's Democratic Club rented a clubroom in preparation for the coming campaign.

The *Whig* reported on the activities at the Republican State Convention, which had convened in Baltimore to nominate an electoral ticket and to send delegates to Chicago. "The meeting was attended with great disorder, and the morning session broken up by Erasmus Levy, and others, who overturned the secretary's desk and pushed and hustled the members. Wm. P. Ewing of this town, is reported in the *Sun* as having been pushed over, which he denies. Levy pushed him, but did not push him down. A member named Bunnison took the street and did some hard running, the crowd pursuing."

A short paragraph mentioned that black Republicans in Chicago nominated Abraham Lincoln for President, but the nomination for his running mate had not been made.

Of more import, if one is to judge by the space allotted to it, was a notice that there had been a great haul of mud turtles from the millpond at Back Creek, where several hundred snappers were captured. "About twenty of them were brought to the market, and went off like hot cakes. The largest weighed 23 pounds."

**A New and Elegant Hall
IN PORT DEPOSIT**
50 BY 21 FEET, has been recently erected and handsomely fitted up, for public purposes.
Apply to
EDWIN WILMER,
Port Deposit

The *Democrat* boasted in May that public schools of Cecil County were open all year long and cost less than those in Pennsylvania, which are open only six or eight months a year. "One of the reasons for the result," the paper speculated, "may probably be found in the fact that we have no county superintendent, at a heavy salary, riding around and lording it over our schools."

Educational institutions advertised in the weeklies. In 1858, the Elkton Academy ran the following:

> The Trustees would announce that the Fall Session of this Institution commenced on 25th ult., under the supervision of J. Q. A. Jones, A. M., assisted by Mrs. J. Q. A. Jones, both experienced Teachers. In order to place the best educational advantages within the reach of all, they have considerably reduced the rates of tuition. They would therefore hope that the public will give increased patronage to the School, that it may be enabled to sustain itself and be made a *First Class Institution of Learning*. The branches will be such as are taught in all our higher schools and colleges, and pupils may obtain a thorough English or Classical Education without going from home.

RATES OF TUITION

1st Class—Spelling, Reading, Writing, Elementary Geography, Arithmetic and Grammar, per term, $3.00.

2nd Class—Including Grammar, Geography, Arithmetic, Book Keeping, Mensuration Algebra, Geometry, Nat. Philosophy, History, and Botany, per term, $4.00.

3rd Class—Trigonometry, Surveying, Political Economy, Science of Government, Rhetoric, History of Literature, Mythology, Logic, Geology, Meteorology, Mental and Moral Philosophy, Natural Theology, Evidences of Christianity and the Latin Language, per term, $5.00.

Any of the above named branches with the Greek, French or German Language and Literature, per term, $7.00

EXTRAS

MUSIC on the Piano or Melodeon, per term,	$3.00
Pencil Drawing or Monochromatics,	3.00
Painting in Water Colors,	3.00
Painting in Oil Color,	5.00
Embroidery and Needle Work,	2.00

An extra charge of 50 cents for each of the two Winter terms to defray expenses of fuel, &c., will be made on each pupil.

Eleven weeks constitute one term.

No deduction for less than a week's loss of time.

    F. A. Ellis, Secretary   GEO. R. HOWARD, President

Mrs. [Kate] Porter's School was located next to the Methodist Church. "She teaches all branches of a common English Education, and the rudiments of Natural Philosophy, Chemistry, and Astronomy. She can produce testimonials of her capabilities to teach, from the best sources."

Ads also appeared for the Newark Academy, Deer Park Seminary [also in Newark], Wesleyan Female Academy in Wilmington, West Nottingham Academy, Lutherville Female Seminary, and New London Academy. Josephine Carter's obituary indicated that she attended the Wesleyan Female Academy in Wilmington, Delaware, but most other obituaries were such models of brevity that it is difficult to establish much about what schools the deceased attended.

A notice in the *Democrat* for that institution pointed out that the buildings were well ventilated, lighted with gas, and there was a room for bathing on each floor. Expenses for board, room, light, fuel and tuition in studies of regular courses were $152 per year. Drawing, painting, music, and modern languages were extra.

> **O, my Head! O, my Tooth!**
> It is true that Dr. Stevens' Magic Lotion cures Tooth and Head Ache in 1 minute. For Sale at Dr. Mitchell's Drug Store.

When E. F. M. Faehtz left New London Academy to accept a post at Elkton Academy, the *Whig* noted that three Cecil Countians attended the former institution: H. C. Whitaker of Principio Furnace and Samuel Purnell and J. Layton Regester of Elkton.

The papers carried notices of weekly meetings of various lyceums. Men [women did not attend] got together and discussed issues of the day. The usual exercises included the reading of an essay and a debate. In 1856, the town was invited to hear men of the Elkton Lyceum debate whether or not prohibition of liquor by legislative enactment was in accordance with sound principles of government.

For the affirmative: J. B. Rowan, who later joined the Confederacy, and W. Pinkney Ewing, whose name figured prominently in local debates.

For the negative: Wm. Jones, admitted to the bar in 1855, who within a few years would defend the character of his boyhood friend, Ben Ricketts; and Jas. T. McCullough.

Henry Torbert, Esq., delivered an original composition; Charles Manley Ellis, already mentioned as secretary for the Juvenile Temperance League, later a surgeon with Rush's Lancers, was recording secretary.

The Lafayette Library Club formed to advance the knowledge of its members and to establish a library. Officers J. J. Poole, Wm. McCullough, C. E. Massey, Harrison Bennett, and Kennard Aldridge solicited donations of money and books.

When the Port Deposit Library Association paid a tribute of respect on the death of John B. Abrahams in 1858, members wore a badge of mourning on their left arm and the hall was draped in mourning for 30 days. Committee members included James Touchstone, later quartermaster for the 6th Maryland, William Parker, and David C. Way. John W. Taylor was the recording secretary.

Cherry Hill Methodist Church provided a lending library for its members. The ledger in which those records were kept is found in the Historical Society of Cecil County.

Although newspapers did not contain forecasts, the weather was an area of constant concern. The first winter snowfall and the first spring blossom annually elicited prose that would find no place in a modern newspaper. The *Democrat* observed a beautiful and unusual "lunar rainbow" in the issue of July 7, 1855. Very often the reader got firsthand accounts from correspondents who witnessed blizzards, floods or other disasters. A letter from Port Deposit to the *Democrat*, dated May 16, 1860, told of great damage the town sustained when the Susquehanna went on a rampage.

> Our river has been doing great havoc since I last wrote you. The heavy rains of the past [*sic*] week or two, caused a most extraordinary rise in the Susquehanna on last Friday and Saturday. On Friday afternoon the river rose about three feet, and continued to rise until the next day in the afternoon. So sudden was the rush of water that everyone was unprepared for it, and per consequence, great loss has been sustained. The fisheries on the river were inundated, and nearly all the salted fish were lost. Mr. William Berlin on Stull's Island and fishery, lost all his fish. His horse was saved by swimming to the shore.
>
> Mr. Devens has lost several on his Battery. All the rafts, except a few, were swept away. Several hundred, comprising a considerable fleet, took their departure on their own hook. The most of the rafts have been found below on the bay shore, scattered promiscuously. It will cost a heavy figure to rearrange the lumber and timber thus thrown about, and bring it back. On Saturday morning the Williamsport boom gave way and down came oceans of saw logs of various sorts. It was estimated that the boom contained about 90,000,000 feet of logs, the whole of which came down. The timber was so thickly strewn in the river during the whole of the afternoon that the steamboat could not cross. Many logs were caught, and many grounded on the Harford shore, but the principal part went outside. It is said that the boom contained, at the time it gave way, timber covering a solid surface of from four to five square miles. The boom company are trying to collect their timber, but they will be apt to lose the half of it, which will be an enormous loss. Our harbor has been completely "gutted." The river has fallen considerably, but it is at a high stage yet. The large fisheries have not been able to resume their hauling, but since the fall of the river, the "gillers" have been catching great quantities of herring, and a good many shad.

The regular correspondent from the town added that druggists, doctors, and clerks were on the wharves scooping up these "finny treasures." Some caught as many as 500 fish.

Those concerned with the vagaries of weather purchased an Armitage's Patent Lightning Rod, as advertised in the *Whig*. The seven-pronged device looked evil enough to scare lightning away.

A matter of perennial debate during the 1850s and early 1860s was the construction of a plank road from Elkton to Lewisville, Pennsylvania. This innovation was touted in the local press as a panacea for travelers converging on the town to catch trains bound for larger cities. Farmers, too, would benefit from a good road when they brought their produce to market.

One local letter writer stated in the *Whig* that a team could pull three tons on a macadamized road, one or at the most two tons on a common road, but six tons on a plank road.

He described the building of a plank road. First, clear and level the roadbed. Then lay down three string pieces—six inches in width and three in thickness. Over these run a heavy roller until everything is smooth. Now put planks—8 feet by 3 inches in thickness—at right angles to the stringers. An embankment at each side completes the project.

In 1853, the Elkton, Andora and Lewisville Plank Road Company sold stock to raise $16,000. The *Whig* opined: "It would seem to be an improvement, and one that would pay well. Several heavy manufacturing establishments lie along the route and a large amount of travel occurs in that direction, over a road celebrated for its uniform badness...."

By mid-May of 1854, the managers selected James McCauley, Esq., to be engineer of the road. The managers themselves were responsible for constructing the first three miles from Elkton. They appointed Joshua L. Gatchel to supervise that segment. He set to work immediately, employing from 20 to 30 hands to do the preparatory grading.

In June stockholders elected managers for the upcoming year: George Earle, Samuel B. Foard, Joseph Miller, Francis G. Parke, Wm. G. Carter, Nicholas Hiss, Joshua L. Gatchel, E. T. Richardson and Wm. Rudulph. Then the managers elected Earle president and Parke vice president.

Planks, some of hemlock, some of oak, were rafted from Port Deposit to Elkton. In summer, laborers worked in 102-degree heat.

> **SHERIFF'S NOTICE**
> For the convenience of those who may have business with me, I may be found at home in Elkton, on Saturday of each week in this month, except the last Saturday in the month. R. W. WALMSLEY
> Sheriff of Cecil Co.

The managers contracted Francis Green to grade and lay the next four miles of the road [beyond the first three miles being done by Gatchel]. Green was to grade the balance of the road as far as the Pennsylvania line for $500. By then the whole road had been surveyed to the state line, and the distance was ascertained to be just over eight miles.

Everything seemed to be going along fine. A stage was established along the route of the projected road, and people looked forward to its completion. The *Democrat* remarked: "There is every prospect of the speedy establishment of a daily mail between these points, and when the plank road is completed, it will greatly facilitate the transportation of mail and passengers."

Travelers occasionally fought over the right of way. For the most part, people agreed that an unloaded wagon should yield to a loaded one. When both wagons were loaded or both empty, each team was expected to go to the right. Disputes escalated to the drawing of pistols when wagoners disagreed about who was taking whose half out of the middle.

As late as November the *Whig* was pleased with the progress. "This work is steadily progressing and will soon be completed to Cherry Hill, a distance of four miles. Tolls have been collected on two miles of the road for a few weeks, and the receipts are quite flattering, and leave no doubt but the road will pay well—that it will besides paying a good interest on the money invested, furnish a fund for relaying the track by the time it is required."

The company advertised the selling of stock at $25 a share for three days in Elkton and then in Fair Hill at Thomas P. Sutton's hotel. Two dollars cash had to be paid on each share at the time of subscription.

In January 1855, the stockholders received the good news that they would be paid dividends. The *Whig* lauded the company: "The Plank Road Company was organized on the 8th of last April, and commenced operations under disadvantageous circumstances; it has succeeded beyond the expectations of the most sanguine. The Plank Road is bound to do well."

But that was about the last favorable remark one ever reads about the ill-fated road. People did not mind paying for traveling on the completed road. But the previous fall, the men got only so far as grading the roadbed before cold weather made further work impossible. In January, travelers began to complain. After passing through the quagmire, one writer called it "the worst road in North America, almost impassible on horseback."

In March 1855, George Earle resigned as president and manager of the company, all the while declaring that he left with undiminished confidence in the project. Over the summer, the *Whig* urged people to find a way to complete the road. One writer blamed the road's condition on careless wagoners who kept their westerly wheels outside the plank. A heavily loaded team with its west wheels grinding against the ends caused planks to slip, some nearly 18 inches out of place.

Finally, in 1858 the road was put up at trustees' sale and withdrawn when the highest bid was only $5,350. The next year it changed hands with heavy mortgages against it.

Despite the new company's determination to enforce the provisions of the charter, Sheriff Cosgrove and deputy, E. W. Janney, arrested two teamsters for cutting down a toll gate. The *Whig* grumbled: "We don't think the act much of a misdemeanor in view of the condition of the road."

It was penitential to ride what was left of the plank road during the early 1860s. A writer to the *Democrat* demanded that the company that owned the road should keep it in order. "We passed over it," the letter continued, "or rather alongside it, on Saturday evening last, when it was really in a condition dangerous to travelers. Should the public be compelled to pay for traveling over such a road as this?"

The road's poor condition was not enough to deter those bent on nefarious deeds, however. Constable R. E. Cantwell arrested George Oneal and Susan Crony for breaking into the dwelling of

---

Bottling Establishment.

THE undersigned are prepared to furnish a superior article of Philadelphia Porter, Ale, Cider, and Lager Beer. Also, MINERAL WATER and SARSAPARILLA of superior flavor and quality.
☞ All orders per mail to the address below, promptly attended to.
C. P. BURRIS & CO.,
Perryville,
Cecil county, Md.

Mr. White, residing on the plank road, a short distance from town. The *Whig* added: "The burglary was committed on Friday evening. The parties are reported to have stolen $10, and a shawl, petticoat, and bonnet. They are from the county alms house, and are now confined in Elkton jail."

By 1864, the planks were torn up and piled along the road. The *Whig* railed: "Having long served no other purpose than to wreck vehicles, they are now placed in a position to frighten horses. This is all that remains to show that a plank road ever existed here. It is the first one ever constructed in this part of the country, and its fate will most likely be a damper on all future enterprises of the kind to put our roads in a good condition. It is believed that had this road been laid no further than Cherry Hill it would have paid well, and the company could have kept it up."

Finally in 1865, the *Democrat* noted: "The road from Elkton to Cherry Hill—formerly the plank road—is now in a horrible condition. It is almost worth a stranger's life to drive over it. The old planking has been taken up, and the large teams traveling over it this spring have cut it up in shocking condition. The road is out of the hands of the county, and a late session of the legislature, we believe, gave the company who have control of it, two years in which to turnpike it."

The *Whig* mentioned the passing of Miss Catherine Dysart, age 83, on January 19, 1856. The editor hoped Dysart's Tavern would cease being a place "where liquid poison is sold." Then as if having vented its spleen, the paper struck a more tolerant pose the next month.

COACH MAKING
AT THE
BRICK MEETING HOUSE.

WM. J. MARSHBANK.

> In the oldest maps I have seen of Cecil county, Dysart's Tavern is marked, but of the date of its erection I have not the means at hand of ascertaining. It is situated about one mile north of Cowantown [or Turkeytown] and on the road from the Brick Meeting house to Wilmington, and within a short distance of Mason and Dixon's line.... That old tavern has been a rallying point of politicians, for a period to the contrary whereof the memory of man runneth not. In the time when all the county came to Elkton to vote, and the election lasted three days, Dysart's had its champions, as well as Battle Swamp. There many a patriot expatiated on liberty and reform—on the good of the country, and the rights of the poor man.
>
> There are many reminescenes [*sic*] of the old hotel; and the stranger who has stepped into the old bar-room, and seen the stove strapped to the floor with iron to prevent its being overturned, may have imagined what jolly times have been there.
>
> One of the old proprietors used to entertain his guests with the most marvelous incidents and adventures; some of which are still extant, viz: "He went to the woods with his sled for a load of wood which he loaded up, but a rain coming on so softened his rawhide traces

that they stretched until he reached home without the sled ever starting; he took them off the horse and threw the harness over the gate post. After awhile the sun came out and the traces began to contract and the sled came sliding up.

On someone complaining that his chimney did not draw very well, he said it had formerly been a wonderful chimney to draw, but that one hard winter they had brought in the grindstone to grind their axes and had incautiously left it on the hearth; from where it had been drawn up and stuck in the throat of the chimney which had never drawn so well since."

It is hard to estimate the amount of evil that an old drinking house has spread around it, the traces of which are as visible as the traces of fire.

There is one circumstance in connection with Dysart's that is not generally known, that it was proposed as a proper situation for the Capital of the United States at the time Washington was adopted. Had Dysart's been selected, a part of the "ten miles square" might have run into Pennsylvania, and there the Congressional abolitionists could have slept soundly on free soil.

During the fall of 1860, some young ladies in Elkton engaged in a morally questionable practice that elicited a warning from the *Democrat* in bold headlines: "Girls, Don't Do It." In a flagrant display of wantonness, they gave daguerreotypes of themselves to young men who were merely acquaintances, a practice the editor found "indelicate to the highest degree."

The Presidential election of 1860 presented voters with four choices: the Democrats split in two. Stephen A. Douglas and Herschel V. Johnson represented one wing, and John C. Breckinridge and Joseph Lane, the other. The Republicans nominated Abraham Lincoln with Hannibal Hamlin as his running mate. Then a relative newcomer to the political scene, the National Constitutional Party, nominated John Bell and Edward Everett.

The *Whig* commented sardonically: "The Democrats used to be satisfied with one candidate for the Presidency. Perhaps it was Calhoun who said that 'they were held together by the cohesive attraction of public plunder....'"

Two important threads ran through the political fabric of the nation: slavery vs. abolitionism; and secessionism vs. unionism. But position on one continuum did not necessarily predict one's place on the other. Some people viewed secession as thoroughly reprehensible, while finding the South's "peculiar institution" acceptable. Especially in a border county in a border state, it was not unusual to find an individual at a 5 on one issue and a 2 on the other.

Working Oxen, Cows and Heifers,

FOR SALE.—2 Yoke of good Working Oxen, 6 Milch Cows, nearly fresh; 10 Heifers, 1 and 2 years old, and Devon stock. Apply to me at Elkton, or at my farm. St. John's Manor, Elk Neck.
S. S. MAFFIT.

Pro-Slavery   Abolitionist
1_____2_____3_____4_____5

Secessionist   Pro-Union
1_____2_____3_____4_____5

Disagreements between Pennsylvania and Maryland foreshadowed turmoil on the horizon. Trouble erupted in 1851 when Maryland slaveholder Edward Gorsuch was killed in his attempt to retrieve three runaway slaves in Christiana, Pennsylvania. On January 10, 1852, the *Whig* ran the following:

> THE SLAVE ARREST, OR KIDNAPPING—AS THE CASE MAY BE.—We gave last week a paragraph from *The Baltimore Clipper*, stating that Thomas McCreary of this town had been arrested in that city, charged by a Mr. Miller of Chester county, Pa., with forcibly carrying from his premises a free negro girl, which girl was, nevertheless, claimed as the slave of a Mr. Schoolfield of Baltimore; and that McCreary gave bail to appear in that city on Wednesday last, to answer the charge.
>
> McCreary was arrested on the 1st inst. On the 2nd the lifeless body of Miller was found suspended to a tree on the line of the railroad near Stemmer's Run. In company with others from Chester county, he had the previous night taken the cars for Havre-de-Grace. A jury of inquest was summoned in the case, and a verdict of suicide rendered. About the case much mystery hangs. It is strange why Miller left the cars to hang himself, and it would seem strange that he should be taken from them by violent hands unseen. Some think that, fearing the consequences of the false oath which they allege he took, like the conscience-smitten Judas, he went away and hanged himself. Others that he was seized and hung by the avengers of the murdered Gorsuch. It seems that he was hanging, tied *to the body of a tree*, with his feet on the ground. His own handkerchief was looped around his neck, and another tied to it and around the tree, which, we must confess, seem indicative of foul play.
>
> We have elsewhere referred to the progress of the trial in this case. How it will terminate, remains to be seen; *but in no case will McCreary be given up to the authorities of Pennsylvania.*
>
> The remark made by us last week relative to McCreary's sorties into Pennsylvania, was copied by *The Village Record*, which speaks of it as encouraging the lawless and daring actions of McCreary. We have a word to repeat, and another say on this subject. First: that as the people of Pennsylvania will not give up slaves to their owners, when they appear

agreeably to the laws of the country to claim them, but on the contrary *murder citizens of Maryland* when they go legally, by day, to recover their property, the circumstances, of necessity, create such men as McCreary, who, for money, will go by night and carry off runaways and sometimes by mistake, it may be, those who are free. This is the inevitable result of the action of the abolitionist citizens of Pennsylvania, men who are the veriest curse ever yet inflicted on the Negro race; and for lawless and daring actions of McCreary. If so, so be it.

Even yesterday, [we write, Friday night,] Gov. Johnson, it seems, vetoed the bill allowing the use of the prisons of the State to secure fugitives, arrested under a law of the General Government. Look at the case—a citizen of Maryland goes to Pennsylvania to arrest his slave; a right guarantied to him under a writ from a U. S. officer—the State refuses to allow him to secure the slave in its prisons, and a mob of its citizens collect, rob him of his property and leave him *murdered* on the ground.

Another citizen, warned by the fate of his murdered neighbor, hires a man—a *borderer*—created by the times, who goes in the night and by daring and speed carries the slave to his owner;—perchance, sometimes mistaking the description, he carries off a free negro. Whose fault is it?

As to the death of Miller—there are those who hold it, even if brought about by violent hands, to be a just retribution for the death of Gorsuch. We join in no such feeling, but such feelings exist; and what wonder!

And with all these evils, and others which are to come—for fugitive slaves will in the night-time still be carried from the very inner temples of the abolitionists—we charge the people of Pennsylvania, and we shall hold them to answer for it. If this be "encouraging the lawless and daring actions of McCreary" or of others, let it be so. We had much rather the laws should have their course, but Pennsylvanians have rendered that impossible.

But by December 17, 1853, a writer from Chesapeake City addressed the *Whig* editor.

The only "item" peculiar to the time and place is the seizure, capture and detention of four free negroes employed on the works of the Canal Co. The officers of the law—prompt in the execution of duty—made a dash at twelve, but eight escaped, and the *State* pocketed eighty dollars. This law [and I dare proclaim it,] is barbarous; uncivilized. It may do to talk about, but when the actual thing is done—the "lex legis"—executed—it is time for men and communities to rise up in voice and deed against it. Your correspondent, as you well know is no *abolitionist*, but strongly the reverse; yet when a tyrannical, contemptible law is exercised to the injury of a whole community, I dare raise my pen to decry it, in the very face of prejudice and sectional feeling.

In November 1858 the *Whig* reported on the Eastern Shore Slavery Convention.

> We publish in full, as made out by the Secretaries, the proceedings of the late Convention of Slaveholders, held at Cambridge. The people of Cecil sent no delegates there. Generally speaking, both those who own slaves and those who do not, in this county, are opposed to the continued agitation of the negro question; but as the Convention of Slaveholders devoted its attention more particularly to free negroes, the subject is materially changed and will not fail to create much interest here. Cecil has fewer slaves to be tampered with than any other county on the Shore, but she has a large free colored population, on which many of our citizens depend almost entirely for labor, and any legislation materially affecting them will affect the interests of the whites and the business of the county. It becomes important, then, for us to consider whether they would be expelled from the state, or legislated back into slavery again; the voice of Cecil should be heard in the proposed Convention in Baltimore and men who understand the interests of the county, and as an integral part of the state, should be chosen to represent us in the General Assembly ....
>
> We shall not now undertake to discuss the question but expect to refer to it hereafter. It is one to which attention should be given, and we invite any gentleman who may be disposed to examine it, to a free use of our columns for that purpose. That there should be some legislation in regard to the idle and worthless free negroes, who live by plunder, in some shape, will not be doubted. Probably, it might be a wholesome regulation to legislate, also for the benefit of the white loafers and vagabonds that infest every community. Probably, also, while in the endeavor to correct the lazy and mischievous habits of free negroes, it might serve a good end to abate the multitudes of little groggeries kept by whites, licensed by the laws, around which the negroes congregate, and where they are corrupted and debauched. All these things may form a part of the general subject, and if so, will engage the attention of our citizens, our Conventions and Legislature, in their honest and earnest efforts to correct the evils growing out of the idleness and crimes of the negro population.

In *Maryland in the Civil War*, Harold R. Manakee (1961, pp. 20-21) reviewed the complicated political scene.

> ...Maryland was truly a border state. The ways of life and the points of view of both North and South clashed, not at the Mason-Dixon line or at the Potomac River, but between those boundaries and within the state. On the same issues that were splitting the nation—slavery, states rights, secession and tariff—Marylanders held sharply divided opinions. That division was reflected in their balloting ... in November 1860.

Breckinridge	Southern Democrat	42,497
Bell	Constitutional Unionist	41,777
Douglas	Democrat	5,873
Lincoln	Republican	2,294

Clearly Marylanders had little liking for the anti-slavery stand of the Republican Party. On the other hand, the numbers of Marylanders who voted for Bell, determined to preserve the Union and hoping to compromise the slave issue, was only 720 less than those who voted for Breckinridge, a defender of slavery and the South with its threats of secession. The state's electoral votes went to Breckinridge, but such close totals in the popular vote gave little indication of whether Maryland would remain in the Union or secede.

1860 tax records summarized the value of slaves in Cecil's nine districts. The records also indicated the owner's full name, the slave's first name, and his or her age and value.

Cecil County Tax Records by District Showing Value of Slaves and Election Results

District	Area	Slave Val.	Bell	Breckinridge	Douglas	Lincoln
First	Cecilton	$79,365	234	140	38	0
Second	Ches. City	18,660	169	194	37	8
Third	Elkton	16,400	250	280	86	8
Fourth	North East	2,000	66	251	42	25
Fifth	Fair Hill	19,990	330	102	104	42
Sixth	Rising Sun	1,750	218	176	17	25
Seventh	Perryville	8,135	317	178	46	10
Eighth	Conowingo	1,000	69	94	10	17
Ninth	Calvert	-0-	138	91	13	23
Total		$147,300	1791	1506	393	158

Total votes cast: 3,848. Bell's plurality over Breckinridge: 285.

The *Whig* endorsed Bell, but when Lincoln was elected, it editorialized:

> ... Abraham Lincoln and Hannibal Hamlin are chosen, by a plurality of the popular vote, to conduct the affairs of the government for the next four years. This choice having been constitutionally made, it becomes our duty as good citizens to stand by the President elect, the chosen head of the government, no matter how much we may regret that the result was not in favor of our own candidate.

Despite the good grace with which the *Whig* accepted its candidate's loss, it was not above wetting the tip of its editorial tongue in the taste of sour grapes.

> The success of the Breckinridge party in our own State, brought about by the use of large sums of money to buy off the foreign Douglas and Lincoln votes in Baltimore city, and thus secure its concentration upon Breckinridge, and also by the throwing away of about 1500 votes in the State for Lincoln, is particularly to be regretted. On the other hand it is a source of congratulation that, by the aid of the Union Douglas men, who, under the most unfavorable circumstances, stood unflinchingly by their principles and candidates, we have, outside of Baltimore, a majority of nearly 2000 votes. We congratulate the Union men of Cecil county that they have so largely contributed to that result by their unexpectedly large plurality of 286 for Bell.

That being said, the *Whig* then recommended that everybody rally to the support of "the Union, the Constitution and the Enforcement of Laws, under an Executive, who, though not of our choice, is the choice of a large plurality, at least of the voters of the country." The *Democrat* supported the J. C. Breckinridge-Joseph Lane ticket. After Lincoln's victory, the editor wrote:

> The great quadrennial contest for the Presidency is past and victory is on the side of the cohorts of Black Republicanism. Abraham Lincoln, of Illinois, is the President elect of the United States, and will take his place in the executive mansion, on the 4th of March next, *Deo volente*.
>
> The fanaticism which has placed him in the Executive office will be held in check by a decisive majority against him in both branches of Congress. The evil, therefore, that might have resulted from his election with Congress in his favor, will at least be deferred if not wholly prevented.

Election or no election, life went on and people dealt with mundane matters as they arose. A writer who signed himself "Pro Bono Publico" recommended in the *Democrat* that the bailiff turn his attention away from national politics and toward the improvement

Armitage's lightning rod

of Elkton's sidewalks. "In many places bricks have become loosened in the pavement, thereby making it exceedingly dangerous for pedestrians, in these times of plentiful slugs of 'red eye.'"

Autumn rains, heavier than any in the past 20 years, swelled local streams and wreaked havoc on dams at Roseville Factory on the White Clay Creek in Delaware, at Parke's rolling mill on the Great Elk, and at Priestley's paper mill on the Little Elk. The latter dam sustained the worst damage. Corn washed from fields, and fencing floated away in the maelstrom.

From Elk Neck emerged the plaintive story of a young boy who tried to drive across Plum Creek a horse and carriage owned by Wesley Janney's livery stable. When floodwaters swept them downstream, the boy swam to a tree and clung there for a long time until rescuers extricated him. Horse and carriage were not found until the next day. While the carriage was splintered beyond repair, the horse survived by keeping its head above the swirling waters.

Concerns about the man about to assume the office of President did not go away. Maryland's chief judge of the Court of Appeals, John C. Legrand, wrote a letter to the Honorable John B. Brooks, president of the Maryland senate, describing financial ruin about to befall the South. Legrand's letter concluded:

> In other words, without disguise, he [Lincoln] distinctly avows his purpose and policy to be the annihilation of slavery, to be accomplished by the exercise of every power with which he will be invested as President. He is not merely the representative of so many votes, but of an exterminating policy against the institutions of fifteen of the States of the Confederacy. He announces that free States and slave States cannot remain in the same Union; that one or the other must eventually triumph, and the same system of labor prevail throughout all the States; that the conflict is now raging, and that it will not cease to rage until the equality of the races be established by law, and, as a consequence, the tobacco, rice, sugar and cotton fields of the South be given over to desolation as have been the sugar and coffee plantations of St Domingo. It is this crusade against the rights, property and lives of the South that designates, in the judgment of all men of sense, his election as an event fraught with direful consequences.

The *Democrat* wasted little sympathy on the plight of slaves. It noted that a runaway named Harrison, owned by Wm. Foster, Queen Anne's County, was confined in Elkton jail. When he was captured, the slave wore "four coats, four pairs of pantaloons, three pairs of drawers, four shirts and three vests! A rather better wardrobe we should think than he would have been provided with for the next twenty years, had he succeeded in reaching a *free* State."

Wendell Phillips, the *Democrat* said, recently stirred up antagonism when he gave a speech in Boston. Henry Ward Beecher, whom the paper labeled "another mouthing abolitionist," incurred his share of editorial derision for a speech at the Plymouth Church in Brooklyn.

In the *Democrat's* view, abolitionism led to incalculable financial ruin and social upheaval. A case in point was a recent example of interracial marriage or "amalgamation."

A beautiful young white girl, 17 years of age, a daughter of Mr. Hiram L. Stout, of the town of Sharon, Michigan, eloped with a negro boy who was in the service of her father, and it is thought has gone with him to Canada.—The father of the girl is a noted abolitionist, and is now, with the other members of the family, greatly distressed at this practical test of the doctrines he has taught.

Just in case any Cecil Countian exhibited similar abolitionist tendencies, the paper bade them ponder the example of some misguided Chicago residents. "Nine of those engaged in the rescue of the slave girl Eliza last week... were yesterday indicted in the US District Court for violation of the Fugitive Slave Law."

Banks' suspension of specie payments signaled impending crisis. The *Democrat* warned:

> The election of a sectional President is already bearing its bitter fruits. It has been an additional source of alarm and disquiet to the South. Confidence in the existence of the Union is shaken; capitalists are alarmed; productive industry is paralized; factories are closing; laboring men are being thrown out of employment; and the banks have suspended specie payments. The Virginia banks suspended on Wednesday; the Washington, Baltimore, Philadelphia and Wilmington banks suspended on Thursday; and the prospect is that the suspension will be general in all parts of the Union.

By the end of December, John C. Breckinridge drew up an address to the border slaveholding states, calling them to a convention in Baltimore, "for the consideration of their duty to themselves, and how to preserve the Confederacy in the current crisis." Since the prospect of a confederacy of border states, seemed, in the view of many, to compound the problem, the plan never got off the ground.

Unrest spread through Cecil County. In Port Deposit town authorities imposed a 10:00 p.m. curfew on all black people and confiscated their firearms. From Warwick came news of the formation of a rifle corps. A meeting, convened at the office of Wm. Hunter, Esq., took measures for carrying out that plan. George M. Tyson presided and Wm. R. Lockwood served as secretary.

The *Whig* ran an account of masters who brought their slaves to witness the execution of other slaves, but as 1860 closed, the *Democrat* described local New Year's Eve customs.

Shoes! Shoes!! Shoes!!!

LADIES Gaiters as low as 88 cents per pair; Ladies' Gaiters with heels as low as $1.25.— The best quality of Black Kid Slippers at 95 cts. per pair. Ladies' Morocco Boots in great variety. Misses' Morocco Boots; Misses' Black Gaiters with heels, all received direct from the Manufacturer, and for sale at the Dry Goods and Grocery Store of R. F. May In the "Hollow.

The transition from the old year to the new, was observed in the usual way, in this town. It is customary in the Methodist church to observe it as watch night; that is, to watch and pray the old year out and the new year in. It is generally a deeply solemn and interesting ceremony, participated in at times, not only by members but by many who are not members of any christian denomination, attracted by curiosity and by the impressive character of the services. Meeting about nine or ten o'clock, it is the custom to spend the time in hearing a lecture or a sermon, and in singing and prayer. As the hour of twelve approaches, the whole congregation kneel and remain in solemn audience with Deity, until some minutes after the dial-plate has indicated the ushering in of the newborn year. On late occasion, the colored people resumed a practice which had fallen into disuse for some years back; that is, to march in procession through the town, singing as they go one of their simple melodies. On New Year's morning about 3 o'clock, a procession of about 50 to 100 of them marched through town, their sonorous voices ringing out upon the still air a plaintive hymn in admirable time, the sheen of a cloudless moon glittering upon the frost-enameled snow, imparting additional interest to the scene, as we looked out upon it from our chamber window.

Palmer C. Ricketts
(1817-1860)

2

Cecil County

1861

The *Whig* announced an upcoming meeting of Cecil Pro-Unionists without distinction of party.

> We the undersigned citizens of Cecil County respectfully invite all the Union loving citizens of Cecil to attend a Mass Meeting of the friends of the Union, to be held at the Court House, in Elkton, on TUESDAY the 8th of January, 1861, at 11 o'clock A. M.

James Crawford	Jas. H. Scott	Willlis Rutter
R. G. Reese	P. C. Strickland	Jacob B. Ash
W. T. McCauley	Thomas W. Green	Benj. F. May
John B. Rowan	J. S. Crawford	Andrew McIntire
John S. Stites	Jas. T. McCullough	Geo. W. Boulden
Geo. H. Joyce	M. Y. Eder	W. F. A. Torbert
Jos. P. Cantwell	H. Vanderford	David M. Taylor
Caleb Parker	Wm. P. Morgan	Edmund Brown, Jr.
H. D. Howard	A. W. Mitchell	Jos. R. Brown
Thos. Mosgrove	W. C. Crow	Justus Dunott
Geo. W. Benjamin	Perry Litzenberg	A. J. Scott
Edward E. Pugh		

The paper conveyed a sense of urgency by further noting that Disunionists were pressing Governor Hicks to call the Maryland Legislature together with the "secret purpose of passing a bill declaring the Union to be no longer binding, and demanding back the District of Columbia."

The tempo picked up as volunteers organized companies. A cavalry corps, led by Capt. A. J. Pennington, Esq., formed in Warwick. At Port Deposit, 40 men joined a rifle corps under Capt. John

Taylor. Wesley Wiley was the 1st Lieutenant; John M. Bullock, 2nd Lieutenant; John C. Maxwell, 3rd Lieutenant.

The Cecil Guard, under Capt. John A. J. Creswell, Esq., enrolled 104 men in Elkton. John B. Rowan was 1st Lieutenant; Nicholas Manley, 2nd Lieutenant; Arthur W. Mitchell, Ensign; John Perkins, Jr., 1st Sergeant; Jacob B. Ash, 4th; in all 74 men passed in review before Lt. Col. F. A. Ellis. The week after they organized, Creswell and Rowan went to Annapolis to get arms. They returned to Elkton, assuring the town that 75 "minnie muskets" would arrive soon.

The *Whig* noted a military meeting in the issue of January 12, 1861.

> Division of Maryland Militia, a meeting of the Field and Staff Officers of the 30th and 49th Regiments of the Cecil county, and the 40th and 42d Regiments and Extra Battalion, of Harford county, and the Company Officers of both counties, convened in Elkton, on Tuesday, the 8th of January at 12 o'clock.
>
> Brig. Gen. Henry C. Stites was called to the chair; Col. John J. Heckert, of Cecil, and Col. Wm. H. Dallam of Harford, Vice Presidents, and H. Vanderford, Jr., Secretary.
>
> The following gentlemen were present:—Brig. Gen. H. S. Stites, Col. John J. Heckart, 30th Regiment; Col. Geo. R. Howard, 49th Regiment; Col. W. H. Dallam, 40th Regiment; Lieut. Col. F. A. Ellis, 49th Regiment; Major Robert H. Archer, of Harford; Major J. A. J. Creswell, of Cecil; Capt. Henry Bennett, of Cecil; Capt. John T. Bradbury, of Harford; John N. Black, Adjutant 30th Regiment; Capt. Benedict H. Keene, of Harford; Lieut. E. W. Lockwood, of Cecil.
>
> On motion of Lt. Col. F. A. Ellis, the meeting took a recess till 3 o'clock P. M., at which hour it re-assembled.
>
> Major Archer, of Harford, being in doubt as to which Brigade the 7th Cavalry Regiment belongs, brought the subject to the attention of the meeting. After some discussion, Col. Dallam, of Harford, offered the following Preamble and Resolution, which were adopted:
>
> WHEREAS. There is some doubt as to which Brigade the 7th Cavalry Regiment belongs,
>
> RESOLVED. That we consider it as belonging to the 1st Brigade, and that we request the officers of said Regiment now present to participate in this meeting.
>
> Capt. Bradbury, of Harford, reported the formation of a Volunteer Company, at Havre-

---

SARAH N. CRAWFORD   MARTHA M. CRAWFORD

THE MISSES CRAWFORD,

FASHIONABLE

Dress and Mantilla Makers,

First door above Mr. Fredus Aldridge's,

Main Street, Elkton, Md.

☞ General sempstress work done on liberal terms, and the patronage of the Ladies of Elkton and vicinity respectfully solicited.

de-Grace, of which he was commander. On motion of Maj. Archer, Capt. Bradbury's Company was assigned to Col. Dallam for inspection and review.

Lt. Col. Ellis desired to know what was the practice in reviewing Volunteer Companies, temporarily uniformed; whether it was in accordance with military propriety to review and report a company so uniformed, for the purpose of procuring arms. He had special reference to the Cecil Guards, Capt. Creswell, which he had reviewed on Saturday last.

The Brigadier General, Major Archer, Col. Dallam, and others, thought it was, as there was no particular uniform prescribed, and a company had the right to say what their uniform should be, and must be reviewed and reported, if their uniform consisted of nothing more than a piece of tape around the wrist, or any other thing however simple, provided it accorded with their by-laws. Lt. Col. Ellis thereupon expressed himself gratified; he only desired his duty to be clearly set before him.

Cols. Heckart and Howard, to which the subject was referred, submitted the following adjustments of the Regimental lines of the 30th and 49th Regiments:

At a meeting of the Commissioned Officers of the 30th and 49th Regiments M. M., the regimental boundaries of said Regiments were revised and adjusted as follows, viz: For the 49th Regiment the 1st, 2d, 3rd, and 4th Election Districts and that portion of the 5th Election District lying south of North East river and Little North East creek; and for the bounds of the 30th Regiment the 6th, 7th, 8th, and 9th Election Districts and that portion of the 5th Election District lying north and west of North East river and Little North East creek, all in Cecil county.

J. J. HECKART,
Col. of 30th Regiment.
GEO. R. HOWARD,
Col. of 49th Regiment M. M.

On motion of Maj. J. A. J. Creswell, the arrangements of the Regimental lines in Harford county was referred to the Commissioned Officers of said county, with instructions to report to the Brigadier General, when they shall have fixed the lines of the Regimental districts in said county.

The meeting then on motion adjourned

H. S. STITES, Chairman
H. Vanderford, Jr. Secretary.

In Farmington, the Lyceum debated the question: Is Governor Hicks justified in not calling an extra session of the legislature? Affirmative—Wm. P. Coulson, James Watson, John T. Egan, B. French, T. W. McCullough, Jas. C. Bird, John W. Caldwell. Negative—A. Kirk, O. G. Kidd, C. Brown, Samuel Campbell, Eli Coulson, A. H. Briscoe, J. C. Egan.

Hicks, Maryland's pro-Union governor, resisted attempts to call a special session of the legislature for fear his state would vote to join the Confederacy. Pressure mounted for him to call the assembly and declare Maryland's position one way or another, so at least its own citizens would know where their state stood. Still Thomas Holliday Hicks hesitated. Manakee observed (p. 23):

> From the various beliefs and crosscurrents it is difficult to determine Maryland's true position on the eve of the Civil War. Many of the secessionist leaders were outstanding men in the state, and their voices were heard.
>
> As the fateful month of April, 1861, drew near, however, probably most Marylanders thought that states had a right to secede, but because of their devotion to the Union they thoroughly disliked the idea of Maryland's withdrawing from it. Probably also, most of them hoped that the seceded states might be conciliated and brought back into the Union. Furthermore, a large number, possibly even an actual majority, bitterly opposed the idea of coercion, or the use of force, by the federal government to maintain the Union.

When a Baltimore firm proposed erecting Rosin Gas Works in Elkton, the *Whig* explained the benefits to its readers. But action on the plan did not begin for another two years. If 70 or 80 customers were found, gas would cost $7 per thousand feet, with installation costs added to each consumer. The illuminating power was said to be 30% greater than that of coal. The firm added that burning 2½ feet per hour gave light equal to 17 tallow candles, at less than 2 cents per hour. With proper economy and reduced consumption, the cost could be greatly reduced. Cambridge, Maryland, said the paper, already enjoyed gaslights.

Nearer to home, people in Sassafras Neck were disturbed by reports of rabid foxes. Uncharacteristically, they approached dwellings, where both men and women killed them with sticks, axes or anything at hand.

The county buzzed when push came to duel on the Delaware line. Dr. Jones of Louisiana wounded Lieutenant Wilson of Tennessee when the latter denounced Southern Douglas men.

The Mechanics, Workingmen, Farmers and Merchants also sensed danger in the "sectional controversy now agitating our country." Intent upon maintaining the Union "as it is," they called a meeting at the Court House on Tuesday, February 12. They saw themselves as "men whose interests are all bound up in the preservation of the Union, 'one and indivisible, now and forever.'" Some names appeared on both lists. In ensuing months updates appeared with an increasing number of signers.

Shingles! Shingles! Shingles!

Have just received **40,000** CYPRESS SHINGLES; good article, which we will sell at $10 per M WHITE PINE LUMBER, HEMLOCK RAILS, etc., etc. Cheap for cash, or approved paper.
BOND BROTHER & CO.

Alexander, Andrew
Alexander, John E.
Arison, John B.
Baker, Joseph
Balleu, Benjamin
Barber, James
Bennett, L. T.
Bennett, Charles H.
Bennett, John P.
Bennett, Rudulph
Bennett, V. L.
Biddle, B. C.
Biddle, B. F.
Boulden, Charles L.
Boulden, Lambert
Boulden, Isaac
Boulden, Geo. W.
Boyd, William
Bradbury, J. P.
Brenner, James
Brown, J. R.
Brown, Jr., Edmund
Burke, James
Burnite, William
Cantwell, Jos. P.
Carmer, Samuel
Carter, Timothy
Casho, Wm. H.
Charles, H.
Cleaves, John B.
Cole, Alfred C.
Crothers, Wm.
Crow, Wm. C.
Dunbar, Wm.
Davis, R. W.
Dean, William
Dean, James
Dean, Richard

Drennen, Thomas
Eder, Matthew Y.
Eder, Wm. H.
Foster, Jesse
Gerven, William
Gilpin, John, (of H.)
Harlen, George
Heath, Thomas
Hickey, James L.
Hollingsworth, T. H. B.
Holt, John W.
Howard, Thomas
Hughes, James
Hyland, A.
J. Q. Eder
Jaquett, Robert
Kimble, James
King, Samuel
King, John
Leffmann, Levi D.
Litzenberg, Perry
Logan, Samuel, Jr.
Lort, Isaac J.
M. Cantwell
Mahan, J. L.
Mahanney, James
Marrett, Thos. B.
Marshbank, R.
Maxwell, Chas. W.
May, Benjamin F
McCauley, Wm. T.
McDaniel, John
McIntire, A.
McNeal, Thomas
McNeal, Amos
McNeal, Joseph H.
McNeight, Alex
Miller, S. H.

Mitchell, A. W.
Mohan, James
Nelson, W. R.
Nowland, Wm. C.
Ott, Wm.
Parker, Caleb
Partridge, John
Pearce, Davidson D.
Pearce, Joshua B.
Pearce, George
Perkins, Jr., John
Pogue, William
Price, J. P.
Pryor, Washington
Pugh, Edward E.
Purnell, W. G.
Rambo, Jacob
Reardon, J. V.
Reed, Thomas S.
Reese, R. G.
Rhodes, M. Johnson
Roberts, Jos. H.
Rossell, John S.
Rutter, Willis
Scott, A. J.
Sebold, Emley W.
Senn, Jacob C.
Smith, Samuel
Smith, William
Strickland, P. C.
Taylor, John
Thackeray, Robert
Thackery, Thomas
Thomas, Isaac
Titus, Howard
Torbert, H. R.
Turner, George
Wells, Joseph

Wells, Geo. W.
Wells, Benj.

Edward Wilson, Sr.
R. W. Wright,

Wm. K. Wright

Slaves were mentioned frequently. Five—four women and a child—escaped from the estate of the late Thomas Boulden. "Some underground railroad agent was doubtless present to aid their escape," the *Democrat* surmised "They probably went to meet their family in New Jersey."

There were references to court cases involving slaves. Joseph Simmons, a free negro, was indicted for setting fire to a stack of straw, but he was found not guilty. Jones for the state, Evans for the defense.

Daniel Stout was indicted for petty larceny, found guilty, and sentenced to be sold out of the State for 18 months. Jones for the State, Creswell for the defense.

A typical announcement read:

> Notice is hereby given by
> virtue of an order of the Orphans Court
> for Cecil County, passed January 9, 1861, the
> undersigned will sell at public sale
> on
> Monday, 21 January 1861
> at the Court house door in Elkton
>
> Isaiah Boulden
> free negro to serve as a slave
> Terms: Cash
>
> Jas. E. Oldham
> Sheriff

The next week the *Whig* reported the sale.

> Isaiah Boulden, free negro, was sold as a slave on Monday last, by Sheriff Oldham, under the provisions of sections 41 and 45 of the 66th Article of the Code, which provide that any free negro, not a resident of this State, who shall come into the State, shall be

fined for the first offence $20, and for the second offence $500, and upon failure to pay said fine at $500, he shall be sold to the highest bidder whether said bidder be a resident of the state or not. The law also provides that one half the net proceeds of sale shall be paid to the informer, and the other half to the State Colonization Society. H. A. Silver, Esq., of Harford Co., was the purchaser in the case. Price $100.

From Newark, Delaware, came news of an unusual occurrence at the funeral of one of its leading citizens. It was noteworthy, too, because it involved Professor Edward D. Porter, principal of Newark Academy.

Joseph Dean, a local businessman, died at his residence near Newark and was buried in the Methodist cemetery. At the graveyard, somebody from Philadelphia claimed that the deceased had been a member of the Infidel Society of America. According to the *Democrat*, Professor Porter could not let the remark go unchallenged. "So unusual an occurrence produced considerable sensation, which however, subsided after a while."

Throughout the war, there were references to the raising of hickory poles to draw attention to various causes. On March 8, 1861, a writer described one such ceremony only to find that it was not so "cheerful a character as in former days, when peace and harmony pervaded society....Suspicion, jealousy and animosity threaten to burst asunder the sacred bonds of confidence by which man is linked to man...."

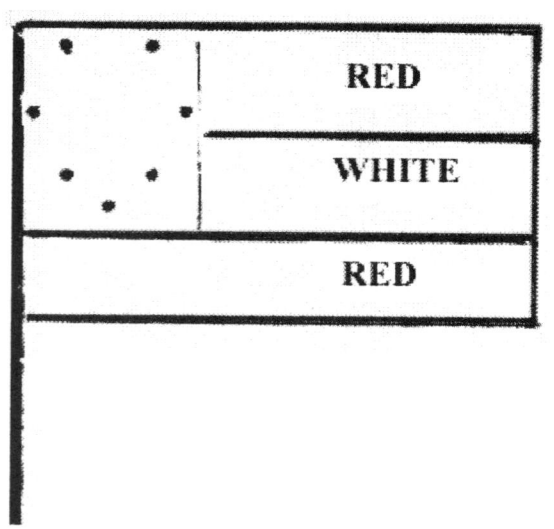

Those sacred bonds were further strained when Charles Murphy held a farm sale. Mr. Scott appeared there under the influence and announced that the calves did not belong to the cow with which they were being sold. Mr. Monohan took exception to these remarks and thrashed Scott thoroughly. Scott's friends swore vengeance and Monohan retreated to the farmhouse until the constable arrived and took him to Elkton for a hearing. Meanwhile back at the auction, 50 men behaved in such a manner that Mr. Murphy was compelled to stop the sale.

The *Whig* printed a diagram of the new Confederate flag: "The above flag has been unanimously adopted by the Southern Confederacy. It is composed of three stripes, the upper and lower red, and the middle white, with a blue union containing a circle of seven stars, the union reaching down to the lower stripe."

In Elkton, Jos. P. Cantwell took over Jacob Heckendorn's foundry, which continued to make plow castings. In fact, "...no farmer should be without the Heckendorn Economical Plow, manufactured in Elkton, which is the best plow in use."

By mid-March, the Cecil Guards were ready for a full dress parade by moonlight. After viewing them, the *Whig* said, "The new uniforms of the corps looked well even by moonlight, but it is hoped the boom-a-laddies will soon give us a better look at them by a daylight parade. Prof. Lancaster's Cornet band accompanied the Guards, and no doubt inspired them with martial ardor by the stirring strains it discoursed."

Other notices in the *Whig* gave additional insight into the lives of two signers of the Workingmen's Petition, Wm. H. Eder and J. L. Mahan. Since Eder was shortly to assume his duties as mail agent on the route from Philadelphia to Washington, he sold "his entire stock of stoves, tinware &c., to Messrs. Cantwell and Crouch, of this town, who conduct the business at the old stand of Mr. Jos. P. Cantwell, corner of Bridge and Main Streets."

> **New Stock of Groceries!!**
> NEW Crop N. O. Molasses, New Crop N. C. Sugar, best Rio Coffee at reduced price fresh Roasted Coffee, Brown Sugar, 4 lbs. for 25 cents; choice Green and Black Teas. Also, the best quality Coal Oil; Burning Fluid; Sperm Oil; Neats' Foot Oil; Window Glass.
> Soap and Candles, &c., &c., always on hand, at   R. F. MAY'S
> In the "Hollow."

The town was not pleased that Mr. McKinsey was appointed Postmaster. He left the State 20 years ago and returned only within the last year and half. Said the *Whig*: "A large number of our citizens are justly indignant that a stranger would have been preferred for this post to Mr. J. L. Mahan, whose recommendation was so generally signed, and whose appointment, it is universally conceded, would have been highly satisfactory....A remonstrance is in circulation in regard to this matter, and is numerously signed."

Thomas Drennen's advertisement brought good news to local fashion plates— a great downfall in the price of hoop skirts. New stock was fifty cents lower than usual and was of an entirely new style to boot.

Three county residents received their medical degrees in March. Thomas F. Cropper of Chesapeake City graduated from the Homeopathic Medical College of Pennsylvania, while Charles M. Ellis and John H. Jamar of Elkton graduated from the Medical Department of the University of Pennsylvania.

In April 1861 the *Whig* noted:

> Since the original call for the County Convention, the President has issued his proclamation for an extra session of Congress, which will make a special election for

members of Congress necessary in this State. It has been deemed advisable in order to avoid the trouble of a second Convention, that the Convention to assemble next Tuesday, shall select delegates to a Congressional Convention. Let the people remember this when they meet in the primary meetings today.

Then, under an editorial entitled "Choose Ye This Day," the *Whig* urged Cecil Countians to support the Union.

> What will you do? Will you continue to be a citizen of the United States, or will you expatriate yourself and become a citizen of the Confederate States? Practically this is the political question now at issue before the people, and it behooves every man to ponder it with all the calmness and seriousness, which its importance demands. All minor considerations, such as slavery extension or restriction, compromise or no compromise, sympathy with the North or preference for the South are buried in the one practical inquiry, which every man must make,—shall I adhere to the government which has thus far protected all my rights both of person and property, which has never oppressed me for a single moment; a government based upon a constitution formed by Washington, Hamilton, Madison, Franklin, Roger Sherman and other of like patriotism and discretion, at a period of profound peace, and with ample time to perfect its minutest details:—or shall I cast loose from it, give up all claim to its protection and confide myself and all my interests to a government—to say the least—untried, conceived in the seething cauldron of Revolution, set up by men undoubtedly able but just as undoubtedly rash, impracticable, and intemperate, the foundation stone of which is the acknowledged right of any fraction of it, great or small, to secede at any time, for any imaginary cause, thereby precluding all ideas of stability. The questions which have heretofore divided us related only to the policy of the government: whether this measure or that was most likely to produce the greatest amount of material propriety, and upon these there were necessarily differences of opinion. But now we are to decide, not what policy the government will pursue, but whether we will live under this government or under the misrule of Jeff. Davis. Can any Maryland man hesitate here?

PHOSPHATIC FERTILIZER.—
Tasker & Clark's Fertilizer, containing all the ingredients necessary to fertility. For sale by
JOHN PARTRIDGE

In the next column, the reader saw the day-by-day report of the first shots fired at Fort Sumter.

A week later Lincoln issued a call for troops. Since Elkton was located on the railroad, people soon noticed mounting evidence of the coming struggle. When the President ordered a blockade of the South, the *Whig* recorded the appearance of more ominous signs in the county.

> Several trains of troops have passed over the Phila., Wil. & Balto. Railroad within the last few days. The road is now under martial law, with troops quartered at all the stations, and guards placed over the bridges at night.
>
> On Monday evening, a dispatch was received from Wilmington requesting the citizens of Elkton to guard the railroad bridges in the vicinity of our town. A company was soon called together, and placed upon duty, until they were relieved in the night by volunteers from Philadelphia.
>
> Major Sherman's—formerly Capt. Bragg's—Battery of Flying Artillery, consisting of four guns, —two twelve and two six pounders—and numbering ninety-four men, with seventy-six horses, arrived here on Wednesday last, and are now stationed at this place. There are also three companies of volunteers stationed at the Depot at Elkton as road guards. A detachment was sent down to Chesapeake City, on Wednesday evening, to protect the locks of the Canal, which were threatened by Secessionists. We understand that secession, which flourished like a green by tree before, has "grown small by degrees and beautifully less," since the gleam of Uncle Sam's bayonets in the neighborhood.

The *Democrat* published the pay of troops per month.

Colonel	$218.00
Lt. Colonel	194.00
Major	175.00
Captain	118.00
First Lt.	108.00
2nd Lt.	103.50
Brevet 2nd Lt.	103.50
First or Orderly Sgt.	29.00
Other Sgts.	27.00
Corporals	22.00
Privates	20.00
Musicians	21.00

On April 23, 1861, handbills circulated around town urging citizens to meet at the Court House at 7:00 p.m. to organize a military Company to stand by the Government of the United States. Col. George R. Howard and Maj. F. A. Ellis declared they would disregard the orders of Major General

Tilghman and would stand by the Union in all circumstances. Seventy people took the oath of allegiance, and a resolution passed: **"Cecil County will stand by the Union if all the rest of the State secede."**

The *Whig* urged, "Let every true man enrol himself at once, so that Cecil may have a regiment ready and determined to meet and crush out Secession."

A call went out for volunteers to join the Howard Guard. H. M. Newton, a Baltimore native who had lived the last 17 years in Cecil County, was headquartered at the Fountain Hotel. Newton enrolled able-bodied men between 18 and 45 years who chose to enlist for three years' service in the Union cause.

> SALT by the sack; Rock Salt; Turk's Island, for Sale.   D. Scott & Bro.

At Colonel Dare's camp in Perryville, over 2,000 troops assembled, quartered in the railroad building there. Many were recruits from Pennsylvania. Nobody crossed the lines in any direction without the written permission of Colonel Dare. Because the soldiers had plenty of everything except uniforms, among some companies the dress was as varied as the men themselves.

Companies of troops ranging from 40 to 300 were stationed at North East, Elkton, Charlestown, Newark, and Stanton, while a patrol kept vigil over the entire line of the railroad.

Periodically, the papers described counterfeit bills. In March, the warnings focused on bogus $5 bills on the Wilmington and Brandywine Bank. The Cecil Bank issued small notes in $1 and $2 denominations in May from plates that were prepared in 1850. The engraving and paper, according to the *Whig*, were of fine quality.

At this point, negative economic repercussions of the war reached Cecil County. Daniel Lord's extensive mills closed for want of cotton. From the South came news that Richmond had become the capital of the Confederacy.

In June, an accident killed an Elkton boy, who had readily signed in support of the Union. Immediately afterward, the *Whig* announced, "Yesterday about noon private McGuire, belonging to Company H, stationed at Elkton, was accidentally shot by one of his companions. Cause—playing with loaded guns." The next week, however, a more compassionate account of his funeral followed.

> Private Andrew McGuire, whose death by the accidental discharge of a musket in the hands of a fellow soldier we noticed last week, was buried on Saturday afternoon in the Catholic burying ground, in this town. After service in the Church, the funeral procession passed into the graveyard in slow-time, to solemn music, with muffled drums. After the officiating Priest, marched a squad of eight armed men under command of a Corporal, with arms reversed; next came the coffin, covered with the national flag and borne on the shoulders of six soldiers; then followed the residue of the company of which the deceased

was a member, unarmed, the commissioned officers bringing up the rear. At the grave the eight armed men wheeled to the right into line, halted on the side, and after the coffin was placed on the supports over the grave, rested on arms, which is done by placing the muzzle of the musket on the left foot, both hands on the butt, bowing the head upon the hands. —The unarmed soldiers opened ranks, and the officers marched between them to the grave, when the funeral service was performed, and the coffin lowered into the grave. The order was then given to load with blank cartridge, and a volley was fired by the squad; this was repeated three times. The soldiers then left the grave to lively music, quick time, and unmuffled drums, with officers in front and the unarmed men in the rear.

The scene was a novel one to most of our people; the slow march of the soldiers, with reversed arms, the mournful music of muffled drums, rendering it very impressive and solemn.

Lest anyone falsely assume that every soldier was of high moral character, the *Whig* impartially pointed out: "A private named Galager, from Danville, Pa., was drummed out of camp last Thursday evening, about 7 o'clock just as the evening train passed up to Philadelphia. He was said to be so worthless as not to have a single redeeming virtue in his character."

After Galager spent several days in jail, he was stripped of his uniform and marched bareheaded with his clothes under his arm, and a bayonet held on either side of him. The fife and drums played "Poor Old Soldier," as the musicians marched behind him. Thereafter followed the rest of the volunteers.

...The fellow 'ornery' as he is said to be, seemed to be quite sensitive to the disgrace, judging from the sluggish manner he trudged along, scratched his noddle, rubbed his nose, turning partially round at intervals toward his grinning camp-mates and assuming a hang-dog expression generally. When the train arrived, the company broke ranks, hustled the cashiered volunteer into cars, and hooted and jeered him out of sight.

Dr. John H. Jamar was appointed assistant at Blockley Hospital in Philadelphia in June 1861. The *Whig* reported a flag raising at Cherry Hill in the June 8 issue.

Parts of two companies of Pennsylvania Volunteers stationed at this town, assisted in the raising of a flag staff and flag at the village of Cherry Hill, in this county, on Friday afternoon of last week.

Captain Terry, of Company I, and Lieut. Hilber, of Company H, each with about 45 men, under command of Lieut. Coulter, left their quarters about 2 o'clock P.M., marching to the soul-stirring music of the "fife and drum," and carrying a beautiful flag given to them by their friends at home. They arrived at Cherry Hill about half-past three, and stacking arms, partook of refreshments prepared for them by the ladies of the village. Raising the pole, which was 78 feet in length, was but the work of a few minutes. When a flag 15 feet, and a streamer 20 feet in length, were presented in a beautiful manner by Rev. J. T. Brown, in behalf of the ladies of Cherry Hill, to the Union men of the neighborhood, and received by Jos. Miller, Esq., who, thanking the ladies in a brief speech, turned to the soldiers present, and spoke of their leaving friends and home and endangering their health and lives to defend and protect that flag, and to raise it from the dust in those parts of the Union where it had been trampled. This part of the speech was received with deafening cheers by the troops. At the close of the speech, the flag was run up by Lieut. Col. Coulter, and greeted with the roll of drums, and loud huzzas of the hundreds who were present. After which the troops left for their quarters, and the citizens for their homes, all no doubt well pleased with the reception given them.

> Prof. Morris' celebrated AZUMEA, or Baking Powder, at WM. TORBERT'S.

Beautiful flag—glorious flag!
Long, long may it wave
O'er the land of the free and the home of the brave.

—By way of returning the compliment of the volunteers who assisted in raising the flag on Friday evening last, the public-spirited and patriotic ladies of Cherry Hill gave the soldiers a handsome supper at their quarters on Monday last.

Now for the first time Ben Ricketts' name appeared in connection with a volunteer company later to be known as the Big Elk Rangers, Company C, 2nd Delaware. He is of particular interest because letters written by him and his wife when they lived at Camp Wilkes, Drummondtown, Virginia, are in the possession of the Historical Society of Cecil County. These letters are included in the Appendix. His family's home still stands on Ricketts' Mill Road. Ben married Charlotte F. (Lottie) Carter in 1861. She lived only until 1863, and he died two years later at the age of 31. Letters, which detail life in the Union army as experienced by soldiers in Company C., 2nd Delaware, appeared in the *Whig* regularly. They were signed "Big Elk," but since some of the speech patterns are identical with those in Ben's letters, it is nearly certain that he is indeed the correspondent. Also, whenever Captain Ricketts was known to be sick, "Big Elk" wrote no letters.

THE BIG ELK RANGERS. Ben Ricketts is raising a company of volunteers by the above title to serve for three years unless sooner discharged. As soon as his company is full it will be mustered into the United States service, and fully armed and equipped at the expense of the Government. There will be a meeting at the Court House tonight to give those who wish an opportunity to enlist. He has opened a recruiting station in Elkton next door to the Register's office, with branches at North East, Fair Hill and Brick Meeting House, at either of which, volunteers can enrol their names. Ben has the requisite energy and ability to make an efficient officer, and from the character of the men already enrolled under him, we have no hesitation in saying his company will do credit to any regiment.

The next week, the men met at the Court House to elect officers. "The Company is now nearly full," said Ricketts, "and will certainly leave in a few days."

> **M**AKE YOUR WIFE and CHILDREN COMFORTABLE, by calling at EDER'S and buying one of his beautiful Chamber Stoves.

A Government steamer cruised the headwaters of the Chesapeake Bay in mid-June and bought up all the local fishing boats for landing troops and supplies. The flat-bottomed boats, each capable of accommodating about 100 men, did not draw more than nine inches of water.

Under the heading, "Stampede of Negroes," the *Whig* described the escape of slaves from Turkey Point Farm. They were thought to be concealed on Watson's Island, and a large reward was offered for their recovery. The "stampede" included all of eleven escapees.

At this point, the *Whig* observed the movement of some volunteers toward the battlefront.

> The three companies belonging to the 11th Regiment Pa. Volunteers, stationed at Elkton and Chesapeake City, were removed toward the seat of war, on Sunday last, and their places supplied by a detachment, composed of Companies C. and G., Captains Layton and Barr, of the 1st Del. Regiment, commanded by Colonel Lockwood.
>
> This Regiment was furnished by the patriotic ladies of Delaware with Havelocks. The Havelock is an article made to fit over the cap of the soldier, with a curtain like that of a sun-bonnet, to protect the neck and face, composed of some kind of white stuff, such as stout muslin. The British soldiers in India used the Havelock, and found it a great protection against the sun.
>
> This appendage to the head-gear of the soldier was adapted by the celebrated British General, Havelock, who commanded in India and is honored with the name of that distinguished commander, who was a Baptist minister, as well as a soldier, and served as acting chaplain to his army. In addition to the Havelock, each soldier is supplied with a piece of soap, pins, needles, thread, etc. All honor to the ladies of Delaware.
>
> Capt. Barr is a representative of the press—being editor of The Commonwealth, a paper published in Wilmington, Del. We find a notice in Wednesday's issue of that paper

announcing to its readers that the Editor is off for the seat of war The present company do not use the depot for quarters, as did former companies stationed at this place, but have formed a "camp" of 145 tents, and named it Camp Andrews, in compliment, we suppose, to the Lieutenant-Colonel of the 1st Del. Regiment, whose name is Andrews.

The *Whig* noted on June 22 that Capt. Ben Ricketts' company left town last Wednesday and were immediately mustered into a Delaware regiment.

This is the first company our county has sent to the war, and Capt. Ricketts deserves high praise for his indomitable perseverance in raising so fine looking a body of men.

Ben Ricketts	Captain
W. F. A. Torbert	1st Lieutenant
John G. Simpers	2nd "
George Hardy	1st Sergeant
Chas. E. Hayes	2nd "
Wm. Sands	3rd "
Thos. Reardon	4th "
E. Jordan, Jr.	5th "
George Turner	1st Corporal
Harrison Bennett	2nd "
Eli Alexander	3rd "
Samuel C. Stretch	4th "
James McCullen	5th "
George W. Wright	6th "
Hugh Armstrong	7th "
Wm. Rementer	8th "

Privates Kennard Allison, Henry M. Bennett, Granville S. Bennett, Samuel S. Boyer, Levis Barbour, Wm. T. Clark, Richard A. Carr, Robert Davidson, Wm. G. Davidson, Geo. W. Davis, William Founds, Benj. F. Farnan, Isaac Foreacre, Albert Furguson, Philip H. Gales, Jacob Grant, Washington Heath, W. S. Harvey, Nicholas J. Honey, Benj. F. Hedges (Co. Clerk), C. H. Jones, Philip Johnson, Philip A. Johnson, Jas. T. Kelley, Wm. Kingston, Joel Lacey, Matthew Lockard, Geo. W. Lutts, J. T. Mahan, Asbury McDaniel, Aquilla Mahan, Jethro T. McCullough, Geo. R. Maffitt, Thomas L. Miller, Amos F. McNeal, Geo. McNeal, James McDonald, H. C. Nelson, Wm. Ott, Geo. H. Pigeon, N. Plummer, Jeremiah Ruxborough, Wm. H. Sowers, Norris Smith, Wm. Sewall, John Smith, E. W. Scarborough, John A. Steele, Heaster Smith, Peter Shannon, Henderson Scott, Richard Thomas, William Tice, Mark Whitcraft, M. T. Whitlock, and Nicholas Wilson.

The Minutes of the Cecil County Commissioners contained the following:

> The Petition of Isaac H. Register, Jas. McCauley, E. D. McClenahan and others, was filed praying the Levy of an amount ($250) to reimburse Capt. B. Ricketts for monies expended by him in raising a company in the County for U. S. Service, in reference to which the following order was passed:—
>
> Ordered that the amount of $250 be added to the incidental funds in the Levy of 1861 which amount will be made payable to Capt. B. Ricketts upon the filing by him, of an account of his expenditures, if after an examination of said account said expenditure amount to the same named, and appear to be just.

In Conowingo at this time a Home Guard formed under Sergeant Cummings of the Port Deposit Rifles. 32 members met at Fair View near Pilottown on Monday and Wednesday evenings to drill. The *Whig* reporter reached Rowlandsville late in the evening and encountered Captain Christie's company as they returned from a flag raising. "The uniforms of this company consist of a red flannel shirt and white pants with a dark stripe," he said. "The sharp contrast of these bright colors gave the company a fine picturesque and martial appearance, as it filed along the road, with measured tread to the warlike music."

A curious accident resulted in the death of Pvt. James Montgomery, of Captain Layton's company of volunteers, 1st Regiment. For some reason, he fell asleep on the railroad tracks. A fellow soldier woke him but continued on his way. However, the hapless Montgomery went back to sleep and was run over by a train at 1:00 a.m. near the culvert over Little Elk Creek. Montgomery was originally from Milford, Delaware, but his wife and child lived in Wilmington.

Whig editor, E. E. Ewing, obliged five girls by printing their ad in his paper. "We are Union girls in every sense of the word," they claimed, "and we wish to form a company of Home Guards to protect our homes and the feeble young men who cannot summon courage or strength to enlist. We reside near Cowantown and our headquarters will be near the Union flag...."

Periodically, the newspapers checked conditions at the Elkton jail. In February, the *Democrat* printed:

> To the Honorable John H. Price,
> Judge Circuit Court of Cecil Co.
>
> We the Grand Jury of Cecil County, in pursuance of our duty, having visited and examined the jail, report that we find it in a dilapidated condition, and unfit for the use to which it is applied; the floors are much broken, the ceiling many places off and the stairs also broken and unsafe, standing in much need of immediate repair.

Recommend new building.
Isaac F. Vanarsdale Foreman Grand Jury

In June, the *Whig* raised its hackles about the unattended pump in front of the jail: "A pool of stagnant water is constantly lying in front of the pump, which will be very likely to generate scarlet fever among the children in its vicinity, and other malignant diseases fatal to both old and young. Humanity, justice and economy, all conspire to induce the Town Commissioners to expend a few dollars in removing this breeding place for mosquitoes and disease."

The next week the *Democrat* said that the Big Elk Rangers, comprising about 80 men under Capt. Ben Ricketts, left to join the 2nd Regiment of Delaware Volunteers in Wilmington. Before they boarded the train, James T. McCullough, Esq., reminded them "of the fame of the Old Maryland Line and exhorted them to bear themselves valiantly on every field."

Big Elk wrote from Wilmington, June 20, 1861.

Capt. Benjamin Ricketts

> We arrived in this city yesterday at half past one o'clock and our Company was duly mustered into the U. S. service in two hours from that time. We are comfortably quartered at Union Hall, on King Street. Take our meals at the Hotel. The Company are all well and all in the finest spirits. We have a fifer and drummer in the Company.
>
> We were mustered into the service by Captain Wharton, U. S. Army: who very highly complimented us on the good appearance of the men: saying, we were the best looking company of men he had seen for a long time.
>
> The men are all orderly and quiet.
>
> You shall hear from us often, and we hope we shall always be able to give a good account of ourselves. Truly yours,
>
> Big Elk

The *Whig* reminded readers to send postage stamps when they wrote to soldiers. Many letters were unanswered simply because stamps were hard to come by in camp.

From the front arrived the disturbing news that the Union army retreated at Bull Run.

The women of Cecil County provided a midsummer's feast for members of Company G, First Delaware, stationed on the railroad in Elkton. They decorated the company's warehouse with flowers and treated the Delaware company to "substantials and delicacies of the season." Company G acknowledged their appreciation.

A CARD. Camp Andrews, Elkton, June 24, '61

The officers and members of Company G, 1st Reg. Del. Vol., on the eve of their departure from the pleasant town of Elkton, feel it obligatory upon them to offer to the citizens of said town an expression of indebtedness for the uniformly kind treatment received while here, and for the numerous favors which were shown them; and especially do they feel it incumbent on them to make an acknowledgement of gratitude to the patriotic ladies of Elkton for the bountiful entertainments supplied, through their liberality, to the company, since no claims, save those of a common interest in a glorious and holy cause, were had upon their hospitality. A generous attention so unexpected to the recipients, and so fully and sensibly appreciated, will serve in its remembrance to smooth the path and lighten the labors of the soldier, in discharge of his duties to his beloved country.

> **PAPER HANGING & FRESCOING**
> Done in the neatest style by DOWNING, GRIFFITH & CO.

Big Elk wrote the following:

Headquarters of Co. C. 2nd Reg. Del. Vol.
   Camp Wharton, near Wilmington, Del., June 27, 1861

Dear Whig—Well! here we are in camp at last. And a beautiful camp it is.
   When I last wrote to you we were in barracks in Wilmington.
   We are encamped at the Agricultural Fair Grounds, about two miles west of town. On Tuesday last we came out, pitched our tents, and prepared a mess hall and kitchen in part of the sheds on the ground. Our table is large enough to seat our company at one sitting. We took supper and slept in town on Tuesday night, started for camp at 3 o'clock Wednesday morning, eating breakfast at camp.
   We are all well pleased with camp life, and with government fare. *Every man of our company is well*, and able to do duty.—We have been visited by several of our Cecil friends, and shall be glad to see more, at any time.
   Every man of the company is fully satisfied with a soldier's life.
   We have had a number of very amusing incidents to happen, but time will not allow my writing them.
   Perhaps some day I will be able to give a chapter of incidents that will amuse your readers.

We all thank you very much for the papers you sent us last week. Newspapers are rather scarce in camp I assure you, and if any of our friends intend visiting we would be glad if they would bring us a paper or two.

Upwards of fifty of our company went to church last Sabbath morning and listened to a splendid sermon from Rev. Dr. Murphy of St. Paul's M. E. Church.

Asking the kind remembrances of our friends at home I am very truly yours,

Big Elk

William Whann Mackall declined promotion to lieutenant colonel and resigned on July 3, 1861. He disguised himself as a cattle buyer and went to Richmond, where he accepted a commission as lieutenant colonel and assistant adjutant general on Albert Sydney Johnston's staff.

As the Fourth of July was at hand, Cecil Countians were invited to a flag raising at Hart's Meeting House in Elk Neck at 2:00 in the afternoon. There were speeches and other ceremonies in which loyal citizens renewed their patriotism.

The Cecil Guards went by the chartered steamer *Port Deposit* to that town. [They bought tickets at A. W. Mitchell's Drugstore at a dollar apiece.] The *Whig* described July 4, 1861 in Cecil County.

The anniversary of the Declaration of Independence was celebrated in Elkton by the citizens generally leaving town. The Howard Guards, Capt. Ash, managed to wake up the whole town about 2 o'clock in the morning, by parading through the streets and firing some swivels they had placed upon the wheels for the occasion.

The Elkton Cadets—this is a military company of juveniles, uniformed in Zouave style and equipped with tin muskets, an excellent imitation of the genuine article—spent the day in Odessa, Del., where several juvenile companies met. The cadets were much pleased with their visit.

The Cecil Guards, by invitation of the Union Rifles, *Port Deposit*, commemorated the birth day of our nationality in and near that granite-bound town. The steamer *Port Deposit* was chartered for the occasion, and leaving Elk Landing at 6½ o'clock in the morning, with her living freight, headed for the Chesapeake. Through the kindness of the Guards we enjoyed this pleasant excursion. The morning being cool and fine, the trip was one of the most agreeable. The scenery on the Elk River is very pretty, and farm houses on its banks, embowered in shade trees, the golden wheat fields, dotted with shocks, or waving with grain ready for the sickle, the green pastures skirted with belts of woodland in the dark foliage of mid-summer, and music by the Elkton Cornet Band, which accompanied the party, all combining lent rare attractions to the scene. The *Port Deposit* reached her wharf between 10 and 11 o'clock A.M., where the Union Rifles, Capt. Taylor, were in readiness to receive them.

After marching through the town, and going through the ceremonies usual on such occasions, the Guards were escorted by the Rifles to the Happy Valley pic-nic ground, situated in one of Col. Heckart's romantic glens, a short distance from the river. There was some target practice near this place, but the competitors made very poor shooting, the glare of the sun and intense heat of the day operating against the marksmen. The Declaration of Independence was read by Capt. Taylor from the stand, after which dinner was discussed—a bountiful repast of both substantials and dainties, prepared by the Port ladies. The pleasures of the day were concluded by music and dancing, which we presumed extended to near the "wee sma' hours." The boat leaving at 9 o'clock, we were compelled to tear ourselves away from our friends, just when the dancers were rising to the height of enthusiasm, and the pic-nic part of the affair began to grow interesting. The party landed in Elkton about 1 o'clock, fully as weary as though it had been on an expedition against some formidable enemy.

And thus the citizens of Elkton celebrated the 4th of July, 1861.

Cecil Countians in Company C, 2nd Delaware, at Camp Brandywine also observed the occasion.

There are still but three companies in camp; one or two others have been mustered into service, but have not yet encamped. There are a great many visitors at our camp, all of whom appear well pleased with the camp and the good order in it.

None of the members of C. Company should complain of not having full enough liberties granted them, for almost every day there are as many as twenty or more on leave to visit Wilmington which is about two miles from camp.

FOR SALE

THE subscriber has for sale about 600 FATHOMS OF SEINE. He will sell the whole, or lots to suit purchasers. Also, a Winter Seine 225 fathoms long, with corks, lines, &c., complete. Apply to
JOHN B. COALE.

Our meals are prepared by cooks, chosen by turns from the company, and all the company mess together. We find the Government rations more than we can eat, and sell enough of the overplus to keep us in vegetables. Mr. Jas. McDonald, son of Samuel McDonald, near Lord's Factory, is the acting commissary.

On Wednesday afternoon the Union ladies of Wilmington sent out to the different companies a *real Union supper*. Indeed the variety was so great that I cannot now think of anything really good to eat that was not sent us. You may suppose the men all enjoyed their suppers *to their utmost capacity*.

Thursday night was very cold for the season of the year, and more so than I ever remember having experienced. One of our men [Benj. F. Farnan,] from North East, is on the sick list, and has been for several days: but now he is better. The rest are all well enough to discharge duty. We were all extremely well pleased to receive a large box of provisions from the *Union* ladies of Elkton and vicinity. The box is a large one, and well filled with good provisions. Tell the Union ladies of Cecil that we will always remember them for their kindness toward us; and tell them we are glad indeed to know that we leave such kind friends at home.

> The subscriber has just returned from Philadelphia and New York with
> **Spring & Summer Goods**
> J. A. ELIASON'S Cheap Corner
> Middletown, Del.

The Fourth is a quiet day in camp; and I believe the city is also very quiet. Hoping our friends at home are all well and enjoying a pleasant and happy Fourth of July, I am very truly yours,

                Big Elk

The *Whig* explained that according to army regulation a ration consisted of 20 oz. fresh and salt beef or 12 oz. of pork; 18 oz. soft bread or flour, or 12 oz. hard bread; 2 1/3 oz. beans or 1 3/5 oz. rice; 1 5/6 oz. sugar, 1 oz. coffee, ground; 1/3 gill vinegar, 2/3 oz. soap and 1/2 oz. salt.

The correspondent in Company C updated the *Whig* on his outfit's activities.

Camp Brandywine, July 12th, 1861

Dear Ewing:—Well! another week has passed, and we are still in camp. Our time passes so pleasantly, and we enjoy our new manner of life so much, that we can scarcely realize the time of a week's passing.

I suppose it is in place for me to tell you so much of our camp life as would interest the readers of your paper.

Since I last wrote you, we have had some very heavy rains, but our tents keep perfectly dry. Each tent has a board floor, raised several inches above the ground and well covered with salt hay, for the men to lie upon. The Brandywine creek runs but a mile from the camp.

There is also a little brook within a hundred yards of the camp, large and deep enough for bathing purposes; a luxury of which our men take the advantage almost every day. There is a well of as good water as I ever drank from, within the limits of the camp.

I do not think that we have passed a day in camp in which some of "C" company have not received some present from home. And I have to year of the first instance in which each has not shown a willingness to share with his friends.

The families in the neighborhood have been very kind to us; and we have a great deal given us; undershirts, havelocks, needle cases, milk, butter, vegetables, fruits, &c., for all of which as a company and as individuals we feel very grateful.

Our arms have come, with belts, straps, &c., all in good order. Our uniforms will be here in a short time; and our men will be glad of it, as they are all very anxious to be dressed in their "*soger clothes.*"

We are still all well, all satisfied, and apparently, all happy. We have plenty of music in our company to enliven camp life. Card-playing and profane language are strictly forbidden, and positively not allowed in "C" company. Any violation of this rule is punished by extra military duty.

A number of kind friends [yourself among the number,] either bring or send us newspapers very often; and they are eagerly read by the men.

Hoping our friends at home are all well, and asking to be remembered kindly by them, I am truly yours,

Big Elk

The *Whig* printed extracts from a private letter "of a former citizen of Elkton,—one of the Faculty—which will interest our readers."

Kennedy Hospital
   Hagerstown, Md., July 13. 1861

Our business has been so brisk that I did not find time yesterday to write. The Hospital is nigh full, in fact is full, and we are obliged to accommodate patients now arriving in tents located on the grounds surrounding. Last night we received a batch of 43 from Martinsburg, sent from the Hospital there, that the army under Patterson might not be encumbered in their onward march, which they expected to begin early this morning.—A good many of these cases are Camp Dysentery.

I was struck with the positions of the wounds in cases where the injury was inflicted in battle; nearly all are wounded between the knee and ankle, and some very curious directions the ball has taken in several of the cases. The standard-bearer of the Wisconsin Regiment was struck on the side of the Tibia, the ball coming out in the calf of the leg, completely perforating the bone; another, the ball penetrated the Intervoscous fascia and passed out without doing scarcely any mischief at all. I could fill an entire sheet in relating the vagaries of the Minie bullet.

SURVEYING

THE subscriber having resumed his former business of Surveying and Conveyancing, promises to accommodate all who desire to patronize him.

JOHN JANNEY.

A soldier's daily schedule at Camp Brandywine follows (Scharff 1888, p. 340).

5:00 a.m.	Reveille. Companies assemble
6:00 a.m.	Police call
7:00 a.m.	Breakfast roll call. Afterwards companies march in order to their mess hall
7:30 a.m.	Surgeon's call. Sick marched to hospital tent by guard
7:45 a.m.	First Sergeant's call
8:15 a.m.	Company assembly of guard detail
8:30 a.m.	Adjutant's call
9:00 a.m.	Squad drill until 10:30
Noon	Dinner roll call
1:00 p.m.	Officers' drill until 2:00
3:30 p.m.	Company drill until 5:00
5:50 p.m.	First dress parade call
6:00 p.m.	Adjutant's call
	Supper immediately after parade
9:15 p.m.	First tattoo
9:30 p.m.	Beat off
10:00 p.m.	Taps

A report, dated July 19, 1861, arrived from the 2nd Delaware, then at Camp Brandywine.

Dear Ewing:—A military camp is as a general thing a very dull place but Camp Brandywine is not, for here we have very much to amuse us. The men are a fine set of lively fellows who from their actions say, that they will do their duty and do it cheerfully.

We now have the Field Officers of the Regiment appointed. Maj. Robert Andrews of New Castle Co., is our major; he is a very intelligent military man, and connected with some of the best families in the county. Our Lieut. Colonel Baily, a native of Wilmington, was for a number of years a commissioned officer in the New York Seventh which is a sufficient recommendation. Capt. H. W. Wharton, of the 6th Infantry U. S. Army has been appointed Colonel of the Regiment.—He is considered to be one of the best tacticians in the army. So, you see, that as a regiment, we will most likely be pretty well cared for, and pretty well

> SALE OF A MILL.—Mr. Robert Dawson has sold his grist mill in the 5th dist., known as Gillespie's Mill to John R. Silk of Baltimore for $2,450.

drilled. The Officers and men of the different companies are well pleased with the appointments. There are now seven Companies of the Regiment mustered into service, and the regiment will be filled in another week, or perhaps less time.

We are sorry to hear of the infamous lies that are circulated in your county about Company C, such as members of the Company being in irons, under arrest &c. *There is no truth at all in such reports.* There has been one man in the guard-house since we came here. His name is Hugh Armstrong, and came from about St. Georges, Del. *He deserted; was brought back as a deserter*, and would have been Court Martialed as a deserter, and punished, if his father and mother had not made oath that he was not 18 years of age.

On Tuesday morning last, every member of the Company was furnished with a copy of the New Testament given them by the Philadelphia Bible Society; application for them having been made by Capt. Christman, of Company B for us. Our men are nearly all well; one or two are slightly unwell—not at all dangerous We have a physician to visit the camp every morning. In my next letter I will give you some account of our daily duty, showing you we are kept at work pretty well. Hoping our friends at home are all well, I am truly &c.,

Big Elk

On July 19, 1861, McCauley wrote: "There is much anxiety to have this war over. There are many in Elkton who sympathize with the South and are traitors in heart."

He added on August 10; "Saw the 15th Massachusetts regiment at the depot. 1014 men Cap. Dev... [name is unclear] of Worcester. The 14th went down this morning—they are young and healthy with woolen shirts and pants, slouch hats and *tin* canteens covered with flannel."

The summer of '61 was a time of patriotic fervor in Elkton. In mid-August the *Whig* reported:

> The rain of last Tuesday having prevented the raising of our flag staff, its erection was postponed till the next day when it was placed in a perpendicular position, and to-day at 2 o'clock the topmast is to be raised to its place, and the large and splendid flag that has been purchased by contributions collected among our citizens, will be thrown to the breeze, to flaunt defiance to all enemies of the country and its blood-brought institutions.

AUCTIONEERING!

The undersigned will sell as Auctioneer, all kinds of property, Personal and Real. Those intending to have sales would confer a favor by calling on the subscriber at Rock Springs, or address him by letter at Battle Swamp, Cecil Co., Md. He will be ready, also, to attend sales in York, Lancaster and Chester counties, Pa., and in Harford Co., Md.

OLIVER G. KIDD

The pole is in two parts, rigged as a vessel mast, smoothly dressed and painted white, and it is an ornament, to the town with that "standard sheet" proudly waving from its spiral top 129 feet above the heads of friend and foe, patriot and traitor, Union men and Secessionists, friends to the Democratic institutions of our country....

Our citizens are much indebted to Mr. B. Wells, Agent of the P. W. & B. Railroad Co., and Capt. Hughes, who displayed much energy and public spirit in procuring the handsome pole and flag, and in attending to all the details of the enterprise.

Not to be outdone in patriotism, the citizens of Rising Sun held a Grand Rally of Union Men. The ladies were invited, too, in hope "they will lend their smiles and soft persuasive influence to push forward the cause of Union." This was to be no "common political gathering," but rather an opportunity for all those interested to hear Hon. Andy Johnson of Tennessee, among others, describe the "horrors of secession."

Despite volunteers' avowed loyalty, opposition to the Union cause surfaced. The *Democrat* noted that John B. Rowan, once a Union supporter, addressed a meeting of all those opposed to "fratricidal war and ruinous taxation." Other speakers at the Peace Party meeting included T. Scott, G. Henderson and William R. Miller.

McCauley wrote on August 25: "The secessionists are combined today in County Convention at Elkton under the name of the Peace Party. John B. Rowan who last season advocated the Union, has turned over to the Secessionists and presented them with a story [?] of revolution and a speech. Maxwell, Veasey, Rowan and Ruth are delegates to the State Convention."

> **ALEXANDER EVANS,**
> **Attorney at Law.**
> May be found at the Office to which he has lately removed, opposite the store of William Torbert, Esq., in the building recently occupied as the Post Office; or at the Office adjoining his residence. Elkton, Maryland.

The *Whig* supported the suspension of *habeas corpus*: "*The Habeas Corpus in Old Times* will be read with interest, and with profit, too, we hope, by those who bawled themselves hoarse in defense and praise of General Jackson, and now make long talks, the burthen of which disquisition is the *habeas corpus*, while they ignore the important fact that traitors and spies are in concert with an immense army of vandals who are scheming to lay the Capital of the Nation in ashes and drench the plains of Maryland in blood."

In the next column, the editor railed against rebel newspapers. He recognized that a free press was the exponent of a free people, but in times of national emergency, "the press must be guarded."

His next words have a familiar ring: "And of late years the American press has been the great foe of popular liberty. Industrious politicians have made it subservient to their corrupt schemes, and it has been given up to virulence, dishonesty and licentiousness. No public man's character has been pure in its estimation, and it has stirred up the people to deeds of mutiny and rage—not even abating its clamor when the Government has been endangered and its flag prostrated."

GROVER & BAKER'S
CELEBRATED
FAMILY SEWING MACHINES.

After the outing on the Fourth, the Cecil Guard got down to the serious business of target practice. At 110 yards, they fired 4 rounds from 25 muskets. Fifty struck the target. Captain Creswell fired 2 good shots, but Pvt. John Gallaher was credited with the best shot that pierced the center of the target.

In the August dog days, readers learned of a new treat from the pen of Charles Dickens. *Great Expectations*, his latest novel, was available from T. B. Peterson & Co., 306 Chestnut Street, Philadelphia, for 50 cents in paper or $1.50 in cloth.

On the 24th, the *Whig* said that "Captain Ben Ricketts, who was confined to his bed for a week or ten days by an attack of fever, is convalescent. He joined company again last Wednesday." Was it merely a coincidence that no news arrived from Big Elk for that length of time? When Captain Ricketts recovered, another letter arrived from Big Elk.

CAMP BRANDYWINE, Aug. 30, '61
DEAR EWING:—From the reports I have from Cecil, you must by this time be tired of looking for us to pass through your place.—And, I suppose, if you soon stop looking for us, about that time you will see us.

When I last wrote to you I fully believed we would leave here very soon. But *we may not leave here for a week or more.*

The men of the Regiment are all ready to go, I believe; although we have not yet received our overcoats; we have everything else necessary for the comfort of the men.—The coats are ordered and will be down in a few days.

The wet and unpleasant weather that we have had for the last two weeks, has caused some little sickness among the men, but in nearly every case caused by their needless exposure. We have had but one death in our regiment; and that very sudden indeed; the man being sick but a few hours. Cause—Congestion of the brain.

There are but two or three of the Big Elk Rangers sick, and neither of them, at all dangerous. The sick are well cared for; attended by one of the best physicians in Wilmington, and draw extra rations of such things as are needful for them, different from the rations with which the men are furnished. The Hospital tent, a fine large tent, is fitted up with berths, so that the men are not allowed to sleep upon the ground.

A Regimental Band has been organized; and will be furnished with their instruments in a very few days. Their instruments will be of the first class. The field officers of the Regiment sent to New York for them. The leader of the band, Capt. Smith, is considered one of the best musicians in the State. The pay of the band is considerably more than the pay of a soldier. Several from our company have been detailed for the band; and, by the way, some of the best men in the company.

Carr, [the fifer] Stretch, [corporal] Sands and Reardon, [Orderly Sergeants], and Hardy [Orderly Sergeant] of the company. Quite a loss, just now; but we have plenty of men in the company, that can fill their places. On account of this we now want a few *good, sober* and *intelligent* men to fill the vacancy.

We can fill up any day, but we want the whole company to be from Cecil county. If you can send us a few of such men as we want, we would be glad. The men are continuing to improve, and are making a fine company of soldiers.

We are furnished with plenty of good wholesome provisions, and have no need to complain of anything.

Hoping our friends at home are well, and trusting that you shall hear a good account of us wherever we may be, I am truly yours,

BIG ELK

According to McCauley, a soldier threw a canteen from a passing train, and the missile hit Benjamin Wells in the chest.

In early September, the dedication of the Elkton Union Hall drew an enthusiastic crowd that filled to capacity the large clubroom on North Street. Club president George Earle, Esq, opened the meeting with brief but spirited remarks. Then John A. J. Creswell, Esq., approached the speaker's platform amid much cheering. Frequently, applause interrupted his stirring oratory, much of which was directed against Rowan's Peace Party.

Mr. Creswell appeared in one of his most eloquent moods, reviewing the whole secession question in a masterly manner, laying the entire blame of the present war where it justly belongs, on the Southern rebels. The keen sarcasm, and fine vein of irony which sparkled through the speaker's remarks, when referring to the "Peace Party" and the manner in which they disgraced the national flag, when that party held its County convention in Elkton, a few weeks since, by appending to the Stars and Stripes a dirty piece of cotton cloth, with the cowardly and humiliating badge of "Peace" inscribed on it, fairly brought down the house with applause....The speaker chained the attention of the audience for an hour and a half....

James T. McCullough, Esq., was next called to the stand, and made a short speech, which carried the earnest convictions of the speaker's own heart to those of his hearers. The orator appealed to the deliberate judgment of every man to decide between his country and its manifold blessings, its brilliant history and sacred institutions; and the devastation of anarchy, the vassalage of despotism, and the overthrow of civil and religious liberty, on which our Government and its institutions rest....

McCauley reflected on the economy in his entry of September 1. He wrote, "trade is paralyzed by war."

Travel became more difficult. In Havre de Grace, a train was searched for deserters and other "improper persons." In that area 2,000 mules were quartered along with 300 wagons.

On the Cecil side of the Susquehanna, residents of Perryville were ruffled by the activity that surrounded their town. There were hundreds of wagons. Their iron axles were uniform in size and pattern. The wagon bodies were painted blue, the running gears dark brown. They were fitted with sturdy canvas covers and required a team of four mules to pull them.

As wagons were fitted up, they were pulled onto the perimeter of a plat of several acres. Several hundred mules grazed within each of these wheeled "fences." An estimated 1,200 to 1,500 mules were in such enclosures around Perryville. The *Whig* mentioned one minor problem: all the mules were green [unbroken] and presented somewhat of a challenge to the persons responsible for breaking them.

There were 25 wagons to a train, with four mules and a driver for each wagon. Each train had its own train master and assistant. As soon as the trains were ready, they moved out to make room for others. Droves of mules, branded on the shoulder with "U.S.," were constantly on the move around Perryville.

McCauley saw the "20th Massachusetts pass at the depot completely equipped with wagons, horses and ambulances."

A *Whig* correspondent described the scene as soldiers left from North East on September 12, 1861.

> Mr. Editor.—Our usually quiet village was the scene of quite an excitement this morning, occasioned by the departure of the Maffit Zouaves for Camp Hoffman, Baltimore City, where they are ordered to go into the camp until the Regiment receives its full complement of men, which is rapidly being accomplished. As was stated in the Whig some time since, this Company is composed of *patriotic* young men who are ready to serve their country, as they have now *fully demonstrated*, of which you would have been satisfied had you witnessed the thrilling scene that occurred at the depot,

---

NOTICE

PERSONS are warned not to trespass on the subscribers with Dog or Gun, as the law will be enforced against all offenders.

H. S. Coudon,	George Gale
G. P. Whitaker,	E. M. Seeley,
H. Chamberlain,	Eli Cosgrove,
Joseph Coudon,	Sam. Jackson
L. H. Evans,	John Stump,
Nathan Layton,	John Sheridan,
John Cunningham.	

this morning, as they impatiently waited for the iron horse to carry them to the point of their destination.

The men were drawn up in line, where the oath of allegiance was administered to them by our venerable Justice of the Peace, Anthony Warton, Esq. Every ear was bent to hear the obligations as read by the old gentleman, and every hand was extended to grasp the sacred book to swear *eternal allegiance to our holy cause.* Present, also, were the mothers and sisters of those men [all honor to them] who were willing to offer on their country's altar their sons and brothers. One mother in the crowd, proud to have a son thus to honor her, expressed the wish that she had an hundred sons to send, "only wished she was a man, to go herself."

The officers of the Company are C. Davis Irelan, Captain. Sam'l Ford, 1st Lieutenant. George W. Benjamin, 2nd Lieutenant.

> **JAMES M. BURGESS, REAL ESTATE AGENT,**
> WHOSE advertisement is in another column of this paper, has on hand at this time and for sale 20 farms: several of them from three to five miles from Port Deposit.

The company will receive a few more men, who will please report themselves either in person, or by letter to G. W. Benjamin, 2nd Lieutenant at North East, who will remain a few days, by command of the Colonel of the Regiment, for that purpose.

It is but justice to add that Chesapeake City is honorably represented in the ranks, as is also Rowlandsville. Yours truly,
Union

[Irelan's name was sometimes spelled Ireland. The Maffitt Zouaves became Company A, 5th Maryland Infantry.]

McCauley wrote on September 21, "Lt. Benjamin is drilling the few Leeds Home Guards."

Meanwhile in Port Deposit, Capt. Alonzo Snow had almost completed the formation of a company to serve in the Gist Regiment, flying artillery, to operate in Maryland. It became Battery B, Maryland Light Artillery. In his five years' experience with the 4th Regiment U.S. Artillery, Snow had served at Old Point, Fort Moultrie, in Georgia, and in Florida.

Several years before Cecil County lost many trees to the ravages of the locust worm. Now the pest returned, completely destroying the foliage of the locusts along the Susquehanna.

In September, John Rowan deserted the Union cause entirely and left to join the Confederacy. The *Whig* politely suggested that other men of the Peace Party should follow their leader to the South.

Loyalists increased their activity. The Jackson Union Club of the Fourth District met at the Fox

Chase Hotel, while the Elkton Union Club heard a patriotic address. Members of the M. E. Church in Elkton met at 10:00 on a September morning for a day of fasting and prayer. Local women raised funds and presented the Public Guard with a regimental flag.

Reid Mitchell in *Civil War Soldiers: Their Expectations and Their Experiences*, comments on the significance of flags made by women at home and presented to various regiments.

> When Americans North and South raised regiments for the army and sent them to war, they saw the soldiers off with almost identical ritual and celebration. The population at large wanted their soldiers to believe they represented all of them. The soldiers of 1861, after all, were volunteers—independent and rational citizens freely choosing to defend American ideals. In a sense, the soldiers' reputation would become the home folks' reputations as well. Nothing made this clearer than the ritual of flag presentation observed North and South. Customarily, particularly in the early stages of the war, the ladies of the community would get together to sew a flag for their boys, which would be presented to the hometown company in a public ceremony.
>
> This ceremony became stereotyped early in the war—a speech given by a leading citizen, a reply by the company commander, and perhaps a picnic or a banquet....
>
> The flag itself was the emblem of the community that sent companies and regiments into the field. These units were almost always composed of men from a single town or county; in a very real sense they represented their communities. Their flags linked them to their homes.
>
> Furthermore, he flags tied the soldiers to an element of society they had left behind when they marched to war. The flag, made by the women of the community, was something to be protected, much as they thought their wives and mothers should be protected. If the men left their communities to protect their homes, as many of them insisted they did, they brought something of their homes with them into battle. The flag was the physical tie between the homelife they had left and fought for and the war into which they were plunged. In Civil War battles the importance of advancing one's flag and defending it from capture—and, conversely, capturing enemy flags—indicates a devotion to flags far beyond what military rationality might...demand (Mitchell 1989, pp. 18-19).

DRESS MAKING.

MRS. MARY A. WOOD respectfully informs the Ladies of Elkton and vicinity that she intends carrying on DRESS MAKING, on Main street, next door to the Episcopal Parsonage, where she will do all kinds of Plain and Fancy Sewing.

Daniel Lord's mill known as Elk Mills resumed operation. But there was enough material to keep going for only six weeks. This time it closed indefinitely to await "more prosperous times." Iron mills fared better. Because he had large contracts on hand, Jethro J. McCullough leased Harvey's rolling mill. [In the previous decade a passerby noted the rolling mills presented a "magnificent appearance at night."]

Company C, 2nd Delaware, according to Big Elk, found itself in new quarters.

Camp Wharton, near Cambridge, Md., September 17th, 1861.
Dear Ewing:—Well! I suppose it is about time for me to write you another letter. And I am happy to say I write it from a new *home*.

I say home because already our camp appears like our home. Our Regiment left Camp Brandywine at Wilmington on Friday last, at about one o'clock, on board the cars, and came to Perryville, where we embarked on board the steamer "Pocohontas." We arrived at this place about sun-rise on Saturday morning, landed the troops and stores, and in an hour or two the tents were all *pitched* and dinner ready for the men.

Our camp is on the bank of Cambridge creek, directly opposite the town of Cambridge. The town is as pretty a little place as we have ever seen. The streets are all shaded with large elm trees.

And to our *unanimous* pleasure we find a great many beautiful little "Eastern Sho" ladies. The prevailing sentiment in this place we find [as well as we can judge] to be strongly Union.

We have a great plenty of fish, oysters and crabs, to be had for the catching. The health of the men is good, but one unwell, and he is able to do most of his military duty. The troopers are rapidly improving in drill, and move and act as if they were regulars. We have a Regimental band, which is under the charge of Capt. Smith, of Wilmington: and the music adds much to the pleasures of a soldier's life, and drives away nearly all the dullness.

The men to a unit are exceedingly well pleased with our Colonel. Having had twenty-five years experience in the regular army, you may well suppose him to be in every way qualified to take charge of a Regiment. The kindness of our Colonel to us all is the most common talked of subject in camp. It reaches to every officer, and to every private in the Regiment.

We were very kindly welcomed by the citizens of the town: and marched through the streets to our camp, cheered by the hurrah of the men and the waving of the handkerchiefs by the ladies. As in the case of troops arriving in Elkton on the 21st of April: and Union men encouraged to stand up for the right; so it is here; for already we are told that the secessionist [cowards and thieves as they are] are frightened into stillness, and honest men allowed to speak for the Union unmolested.

The paymaster of the Regiment will be here on Friday next. Some of our Company have three months pay due them. Our men are indeed exceedingly glad. Hoping to hear often from our friends at home, and hoping they are well,

I am yours truly,
Big Elk

In the same issue the editor castigated the "soulless individual" who circulated the rumor that the 2nd Delaware had been attacked by secessionists in Cambridge and cut to pieces. Understandably, the groundless report caused a great deal of anxiety among relatives and friends of the Big Elk Rangers.

From Camp Blenker, Roches Mills, Virginia, came the following dated September 16, 1861.

FRIEND EWING:—One battalion of our Regiment has at last got into Virginia. It is composed of two squadrons, Companies A. and F. forming the first, B. and G. the second. We left Camp Stoneman Tuesday, at four o'clock P. M., marched over the Long Bridge just before dusk and arrived near this place about nine o'clock, when we halted for the night and were not allowed to quit our saddles all night. Shortly after we halted it commenced raining, and continued until morning. [So you may know we were a nice set of boys when day-light came.] We then marched one-quarter of a mile further on and pitched tents. The situation of our camp is a very pleasant one. We are eight miles from Washington, two miles from Alexandria, four miles from Arlington Heights, and one mile from a Rebel battery, which is directly in front of us. We are in General Blenker's Brigade [formerly Colonel Blenker's]. He has seven Regiments of Infantry, one Battalion of Cavalry, and the Battery of Artillery known as the Bull Run Battery, which was captured by Co. K. of Col. Blenker's Regiment at the Bull Run Battle. It is a splendid Battery of six rifled brass pieces, and the men who have them know how to handle them. They are along side of us. Col. Estien's Regiment, the Garibaldi Guards, the Cameron Rifles, and several other Regiments are within hailing distance of us. There is a long range of hills on our right, which is completely covered with cannon; the trees for miles around are all felled to prevent the advance of the enemy.

> HOPKIN'S Washing Soap, a new article; Chemical Adamantine Soap, warranted to wash in hard, soft and salt water, possessing unusual cleaning properties, particularly for washing flannels and other woolen goods, extracting all gummy matter without causing them to shrink, for sale by   R. F. May

Gen'ls. McClellan and Blenker have paid us several visits since our arrival here, and complimented us very highly on our fine appearance while passing through Washington.

They say we are already equal to regulars. I am acting Sergt. Major for this battalion, and have a great many things to attend to, therefore, I will have to close.

Yours with respect,
J. FRANK CUMMINGS

In Cecilton, 61 young men formed a company under Capt. Thomas P. Jones. They employed Lt. Thomas E. Hurn of the Clayton Light Guards at Middletown as drill master.

Violence erupted in at least two areas of Cecil County that September of 1861. A deadly fight broke out in Port Deposit when a dozen soldiers "on a spree" from Havre de Grace and Perryville showed up at a Peace rally with the avowed intention of breaking up the secessionist meeting. Before the soldiers were ejected, they killed Robert Stephenson and Thomas Kelly and inflicted knife wounds upon John McCullough, George Gorrell and Samuel Aiken.

On October 23, McCauley wrote: "Court progressing. The jury is mostly of the Peace Party and there is some feeling on that subject. The soldiers at Havre de Grace that were to be tried for riot and murder at Port Deposit broke out of guard house and escaped."

The *Whig* reported a lynching near Cecilton:

> Attempt by a negro to commit rape on a white girl. — The negro hung by the citizens.—A negro man, the property of Capt. Pearce, residing in Elkton, attempted to commit a rape on a young lady, the daughter of John V. Price, of Cecilton, on Thursday last. The young lady was out riding, and arriving at a set of bars where the negro was, she requested him to lay them down, when he seized and dragged her from the horse. The young girl fought bravely, and bit the negro's finger in her efforts to resist.
>
> The exact manner of the rescue we were not able to ascertain, but the citizens of Cecilton seized the miscreant and hanged him on the nearest tree.

On October 1, 1861, the correspondent in Company C, 2nd Delaware wrote from Easton, Maryland.

NEW SHIP YARD

THE subscriber having started a yard for building and repairing Boats and Vessels, of all sizes, at PORT HERMAN, hopes to make it an object for all having work in his line to give him a call. Being in good timber country, with a steam mill on the spot by which much of the work will be done, and all of his expenses being very light, he is enabled to do work lower than it can be done in the cities. Please give me a trial.
JOHN BARNABY.

Dear Ewing:—When I last wrote to you we were at Camp Wharton, Cambridge, Md. On Wednesday evening last the 25th ult., we were ordered to this town, under charge of Lieut. Col. Baily, Capt. C. H. Christman Company "B," and Captain Ben Ricketts Company "C." We left Cambridge at 4 o'clock P.M. on Thursday 1st, and arrived at Easton Point, one mile from the town at 7 o'clock. We marched to the edge of town, pitched our tents and posted guards in a few minutes time. And at tattoo [9 o'clock] the camp was as still and as quiet as a camp ever was.

We met with a very cold reception, being in the strongest secession part of Maryland. On our march from the landing up to town we heard a number of the infamous traitors cheer for Jeff Davis and Beauregard. Having come here to aid in enforcing the Laws and to stop all unlawful proceedings, the Col. properly concluded to commence right. Consequently about 11 o'clock on the night we came, Captain Ben. Ricketts with a detachment of twelve men from his Company, accompanied by our quartermaster Geo. Plunkett of Wilmington, and guided by a gentleman of the neighborhood with hacks proceeded to the residence of Gen. Tench Tilghman [14 miles from here] and there arrested him in the name of the U.S. Government. The men of Capt. Ricketts Company who went with him were Harrison Bennett and George Turner of Little Elk, Wm. Founds, Myers Whitlock, Thomas Kelly, Wm. Sewall, Amos McNeal, Wm. B. Smith [son of John L.], Geo. Pearson, James Murry, Thomas Jeffries, and Chas. E. Hayes.

Arthur's Patent Air-Tight, SELF-SEALING CANS & JARS FOR PRESERVING FRESH FRUITS AND VEGETABLES. WM. TORBERT, Agent for Elkton

The whole company to a man were anxious to go along, and not one but the Captain knew where they were going. We left our hacks about a half a mile from the General's house, and marched up silently surrounding the house, every man armed with both gun and revolver. It was then about 2 o'clock in the morning. Captain Ricketts knocked at the door, and was answered by the General himself. He was then brought up and given in charge of Col. Baily. The Col. immediately sent him to Cambridge, under the charge of Lieut. Torbert of "C" Company, who safely delivered him to the care of Gen. Lockwood. The Gen. was very much surprised when arrested, but made ready to leave his home immediately. I have been told by several residents of the neighborhood that he had not been sleeping at his own home for four months. Unlucky night for him! I know the Union people of your county will be glad to hear of his arrest, and if justice is dealt out to him as he deserves, he will not trouble the Easter Shore of Maryland much for a while.

On Saturday last we moved to another camp, immediately adjoining the town, water and shade being very close. Our camp is a very pleasant one. The men are all well, and all appear to be enjoying themselves—We hope to soon to have something to do in the way of arresting traitors, and disarming secessionists. I tell you what it is, the arrest of Tilghman appears to have frightened them: for now we hear no more hurrahs for Davis or the South. And they had best be quiet. The scoundrels so brow-beat loyal men that they were in personal danger if they attempted to publicly speak for the Union.

There are some, however, who have not been cowed, but who in the face of all things publicly avowed their principles of the Union and Constitutional rights. Dr. Cox, Hardesty [the Post Master], Rasin, [Merchant] and a few others are as good, as loyal, and as true Union men as the sun ever shone upon. We who have voted in your county all wish we were there this fall to help your cause a little; but from the *cheering* news we hear of the *downfall* of the peace party, we suppose we will not at all be needed.

> **Increased Inducements offered to**
> Purchasers of
> DRY GOODS,
> **GROCERIES**
> BOOTS AND SHOES
> &C., &C., &C.
> BY
> **J. L. CARHART,**
> ZION MD.

We expect to be more regular in our correspondence with you; and we hope to have, every week, something of interest to write about.

We do not know how soon we may leave here, or how long we shall stay; our friends who may write to any of "C" Company, will please direct their letters to Capt. Ben. Ricketts, 2 Reg. Del. Vol. Then they will be immediately forwarded to us if we should not be in that town.

Hoping our friends at home are all well, I am truly yours,

Big Elk

The *Cambridge Intelligencer* praised the 2nd Delaware for unselfishly sending the greater portions of their paychecks to their families. Colonel Wharton reminded them of the probability of a hard winter for their loved ones at home.

The Government continued to advertise for teamsters, and the Eastern Shore Home Guard, and the Public Guard regiment recruited as well. "Captain Faehtz, long a resident of Elkton, and an experienced German officer, is raising a company for Colonel Schley, of the latter Regiment, offering a splendid opportunity to those who wish to serve their country."

Under Military Matters, the *Whig* explained insignia, rank, pay and weapons. The first section was entitled "Distinguishing Insignia of Rank in the United States Army."

The highest rank in our army is that of Lieutenant-General Winfield Scott, General-in Chief, the only one who occupies this position at present. The principal distinguishing marks of uniform are three silver embroidered stars on the shoulder strap or epaulette—a large one in the middle, flanked by two smaller ones—a double row of nine buttons on the coat, disposed in threes, a buff sash, a straight sword, and a sword knot terminating in acorns. A Major-General is the same, but with only two stars on the shoulder. A Brigadier-General has one star, and the buttons on his coat number but eight in each row, disposed in twos. The Colonel is the highest in rank in a regiment, and wears a silver embroidered spread eagle, having in the right talon an olive branch, and in the left a bundle of arrows on his strap, the buttons on his coat in double lines numbering eight at equal distances.

A Lieutenant-Colonel is second in command of a regiment, and is known by a silver-embroidered leaf at each end of the strap, otherwise his uniform is the same as a colonel's. The major's is also the same, the leaf being of gold.—His duty is to act as aid-de-camp of the Colonel, and in the event of his two superior officers being disabled or absent, he takes command of the regiment; these three constitute the field officers of a regiment, and are mounted. The Adjutant, whose position is the same to the regiment as that of orderly sergeant to a company, generally ranks as a lieutenant. Captains are commandants of companies, and are distinguished by two bars of gold on the shoulder strap, and eight buttons at a regular distance in a single row on the coat; the First Lieutenant the same, but with one bar on the strap, the Second Lieutenant having a plain strap without marks. These last are called line officers: all regimental officers wear a red sash.

FOR ROAD SUPERVISOR

I offer myself to the Voters of the Third Election District, as an Independent Candidate for Road Supervisor, and respectfully solicit their support; pledging myself in case of election to perform faithfully the duties of that office.
THOMAS H. DAVIS

The Surgeon has the letters M. S.—Medical Staff—embroidered on his strap; also wears a green sash. The quartermaster also takes a Lieutenant rank, and has the letters Q. D.—Quartermaster's Department—embroidered on his strap; the paymaster the same, with the letters P. D.—Paymaster's Department—and the Commissary with the letters C. D.—Commissary Department.

These constitute [with the Chaplain, who wears no marks, only plain clothes of uniform cut] the regimental staff, and are all allowed to have horses.

Chevrons.—The rank of non-commissioned officers is marked with chevrons upon both sleeves of the Uniform coat and overcoat, and above the elbow, of silk or worsted binding, one-half an inch wide, same color as the edging on the coat, points down, as follows:

The Sergeant-Major is first Sergeant in the regiment, and acts as orderly to the Colonel. He wears three bars, and an arc in silk. The Quartermaster-Sergeant's business is the management of the details of that department. He wears three bars and a tie, in silk. The Orderly Sergeant is first Sergeant in the company, and commands it in the absence of commissioned officers. The Chevron is of three stripes without connection, and a diamond or star above.—The Second Sergeant takes charge of half a company, called a platoon; and has the same chevrons as the first, but without a diamond. The corporals are in charge of sections or quarters of a company, and are distinguished by two bars in worsted.

Of the swords the cavalry sabre is the longest and has a steel scabbard. The field officers come next; the scabbard being of chocolate enamel with gilt trimmings. The line officers' shorter and plainer, with sheath of black leather.—A general officer's weapon is straight and short. Musicians' and non-commissioned officers' being shorter still and more for show than use.

The color of the cloth used for the strap of the general staff and staff corps is dark blue; of the cavalry, yellow; dragoons, orange; artillery, scarlet; riflemen, medium or emerald green; and infantry, light or sky blue.

FOR RENT

THE STORE and DWELLING, on Main Street, opposite the Fountain Inn. It is now occupied by Mr. Leffman for Millinery. Possession given on the 25th of March, next. Apply to J. McINTIRE

Light Artillery

Light or Field Artillery is that branch of the war service that manoeuvres with the batteries, on the field of battle, in connection with troops of infantry or cavalry.

A battery consists of six or eight pieces, four of which are guns, and two are howitzers.

Six-pounder batteries are composed of six-pounder guns and twelve-pounder howitzers, and twelve-pounder batteries are composed of twelve-pounder guns and twenty-four or thirty-two pounder howitzers.

Six or eight horses are assigned to each piece with ammunition carriage or caisson.

The number of men in a company of artillery varies from eighty to one hundred and fifty, including one Captain, three or four Lieutenants, four to eight Sergeants, eight to twelve Corporals, two to six Artificers, two Buglers, twenty-four to fifty-two drivers, and thirty-four to seventy cannoneers.

Cannon are cast from iron or from bronze, commonly called brass. Brass pieces are preferable to iron, because they are less liable to burst.

Projectiles for field artillery are round shot [solid], shell [hollow], canister, grape, and spherical case shot. The shell is filled with powder, which is fired by means of a fuze, and the fuze is ignited by the discharge. The length of fuze is graduated to the distance traversed.

The canister consists of a tin cylinder filled with cast-iron shot which vary in size with the calibre of the pieces.—Canisters for guns contain 27 shots, for howitzers 48.

Grape consists of large shots, usually nine, sewed in cylindrical bags.

The spherical case shot differs from the shell in having in having a thinner shell or case, and in being filled mostly with musket balls, only sufficient powder being inserted to burst the shell and scatter its contents—this is intended to take place 50 or 75 yards short of the object aimed at.

In a six-pounder case shot, there are 27 musket-balls; in a twelve-pounder, 76; in a twenty-four pounder, 175; and in a thirty-two pounder, 242.

> **FOR CONSTABLE**
> At the request of many Voters, I offer myself as an Independent Candidate for Constable of the 2nd Election District of Cecil county, at the ensuing elections.
> LAWRENCE SIMMONS

Each battery is attended by one traveling forge and one battery wagon, containing tools and materials for shoeing horses, repairing harness, saddles, &c.

A battery thus fully equipped, and served by active, strong and intelligent men, becomes the most formidable weapon of modern warfare.

Called into action usually at the most critical moment, at a time when the forces of the enemy are advancing exultingly, perhaps in the hope of an easy victory, at a moment when the destiny of an empire is quivering in the balance, the light artillery sweeps forward to its position at the bugle-call for "advance"—the earth shaking beneath the tramp of the horses and the heavy rumble of the guns.

In a moment the pieces are unlimbered, loaded, and pointed, with a rapidity too great for the eye to analyze the different movements; and then commences the almost continuous explosion, the cannon vomiting forth incessant charges of shot and shell, or canister and grape, until the proud lines of the adversary are riddled and shivered, and hurled back on themselves in dismay; while the ground is strewed with human beings quivering in the agonies of death.

At this moment it only remains for the infantry to charge and sweep the field with the bayonet, and the day is gained.

It is the suddenness of the attack, the rapidity of the movements, and the terrible effect with which the shot tells upon the ranks of the enemy, that render this kind of service so attractive to old gunners; hence, they will never enlist in any other branch of the service if there is a possible opportunity for them to get into the light artillery.

The amount of labor to be performed by the artilleryman differs very materially from that required of an infantry soldier—having no musket, he is not required to do general *guard service*, so while detachments of infantry are pacing back and forth, at their posts, through the long weary night, the artillerymen are sleeping quietly in their quarters.

Army Pay

Lieutenant General's total monthly pay, inclusive of rations, is $758 per month; his aid-de-camps receive $195 per month each; Major-Generals, $457; Brigadier-Generals, $314.50; Colonels of Engineers and Dragoons, $229; Lieutenant-Colonels of the same, $205; Colonels of Artillery and Infantry, $212; Lieutenant Colonels, $188; Majors of Engineers and Dragoons, $181; Captains, $134.50; Lieutenants, first and second, and brevet second, $125.83; in the Artillery and Infantry, Majors receive $169; Captains, $115.50; first Lieutenants, $105.50; second and brevet-second Lieutenants, $100.50; The Surgeon-General is paid $288.33, and his assistants from $217 to $317.33, according to their time of service—the older Surgeons, of course, receiving the largest pay. The Paymaster receives $228.33, and common Paymasters, $181 per month. Non-commissioned officers are paid as follows, by the act of August 4, 1854; Sergeant-Majors, Quartermaster-Sergeant, Chief Musician, and Ordnance Sergeant, $21 per month; first Sergeant of a company, $20; all other Sergeants, $17; Artificers, $15; Corporals, $13; Musicians and privates of Dragoons, $14; Musicians or privates of Artillery or Infantry, $13—one dollar per month of each private's pay being retained to the expiration of his term of service.

On October 15, 1861, Big Elk added his description of camp life.

Dear Ewing:—I declare I would write to you every week, but I have really nothing of any special interest to write about. When we first came to Easton we thought we were to have *stirring lively times*; but we find we are to be disappointed. The three Secession companies that were here have all disbanded and given up their arms; and we have no show at all for a

---

SPECIAL NOTICE

OWING to the great difficulty in making collections, on and after Monday, September 2, [1861], I will sell Goods only for Cash or country produce. There will be no exceptions to this rule.

R. F. MAY

brush with the scoundrels at this place. The men appear to be all anxious to remain—as they are—detached from the regiment. They all appear to enjoy themselves, and every night our little camp is made to ring with songs, and shouts of pleasure, frolic and fun.

We have a violin or two in the company, and many a good dance we have.

We hear at times as good singing in camp as we ever heard in our lives. Lt. Col. Baily, [the officer in charge,] is immensely popular with both officers and men. Col. B. is a native of Wilmington, Del., where his parents now reside. There were one or two drunken worthless fellows here who when drunk would occasionally hurrah for Jeff Davis. One named Hamilton was arrested by Capt. Ben. Ricketts and a file of men on Friday last, and kept in the guard house for a few days, fed on bread and water. The poor old devil begged hard to get off, and I am willing to bet that he'll not hurrah for Jeff, very soon again. He was discharged yesterday.

Last Saturday night, when Sergeant Chas. Smith [son of Jno. L.] was Sergeant of the guard, a man from Easton tried to smuggle into camp about two dozen bottles of whisky. But Smith was a little too sharp for him.

He was put in the guard house also, and kept there on bread and water; during the day he was made to stand in an empty barrel in front of the camp, marching between a file of men with bayonets.

Our men are all well, except one or two who are slightly unwell. There is one other little matter I will write of before I close this letter.

There is a little *one-horse* paper published here called "*The Easton Star;*" and the editor must be very one horse, to judge from his editorials. He appears to be a sort of a tool [and an awful dull one,] for the secessionists of this part of the State. I would advise them to get one of better metal, or else give up the job. He has published quite a number of little lies about us since we came here, but they are not at all worth minding. His name is Robinson. I do not know where he came from. He is perfectly harmless, however. For when he does get a *little high*, Council, the Editor of the *Gazette* polishes him off to the great pleasure and gratification of all honest men. We are not much of a judge of the qualifications of an editor; but we really think Robinson of the Easton Star has missed his calling.

Hoping yourself and all our friends are well, I am very truly yours with respect,

Big Elk

Tench Tilghman was released following his arrest by Capt. Ben Ricketts when he took an oath to support the Union. The *Whig* published the "Parole of Honor."

Be it known, that on this fourth day of October, A D. 1861, I Tench Tilghman, having been arrested by the military forces of the United States, on the charge of being engaged in enterprises hostile thereto; and being required to give my parole of honor as the

condition of my release; Now, therefore, I give this my solemn pledge, that during the existence of the present troubles between the Government of the United States, and the people of some of the Southern States, I will support the Constitution of the United States, and will make no opposition to the military forces thereof; and that I will not visit Virginia or any of the seceded States: that I will not advise against or do anything to oppose the disarming of any volunteer company on the Eastern Shore of Maryland.
[Signed] Tench Tilghman

From Camp Blenker, Blenker's Brigade, J. Frank Cummings described the war as seen from Roches Mill, Virginia. The letter was dated September 29 and ran in the *Whig* of October 12, 1961.

Friend Ewing:—Since last writing to you, our Brigade has been considerably increased by the arrival of the 45th Penn. Regiment and the Regiment of mounted Riflemen [one thousand strong] of New York. We have now as fine a Brigade as there is in the service, and I think our General will never lose his reputation as a General, as long as he has such men to fight for him. We had quite a time in camp last night. Orders were received about 9 o'clock for us to send 24 men in charge of a Lieutenant, immediately to Mansion Hill, which we did in double-quick time. In about fifteen minutes after, another order came for 75 more men, well armed to report to Headquarters, which they did also in quick time. Then came an order for all to hold ourselves in readiness and be ready at a moment's warning. The boys were all eager for a fight, and were very much put out when they got there and found our men had peaceable possession of the Secession Hill, and all the forage, &c., belonging to the rebels. The march of our troops was made about two or three o'clock yesterday P. M. They marched to an old barn and blacksmith shop this side of the Hill and took possession of them, then they halted for some time for the purpose of reconnoitering. Shortly after they started for the Hill, when they got within gun shot they fired three volleys, but the enemy did not hear it, so they did not answer; of course if they had heard it they would have fired into our men; but they fired *nary* time, and concluded they would *retire* and let us take quiet possession. Orderly Morris and

HELMBOLD'S GENUINE PREPARATIONS.
HELMBOLD'S highly concentrated compound Fluid Extract of Buchu, for diseases of the Bladder and Kidneys, Obstructions of the Urine, Chronic Gonorrhea, Strictures, Gleets, Weaknesses, and all diseases of the Sexual Organs, whether in male or female, from whatever cause they may have originated and no matter of how long standing.

Serg't Gillingham of our company were whithin [sic] half a mile of the Hill all afternoon.

They went out for the purpose of seeing some of their friends in the other camp and came very near not getting back again, as they got out side of our pickets. Our men must be careful how they travel, as we are not far from the Rebels. I was in Alexandria on Thursday last, and such a place you never did see, as it is, everything is deserted and the streets are all grown full of grass.—there is no kind of business doing. I met one of my Port friends there, Dr. Wakeman.—It did me a great deal of good to meet an old friend from home. I paid a visit to the house where Ellsworth was shot. The house which has been a fine large one is now nearly cut to pieces, by persons taking pieces as relics, the floor of the room where he met his fate, is all gone and nearly all of the joists. Everybody in the town wears a hang-dog kind of look. Whether Secession has that effect on people I know not, but it seems so in this community at any rate. I see the good people of Cecil have made their nomination and I think a better choice could not have been made by any set of persons and if they do their duty at the coming election there will be no difficulty in the election of the gentleman you have placed at the mast head.

More anon. Yours &c.

J. Frank Cummings

> **GRAIN DRILLS.—**
> Willoughby's Gum Spring DRILLS.
> for sale by   JOHN PARTRIDGE

Cummings wrote again from Roche's Mill, Virginia, when he had something to write home about. The letter ran in the *Whig* on October 19, 1861.

FRIEND EWING:—Since last writing to you, I have had the extreme pleasure of seeing some of the rebels. It came to pass in this manner, on Sunday morning last, the 6th inst. Sergeant Nangle, Gillingham, Baily, myself and three privates led by Orderly Sergeant Morris, got a pass to go outside of our pickets, for the purpose of reconnoitering. In the first place we went to Alexandria, from thence we took the road leading to Fairfax Court House, [which is 14 miles from Alexandria], and went on until we came to our outposts on Mason's Hill, four miles from Alexandria, after parleying with the Captain of the Picket Guard for some time and showing our roving papers, he let us go on. We advanced then some three miles and just as we raised the brow of a small hill, we discovered several horses picketed to the fence around a frame house, to our right and a few hundred yards ahead. It seemed as if the riders ever keeping a sharp look out, for no sooner had we raised the hill than eight of them mounted and one went some ¼ of a mile to our right, and then dismounted for the purpose, we supposed, of taking observations, but fortunately there were too many trees and they could not see how many there were of us; the other seven came out to the road and two of them advanced down the road toward us, while the others advanced on our left, and came out to the road and two of them through the woods, the two who came toward us waved a white handkerchief and came within three hundred yards of us, and then halted. Thus we stood facing each other, while the other five were going down the side of the woods to surround us and drive us into their lines. But we having *business, and very urgent too*, at home, concluded to bid them good day, and it was not long until our horses heads were where their tails had been, and going down the road.

We had no arms with us but sabres and revolvers, and they had carbines. We could distinguish them very plainly, their uniforms were about the same as ours, with the exception of the trimmings, of which they had none, their hats were low crowned black, hooked up at the side with something, I could not see whether it was an eagle or not, but supposed it to be a rattlesnake. We sent twelve pickets every day, mounted. Monday night last one of the Horses [belonging to H. Deity] of Co. "F" came home without any rider, saddle and bridle on all right and a dispatch to Gen. Blenker, in the saddle bag. It was during the heavy storm; until now we have not heard of him; in all probability he was shot by the rebels and the horse escaped, or he may have been drowned while crossing some of the streams. We had a magnificent parade of Cavalry and Artillery, on the grounds east of the Capitol on Tuesday last. There were 6500 cavalry and 1600 Artillery. It was a sight seldom to be seen. They all manoeuvred well, and I tell you the C. Dragoons were not behind any of them although there were regulars among them. When we have a fight which will be in a few weeks, I will give you some of the particulars, Yours with Respect,

J. Frank Cummings.

> **NOW is the Time to Subscribe THE WHIG FOR 25 CTS. THE WHIG IS EMPHATICALLY A SOUND UNION PAPER**

Not to be outdone by other Cecil companies, a correspondent from the 5th Maryland wrote from Camp Hoffman, on October 17, 1861.

> DEAR Whig:—In looking over your truly valuable paper I have failed to observe any correspondence from "Camp Hoffman."—It would be truly gratifying to many members of the Regiment and particularly to company A, who are without exception, citizens of Cecil county, to have their numerous friends and connections posted, respecting our

movements, past, present, and to come.—Your consent to insert our correspondence, will confer a *special favor*. The Public Guard Regiment is encamped in Lafayette Square, North Freemont Street, Baltimore, and is without exception, one of the most beautiful, healthy and salubrious situations to be found within the limits of the Monumental City. A magnificent panoramic view is had of the city and surrounding country. But what particularly gratifies the eye in the picture spread out before you, is the sight of the glorious old *Flag of the Union*, which waves in triumph from the numerous Military encampments, which surround the city in all directions—*a terror to Traitors*, but the signal of *comfort and encouragement*, to the lovers and friends of law and order. I believe I have already stated that Co. A. are exclusively Ceciltonians. They have been specially and publicly complimented upon their personal, as well as physical appearance and proportions, by officers of high rank in other regiments. I cannot therefore be considered *egotistical*, whilst unequivocally endorsing public opinion. Our Captain, Charles Davis Irelan, is a perfect gentleman, an experienced officer, and a thorough soldier. He is positively idolized by the men, who place unlimited confidence in him as a commander, protector and friend. He manifests the utmost solicitude in their behalf, by promoting, by every means in his power, any and everything which tends to add to their convenience and comfort. As a proof of his attachment for us, I may just state the fact, that very recently he was offered the dignified position of Major of the Regiment but magnanimously declined the high honor, as his acceptance of it would necessarily have deprived Company A. of their favorite. Should we be so unfortunate as to lose our gallant captain, whether through promotion or otherwise, it would be occasion for sincere regret to every officer and man in the company. Whilst endeavoring to convey to your readers, the very highest estimation in which we hold those

---

PORT DEPOSIT
Planing Mill and Sash Factory
Door and Window Frames
Panel Shutters
Wood Mouldings
Hot-Bed Sash
Brackets
Wooden Mantels
Ballasters
Newel Posts
Barn Ventilators
Window Glass
Builders' Hardward
Sash Weights and Cords
Hand Railings
Wood Tube for Chain Pumps
All orders by mail or otherwise,
attended to with promptness by
NOLAND & CO.
Port Deposit, Md.

placed in authority over us, I should be guilty of the basest ingratitude, did I omit to speak of our worthy and respected 1st and 2nd Lieutenants, Samuel Ford, and George W. Benjamin, Esqrs. Both these gentlemen are popular citizens of North East, and deservedly esteemed and respected by a wide and numerous circle of friends and admirers in their native county; but by none, are they more highly appreciated and respected, than by the members of Company A., who were raised altogether through their instrumentality. I feel proud in having the honor of representing their feelings on this occasion, and thus publicly bearing testimony to the high estimation in which they are held by the company.

> **To Paint Kitchen Floors.**
> One quart boiling water, one ounce glue. When thoroughly dissolved, stir in paint the color you wish, while warm. It should be the thickness of other paint. Spread it on, and it will dry in a few hours; then go over it with a coat of boiled oil, and it is ready for use.

Next in importance to good officers, is having good Non-Commissioned officers—Their duties are of a very onerous nature,—the drill and discipline of the men, is under their immediate surveillance. I have much pleasure in stating, that our Orderly [Wm. Jeremiah Morris], Sergeant and Corporals, are special favorites, and enjoy the confidence and best wishes of their fellow soldiers.

I shall not intrude with any further remarks at [this] time, but promise to resume the correspondence at an early opportunity.   UNION

The *Whig* noted the return of soldiers for the November '61 election. Their arrival in Elkton, accompanied by music, delighted friends and relatives. Lottie Carter, in particular, awaited news of the return of Company C. and its captain.

Capt. Ben. Ricketts' Company made its appearance in our streets, on Tuesday last about noon, "keeping step to the music of the Union," performed on the ear-piercing fife and soul-stirring drum; their bright uniforms, and still brighter bayonets, gleaming in the sun, presented a grand and martial display. The company landed at Chesapeake City, at 9 o'clock in the morning, from the steamer Balloon, direct from Easton. It will be remembered that the major part of this company are citizens of this vicinity of our county, and consequently on their arrival in Elkton they marched into the very arms of relatives and friends. The fine *physique* of the men was the remark of everyone who saw them. Soldiering has certainly improved their appearance very much. The fact that Company "C" has been mostly detailed on special service shows that it ranks high in the service, and is properly estimated by the superior officers of the Regiment.

Lottie Carter Ricketts

Capt. Ben Ricketts

Capt. Ben Ricketts, while he was home, married Charlotte [Lottie] F. Carter on November 6. Rev. Joseph T. Brown of Cherry Hill conducted the ceremony.

An ad for volunteers in the Eastern Shore Regiment invited Marylanders to rally to the cause. Those who wanted to discourage enlistments, the ad claimed, circulated false rumors that the Government would order the troops far from home as soon as they were mustered in. The Secretary of War expressly pledged that the regiment would be stationed on the Eastern Shore of Maryland to be used only for home protection. [Promises notwithstanding, the Eastern Shore Regiment was ordered into battle at Gettysburg.]

The time of enlistment was to be three years or until the end of the war. A full company comprised one captain, one first sergeant, four sergeants, eight corporals, two musicians, one wagoner, and eight-two privates. The company selected its own officers, subject to the approval of the war department. Troops were mustered into service as soon as their number reached 86 men, but it had thereafter to be raised to 100.

The ad gave the monthly pay for volunteers in the 1st Eastern Shore Regiment of Home Guards.

Captain	$60, four rations (or $36), one servant
First Lieutenant	$50, four rations, one servant
Second Lieutenant	$45, four rations, one servant
Cadet	$24
First Sergeant	$20
Sergeant	$17
Corporal	$15
Private	$13

Those officers who had no rations mentioned were allowed one ration or nine dollars per month for board and three dollars per month for clothing. The same allowances were also made to privates. Further, each soldier received a bounty of $100 upon his discharge from service.

In mid-November the town watched as a Government mule train of 30 wagons passed through Elkton en route from Perryville to Snow Hill, where it transported troops in that area of Maryland.

The women of Elkton presented a flag to Colonel Schley's Regiment in front of the Court House. The silk banner had the Maryland coat of arms painted on one side in the center of a blue field. The other side bore the inscription: "Presented by the Union ladies of Elkton Guards, Capt. E. F. M. Faehtz, to the Public Guard Regiment Md. Vol., Col. W. L. Schley."

A letter writer to the *Whig* praised Mrs. T. H. Knight and Mrs. R. Reynolds. These two Port Deposit women, through the relief association they organized, collected over $50 for sick and wounded soldiers.

The big news about town, though, was the arrest by Capt. Ben Ricketts of a clergyman suspected of disloyalty.

> On Sabbath morning last, the Rev. Mr. Mitchell, pastor of the Episcopal Church of Elkton, was arrested by Capt. Ricketts, by order of his superior officer, on a charge of disloyalty to the Government, having made use of language the substance of which was an invocation to God that the armies of Jeff. Davis might ere long, enter Maryland and drive out the Union men. We have always had a high regard for Mr. Mitchell, and exceedingly regret that, notwithstanding his many virtues, he should so far forget his duty as a christian and a good citizen, as to thus place himself in moral rebellion against a Government which has been to him one uninterrupted blessing. The prisoner was conveyed to Chesapeake City and taken to Easton.
>
> The arrest was the occasion of a "scene" among the secession ladies of the town, some of them even condescending to say bad words. Some called out to have the Captain shot; others shed barrels of tears, and others again, more warlike, charged on the guard, delivering volley after volley of hard words, which however, would not avail against muskets and fixed bayonets. Some accused their male friends of cowardice, and wished they were men till they would knock the guard down. These fighting Amazons had better hasten to don the breeches and shoulder arms in the cause of secession in Cecil, for it is in a very sickly state. In fact, there is nothing left of it in this latitude but the curl in the upper lip. Having that curl taken out of the upper lip appears to be a more severe operation than extracting teeth. But it must come out. Secession is getting out of fashion, and no lady will long submit to be out of fashion.
>
> Secession, to be sure, is an Aristocratic institution; but Aristocracy rests on Royal ancestry or wealth, neither of which the major part of our secession friends are blessed

---

Apple Corn Bread

Mix 1 pint of Indian meal with 1 pint of sweet milk, and add 1 quart of chopped sweet apples, and a small teaspoonful of salt. Bake in shallow pans in a quick oven. To be eaten hot.

with; in fact, the genealogy of numbers of them might be traced back to the *sans culottes*. Verily, the great bulk of our secession coinage is bogus. It would never pass at great Jeff's counter. A miserable imitation is our Cecil county secesh; the only faint resemblance it bears to the genuine article is the bad imitation of a curl on the upper lip. 'Tis quite amusing to see little Misses, whose mothers ought to spank 'em and put them to bed, trying to curl their upper lips. Tut, tut, girls, curl your hair and look pretty, and give up such nonsense. Providence has ordained that you shall be republican mothers, whose sons will adorn the armies and navy of the great United States, and they will be ashamed to hear that their mothers, like the tory women of the Revolution, tried to curry favor with aristocracy by curling their upper lips.

The *Democrat* reported that Ellis Pennington, a free black, was convicted of enticing away the servant woman of James E. Barroll, Esq. As punishment, Sheriff Oldham sold Pennington to an out-of-state buyer, B. C. Pearce, for $79.

According to the same source, the cabinet stood 4 to 3 against freeing and arming slaves to put down the rebellion.

Dry Mush and Milk
Parch corn quite brown, grind it in a clean coffee mill or pound it in a mortar, and let it soak in warm milk until softened; then if too thick, add more milk and eat when cold. Or meal may be browned and eaten in the same manner.

The *Whig* expressed its annoyance with the postal authorities. Subscribers in the upper part of the county received their papers late. "The fault is the Post Master's or the Mail Agent's," proclaimed the editor. "It is very annoying [and perhaps injurious] to us to bear these complaints, and we hope the officers will attend to their business a little better in future."

A few other items drew editorial blood. Those fallen leaves, for instance, that clogged up the gutters and caused unsightly puddles to form in the street! And what about people who dumped their ashes in the street with the idea of covering the mud? Ashes were every bit as miserable as mud to clean from ladies' skirts!

At least one town—Perryville—had the possibility of attaining a place in the history of this war. "At present," said the *Whig*, "it is the great mule school of the country." Then with a burst of civic pride, the paper included the whole county in its encomium. "Cecil has demonstrated by her conduct since the breaking out of the Rebellion that she is the most loyal county in the state, and richly deserves to be entitled the banner county of Maryland. She was the first to declare, on the 28th of April, her determination to adhere unconditionally to the Union, and she has furnished more soldiers to fight for the Flag, and has given a larger majority, in proportion to population, than any other county in the State. Three cheers for old Cecil."

More than 60 women attended the meeting of the Military Sewing Circle of Elkton. The *Whig* urged gentlemen to match the ladies' loyalty by contributing cash.

The population of Perryville swelled as the 11th and 14th regiments of the US Infantry prepared to winter there. Sixteen hundred troops formed a camp of instruction. The *Democrat* correspondent reported on his visit to the encampment.

The Government depot at Perryville is now the most important in the country. It contains 11,000 mules, 3,500 horses, 3,000 wagons and 3,200 teamsters with quantities of hay, oats and corn, of not less value than one million five hundred thousand dollars. The total property cannot be less than five million dollars. These animals and articles are in charge of the 14th regiment of regulars, 800 strong, under command of Major Giddings, and part of the eleventh regiment of regulars, comprising 150 men; in all including teamsters and soldiers, about 4,500 men. The tents are pitched on the brink of the Susquehanna river, sentries are posted on all the adjacent roads, and the most perfect military discipline prevails within the precincts of the camp. To guard the mules and horses is a most difficult duty. Notwithstanding all precautions, stampedes frequently occur and the animals are given to mortality. About 2 horses and 2 mules are dying every day. Uncle Sam has been pretty extensively swindled in the matter of these beasts. Major van Vliet of the quartermaster general's department, visited Perryville on Wednesday and witnessed the battalion drill of the 14th Regiment. The latter is said to be one of the best regiments in the service of the Government. Captain O'Connell is acting drill master.

Perryville captured national attention when a reporter from the *Cincinnati Commercial* visited the site. The *Delaware Republican* quoted the Ohio paper in the following article.

At Perryville, opposite Havre de Grace, a great mule and wagon depot has been established. The American flag at that point waves in triumph over six thousand mules and three thousand wagons, with fresh arrivals every day. A thick, heavy cloud of dust hovers over the region round about, and the air is resonant with multitudinous brays, intermingled with the hoarse cries of the mule-breaker.

THE MULE PENS

Coming down from Port Deposit in a buggy by the river road, in the outskirts of the city, we came upon a vast corral of United States wagons, including a space of five or six acres. Inside the enclosure we noticed a perfect forest of long ears and a compact mass of black mules working and surging to and fro. There are quite a number of these pens near Perryville, each containing fifteen hundred or two thousand mules collected from all parts of the country, and stored in these pens to await the process of breaking.

BREAKING MULES

Some distance from the pen we found the breaking ground, where about a hundred lusty darkies were engaged in the work of taking the mules through a rudimentary course of instruction, preparatory to fitting them for duty in harness. The process of breaking is exciting and interesting, and not unattended with danger.

The mule is driven into a "chute" just the width of his body, with strong wooden bars on each side, which prevent his kicking out laterally, and at the same time admit of his being handled through the cracks. A rope is then fastened to his jaw, and another tied as a girth around his belly; after which one is attached to his forefoot, and passes under the girth and out at the rear, in which condition he is turned out for the preliminary exercises, consisting of a series of frantic plunges, with some ludicrous ground and lofty tumbling, vicious attempts to bite, and strike with his fore feet. This exercise continues for a longer or shorter period of time, according to the intelligence and obstinacy of the subject. But your mule is not altogether such a fool as he looks, and after coming to grief a matter of a dozen times by means of the check-rope, he wisely concludes that plunging and rearing is not remunerative, and lies still, either reflecting or groaning piteously. If unusually obstinate through the first course, he is trotted around the course at a double quick, and his hide copiously anointed with a stout cudgel.

After the first course, the mule then being supposed to have absorbed something of the rudiments of his education, is reconducted to the "chute," where he is invested with harness and again led forth, and another series of gymnastic exercises takes places.

HIDES and HAIR

WILLIAM T. GILES at his Grocery and Provision Store, Main street, Elkton, will give the highest prices for Hides and will, also, keep on hand and for sale HAIR for the use of plasterers.

After becoming somewhat accustomed to the harness, the mules are hitched up to the large wagons and driven around the course. The operation of hitching up is a delicate one, requiring great care. The negro approaches cautiously and gingerly, with his eyes fixed on the mule's ears. A suspicious movement of the auricular appendages is seen, and the startled African springs backward quick as lightning, just in time to escape a flashing pair of heels. Again he approaches, and finally succeeds in hitching up. A brace of broken mules are usually put in the rear, with a team of wild ones in front.

Different phases of mule character are developed in the process of starting. Some plunge and rear all the time, others lie down and obstinately refuse to move, others kick out of the traces, face on the driver riding the saddle mule, rear up and viciously strike at him with their fore feet. Again one will remain properly quiet for a time, and then spring forward to the full length of his traces with such violence as to bring him to his knees. Nothing but the natural obstinacy of the mule prevents a general smash up. Fortunately, while one plunges forward, the other, through sheer perverseness, will pull back. Sometimes a forward mule will turn round in his traces, come to a dead halt, and stare at the driver the most ludicrous and side-splitting manner.

SHOEING THE MULES

A broad leather belt is passed around his belly and the mule hoisted clear, when his feet are drawn back and fastened, when he helplessly submits to the operation of shoeing, entering sundry protests in the way of snorts and groans.

CURRYING

This is an operation which hardly pays for the danger incurred. The mule is altogether too handy with his heels to render it desirable employment. Sometimes a currycomb is fastened to an eight-foot pole, when the groom stands out of range and rakes him down from the long taw.

WATERING THE MULES

This is not the least interesting of the operations I witnessed at Perryville. The mules, to the number of a thousand at a time, were driven down a small ravine in front of the hotel, spreading at its mouth to a width of about a hundred yards into the river. They rushed far out into the stream so that most of them were covered with the exception of their heads floundering and plunging, and lashing the water into foam, and all braying continually. They remind me forcibly of a school of immense porpoises sporting in the water.

Negroes are exclusively employed in the breaking and training of mules at Perryville. I asked one of the men superintending the matter why this was so. "Well," said he, "a nigger is the next thing to a mule, anyhow. They understand each other better, and there is a natural affinity of character between them. The niggers like it and—if I don't believe the mules like it, too. At any rate, a nigger can break a mule twice as quick as a white man, and get more out of him after he is broken. We tried white men, but it wouldn't do. The mules have no confidence in them."

They break about a hundred and twenty long ears a day at Perryville.

A great many people wonder why General McClellan does not make a forward movement. If they will go to Perryville, and see the vast pens of mule flesh, the wagons and the stores of forage, forges, harness and equipments, they can see what he is waiting for.

CONCLUSION OF THE DISSERTATION ON MULES

Notwithstanding all I saw at Perryville, as yet, I have no cause to modify the opinion I have long entertained of this interesting animal: "Well—a mule anyhow!"

In the fall, the *Whig* [11/30/62] added details of the Perryville operation. The horse camp, also located there, was under the direction of Arad Alexander of Northfield, Massachusetts. Two thousand horses, many of which had been drawn from the Perryville depot, were stabled there for the use of Cecil and Harford cavalry and artillery companies. Alexander grouped the horses according to color and appointed a squad of men to take care of a certain color. If a horse got loose, two facts were immediately evident: where he belonged, and who was so careless as to let him escape. The horses were fed at boxes and troughs.

At the mule camp below Mr. Stump's mansion, the same order did not prevail among the residents. Hay and grain were dumped on the ground, and a great deal was wasted. The mules, kicking and squealing, tore into the provender in a grand display of survival of the meanest.

NEW PLASTER MILL, AND COB GRINDER

THE subscriber having at considerable expense fitted up a NEW
Plaster Mill and Cob Grinder,
In connection with his Mill, at
NORTH EAST,
would inform FARMERS and others, that he is prepared to
GRIND CORN ON THE COB,
at all times, and will keep constantly on hand
GROUND PLASTER,
at the Lowest City Prices; to which he respectfully solicits a share of their patronage. GEORGE CHANDLER, North East

Mr. Stump received $4,000 per year from the Government. After the war was over, the *Whig* optimistically speculated, he would also be able to reap a rich monetary harvest from the great stacks of manure, which were piled in "immense heaps."

A. J. Scott of Elkton was the carpenter in charge of constructing barracks for the 1,400 Regulars encamped on the Stump farm. The writer noted a great deal of coughing from the men, an indication that better protection from the elements was required.

Quartermaster Sawtelle [Sautelle] was headquartered in the Stump mansion. With 14 of his staff he formed a "club." Government rations included more than the men could eat, so they sold the surplus, putting the surplus into an "etc. fund."

Mr. Townsend, chief commissary of the station, conducted a tour of the store house.

> THE NE PLUS ULTRA GLASS FRUIT JAR, said to be the best GLASS JAR in use, for sale by CANTWELL & EDER.

Here, the reporter observed barrels of flour, coffee, molasses, sugar, rice and biscuits. There were boxes of bacon and quarters of beef, too. At first the bread was baked at Havre de Grace, but then a new oven on the site supplied the post with fresh bread. An 80-foot by 40-foot commissary building was constructed to replace the "present wretched storehouse."

> It were impossible to give the reader a fair conception of the enormous amount of hay and straw that is piled round about the place. Perhaps if we say there are mountains of this kind of provender it were the best figure, to convey the idea, we can make use of; while out on the wharves are piled bags of grain and boats unloading more, and far out on the river and bay steamers may be seen towing barges piles up with bales, to keep up the supply which is daily consumed by so many thousand pairs of jaws.
>
> At 3 o'clock the steam whistle blew, and stepping into the cars we took leave of Perryville and the sight and sounds of that military depot of instruction to man and animal.

At Fox Chase, there was a flag raising on November 23, 1861. [1]John A. J. Creswell gave the flag to the Union men of the Fourth District to acknowledge their gallantry in the recent campaign.

---

[1] A marker identifies John A. J. Creswell's house on the corner of Main Street and Jacob Tome Highway in Port Deposit. It reads: "Born at this house at Creswell's Ferry, now Port Deposit, in 1828, John Creswell graduated from Dickinson College and became a lawyer. He was elected to the General Assembly in 1861, became Adjutant General in 1862, was elected to Congress that same year, and to the US Senate in 1864.

"He served as President Grant's Postmaster general from 1869 until 1874, in charge of Republican Party patronage. He returned to Elkton, where he was the acknowledged head of the state's Republican Party until his death in 1891."

Creswell had promised the flag "to the district that led the most gallant fight against disunion." The "Old Gibraltar District" was named the "Banner District," and the flag of honor was awarded to her.

R. E. Jamar received an appointment to the Naval School at Newport, Rhode Island, He set out for school at the end of November with the *Whig's* faith that "he will justify his selection."

At the end of the year, the *Whig* ran a Church Directory for several issues. It listed the following churches and clergymen in Cecil County.

EPISCOPAL: Augustine Parish, St. Augustine's Church, Rev. R. L. Goldsborough, *Rector*, [Dioc. Delaware,] 2nd District; North Elk Parish, St. Mary Anne's Church, North East; St. Mark's Chapel, near Perryville, 7th Dist.; North Sassafras Parish, St. Stephen's Church, Rev. Mr. Shields, *Rector*, 1st Dist.; Trinity Church, Elkton, Rev. Richard H. B. Mitchell, *Rector*.

CATHOLIC: St. Francis Xavier, Bohemia, 1st Dist., Rev. Geo. Villiger, S. J., 2nd and 4th Sunday in each month; St. Patrick's, near Conowingo, 8th Dist., Rev. Lawrence Malloy; Immaculate Conception, Elkton, supplied from Port Deposit, 1st and 3rd Sunday in each month; Port Deposit, Rev. Lawrence Malloy.

METHODIST EPISCOPAL: The District is presided over by Rev. Jos. Mason, Presiding Elder. Cecil county is included in the Wilmington District.

Elkton, 3rd Dist., Rev. W. H. Elliott; Cherry Hill, 4th Dist., Rev. G. W. Lybrand; Bethel, 2nd Dist., Rev. W. J. Paxson; Chesapeake City, and Manor, 2nd District, Rev. J. Smith; Cecilton, 1st Dist., and one church in Pond Neck, Rev. Solomon C. McClintie; St. John's, 4th Dist.; Union, 3rd Dist.; Rising Sun, 6th Dist., Mt. Pleasant, 6th Dist.; Hopewell, 7th Dist., Asbury, 7th Dist., Zion, 9th Dist., Rev'ds Geo. Quigley and Wm. Throff; Charlestown, 5th Dist., Principio, 7th Dist., Wesley Chapel, 5th Dist., Hart's Chapel, 5th Dist., Rev. Thos. Sumption; North East, Rev. John Allen; Port Deposit, Rev. R. H. Pattison.

METHODIST PROTESTANT: Cecil Circuit—Shelemiah, 9th Dist., New Leeds, 3rd Dist., Harmony, 7th District, Bethesda, 8th Dist., Rev'ds J. E. T. Ewell and E. King. The only Cecil church embraced in Warwick Circuit is Warwick, Dr. D. F. Ewell and Rev. G. S. Battersby.

PRESBYTERIAN: Elkton, Rev. Henry Mathews, Port Deposit, Rev. John Squier; West Nottingham, Rev. S. Gayley; Rock, Rev. A. DeWitt; Chesapeake City, Rev. Henry Mathews; Zion, Rev. J. Napier Husted.

The Elkton Presbyterian Church is connected with the Southern Synod. All the others in the county, with the New Castle Presbytery.

UNIVERSALIST: This denomination has two churches in the county—one of them at Chesapeake City, and the other between that place and Elkton; both of which are occasionally supplied from the cities.

QUAKER: There are four Quaker of Friends' Meeting Houses in the county, viz: Brick Meeting House, 9th Dist., East Nottingham in the 6th Dist. and Octoraro in the 8th Dist. These belong to the Hicksite denomination. There is also one in the 6th District, belonging to the Orthodox society.

AFRICAN CHURCHES: Mt. Zoar, 8th Dist., Rev. J. J. Herbert; Port Deposit, 7th Dist.; Coax Berry, 7th Dist., Rev'ds Robert Howard and Henry Nelson; Frenchtown, 3rd Dist.; Bohemia Manor, 2nd Dist.; Cecilton, 1st Dist.; North East, 5th Dist., Elkton, 3rd Dist., Sandy Branch, 2nd Dist., Benjamin Scott.

William Torbert, Esq., was appointed Secretary of the Board of School Commissioners to replace Charles Manley Ellis, who resigned when he joined Rush's Cavalry as assistant regimental surgeon.

Company C, 2nd Delaware, was assigned to Camp Wilkes, Drummondtown, Virginia. Capt. Ben Ricketts with his wife Lottie moved down to live there in a log cabin. Big Elk wrote:

Dear Ewing—It has been a long time since I have written you a letter, and I think I will write you one today. It has been but a few weeks since you saw the "Big Elk Rangers." When they were up to your late State election, I guess, from the remarks I heard concerning them, they did not look any the worse on account of going a-soldiering. What did you think about it?

Well, we left your town on Sunday, the 10th of last month. Arrived at Cambridge the next morning. Left there on Sunday, 17th, and arrived at Newtown the next evening. Left there on Tuesday, 19th, and arrived at Oak Hall, Va., [Sacred Soil], same evening, at 5 P.M., passing on our march a deserted rebel battery. Left there on Thursday, 21st, and arrived at this place on the same evening at 5 P. M. We passed one or two more rebel batteries this day.—On Friday, the 22nd, there was a grand review of the brigade.

> ☞ Hens can be prevented from eating their eggs by making their nests in nail kegs, half filled with straw.

Well, we have not been doing much since we came here, except capturing a lot of cannon and small arms, arresting secessionists, and confiscating rebel property.— The Brigade Quartermaster has his hands full of contraband; a little of everything, except *niggers*. We let them alone, not even allowing them to enter the line of sentries.

I would like very much to be able to give you a description of this part of the country, but I cannot. "*Suffice it to say,*" as the preachers say—it is the most sandy, swampy, poverty-stricken, God-forsaken looking country I ever saw,—and I have traveled some little. And the people—my Lord what people! Why they are lazy, ugly, ragged, dirty, ignorant, and almost as poor as Lazarus. I hope they may, at last, get as good a home as

Lazarus did. But I see so many of them drunk and see so many who go about lying and swearing, that I fear they will never get up where Lazarus did.

But it is astonishing what pleasant weather we have down here. Some days it is quite warm. We are still in tents, but as our barracks are about finished, we will move into them in a few days. There are two buildings to each Company; each being 37 feet by 21 feet in size. We have quite a town here now. Our Regiment now consists of 12 companies.

There have been some changes in Company "C" since we left Elkton. Lieutenant Torbert is now Adjutant of the Regiment. The appointment is considered an excellent one, and I have heard Col. Wharton [who made the appointment] say a number of times that he could not have made a better appointment. Lieut. Simpers is now 1st Lieutenant of the company, and a better officer cannot be found in the Regiment.—He is always at his post when needed. He is one of your free, open-hearted men, frank and courteous to every one; respected by his brother officers, and a perfect idol of the men of his company; joining his hearty laugh with theirs in their sport, and sympathizing with them in every little trouble or sorrow. And you may depend upon it, he will be found at his post in the hour of danger. Our 2nd Lieutenant is named Richards, from Delaware. He is considered one of the ablest civil engineers in the country.

The men of our company are well, except our Orderly sergeant; he has been sick for several weeks at the hospital, but is now better, I think. His name is Benj. Sands of Westville, N. J.

We as soldiers do not fear armed men; we expected, when we enlisted, to have met them before this time. But the cowardly scoundrels scattered and fled before us, while on our march down like chaff before the wind. And now, with black hearts of treason, and mouths full of lies, they come sneaking around us—pretended friends.— So mean, so cowardly are they, that they send their negroes to our camp, and sell pies and cakes, in which is mixed broken glass and poison. And they have poisoned one or two of the soldiers of the Regiment.

I hear the arrest of the Rev. Mitchell caused quite a *stir* among the people of your town, especially among the secession ladies. Now as to the doings and sayings of the ladies, we have nothing to say. But it is *my* candid opinion that if Capt. Ben Ricketts were in your town a few days, the *men* would have to hold their "Secesh" gabbling.

> **NOTICE**
> **R**AN AWAY from subscriber, an Indentured Apprentice, named Andrew Johnson, a mulatto boy, on the 1st of the present month, and is now skulking about the county. I hereby forbid all persons from harboring or employing said boy under penalty of law.
> ROBT. THACKERAY

Well, my old friend, I have written you a long letter this time. I will try hereafter to write oftener, and to write shorter letters.

I hope you and all our friends at home are well. I wish you all a merry and a happy Christmas. Many a vacant chair will there be at the Christmas feast this year. I have several things to write about, which I will put off until my next letter. So good bye for this time.

Yours truly,
Big Elk

The *Delaware Republican* on December 23, 1861, carried a reference to the Ricketts.

Capt. and Mrs. Ricketts, who have arrived at Washington, state that nine thousand sick rebels are represented to be in the public hospitals and under private care in that city. Indeed, nearly every house has its sick or wounded soldier. There is a great lack of medicine and in many of the Secession regiments a disease called "camp-fever" prevails to an alarming extent. The soldiers are sadly destitute of shoes. Good boots sell in Richmond at $25 a pair; ladies' do. at $10; and ladies' shoes at from $4 to $5. Provisions of all kinds are scarce and command exorbitant prices. Army stores of certain kinds are much needed, and a supply is confidently expected from Washington by way of the Potomac. Mrs. Ricketts thinks there are active agents of secession and correspondents of President Davis still in Washington.

The *Delaware Republican* also mentioned that Cheap John would distribute another thousand loaves of bread this year on Christmas as he did last year. "Quite a rush of people may consequently be anticipated. He made a great many happy last Christmas, and a recollection of that fact doubtless prompts him to a repetition of his kindness. He certainly must believe in the Scriptural injunction, 'Cast thy bread on the waters and after many days it will return to thee again.'"

While Cecil Countians prayed for the safety of their soldiers in battle, they also worried about dangers to combatants' well-being in camps and prisons, where diseases spread rapidly. Anxiety at home was certainly intensified when the *Democrat* reported that there were 60,000 sick soldiers, an army within the U.S. Army.

TO PICKLE APPLES.—Take the Swar apple, Roxbury Russet, (some prefer the Tolman Sweeting,) steam them until soft, put into a crock, then take vinegar and sugar, with spices, and pour over them hot. Put on enough to cover. If the vinegar is too strong, reduce it, and pickle as peaches, or other fruit.

J. Frank Cummings told the *Whig* how a Virginia miller deliberately misdirected his squadron to a nest of rebels, "but tomorrow we will get the scoundrel as we are going after him expressly."

President Felton of the P. B. & W. Railroad granted free passage to some soldiers so they could visit their families over Christmas and return to their posts afterward.

The *Whig* reminded subscribers that it incurred the expense of new type to print an almanac for 1862. Subscribers received calendars free of charge.

With the advent of cold weather in December, rodents sought shelter in the barns and farmhouses of the area. Not to worry, because the exterminator made his annual visit to the county. Said the *Democrat*: "Anges Nicholas, known about Cecilton and Delaware City, visited our town with ferrets and made havoc among these destructive rodents. He will keep a barn free for a year for $5." For the convenience of 19th-century do-it-yourselfers, Nicholas also sold ferrets at $5 a pair.

> *Whitpot (Indian).*—Take 1 quart sweet milk, ½ pint Indian meal, 2 or 3 eggs, ½ teaspoonful salt, and 4 tablespoonsful sugar. Boil 1 pint of the milk, stir in the meal while boiling, cook 5 minutes, and add the remainder of the milk. Beat the sugar and eggs together, and when cold stir the whole thoroughly, and bake 1 hour in a deep dish. To be eaten either hot or cold.

On that encouraging note, 1861 faded into history as people braced themselves for whatever the threatening clouds might bring: escalating war on the national scene or even, God forbid, in one's own town, or widespread economic devastation.

3

Cecil County

1862

As the new year dawned, Cecil Countians flinched at the high price of coffee. The lowest grade sold for 25 cents a pound and there was every expectation that the cost would continue to rise. Families boiled wheat as an affordable substitute. Some used half the usual amount of grounds but added Waring's Extract for Coffee, manufactured by a county resident, to enhance the flavor.

The cold weather was perfect for the ice harvesters. They cut, hauled and stored the ice, an indispensable product for summer. The yield was estimated to be of a "very superior quality."

People picked up a free copy of Ayer's American Almanac at drug stores. The *Whig* declared, "It gives the best instruction for the cure of prevalent complaints that we can get anywhere. Its anecdotes alone are worth a bushel of wheat, and its medical advice is sometimes worth the wheat's weight in gold."

2nd Lieutenant Alexander of Company H, 2nd Delaware, was promoted to 1st Lieutenant of Company C. Lieutenant Simpers, Company C, 2nd Delaware, returned to Elkton to recruit.

Cheap John offered to furnish coal oil for one month free if the Elkton Commissioners would install street lamps. Another philanthropist would supply a portion of the posts [not exceeding 12]. "Come," urged the *Whig*, "let us have the street lamps, now that the fire engines are in good order, and are not to be any more expense."

John Robert Campbell of Captain Snow's Artillery died of typhoid at Drummondtown, Virginia, and his remains were brought over the Delaware Railroad by way of Wilmington and Perryville. His body was interred at Hopewell Cemetery in January.

From Drummondtown, Big Elk wrote a letter, dated January 21, 1862.

Friend Ewing:—You would think your paper was of considerable account if you could see how eagerly the Big Elk Rangers look for it. I am sorry I am not more attentive in writing to you; but, really I have so very little to write about is the cause. The Regiment is now very comfortably housed; and well fixed to "stand the storms." But we do not have many to stand down here; for during the last week or two the weather has been very pleasant; a number of days it was so warm we needed no fires during the day.

Our friends have been very kind to us, sending us stockings, mittens, luxuries for our sick, &c., for all of which we are very thankful. But until the present time there has been very much delay in getting the boxes down here from Salisbury, the terminus of the R.R. The two large boxes that were first sent to us, would not have been here yet, had it not been for the kindness, and energy of Mr. Henry R. Carter of your county.

[In reading Lottie's letters in the Appendix, one might conclude that her uncle, Henry Carter, accompanied her to Drummondtown to join her husband. On that trip, perhaps, he made the arrangements that Ben mentioned.]

He had the boxes for our regiment that were lying at the depot, hauled two miles, and then shipped on the steamer Balloon to this place. Now we have Government wagons running, which will bring all articles to us from Salisbury without charge.

Our Regimental Hospital is now finished; and anything our friends may send to the company for the sick, will be faithfully given to them. We do not need any such things as quilts and pillows, we have plenty of them, but socks, mittens, and little luxeries [*sic*] however common for the sick will be thankfully received. The Society in Elkton have been very kind, indeed, to us; and have sent us a great many different things.

The flag sent by the loyal ladies of Cecil to us by the hands of Mr. H. D. Carter was received in the best of order. A splendid flag it is, but by the inscription, I suppose it is for the Regiment.

Battery "B" of Purnell Legion, Captain Snow, is encamped with us. This battery is from Cecil county, and the men are as fine a looking body of men as we have ever seen together. The officers are all pleasant and sociable; and together with the men, are of the material that will do their duty in the hour of danger. Well, what do you think? we have a newspaper

---

REMOVAL

DR. T. H. MUSGROVE has removed his
Office to the new
Brick Building
opposite Col. Groome's.
He is prepared to perform all operations in
DENTAL SURGERY, in the best manner.
Artificial Teeth Inserted, from one
to a full set.
CHARGES MODERATE
P.S.—Persons from a distance, by informing
him by mail or otherwise, may have set
times reserved, and thereby prevent the
liability of disappointment.

published by our Regiment; and a credit it is, I assure you. We have our news carriers going around crying "paper, sir;" "this morning's." Captain Barr of Company K is the editor, formerly editor of a paper in Wilmington. We sent you a copy and would be glad to have you exchange with us.

Our garrison is favored with a little society of ladies which causes the time of *some* of the officers to pass more pleasantly than if the ladies were not here. Mrs. Col. Wharton, Mrs. Col. Baily, Mrs. Capt. Ben. Ricketts, Mrs. Condron, the wife of our chaplain, and the accomplished little Miss Nellie Wharton, the daughter of our worthy Colonel constitute our society of ladies; not very large, but *very* select. The ladies all enjoy camp life very much. I am very happy to state, that Sargt. Sands is much better; he will leave for his father's in a few days, and visit, when we all hope he will soon entirely recover his health. The health of our Company is good, as is also the whole Regiment.

Hoping you and all our kind friends in Cecil are well. I am very truly yours,

BIG ELK

At Perryville, Quartermaster Sautelle advertised for 200 teamsters. The pay was $25 a month, but he accepted only "experienced drivers, willing to go where ordered. Recently some were ordered to join Burnside's expedition and refused to comply."

A soldier belonging to a Norristown company was shot to death in Perryville. He asked his lieutenant for permission to cross the river and was told that it was too dangerous to do so. When he argued the point, the officer told him to be quiet and turned away to signal the end of the discussion. The soldier angrily fired at the officer, and the ball cut off the rim of his hat. The captain, who stood nearby, did not look approvingly upon such shenanigans in his company. Somewhere, he recalled, there was a rule about shooting at, or even missing officers. He drew his revolver and shot the offender on the spot. "The Captain's conduct is generally approved by his company," reported the *Delaware Republican*. "The corpse passed through this city on Tuesday night last, en route for Norristown, where it was interred."

Lest anyone believe that camp life allowed no time for horseplay, the *Delaware Republican* reprinted the details of a snowball fight at Drummondtown.

JAMES BLACK GROOME,
ATTORNEY AT LAW,
OFFERS his professional services to the public. He may be found at the office of his father,
John C. Groome, Esq.
ELKTON, MD

A Snow Ball Engagement.—A correspondent of the *Peninsula News* thus describes the great Snow Ball Battle that occurred in the Second regiment, at Camp Wilkes. His letter is dated January 18th. He says:

Yesterday about 5 o'clock, the Delaware Second received orders to attack Snow's

Battery, a part of Purnell's Legion encamped near Camp Wilkes, and very soon officers and men were ready for action. At the command of our Col. we took up the line of march for the field of battle which was covered about five inches in snow, which on gaining we found the enemy ready for us, receiving us with a volley of well wadded balls. Our Col. commanded "forward men," ... our boys "waded right in," and the way the balls flew was destructive to any host. After about an hour's hard fighting the enemy began to give way, and amidst the cheers of our boys and well directed balls they were completely routed and driven into Camp, when a flag of truce was sent, and we were ordered to cease firing.

Col. Wharton was slightly wounded by a ball in the face. He also received several in the breast and side.—[none in the back] amid all his clear voice still rang out "forward men," until he led us into the very Camp of the enemy. Lieutenant Col. Baily, an active officer, rushed in with slippers, without coat and hat, and was in the thickest of the fight during the engagement—a brave man, one that we will follow in any battle. Lieut. Haughy, of Company L. showed himself bravely, receiving twenty or thirty balls, but not wounded badly. Sergeant Major Brady fought desperately, was slightly wounded, Corporal Aldred, of Company M, securing a prisoner, but released him for reasons not mentioned. Our Chaplain arrived timely at the scene of action with a relief corps from Company C. and flanking the enemy on the left, led them bravely into action, himself receiving several balls. Company M., though not drilled, were in the front ranks and fought at will and well. Corporal Edmondson deserves special notice for bravery displayed on the occasion.—The men fought well generally, and our wounded are fast recovering, and should a battle come off with leaden balls, you would see the boys of the Delaware Second acting with the same bravery that is ever characteristic of the Blue Hen's Chicken. Thus ended the Snow Ball engagement of the Delaware Second.

> ☞ Mr. C. P. Ward will offer at public Sale, on the 21st inst., stock and farming implements, on the Creswell farm, near Port Deposit.

Free black people obtained "leaving slips," if they traveled beyond the confines of the county. Before departing, they tacked a notice to the Court House door describing their destination and purpose in going. They were fined for failure to comply.

Punishment for a variety of offenses resulted in the person's being sold into slavery. For example, Deputy Sheriff E. Wesley Janney, "captured" five black men on Back Street and took them to Justice Torbert for a hearing. Three were released upon proving that they were gainfully employed, but two, Jake Raison and Jim Wilson, were sold under the Vagrant Law, on Tuesday, February 11.

Unionists were encouraged by news that Forts Henry and Donelson had fallen to General Grant. The *Whig* observed that "rebel ladies of Elkton are offering gingerbread and cider as an inducement to Union beaux. It won't do, ladies. Rebeldom is a dreary old place to inhabit. 'Tis getting very uncomfortable, no doubt, out there in the cold; but ginger cakes and hard cider won't purchase redemption or bring Union beaux to conduct you out of this land of Egypt. You must renounce your secession heresies...."

> ☞ A Horse and Buggy will be sold at Public Sale, at the Court House door, on the 24th inst.

Ben Ricketts mentioned [see Appendix] in a private letter that the 2nd Delaware published a paper called the *Regimental Flag*, which the *Whig* [February 15, 1862] quoted in assuring the friends at home that General Lockwood was purging John Barleycorn from the ranks.

It having been found impossible to allow the sale of intoxicating liquors to the troops of this command, without great abuse, it is hereby ordered that hereafter no one within the limits of this command will be allowed to sell or give liquor to any officer or soldier thereof, except by the express permission of the Commanding General, or the Commanding Officer of Infantry Regiments, or Artillery and Cavalry corps. Anyone violating this order will be punished according to the terms of General Order No. 18, with labor for one month, or if that be impracticable, with imprisonment on bread and water for the same time.

Every Commissioned Officer found intoxicated will be brought before a General Court Martial for trial, and every enlisted man will be punished with imprisonment and hard labor.

It shall be the duty of every Commissioned and non-commissioned Officer knowing of spirituous liquors having been given or sold to his inferior, to report the same promptly to his commanding officer: and official notice will be taken in all cases where such officers connive at such gift or sale, or knowing of the same, fail to report as aforesaid directed.

Big Elk wrote again from Drummondtown to describe life in camp.

Camp Wilkes, February 18, 1862
Dear Whig: Do you know anything about Camp life? If you do not, I can tell you that as a general thing it is rather dull. Sometimes, however, we have something to enliven us. Only a week or two ago, we had the Paymaster to visit us. That was quite an *interesting* time. Now we have drills on rather an enlarged scale; evolutions of the Line. The Regiment is divided into three battalions; each under the command of Acting Colonel, taken from the officers of the Regiment. Lieutenant Col. Baily, the first battalion; Captain Sticker, of Company "A," the second; and Capt. Ben Ricketts, of Company "C," the third; all under charge of Brig. Gen. Lockwood. These drills are very interesting, and of much advantage to the officers of the Regiment. Company "C," Second Delaware Volunteers, *alias* "The

Big Elk Rangers," are getting along finely. A few of the men are sick, the principal ailments being rheumatism and colds.

Our company received last week, a large box well filled. Besides a number of socks and mittens for the men, there was also a great quantity of articles for the sick: bread, cakes, pies, jellies, currant and blackberry wine, canned fruits, apples, and a number of packages for some of the company. I tell you what it is the company is grateful for such favors: and our poor sick fellows fully appreciate the kindness of our friends at home. One of our sick [Wm. S. Harvey] of North East started in charge of his sister. She heard her brother was sick and came down alone; nearly a hundred mile of the route being by stage. I tell you old Whig that's what I call the right kind of a sister; I would not mind having a dozen such myself, *in case of accident you know*.

Private Ott has been discharged from the service on account of physical debility, also Private Poulson. Poulson has never been of any use to the company, having been in Wilmington *playing* sick for several months. The men are sorry to a man on account of Ott leaving us; for we all considered him a first rate fellow.

PROF. WOOD'S RESTORATIVE CORDIAL AND BLOOD RENOVATOR

Our Colonel has not come back yet; his leave of absence has been extended until the 22nd. We are getting along finely under care of our Lieutenant Colonel Wm. P. Baily.

Private Lilly has been sick, but he is now about able to do duty again. There is no contagious disease among us. We had a few cases of measles a few weeks ago, but there are none now.

What do you think of our paper *The Regimental Flag*? I guess a good many copies are sent up to Cecil by men of the company.

There is no talk of us leaving here yet; but I believe the men are all anxious to do something; and I fully believe they will fight if we ever have a chance.

Hoping our friends at home are well, I am very respectfully Yours,
Big Elk

In March, the people read with dread that the Government took over by law of Congress the possession of all telegraphs and railroads in the states under its control. War news was sparse, of course. The fear was that the Government's move portended a terrible battle, the news of which would arrive at any time. The telegrapher in Elkton was Mr. McSorlie.

The women of Port Deposit continued their efforts to supply the sick and wounded members of Battery B with necessities. The *Whig* noted that they sent the following: one dozen flannel shirts and drawers, 7 quilts, 2 dressing gowns, 9 pillows and cases, 8 pairs of socks, and a number of needle cases and mittens.

The *Whig* published a lists of dentists and physicians in Cecil County. "All the Physicians belong to the allopathic or old school, except one. Those marked with a * are not practising."

1st Dist.: Thomas A. Roberts, S. V. Mace, S. E. Wills, J. F. Cunningham,* M. A. Durney,* W. C. Pennington, W. C. Perkins, J. J. Wright, Dr. Thayre, [Indian]

2nd Dist.: Jospeh V. Wallace, W. Karsner,* _____Oldham

3rd Dist.: H. H. Mitchell, Justus Dunott, T. Musgrove [dentist], John Gilpin*, Joseph Wallace*

4th District: Robert C. Carter

5th District: C. J. Simpers, S. M. Harry, N. B. Morrison, J. J. Buckley

6th District: Eber Heston, S. B. Stubbs, John Haines McCullough, Jas. Whiteside [dentist]

7th District: J. Glacken, S. Norris, W. Loag [dentist], M. Glacken, R. Wakeman [dentist]. Cornelius S. Knight

8th District: W. B. Rowland, A. M. Jordan

9th District: Joseph Hopkins, James Turner.

Shortly afterward, the paper apologized for having omitted the name of Dr. Bromwell from the list of practicing physicians.

Now the ingenuity of Union men was put to the test. It seemed that a little rebel flag was hoisted at Fox Chase "by attaching the contraband to the halyard, cutting the cord and then drawing the diminutive emblem of treason to the top of the pole." Since there was no way to lower the flag, it flew in the face of all passing Union men.

But the latter had the last laugh. They placed an iron ring around the pole, with a pair of spring nippers attached to it and a cord to draw the jaws of the nippers together at pleasure. This machine was pushed up the pole by splicing strips of boards and pushing the machine up the flag staff till it reached the top. The iron beak seized the fabric, and brought it to the ground.

Rebel sympathizers then put a charge of powder in the pole, but the explosion only slightly injured the flagstaff. The *Whig* noted that the Treason Bill would go into effect after April 15. "After that, quarters will be found fitted up for the accommodation of such

---

RUNAWAY NEGROES ARRESTED.

TWO Negroes, calling themselves respectively Joseph Stewart and Isaac Johnson, were arrested as runaways and confined in the Jail of Cecil county, on Tuesday, the 1st instant.

Johnson is about 35 or 40 years of age, slightly gray, about 5 feet 10 inches high, dark copper color, and has on a suit of heavy drab kersey or home-made cloth. Stewart is about 25 years of age, 5 feet 6 or 8 inches high, dark copper color, has a coat of same material as Johnson and blue striped pantaloons. These negroes are supposed to have come from the neighborhood of Winchester, Virginia.

ELI COSGROVE
Sheriff of Cecil county.

apostates to Liberty, where they can amuse themselves by manufacturing miniature emblems of treason out of their worn out party-colored convict garments."

The papers carried two references in March to hay purchased by the Government from local farmers. 12 tons of government hay burned at the Elkton Depot. Said the *Whig*: "The train that caused the mischief was an extra, and running with great speed, having two engines attached, old wood burners, which scattered sparks in showers along the road, setting fire to fences and everything else combustible they reached."

Two weeks later the *Democrat* reported on the use of Wakeman's Patent Hay Press. "One of these machines, patented by Mr. B. Wakeman, of Port Deposit, has been in use here for some time, among our farmers, in preparation of their hay for market. It belongs to David Scott and Bro. of this town, who have purchased a considerable quantity of hay in this neighborhood for the government, all of which has been baled by the Wakeman machine. It costs eighty dollars."

When people learned that the *Monitor* and *Merrimac* fought to a draw at Hampton Roads, they wondered what fearsome technological changes waited just over the horizon.

As quickly as the population of Perryville increased, it declined in 1862, when the Government moved wagons, ambulances, mules and personnel. Depots were established farther south to meet the needs of the army as it moved. The camp of instruction, however, remained near Perryville.

Big Elk wrote again from Camp Wilkes in a letter dated March 11, 1862.

> Dear Whig:—Our camp was thrown into a state of great excitement a few evenings ago by the reading of a dispatch by our Colonel, which was received from Headquarters. The dispatch was an order for us to immediately get ready for a march to Baltimore. You have no idea of the amount of cheering the order caused, and if you had heard us you would have thought we were ready to leave this miserable part of the country. We at once supposed we would from Baltimore be ordered away on the expedition that is now fitting out. But we are for a time disappointed, as the order was countermanded, news of which we received today.
>
> The Second Delaware will compare favorably with the other regiments in service I should think, as we will not have to remain there long.
>
> Six or eight of Virginia sprouts (or F. F. Vs.) being a little jubilant from the effects of tangle-foot commenced hurrahing for Jeff Davis last night, in Drummondtown, when they were taken charge of by the Provost Marshal and placed in jail. They were out at work to-day along with a number of negroes, cutting wood for the soldiers, and guarded and made to work, too. Served them right; although a man who would betray his country is not fit to be kept in company with a decent negro. But before many years a personage will have charge of them all, who will have no need to use them as wood-cutters, because HE has no need of wood.
>
> I would return our warmest and most hearty thanks to our kind lady friends at North East Iron Works for the contents of a large box received today. It was the best filled that I have

yet seen come to this regiment. You would be surprised at the variety of useful and necessary articles the box contained. I tell you what it is, the soldiers appreciate the kind remembrance of our friends at home.

Well, I have to stop now. I hope that the next time you hear from me I will be away from this county, at any rate.

Hoping you and all our friends are well. I am yours very truly,
Big Elk

At the same time, the *Delaware Republican* ran a letter from a correspondent in Drummondtown that evidently referred to the same incident in which Secessionists were punished. It is included in its entirety because it gives insight into the happenings in the Second Delaware, although perhaps not of Company C specifically.

Drummondtown, Va.   March 7th, 1862

Mr. Editor:—There is but very little of interest to write about this week; but that which is transpiring, I cheerfully send you. During the severe storm of Monday last, the water broke the breast of a mill dam near Bobtown, 9 miles from here, and in its course trees were swept away as if by magic; the earth, too, was washed away to the depth of six or seven feet. The telegraph line passes down the road; and just where it crosses the dam, the poles were torn up, and the wire not only broken in several places, but a considerable portion of it was buried deep in the sand and entangled around the stumps of trees. Mr. Nunan, the operator, and myself went down to repair the break, which we finally accomplished, temporarily, but we had a happy time before we got through with the job. In the neighborhood of Bobtown there are a great many quag-mires; and before we got to our place of destination, the horse we drove, which was a noble animal, sank up to his flanks in one of those deceptive places. After we arrived at the dam, we had to walk across the gully which had been made by the water. I was standing about midway, with one end of the wire in my hand, hauling away with all the strength I was possessed of, in order to extricate it from some brush in which it had become entangled; all at once I found myself gradually sinking, and before I was hardly aware of it I was nearly up to my knees in sand. Well, if I didn't get out of that uncomfortable position quick then there's no use of having trotters. I really believe that if I had remained in that quick-sand much longer I would have been over the other side of Jordan sooner than I had made arrangements for.

WILLIAM R. MILLER
ATTORNEY AT LAW
ELKTON, MD.
OFFICE—First story of
The Cecil Whig Building.

Upon looking around, I saw that Mr. Nunan was in very nearly as bad a fix as myself, for he, too, experienced what Virginia quick-sand was. He remarked that it might have been intended as a very good joke, but for the life of him he could not tell where the laugh came in. After the break was repaired, Mr. Nunan, with his field instrument, which he had along with him, had the pleasure of conversing with the operators at Eastville, Va., and Harrington, Del. In a few days Mr. John White of the corps of telegraph builders, came down and repaired the break permanently, setting new posts &c.

GRAND REVIEW

On Sunday morning last, there was a grand review and inspection of the troops stationed here, by Brig.-General Lockwood. This was the first time that I had ever witnessed anything of the kind, and I can assure you that I was highly pleased with it. The noble bearing of Gen. Lockwood was the subject of general remark by all who were present. His extensive military knowledge qualifies him for any position in which the Department may see proper to place him. If the General is ever so fortunate as to lead his men in a battle, he will most assuredly bring them out victorious; and fame, ever ready to do justice to the loyal, brave and noble, will entwine a wreath around his brow which can never fade. The honor and dignity of Delaware is safe in Gen. Lockwood's hand. Col. Wharton, too, was the recipient of much merited praise, for the state of perfection in drill to which he had brought the 2nd Delaware. The men of this Regiment speak in the highest terms of praise of the Colonel. In fact, he is thorough soldier and though a strict disciplinarian, I have yet to hear, for the first time, any one of the men speak ill of him.

THE CASE OF PRIVATE ROGERS

In your paper of the 6th instant, I saw a notice about the shooting of private Rogers, of Capt. Hackett's company, which does Brigade Surgeon Jones and Dr. Babb great injustice. Dr. Babb has charge of the hospital here. Rogers, as I learn, is a troublesome fellow, and no reliance whatever can be placed on his word. After he was taken to the hospital Dr. Babb advised him to have the bullet removed, and told him that it might not cause him trouble just now, but that ere long suppuration *would* take place. Rogers positively *refused* to have the ball removed. Brigade Surgeon Jones was made acquainted with the facts of the case, and in a day or so thereafter went to the hospital, taking his case of instruments with him, and not only *advised* Rogers to allow him to remove the ball, but *insisted* on doing so, telling him of the bad results which might ensue by allowing the ball to remain embedded in his flesh. Dr. informs me that he could extract the ball almost instantaneously, and that it would be attended with very little pain. Rogers still refused to have the ball extracted; and as he was very insulting in his language, Drs. Jones and Babb concluded to have no more trouble with him, and permitted him to have his own way. This is a true statement of the case. As to the skill of Drs. Jones and Babb, I have nothing to say, further than to remark that they could not now hold the positions they do had they not been successful in their examination before the Medical Board.

An evening or so since Provost Marshal Wm. E. Appleton arrested five notorious secessionists. They were going around the streets of Drummondtown shouting for Jeff Davis, singing secession songs, flourishing Bowie knives, and swearing that any one of them could whip ten Yankees. Marshal Appleton was informed of the rudeness and taunts of these bragadocias [sic], and started alone, well armed, in quest of them. He overtook them on the outskirts of the town; no sooner, however, did they catch a glimpse of the Marshall, than they made a break for the woods. He succeeded, however, in catching them, for he was pretty close to them before they were aware of it. He compelled them all to follow him to jail, where they were locked up for the night. The next morning after making a hearty breakfast of Commissary Kent's "jumbles" and invigorating cold water, they were placed in the gang of woodchoppers under charge of a guard, and marched off to the woods, in order to show the Yankees that they were much better at felling trees and singing secession songs than they were at fighting. It was really amusing to see these Virginia gentry going out to the woods with axes upon their shoulders. As they passed out of the town they were saluted to just such a manner as they deserved—with hisses and groans.—There are so many loyal people here, and it is not right that they should be insulted by such bragadocias as those I have mentioned above. On going out to the woods I noticed that these men were attired in rich, fashionable garbs; the rain, which came down shortly after they arrived there, no doubt soiled their broadcloth....Respectfully yours, &c, J. G.

> W. J. JONES   W. P. EWING
> JONES & EWING
> **ATTORNEYS AT LAW,**
> ELKTON, MD.
> Having associated ourselves for the practice of our profession, we will attend carefully and promptly to all business placed in our hands. We will practice in the Courts of Cecil, Kent and Harford, and the Court of Appeals. Office on NORTH STREET, opposite the Jail.

A week later J. G. wrote another letter in which he compared the two Drummondtown hotels. These establishments would have been familiar to the members of the 2nd Delaware.

There are two Hotels in this town; one [the Union] is kept by a widow lady named Lilliston; her table is well supplied with everything a man could wish for or expect to find in a boarding house; and what is still better, both herself and pretty, agreeable daughter Emma are Union women out and out; yet still the "Union" is not patronized to that extent to which it is justly entitled. The other hotel is kept by a rabid secessionist, who proclaims himself such on all occasions; and yet he is patronized by Colonels, Captains, Lieutenants, &c. How is this? With all my knowledge of human nature, I find myself slightly at fault in this instance. If men have no respect for themselves, they should, at least, dignify the offices they hold and not patronize traitors.

In the issue of March 29, 1862, the *Whig* noted that on the previous Thursday night, the 2nd Delaware, which included the Big Elk Rangers, passed through Elkton at midnight on its way to Baltimore. In that same issue appeared a letter from Big Elk in which he reflected on the death of a fellow soldier.

> Dear Ewing:—Were you ever present at a soldier's funeral? We burried [*sic*] one on Sunday last from this camp. We saw his body wrapped in the American Flag, going to the grave. Solemn and sad were our thoughts as the funeral procession passed by us. The music of the fife and drum, generally so gay and lively was changed to the plaintive and melancholy notes of the Funeral dirge, and to the slow and solemn roll of muffled drums. Poor fellow, thought we, your grave should be marked as the grave of a hero. Your name should be remember[ed] as that of a patriot. He died, not on the field where red war run[s] mad, not where the balls like hail stones were flying, not amidst the groaning of the wounded, nor the shriek of the dying. But in the stillness of the night, when all was quiet around him, save the soft step and whispering voices of his attendants; or, perhaps, the stillness of the midnight hour [the hour when his spirit fled] was broken by the watchful sentries cry of who comes there? May his spirit soul when challenged at the throne of his Creator, answer "Here comes a spirit with the countersign." and may he safely enter into joy, and be at rest, in that blest world above where the noise of war is not heard, but where peace flows as a river, and where all is love. The soldier's name was John Berlin, Battery "B," First Maryland Light Artillery, a native of Port Deposit in your county.

> Although we received orders more than a week ago to get ourselves in marching order immediately, we are still here. Many safely say no one knows when we will move, or

---

COLLECTING

THE undersigned having been elected to the office of CONSTABLE in the Second Election District of Cecil County, Md., offers his services to the Public in that capacity. Prompt attention will be given to the
COLLECTION OF CLAIMS,
and all other business entrusted to him.
N. ALEXANDER COLMARY,
Post Office, Chesapeake City.

where we will move to; although, the general impression seems to be [among the officers] that we will go from this place to Baltimore.

There is nothing new with us of any account. The regiment is being drilled in bayonet exercises; which is not at all difficult to learn; but which would be of very much advantage to men in close quarters with bayonets.

The discipline of our regiment is good; and the men are well drilled. There is but very little sickness among us. But one or two of the Big Elk Rangers are sick; none very sick.

There has been great rejoicing during the week among our men on account of the brilliant victories of the Federal troops.—The only regret of the men being that we are not permitted to take part in the advance of our army.

Occasionally we hear from your town of open remarks made by those who profess to be opposed to the Administration in its determination to put down rebellion, which are treasonable in spirit if not in language; cowardice alone preventing them from saying what they would wish. Is there not *spirit* enough in your Union men to *drive* them from among you[?] Or are many of your Union men like *some* we have heard from, who think it perfectly right to arrest and confine secessionists; *but who do not want to have their names mentioned in the matter*. I tell you you have some such; and, the Big Elk Rangers know who they are. It may suit *them* to be *everybody's* friend, but I tell you what it is, it don't suit us. We call no man our friend, who is a friend to the enemies of our country.

Having lengthened this letter much longer than we intended, we will close, by asking you to remember us kindly to our friends. Hoping you, and all our friends are well, I am truly yours,   Big Elk

> Coaches.—A few children's coaches received to-day and offered cheap by McCAULEY & CO.

J. G. embarked with General Lockwood and staff, Mrs. Wharton and her daughter Nelly, and Mrs. Jones for Baltimore on the steamship *Balloon*. They left at the same time the rest of the 2nd Delaware boarded the train for the same destination. The rail route took the regiment up the Delmarva Peninsula to Wilmington, where they changed trains for Baltimore. News from the front the first week in April indicated that both sides suffered heavy losses at Shiloh, although the Union claimed victory. A few weeks later Farragut's Union fleet captured New Orleans.

From Newport News came an unsigned letter dated March 28, 1862.

Dear Editor: This is the third attempt to provide your columns with some items of interest about the weal and woe of two Cecil companies, who now tread the sacred soil of the Old Dominion, but, as I understand my former communications did not reach you, I hope that these lines may find their way to the eyes of those of your readers who have friends in our midst.

Our arrival here two days after the Merrimac had made her appearance, was in every way a cheerful one for us, notwithstanding that we had to exchange the comfortable barracks of Camp Hoffman for chilly tents without stoves and without floors. We were at once brigaded under General Mansfield, together with several New York, Massachusetts and Indiana regiments, and our Brigade belongs to the Division of Gen. Wool.

Our Camp is very prettily situated between the beech [beach?] and the skirts of a picturesque pinegrove, and the inclined masts of the unhappy Cumberland are within rifle shot of it. The Congress lays about a half a mile further below in the river, and shows nothing more of its existence than the black charred edge of its burned deck, on a level with the water at ebbtide. We found in our campground several pieces of shells, which the Merrimac had sent hither, perhaps in anticipation of our arrival and some of the boys collect freely, relics of the last combat and of the different ruins of houses, ships, etc., around us. We had hard work the first few days to get along on a level in drill and field service with those regiments which had been seven to ten months, here, but we are acknowledged a fine regiment, not only in appearance, but in every branch of the whole material, our holiday clothes begin to assimilate already with the weatherworn and threadbare garments of our neighbors, and smooth fair countenances change into beardy chins and sunburnt complexions.

Some of our boys were a little homesick at first when they chewed the ancient biscuits, and found the sacred soil of Virginia as wet, muddy, and when dry, as hard, as that of old Maryland. But sunrise with the warbling of the songsters in the trees dispelled all blues, and there is no one in the regiment who is not anxious to give a good report of himself when we shall have an opportunity to show our love to the Union by more than marching and drilling.

The climate here is very changeable. We have many rains, but short ones, with warm days and cool nights. Hence we had the first two weeks a great many colds, and other slight indispositions; but the general health among us is good and our comfort increasing, as we have learned that once more it lays in our hands to improve nature and government supplies as long as we are willing to make use of spade and axe. Our hospital arrangements are, however, insufficient, and if the generosity of your Union ladies is not exhausted by their free contributions to the Eastern Shore, they may be persuaded, that some of the bounty of their good hearts, will find here, perhaps less worthy, but not less needy or less grateful receivers. A small supply of *The Whig* would also be thankfully received, as our boys do not cease to take an interest in their home affairs, even if their native county should cease to take an interest in them.

We have heard that there are many reports circulated concerning our regiment, not very complimentary for it, but we do not condescend to enter into any answer of them, as facts always speak for themselves and we suppose that you know as well as we, who has an interest to revile the Maryland regiments as much as possible. Goodbye. Give the love of all Cecil boys of 5th Maryland regiment to their friends, and send us in return soon some county news.

***

The P. W. & B. Railroad added a refreshment car for the convenience of its passengers. They might, said the *Whig*, "be regaled with hot coffee, oysters, cakes, pies, sandwitches [*sic*], without having to scramble at the stations for a few bites while the cars stop, or bold a half chewed lunch on the boat while crossing the Susquehanna, or fast till the end of their journey. Ladies are supplied in their seats, with refreshments by waiters who thread their way through the cars with platters bearing cups of coffee, Etc., etc. Improvement is the order of the day. The age is onward."

> **W**ANTED.—Wanted old Lead, Copper or Brass in exchange for stoves or Tin ware.   E. W. STAPLES.

Mrs. Tollinger's "house of ill fame" was cleaned out in Port Deposit, much to the *Whig*'s relief, when local citizens deluged the premises with the fire engine.

The first week of April in Elkton was expected to be busy because all three courts—circuit, orphans' and commissioners—would be in session. Merchants and innkeepers braced for a welcome surge in trade.

The *Delaware Republican* printed a letter from the 2nd Delaware on April 10.

Baltimore, Md., April 7, 1862

I have but very little to do since I arrived here but walk about the city. In fact, I am physically incapable of doing anything else, unless it is writing. Things are slightly different here now from what they were a year ago. Rebels and rowdies then did just about as they pleased. Now, however, through the better judgment of the prevailing authorities, order and quietude hold sway. This is owing in a great measure to the excellent police arrangements lately inaugurated. No man can hold the office of policeman who is in the least suspected of disloyalty to the General Government; and this is exactly as it should be. In a conversation with an old resident of Baltimore, a few days ago, he informed me that the city was quieter now than it had been for the last twenty years. It is a great pity, indeed that Baltimore, as a first class city, did not see the right course to pursue before the blood of Union men was suffered to stain her streets. But if she will only conduct herself in a proper manner hereafter, probably that crime will be only slightly punished—insane persons are not altogether responsible for their acts.

About one of the best conducted establishments here is the rooms of the Union Relief

Association, situated on Eutaw street, a few doors from Conway st. The building is four stories high, about 15 feet front and runs back about 75 feet. The first, second and third floors contained the tables, at which the troops are fed who pass through the city. The fourth floor is occupied as a sleeping room. I am informed that no less than 5,000 troops have been fed there in the course of one day. They are furnished with good strong coffee, bread, butter and ham. This is a great benefit to the weary soldier as he passes through the city. Any soldier can go in there at any time and get a good meal without being asked for pay. The Union Relief Association is composed of wealthy Union men of the city, and they contribute freely of their money to purchase food for the soldiers. Not one cent do they expect or receive from Government. They are doing quite as much good as those who are bearing arms for the preservation of the Union—the crushing of rebellion—and ask no other reward than a consciousness of doing right. I am sorry that I cannot give you the names of these gentlemen now; but I will endeavor to learn them, so they may be placed on the record.

Yours & c.,
J. G.

Wanted, A Boy,
ABOUT 16 or 17 years of age, to learn the Blacksmithing business. Apply to
W. T. Weldon
Cecilton.

By mid-April, Enoch Cantwell, son of John Cantwell, returned to Elkton from Leesburg, Virginia, where he had resided for some time. He said that he was impressed into Confederate service and was wounded in the shoulder at Bull Run by a random musket ball fired from a Mississippi regiment behind him.

Mitchell F. Jamar, son of Reuben D. Jamar, Esq., received an appointment to the Naval School at Newport, Rhode Island In supporting the best and brightest of the county, the *Whig* of April 19 wrote: "Young Jamar is a smart and studious boy and will doubtless, if he lives, make a good officer."

Sometimes aid reached the troops by a circuitous route. In the same issue, the *Whig* observed:

> The Grand Jury of the April term of Court, bestowed to the Ladies' Relief Association of Elkton, the sum, arising from fines imposed upon members of the Jury for violating the by-laws. The custom of imposing fines on the members of the Grand Jury is an old one. The fines were formerly spent in "something to drink" or in a dinner at the close of the term. This "contingent fund" by the last Jury has been appropriated to a more patriotic purpose.

A sure sign of spring appeared in Perryville—11,000 shad from different fisheries. They sold at ten and fifteen dollars per hundred.

In May, the body of Wm. David Hutton, Company K., Captain Patterson, Purnell Legion, was brought home for burial in Elkton Methodist Cemetery. He died in a camp near Baltimore.

Cheap John and Enoch Crouch hired Jacob Rambo to build a "large Ice Cream Saloon and Refectory" at the east end of Elkton on Crouch's lot. It was a 20-foot by 35-foot frame. There was an octagonal pavilion for picnics and cotillion parties, and the site featured a bowling green and other recreational facilities as well.

Another change in Elkton business occurred when Edward B. Johnson took over the Howard House from his father, Jacob Johnson.

An unsigned letter from the 5th Maryland, dated April 19, ran in the May 3 issue of the *Whig*.

> Dear Editor—It requires more than an ordinary effort for any but a regular correspondent to write for a newspaper under circumstances by which we are surrounded. The life in tents, under the influence of a changeable April weather, varying from cold rains to really oppressive heat, without stoves against the one and shade against the other, reduces considerably poetic inspiration; and the restriction of political or rather military communications on the other side, leaves to the author but a narrow scope of topics which might be of interest to your readers. However, it may be pleasant to the Union men of Maryland and to the friends of our Regiment to hear, that to-day, on the anniversary of the Baltimore riot, the State flag of the old State waves on the side of the Union banner over the soil of Virginia, and that good spirit, discipline and love of the Union are undisturbed in our ranks, notwithstanding discourtesy of some of our northern fellow-soldiers. It is true that we have not yet had a chance to prove our valor in the field, yet our boys have seen the enemy's shells flying in close proximity to their heads, and their unflinching hurrah in expectation of approaching fight gave no bad prognostication for their behavior in a more serious combat. Our army before Yorktown keeps aloof all imminent danger from one side, yet the still formidable Merrimac threatens our post in a manner that we have little hope, that our brigade may have the honor of advancing and taking a share in climbing the breastworks of the enemy's stronghold at Yorktown.
>
> Our colonel and other regimental officers do not lose the time, however and frequent target practice with regular drill improves our Regiment visibly, and our Cecil boys are by no means behind their comrades in any military branch. They have noticed with pleasure in the last numbers of your Whig that they are not forgotten in their native county, and as

---

COAL OIL LAMPS, WITH PARAGON Burners, also the best Coal and Carbon Oils, at T. DRENNAN'S.

well as they show, when pay day comes, that they remember Cecil, they will show on the battlefield, that they wish to keep up their good reputation.

Their health continues to be good, and since they have seen McClellan's army pass, deprived of many more comforts than ourselves, they are much less susceptible to the annoyances of the tented field. There are however many such in this part of the sunny South, as snakes, ticks of gigantic size and poisonous breath, and other such venomous creatures of more or less microscopic character.

We still hear that uncharitable reports, circulated by treacherous slanderers in disguise, leave little honor and credit to our Regiment; and at other times again try to frighten and alarm our friends by false tales concerning our dangers and sufferings. But no answer is the best answer to such illwilled gossip. Good-bye to you and all friends from your correspondent and from all Cecil boys in the 5th Maryland Regiment.

A letter from Capt. E. F. M. Faehtz, commander of Company I, 5th Maryland, publicly thanked the Ladies Union Relief Association for the flag they provided. The soldiers made a gift in return.

Mrs. Nicholas Hiss, President of the Ladies Union Relief Association, Elkton, Md.:—Madam:—In thankful remembrance of the kindness of the Union Ladies of Elkton, the officers of the regiment to which I have the honor to belong, wish to present to them a small token of gratitude, and not yet having had an opportunity to carry by their own bravery trophies from the battle-field, they think it not unbecoming to send a gift reminding you simply of the scenes surrounding the spot, where now waves that beautiful flag, by which your generousity [sic] has honored our Regiment. This humble gift, made roughly by us out of the relics of the unhappy Cumberland and Congress, and of the crowns shaken from the trees around us by the shells of the Merrimac, has been forwarded to-day by Adam's Express to the Treasurer of the respected Association of which you are President. May it cause some pleasure to the fair receivers and be considered as a pledge, that wherever the 5th Maryland regiment will be carried to by the god of war, they remember you.

In the name of the officers of the 5th Reg., most Respectfully,

CAPT. E. F. M. FAEHTZ   Com. Co. I.

Big Elk wrote again on May 14, 1862.

Dear Ewing:—It has been some time since have written to you; why it has been so I

BIRD CAGES and RAT TRAPS, for sale by CANTWELL & EDER.

cannot tell. But you must remember, we have but little to write about, that will be of much interest to our friends; while we are quartered in a quiet place. Fort Marshall is about half a mile east of the city limits; on the east side. It can be plainly seen from the P. W. & B. Railroad, as the cars approach the city. The Fort is of earthworks; the banks being very thick; and it is mounted with 24 and 32 pounder siege guns; and 8 or 19 inch Columbiads. In all, about 30 guns.

The men in the Regiment are being drilled with the heavy guns; and are becoming quite proficient in the drill.

As regards Co. "C." there has been some changes made in the officers of the Company. Lieutenant Richards has resigned, and Ephraim Jordan [who has been a Sergeant in the Company since its organization] has been appointed 2nd Lieutenant in his place. Mr. Jordan appears to be the unanimous choice of the men of the Company, and he is a fine looking officer, and is one that will do his duty. He is a son of Ephraim Jordan, of Rockville Paper Mills. Ebenezer Alexander, from Scott's Mills, has been appointed Sergeant; vice Jordan, promoted. Thomas Jeffries, Samuel Biddle, Asbury McDonald, and John Rose have been appointed Corporals to fill vacancies. The men of the Company are as well as usual. We are quite comfortably fixed; and have a fine large stove for our cooks. Our provisions are now fresh and of the best quality. There has been one thing happened with us all, that we want to have done soon again; and that is to be paid off. The paymaster came a few weeks ago; and many a long wish was made for him before he did come. Of course a number of the men have had their pay-day spree, but things have settled down again; and the camp is as quiet as usual.

I am very sorry to tell you that one of our[s] was shot last week. The circumstances are about these: the man [William Mahan, private of Company "A."] attempted to cross the post of one of the sentries, and would not stop when ordered to do so by the sentinel. The sentry in fulfilling his duty, fired; the ball striking Mahan in the right arm near the shoulder: and shattering the arm very much. The poor fellow is now in the hospital, and is quite likely that his arm will be taken off, although everything is being done for him.

The men of the Regiment have been furnished with the new regulation pants—light blue. The cloth is good, and looks very well, indeed.

PATENT MICA LAMP CHIMNEY
A Lamp Chimney that will not Break!
This great invention commends itself to everyone using COAL OIL LAMPS. It gives more light, requires less cleaning and will not break by the heat or cold, falling or any ordinary usage.—For sale by storekeepers generally throughout the U.S. and Canada and Wholesale by the Manufacturers and Patentees.
HORNING & HUMPHREY,
No. 321 N. Second Street, Philadelphia

I am sorry to tell you that our Major [than whom, a finer man never lived] is quite sick; he has been confined to his room for some time. I sincerely hope he may soon be entirely well again.

The men of the Company are beginning to think that the war will soon be over and that they will soon get home. I hope it may be so; but I do not want to see the war stopped until rebellion is put down forever. In other words, I do not want them to stop whipping the infernal rebels until they are thrashed.

The men of Company "C," [Big Elk Rangers] often, very often, talk of the kindness of their friends: especially of the great interest Mrs. Hiss, of your town, has taken in our health and comfort. She may rest assured her kindness will never be forgotten by the men of Company "C."

Hoping our friends at home are all well.—I am yours very truly,

Big Elk

Deputy Sheriff E. W. Janney arrested John Manluff, a free black, who came into the state contrary to law. The case was listed under the Proceedings of the Orphans Court. Manluff was delivering a wagonload of goods, which Cheap John wanted to be taken from his store in Wilmington to his other in Elkton. The unfortunate driver, whose only crime was doing his day's work, was fined $20 and costs.

Calling the case an outrage, the *Delaware Republican* added: "Such a statute is disgraceful to that State, and a reproach upon her people. There is a similar provision in our State, but we hope that it will soon be repealed."

The *Whig* expressed hyphenated displeasure with those female secessionists sympathizers who formed a Rebel Relief Association. Their president was Miss Eliza Leech, "than whom a more whole-souled, thorough-going, unpromising, tee-total, out-and out, whole-team and a quarter over, secech cannot be found among the high-born dames of the cotton aristocratic States."

With Miss Leech at the helm, the prisoners at Fort Delaware were assured of "many palatable little extras to their bill of fare, which will doubtless be keenly relished by palates that have been accustomed to nothing more inviting for a twelve month than hard corn dodgers and salt bacon."

On May 24, 1862, the *Democrat* reported the death at Fredericksburg, Virginia, of John A. Wherry, a Federal soldier.

DR. N. B. MORRISON
CHARLESTOWN, MD.
HAVING permanently located in Charlestown, offers his Professional Services to the citizens of that town and its vicinity.
☞ He will be found at all times, unless profesional [*sic*] engaged, at his office.

One hundred twenty-five men under Captain Ricketts arrested Judge Richard Carmichael and prosecuting attorney James Powell in Easton on charge of treason. The secessionists had threatened resistance, but the marshal telegraphed General Dix, who dispatched the soldiers, and the arrests were made without incident.

Now that the mule school moved from Perryville, an auction was advertised at which property of the U.S. Government was to be sold. A partial list included: 23 mules; 12 horses; 15 mares with foals; 50 cooking and heating stoves; 15,000 grain sacks; 60,000 old tire irons; 8,000 lbs. old tire iron; 175,000 feet assorted lumber; 15 barracks; 271 neck halters; 200 lbs. horse shoe nails; 112 stable forks; 82 lanterns. Terms: Cash, in coin or U.S. Treasury notes. Symmes Gardner, Captain and Assistant Quartermaster, U.S. Army. Auctioneer Samuel Burns.

The 2nd Delaware left Baltimore to join the army of General McClellan before Richmond. "Company C., Captain Ben Ricketts," said the *Whig*, "which is composed of Cecil countians, is the crack company of the Regiment."

The son of Professor Loman, root beer manufacturer in Elkton, narrowly escaped injury when his root beer stand, located near the Court House, blew to smithereens in the hot sun. The barrel was found among the treetops, but the enterprising youth was unharmed.

Jacob Johnson, previously identified as proprietor of the Howard House, appeared in print again, this time because his slave ran away.

> PRIME
> **SUSQUEHANNA HERRINGS,**
> IN Barrels and Half-Barrels, by
> STEELE & COULSON
> Port Deposit.

> On Monday last Mike Harris a negro man... having an attack of the contraband mania, decamped. Mike has a wife in Back street, and he is believed to be still lurking about town. W. E. Janney is on the look out for him.
>
> On Tuesday last a strange negro was found lounging about Elkton, who said he belonged to Judge Price, residing in Harford county. The negro being somewhat intoxicated, was pretty gabby, and stated that he had left the Judge's horse at Havre de Grace the day before. Mr. Janney arrested him, and lodged him in jail.

There were, no doubt, raised eyebrows nationwide when the papers reported that a teamster in an Ohio regiment was a woman, Ann Scaddy.

Sergeant Samuel P. Stewart, suffered injuries at Chickahominy. He was in Company I, 61st Pennsylvania Regiment. Before leaving Elkton, he had worked as a carpenter for J. C. Rambo.

In the same battle, James M. McCarter, 93rd Pennsylvania Regiment, was slightly wounded. A Methodist minister, Colonel McCarter had preached on the Newark circuit. At the outbreak of the war, he served as chaplain for a regiment of three months' volunteers. When that time expired, he raised a regiment, which he commanded at the battle before Richmond.

James H. Davis, son of Thomas Howard Davis, died in Camden Street Hospital, Baltimore, of inflammation of the brain. He had left New Leeds with Company I, Purnell Legion, on March 14. When his Legion left for Harper's Ferry, he was too sick to go with them. "He was a quiet and orderly young man, much attached to the service, and was a favorite with his comrades. His remains were interred in the Loudon Park cemetery." (*Whig*, June 7, 1862) At this time, the Legion is encamped on Bolivar Heights on the Shenandoah, near Harper's Ferry.

Just to make sure there was no mistaking his political sentiments, proprietor James B. Wells put up a new sign before his Fountain Hotel in Elkton, renaming it Union Hotel.

Marley Paper Mill retooled for the manufacture of paper from straw. Additions were made to the main building for bleaching, and large rotary boilers installed. When completed, the mill required an estimated one thousand tons of straw per year. No longer would large quantities of rags have to be imported form Italy and Egypt for paper making.

Cheap John promised to hold open house for the poor, if he settled to his satisfaction an estate in Europe valued at $21,000.

On June 14, the *Democrat* noted the death of Peter Tilloston, a local black man, a teamster with the army in Virginia; Sam Stewart, another black teamster, was wounded.

Big Elk wrote a short note, published in the *Whig* of June 14.

> J. T. WELLS,
> **WITH JACOB REED**,
> S. E. Corner of Second and Spruce Streets,
> PHILADELPHIA
> FINE CLOTHING, wholesale and retail.
> Also, a well selected assortment of
> CLOTHS, CASSIMERES, AND VESTINGS,
> kept on hand for customers' orders;
> Army, Navy and Volunteer Uniforms.

> In camp, on way to Grand Union Army, June 1, 1862.
>
> We are about nine miles from White House. We left Fort Marshall on Thursday last, May 28. We will soon join the main army, perhaps tomorrow. The roads are perfectly awful; you have no idea how bad. No wonder General McClellan has to move so slow.
>
> We left four men of Co. C at the Patterson Park Hospital in Baltimore: McCullough, Thompson, Thomas and Shannon. We buried one man to-night, Robert McGowan of Philadelphia. He died from sun-stroke.
>
> We are soldiering in earnest now. Each man carries half a tent, two tenting together, and joining parts of tents. The officers and men all tent together and eat together. We are all in the best of spirits and ready to do our duty.
>
> We all wish to be kindly remembered by our friends at home.
>
> Yours very truly,
> Big Elk

Those who cringed at the battle of the ironclads, now had something else to think about when the papers reported aerial reconnaissance. Professor Lowe with the balloon *Intrepid* was in advance of Gen. McClellan in the environs of Richmond.

Residents of Charlestown were saddened to learn of the deaths of two of their soldiers, Barney McIntire and S. B. Tuttle, who drowned in attempting to cross Hampton Creek in Virginia during a violent storm. Three others in the capsized boat survived, but they were unable to save their Cecil County companions.

In June 1862, Col. Geo. R. Howard of Elkton was commissioned Colonel of the 6th Maryland Regiment, which geared up immediately for active service.

The *Whig* wrote:

> FINE BLACK SILK HATS, late style at $2.50 at R. F. Mays.
> In the "Hollow."

> Captain Hill, whose advertisement will be found in the *Whig* is recruiting a company of Cecil boys for the war. Cecil has already given some 700 of her sons to the armies of the Republic. She has, doubtless, a few more left who would count their lives nobly spent if given to their country. Rally, then, brave sons of Cecil, and enroll yourselves in Cpt. Hill's company, which is to bear the name of "Howard Guard," in honor of the commander of the 6th Maryland Regiment.

The Ladies Relief Association of Elkton sponsored a strawberry festival. The Elkton Cornet band provided music, and the organization cleared $277 for their efforts.

Philip H. Ellis left to accept the post of Sergeant Major in the 2nd Delaware, but returned when the position was already filled.

Big Elk wrote from camp on the battlefield at Fair Oaks Station, near Richmond. The letter ran in the *Whig* of June 21, 1862.

> Dear Whig:—A few days ago, I hurriedly wrote you a line or two, simply to let you know of our whereabouts.
>
> We are encamped on the battle-field of Fair Oaks. We are near the Railroad station of that name; in French's brigade, Richardson's Division, Sumner's Corps.— So you see that our General Officers are *all right*. We are soldiers now; and no mistake. Not a man of the Regiment is allowed to take off his clothes at any time. Every man's rifle is kept loaded, and we never think of sleeping without our cartridge boxes are buckled upon us. In fact we are with the advance of the center of the main army; and know not at what hour we may be called upon to take part in our first battle. Often during the day or night we are called into line of battle.
>
> Last Sunday was a day that the 2nd Delaware will never forget. Nearly all day we lay upon our arms, waiting for the rebels to make their appearance from a woods in which they

were enclosed. Part of the time their bombs and bullets were flying around and over us, but the day passed without a general battle, the fight being mostly between the pickets.

When we arrived on this ground a week or more ago, the dead and wounded were still lying around. Many of the dead rebels had not been burried; dozens of dead horses lying around, causing a dreadful stench. The slaughter of the rebels on Sunday of the fight was awful.

Fair Oaks is a station to which immense quantities of army supplies are brought.— There is almost a continual fire kept up between the sharpshooters of the armies and many a poor fellow is picked off.

Often we have a lot of shells sent over to us; I suppose to let us know they are still about. None of our Regiment have been killed yet; although a number of a Minnesota regiment were killed this morning by the enemy's shells. There is a tall tree near our camp used by our soldiers as a lookout tree; but it is a dangerous place to go up on that old tree. Occasionally some one ventures up, but they always get down much sooner than they got up.—The tree is in range of the rebel sharpshooters, and this is why any one who gets up always gets down so fast. I hear a sight of Richmond can be had from the tree-top. *I have not been up yet.*

Snow's Cecil co. Battery of field artillery had a furious artillery fight a day or two ago. They were protecting a working party, who were bridging the Chickahominy, opposite Porter's Division; so that Porter might cross over the stream. There were four rebel batteries opposed to them, and Capt. Snow with his six guns made them leave. The battery was under fire for three hours; and during that time fired nearly one thousand shells and shot. They lost a number of horses and had one or two men slightly wounded. The coolness and bravery of the men of the Battery is much spoken of along the line. From a deserter from the rebels, Gen Porter learned that a number of men and officers of the rebel batteries were killed, and a number of their guns disabled and silenced. At any rate they retired in

---

Steam Dyeing and Scouring
ESTABLISHMENT
MRS. E. W. SMITH
No. 28 N. Fifth Street, between
Market and Arch,
PHILADELPHIA

PIECE Goods of every description dyed to any color. Ladies wearing Apparel of every description, dyed in the most fashionable and permanent colors, and finished in a superior style. Merino, Cashmere and Crape Shawls, Table and Piano Covers, Carpets, Rugs, etc. Scoured. Pongee and Silk Dresses Re-Dyed all Colors, and warranted equal to new.
N. B.—Gentlemen's Clothes Cleaned or Dyed on reasonable terms.
The Passenger Railway Cars pass the door.

the greatest confusion. We were standing in line of battle this afternoon when General McClellan rode by; he is a fine looking officer, and without a shadow of a doubt he is the favorite of the army. As to Co. "C." I have not much to say; I have not the least doubt, that if we are ever brought into action, we will do our duty nobly. You would have been surprised at the coolness of the men calm and cool; the mark of a brave and determined man when in danger.

Our Regiment was paid off this afternoon. The men of Co. "C." have sent to their homes about fifteen hundred dollars. This is a very poor place to spend our money.—Only a few sutlers are near us, and they have very little except tobacco, and paper and ink.

We all wish to be kindly remembered by our friends. Around our little camp fires, the usual talk is of the old folks at home, and of the pleasant times we used to know. May the good Lord take care of us all. In all probability we will not all get home again.

DR. COWAN
DENTIST.
Rooms at the Fountain HTL.

The boys are merry and ready for anything that may turn up. Good by for the present.

Tell our friends to direct thus: French's Brigade, Richardson's Division, Sumner's Corps, Co. "C." 2nd Del. Vol.

Yours very truly,

Big Elk

The *Democrat* reminded its readers of important town ordinances. "No litter, no driving on the sidewalk, no shooting firearms in town. Dogs must be muzzled from August until November. No disorderly meetings of negroes, and no disorderly meetings of men or boys."

Adj. W. F. A. Torbert, 2nd Delaware, fell ill of typhoid, and Henry R. Torbert, Esq., traveled to a point near Richmond to bring his brother home. Rumor had it that Colonel Wharton of the same regiment also had typhoid.

James B. Wells, owner of the Union Hotel, offered his house to Colonel Crosson of Philadelphia as a hospital for soldiers. If Colonel Crosson would not be able to accept, Wells planned to make the same offer to General Wool. The *Democrat* noted on June 28, the passing of General Pope and President Lincoln on a special train the previous Wednesday.

War or no war, horse racing still absorbs the interest of the local gentry. The *Whig* published a list of owners and their licensed horses: Benj. Green [Dare Devil, Jr.]; Ezekiel C. Boulden [Stranger]; James Ginn [Bleak House]; Jas. H. Benson, Jr., [Montreal]; Jacob Fite, [Godolphin Lion]; John T. Skirven [Young Priam]; Joseph Wells [Henry May Day, Jr.], James Marrett [Young Archy]; Alexander Hamilton [Tilboy]; Samuel Gillespie [Silver Heel's Messenger]; John L. Pearce [Prince Albert]; Perry Wilson [North Star, Jr.]; Joseph Galloway [Sir Archy Reynolds]; Joseph

Worrick [Morgan Black Hawk]; Samuel G. Mackey [Cruiser]; William Foster [John Prime]; J. N. Black [Mazeppa]; Enoch Ferguson [N. Lawrence]; John B. Arrison [Tom Morgan, Jr.]; John A. Mackie [Louis Napoleon]; James Armstrong [Zack Harvey]; L. B. Anderson [Z***]; John W. Simpers [Tom Rinaldo].

Camp Desk [Reenactment Photo]

♦ CECIL COUNTY: 1862 ♦

EXHIBITION

BY THE

STUDENTS

OF THE

ELKTON PUBLIC SCHOOL,

Thursday Evening, March 27th, 1862

Singing—Good Time Coming

1. SALUTATORY.
   John H. Frazer.   George T. King.

3. Young America on Progress
   James McNeal.

4. Cowardice and Knavery.
   Landlord.—Calvin Boulden.
   Trusty.—Alfred Gallaher.
   Hector.—John K. S. Lodore.
   Hamburg.—Charles M. Boulden.
   Simon.—Davic T. Strickland.

5. **SINGING:** Multiplication Table.

6. The Seminole's Reply,
   Thomas E. Howard.

7. Early Retiring and Rising,
   James A. Cantwell

8. Intellect not Everything.
   Carrie K. Cosgrove,   Emma Thomas,
   Mary A. Cosgrove,   Mary A. King,
   Ellie F. Cloud,   Mary J. Cantwell,
   Mary A. Wells.

9. **SINGING:** Song in Motion.

10. Foolish Ambition.
    Thomas A. Crouch.

11. The Three Black Crows.
    David T. Strickland

12. The Book Convention
    Chairman.—William Veach.
    Mr. Spelling Book.—Calvin Boulden.
    Mr. Analysis.—John H. Frazer.
    Mr. Grammar.—Joshua M. Ash.
    Prof. Dictionary.—William J. Collins
    Prof. Botany.—Joseph H. Taylor
    Mr. Geography.—Henry Gallaher.
    Mr. Political Economy.—John Morgan.
    Dr. Physiology.—John Moke.
    Mr. History.—John K. S. Lodore.
    Mr. Astronomy.—Thomas W. Thackary.
    Dr. Philosophy.—William H. Bennett.
    Mr. Mineralogy.—Alfred Gallaher
    Secretary,—Lemuel Dilks.

13. Singing: This World Is Not so Bad a World.

14. Our National Banner.
    Robert C. Thackary.

15. Grammar Speech
    William P. Buchanan

16. Novel Reading.
   Ellie F. Cloud,   Mary R. Crawford,
   Mary E. Buchanan

17. Curiosity
   Leora G. McKinsey,   Ellie M. Biddle,
   Lidie J. Marshbank,   M. E. Buchanan

18.   SINGING. Music

19. Liberty and Union.
   Alfred Gallaher.

20. Trouble and Nervousness.
   ******—Emily D. McCoy.
   Aspen.—John K. S. Lodore.
   Dr. Oryde.—Thomas W. Thackary.

21. SINGING: Come Let Us Ramble.

22. Our Country.
   David M. Frazer.
23. The Street of By-and-By.
   Emily D. McCoy.

24. Value of Knowledge
   Lidie J. Marshbank,   Annie R. Moore,
   Lidie C. Aldridge,   Ellie M Biddle,
   Leora G. McKinsey.

25. SINGING: Never Late at School.

26. America.
   John. K. S. Lodore.

27. An Oration.
   William H. Bennett
28. The Two Lecturers
   Teacher.—Joshua M. Ash.
   Timothy Dobbin.—John H. Frazer.
   Jonathan Puff Stuff.—J. K. S. Lodore.
   1st Const.—Calvin Boulden.
   2nd Const.—Willliam Veach.
   Jake.—Willie P. Buchanan.

29.   SINGING: Beautiful Star.

30. Essay on Public Schools.
   Leora J. McKinsey.

31. Writing Composition.
   Emma D. McCoy,   Clara Hughes
   Hannah B. Merrey,   Mary R. Crawford.

32. SINGING: Hoe Out Your Row.

33. ESSAY.—Home.
   Lidie J. Marshbank

34. Impressment of American Seamen.
   Captain Martinet.—Willie Johnson.
   Lieut. Berley.—John Morgan.
   Hiram Handy.—David T. Strickland.
   Capt. John Luff.—Henry Gallaher

35.   SINGING: The Blind Girl.

36. An Address.
   John K. S. Lodore

37. Time's Changes.
   Lidie Aldridge,   Clara L. Hughes,
   Hannah B. Merrey,   Robt. C. Thackary,
   Annie R. Moore,   Thomas E. Howard.

38. SINGING: GRANDMA'S ADVICE.
39. VALEDICTORY,
   Charles H. Cantwell

☞Exercises to commence at 7 o'clock.
☞Tickets of admission may be obtained from Mr. Ellis, Commissioner, or any of the Teachers.
The next Quarter will commence march 31st, inst.
M. JOHNSON RHODES, Principal.
Miss CARRIE T. BROCK,   Miss CARRIE H. MOORE,   Assistants.

M.'s letter to the *Delaware Republican* (7/3/62) told not only about the location of the 2nd Delaware, which included Cecil Countians, but also about their treatment, the sanitary conditions, and contemporary medical myths.

FAIR OAKS, JUNE 23, 1862

Dear Vernon: I suppose things in Wilmington continue as of yore. If, however, it is as hot there as in this detestible swamp, I pity you. I do not know whether it is contraband of war or not, but I will tell you, hoping you won't tell anybody: WE have a piece of Ice about as big as a water pail, where it came from I am unable to say. It is the first piece I have seen since we came here, no one knows where we can get another piece, so we are very economical of it. But alas, before noon it will all be gone, never more to return. The water here, although very palatable, is exceedingly injurious. It is what is termed surface water; by digging two or three feet, abundance of it is obtained. But upon this comparatively small area of ground, is crowded over one hundred thousand men, besides thousands of horses.

All their excrescence falls upon and is speedily absorbed by this spongy soil. Hundreds of beef creatures are killed here daily, their blood and entrails, and hides are slightly buried, and to make matters still worse, within a month this has been the scene of a terrific battle.

There are on every hand immense trenches filled with human dead. At any time this would be at this season of the year, an unhealthy place, but now it is doubly so. Yet strange to relate, there is not near the amount of sickness one would suppose. Our Regiment turns out in nearly full number, actually more than at Fort Marshall. The prevailing disease is Diarrhea, accompanied with colic. It soon knocks the legs from under one, and leaves him as weak as a kitten, but it yields readily to blue mass and quinine. I think our soldiers would suffer much less, did they drink tea at least once a day. This black, bitter soldier's coffee is like so much aloes. The mixture is swilled down three times a day. I believe that it would kill a horse. I live in this place, undergo the same hardships and deprivations with the rest, yet I enjoy very good health. I wash frequently and put on clean (?) clothes, i.e. as clean as clothes can be made in muddy water. I avoid cheese and pickles, except in small quantities. I sleep whenever I get a chance, drink tea twice a day. Not more than three

---

For Baltimore and Philadelphia
The Steamer Port Deposit
CAPTAIN D. VANNEMAN,
Having resumed her Regular Trips, will leave Mr. J. J. Heckart's Wharf, Port Deposit every day (Sunday excepted) for Havre de Grace at 9 A. M. 1:15 and 5:30 P. M., connecting with trains leaving Baltimore at 8:30 A. M., and 5:10 P. M.; from Philadelphia at 8 A. M., and 12 M., returning on arrival of trains.
☞ Travelers will be accommodated to Lapidum at 8 A. M., and between trips to Havre de Grace.

times have I tasted ardent spirits, and that after long abstinence and fatigue, since our arrival. There is no doubt if these simple matters were rightly observed, much sickness would be avoided. The soldiers can draw tea in place of coffee, and by economy they can purchase many luxuries. I have known soldiers to pay $2.50 for a pint of whiskey. They could have gotten three quart cans of roast chicken, beef or mutton for that price, which would have benefitted them.

We have now two new hospital tents, and the men have constructed cots of sticks for the sick to lie upon. We manage to get for them lemons and such articles. Our Colonel insists upon cleanliness, so our sick are quite comfortable. We have no serious cases as yet, and I trust we may not have.

We live in constant alarm. The other afternoon the enemy drove in our pickets, and showed themselves in large force in the edge of the woods; but we opened upon them with grape and shrapnel, and drove them back. I was standing not 20 feet from the battery. It was the first time I had ever seen a cannon fired at a human being, and this time it was at hundreds. It is impossible for me to describe my feelings. To say that I had no thoughts for my own safety would be untrue; but to confess that I had nothing like fear or a disposition to betake myself to a place of safety, would be equally untrue. I was filled with mingled pity for those under the fire, and a desire that our gunners might successfully drive them back. If here is not a paradox I never saw one.

During the whole subsequent night our pickets kept firing, and the whole camp was in alarm. In the morning I learned that the cause was the enemy trying to recover their dead and wounded. Had they asked for this under a flag of truce, no doubt but it would have been granted. They frequently send shell over our camp, and one exploded in a tree not 20 yards from the Colonel's tent

I have thought what will become of Delaware troops when wounded? Every State has made some provisions for theirs, and there are hospitals for the regular army. That the noble patriotic and humane of other States will permit our men to suffer, if they can prevent it, I do not believe; but they will naturally look out for their own first. I wish I could effectually appeal to the people of Delaware to do as other States do: look out for their own first. Give me two or three good doctors, provide us transportation for our sick, independent of the slow delay of the General Government; let every man feel when he falls sick that the arms of all Delaware are open to receive him and console him, and you make him doubly

the soldier. We know not the hour that we may be precipitated into an awful battle. Even while I am writing the rattle of musketry is very sharp. One year ago, that which has taken place since I commenced writing this letter, and within my hearing, would have been termed a battle; but so warlike have we become this skirmish is not noticed, and the telegram possibly may announce to you at your tea-table, "All quiet in the army of the Potomac!"

Our Chaplain has not distributed to us lately any relibious books or tracts; in all probability he has none to give....

Yours, M.

In July, Rev. Joseph T. Brown of Cherry Hill was appointed Chaplain of the 6th Maryland. Union tempers flared at a demonstration of "disloyal sentiments" on the Fourth of July in Elkton. The *Whig* did not hold back its scorn:

This spirit of arrogant treachery and malignant devilishness, on the part of the secession element of Elkton, came nigh producing serious consequences to the Jeff. Davisites last week.

On the night of the Fourth of July, after the hour when honest folks are supposed to be in bed, a party of secesh got to ventilating their "southern sympathies," by perambulating the streets and shouting for Jeff. Davis. This had the effect to arouse a party of Union men about fifty or sixty strong, who turned out the next evening in search of these "southern sympathizers," but said sympathizers were not found.

While Union people generally are quiet and respectful to all, the secession element everywhere has shown an arrogant, snobish [sic] impudence which seems to be intended to provoke good citizens. Measures are being arranged in future, and those who want to shout for the traitors and show derision for the government, will have to seek more congenial localities than Cecil to enjoy their penchant for the traitor contheiveracy.

This street buffoonery is not only practiced by fuddled men, but we have heard frequent complaints from the Union people, of a practice that is persisted in by little Misses who have just doffed their swaddling clothes, making a business of, parrot-like mouthing secession which they have doubtless picked up, like the tropical bird of green and gold, from their teachers, in the streets when passing loyal citizens. Such immodest conduct is evidently intended as taunts

---

HEALTH. HEALTH. HEALTH.
Swayne's Compound Syrup of Wild Cherry. The Great Remedy for Coughs, Colds, Croup, Bronchitis, Asthma, Blood Spitting, Sore Throat, Hoarseness, Consumption.

and insults, from those children whose parents and guardians fear the responsibility of openly acting against their country, and in too many instances claiming to be Union men.

This revolting obscenity was carried to the most disgusting lengths one evening last week, at the depot, on the occasion of a party of several hundred secesh prisoners passing through on the train. One of these little Misses so far forgot that respect due to her sex as to raise a hurrah for Jeff. Davis, in the presence of these dirty, ignorant ruffians.

Big Elk wrote from Fair Oak Station, Virginia, Monday, June 22, 1862 (*Whig*, July 5, 1862).

Dear Old Whig:—I feel confident that we have plenty of friends up in good old Cecil, who are always anxious to hear from us; and of course we are always anxious to hear from them. We received a small mail for our Regiment a few days after leaving Baltimore, and heard nothing more from home until last Friday, when we received a large mail bag filled with letters and papers, only a few papers to be sure, but then a part of the few, were the welcome old Whig, welcome anytime, but doubly welcome now. With what haste do we unfold it, that we may see the column of locals and the column of deaths and marriages. And by the way, we would advise the friends of some of our men, for God's sake, to have a little more local news in the letters they write down to us. We took particular care to notice the expression of the men after reading their letters. Some would call around them a crowd of their companions, and with a shout of laughter tell them of good jokes that had just happened up home. How John Smith tried to go see Sarah Ann _____; and Sarah Ann's mother drove him off. How the young folks all enjoyed themselves at a certain party. How such a young man was getting along at his trace, and then some one would tell the other, that the black colt had been sold; that the bay mare ran off and threw Bill and Sam out of the carriage; how well the corn looked; how soon they would commence mowing, and a thousand and one little matters that would serve to talk of, and to tell each other.

Some of the men after reading their letters we would notice would go quietly away and lay down in their tents, or else go slowly walking out of camp, and sit down alone under the shade of some tree or bush, to weep perhaps, and when we ask them, what's the news from home? they would answer, perhaps with tears in their eyes "Oh! there ain't much

---

Lecture at the Court House,
ON THURSDAY EVENING,
the 6th inst. at 7½ o'clock by
Wm. Pinkney Ewing, Esq.
SUBJECT,
"THE AMERICAN CITIZEN."
Admission 15 cents.
Children 10 cents.
☞ Proceeds for the benefit of the Presbyterian Sabbath School.

news. I got a letter from my mother," or perhaps "my sister. They all say, they wish I was home once more; if they could only see me once more," or some sister will write, "your poor mother is almost heart-broken about you, your mother will never get over your going away from home;" or else "There are so many poor fellows sickening and dying and you are so weakly you know that we never expect to see you again."

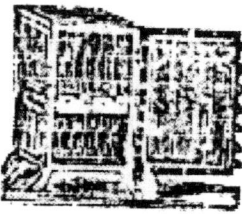

Evans & Watson's
Philadelphia Manufactured
SALAMANDER SAFES.

Now we would ask our friends, which is the best way to write us? You all know we are here; and here we will be apt to stay for a while; and what is the use of making the hearts of the boys so sad, and making them feel so lonely. We all know our mothers and sisters love us; and we all love them; but it does the men more harm than good to get some letters from home that I have seen. WE would tell our mothers and sisters do not be uneasy about us; we are getting along first-rate. If we do get a little sick, we are well taken care of.—There are plenty of Government Hospitals near us, to which we would be sent, if we get sick. There are very few of our men sick, not more than twenty or twenty-five, and none of them dangerously sick, as I can hear of. There has been but one death in the Regiment since we left Baltimore, that was McGowan of Company D. that was mentioned in your paper a week or two ago. There is a poor chance to get any kind of provisions here; except Government rations. The men and officers are obliged to fair alike, but the provisions furnished by the Government are of the best kind, and very healthy. A number of the officers find it rather a rough way to life; and it is begining to *tell* on some of them. There are, out of the officers of the Regiment, twelve or fifteen of them sick.—The captain of the Big Elk Rangers, having for several years of his life been accustomed to a rough way of living in the west, is enjoying excellent health; eating where his men eat, and sleeping where they sleep.

Our Regiment is in good fighting trim, and will do its duty, when *the day* does come.—We were highly complimented last evening by Major General Sumner, to whose corps we belong. We have changed the Austrian Rifle for the Springfield Rifle; said to be, and is, the best rifle in the world. They are the best finished pieces we have ever seen, they carry a heavy conicle ball, their greatest range is eight hundred yards, but will carry one thousand yards.

None of Company C. are much sick. The water is not very good, and the sickness we have is caused mostly by the water, I think. Tell our friends to write often to us, for letters from home are very welcome indeed.—Our Colonel has been very unwell, but is better now. Very truly yours, Big Elk

Cecil County physician Dr. Cornelius S. Knight, recently appointed army surgeon, died at a hospital near Washington of typhoid fever.

Lt. Col. Henry McIntire of the 1st Pennsylvania Reserves, McCall's Division, was wounded at Savage Station (*Whig* 7/12/62). He was captured by the Confederates and was believed to be in the Richmond area. He had lived in Elkton before becoming a member of the bar in West Chester, Pennsylvania. His servant, Charles McCabe of Elkton, brought his horses home. Colonel McIntire lost a leg in the Seven Days' Battle.

Farmers found themselves behind schedule in the harvesting of crops that season of 1862. With their regular help away at war, they hired others with little experience and the yield dropped. After six to eight years of failure, the apple crop rebounded and was deemed the "only full crop this year."

The *Democrat* occasionally offered advice in caring for animals. [*Bots* are worms, and *to drench* means to administer a dose of liquid medicine to an animal.]

When your horse has the bots, first give him some sage tea. Boil the sage in a quart of milk, and sweeten with molasses. Half an hour after, drench your horse with two ounce phials of laudanum; in three quarters of an hour, drench with three fourths of a pound of salts and your horse will be well in three hours, or as soon as the salts operate. The tea will make the bots let loose, the laudanum will put them to sleep, and the salts will cause them to pass from your horse.

In the *Delaware Republican*, Capt. J. J. Barr, of Company K, 2nd Delaware, appealed for help in a letter from Harrison's Landing, dated July 5, 1862.

SAMUEL BIDDLE, Esq.—Dear Friend. I write to say to you that if there is any reality in the profession of Delawarians of sympathy for our troops, let them at once charter a steamboat and send it to this place and take away our sick. It is really heart-rending to behold them, with their pale, emaciated countenances, sunken cheeks and glassy eyes staring out of their heads.

Ever since we left Baltimore we have been exposed to the most dreadful hardships; strong men, the most hearty-looking, have had to succumb to the exposure, and are broken down in body and mind; and their number is so great that there are not surgeons, nurses, nor hospital accommodations for them, so that the sick and wounded are forced to lie out in the woods, and have to dress their own wounds. It really is awful to behold, and makes one's heart bleed to witness the scenes of misery. It keeps the grave-diggers busy every day interring the dead at this place, and it seems to me that the number increases daily.

We have retreated and fought the enemy every day for the last eight successive days and nights, and I, like others, have lost everything, not having so much even as a second shirt, or indeed a change of clothing of any kind. We have had several killed and wounded in our regiment. Let the Wilmington people come to our assistance; get a steamboat, doctors, surgeons, nurses, medicines and delicacies for the sick, and start without a moment's delay, or we shall bury a number of our poor fellows in unknown and forgotten graves. Come to Fortress Monroe with the boat and report there for directions how to get here, and for a pilot if necessary. But if you wish to be of service, no time must be lost. I suppose there is from 75 to 100 men here to go away. I beg of you to come. I write with the approval of our Colonel and our surgeons so don't delay.

J. J. Barr,   Captain of Company K.

Word arrived in July that Dr. Charles Manley Ellis, assistant surgeon in Rush's Lancers, fell into rebel hands in the battle near Richmond. He had been in charge of a hospital at Mechanicsburg and refused to leave his patients when the hospital was taken. His servant, Ned Boyer, a free black man, was sold into slavery. Ellis was confined to Libby Prison.

From Spotswood House, Richmond, Dr. Ellis wrote to his father, F. A. Ellis:

> I am safe and well. I was left in charge of my Hospital when our army retreated and was taken by General Stewart. I have walked from the Hospital to Richmond, a distance of 12 miles to make provision for the wounded left on the field by our army, and through the influence of General Reynolds, in whose room I am writing this note, have been able to do much for their comfort. When I will get into our own lines again, I do not know. It will probably be some time, however, as we have many wounded—about 1,700.

A New and Entire Stock of Seasonable
DRY GOODS,
JUST OPENED BY
J. L. CARHART,
ZION, MD.

A sketch in *Portrait and Biographical Record* (1897, p. 551 ff.) contained the following:

Before he was of age Dr. Ellis was elected secretary and treasurer of the board of school commissioners of Cecil County. In the spring of 1858 he began the study of law in the office of Hon. Alexander Evans, but in the fall of the same year he matriculated in the medical department of the University of Pennsylvania, of which institution his great-great-grandfather was an original incorporator. He pursued a graded three years' course, and graduated in the class of 1861, amidst the din and turmoil of the early days of the Civil War. He immediately entered the military service of the United States as assistant surgeon of Rush's Lancers, a favorite Philadelphia organization, subsequently known as the Sixth

Pennsylvania Cavalry. Three of his brothers, Howard, Rudulph and Philip, were also officers of the same regiment. He served with the Army of the Potomac, and in May, 1862, was detached by order of Gen. Philip St. George Cooke in command of the cavalry division of the army, to take charge of the hospital of the division located by General Cooke on the "Johnson" farm, near the Chickahominy. He was captured, with his hospital, by the advance of Stonewall Jackson's corps the day after the battle of Mechanicsville, which ushered in the Seven Days' fight on the peninsula. His hospital, being immediately in the rear of the rebel lines, was overrun by wounded Confederates, to whom he rendered surgical aid. Before his removal to Richmond he went into that city through the Confederate line in disguise and made known to General Reynolds [then a prisoner at the Spotswood Hotel] the starving condition of the officers and wounded prisoners on the battlefields. His mission, although one of great danger, was entirely successful through the courtesy of General Winder, Provost-Marshal of Henrico County. He was subsequently removed with many others to Libby prison and occupied his time continuously in devoted attention to the wounded prisoners in Castle Thunder and other prison houses, a service that attracted the favorable comments of the Richmond press.

> **Blackberry Wine**
> Measure your berries and bruse [sic] them, to every gallon adding one quart of boiling water; let the mixture stand twenty-four hours, stirring occasionally; then strain off the liquid into a cask, to every gallon adding two pounds of sugar; cork tight, and let stand till the following October, and you will have wine ready for use, without any further straining or boiling, that will make lips smack as they never smacked, under similar influence, before.

Philip Ellis was wounded during the Spanish American War. The *Whig* (July 23, 1898) indicated that he was recuperating at the home of Dr. Ellis after being wounded in the Battle of Santiago.

The *Democrat* reported on July 12, 1862, that Robert J. Rink was killed near the James River, and his body was left on the field Jos. C. Abraham's body was recovered and buried in camp.

There was frequent mention of the peach crop in Maryland and Delaware. Heirs of Daniel Combings chartered Capt. Jos. M. Balance's steamer *Fairy* to freight peaches from the estate near Smyrna to Philadelphia.

Capt. Ben Ricketts was hospitalized and ugly rumors circulated around Elkton accusing him of cowardice. For the next several weeks, he wrote letters and submitted documentation verifying his confinement to area hospitals.

The matter first surfaced in the *Whig*, July 12, 1862.

Capt. Ben Ricketts of Company C., 2nd Del. Reg., is sick at Norfolk.
Capt. Ricketts' Company has been heard from since the recent battles, through letters

from members of the company. From some cause, not fully explained, the company officers were all missing during the fighting, and a Lieutenant from another company commanded the men of company "C." Two men, Sours and Lockard, both of Elkton are missing from the company since the battles. No inteligence [*sic*] has been received by their comrades. With the above mentioned exceptions, all are well, and encamped in a pleasant situation on the James river.

Sours' name is spelled Sowers in other places. In the next issue, July 19, 1862, the *Whig* observed:

> We are much gratified in being able to announce the promotion of our townsman, W. F. A. Torbert, Adjutant of the 2nd Delaware Regiment. Adjutant Torbert has been detailed from that Regiment and appointed Aid-de Camp upon the staff of Brig. Gen. French, U.S.A. The promotion of Adjutant Torbert does not accord with the infamous statements which were written home by some of the members of the 2nd Delaware, charging their officers with cowardice, and which is so flatly denied by Captain Ricketts in to-day's *Whig*, of whose integrity and courage no man among his large circle of acquaintances ever for a moment doubted.

In an adjoining column, Ricketts responded from Annapolis, July 16, 1862.

> Friend Ewing:—Meeting a friend of mine this evening, who had just come down from Cecil, I learned a number of reports were in circulation in and around Elkton, concerning the action of the officers of Company "C.," 2nd Del. Vols. Also, from *The Whig* of last Saturday, I found a notice, "that from some cause, all the officers of the Company, were absent during the fighting." Now, I will tell you all I know about this thing, in a very few words. Now some part of the letters you get your information from is *the biggest kind of a lie*, as far as myself is concerned.—All the men of the Company, and I expect of the whole regiment know that I was sick, and under the charge of our Assistant Surgeon for some time before the days before the fighting you speak of in your paper commenced, which was Thursday June 26th.—Our Regiment was outlying in the line of battle behind some of the earthworks on our right, from early on Friday morning [the 27th] until about 4 o'clock P. M., when we were ordered to join our Brigade, and then the whole Brigade marched to Gaine's Hill, a distance of five miles, at

---

Jannie's Crisp Gingerbread
Take two cups butter, two cups molasses, one cup sugar, teaspoonful of soda, dissolved in 4 tablespoonfulls of milk, two tablespoonfulls of ginger, flour sufficient to make stiff enough to roll out; roll it out very thin on buttered tin sheets; mark it in squares and bake in a quick oven.

double quick, almost all the way. We were then placed in line of battle, and marched to the support of a battery of artillery that was at the time shelling the rebels. We laid down on the ground until night in rear of this battery and kept our place until about mid-night; at which time all the troops, except the wounded, had crossed over the Chickahominy at this place. Ours was the last Regiment that crossed the bridge. About sun rise on Saturday we reached our camp, which we moved to the line of breastworks near the Railroad at Fair Oaks.

We laid all Saturday night on our arms, leaving the breast-works about daylight of Sunday morning. About noon of Sunday I left the Regiment and went back to the Hospital at Savage Station. After which I hired a horse from an officer's servant, and rode most of the days of Monday and Tuesday. On Wednesday, Major Andrews and I were put on board of a steamboat at Harrison's Landing by our Assistant Surgeon, Dr. Plunkett, of Wilmington, and sent to Fortress Monroe.

> ☞ Stephen B. Ford, at "Cheap Corner," Cherry Hill, reminds the public that he continues to sell new goods at old prices.

Dr. Cuyler, the medical director of Fortress Monroe, sent us to Norfolk, at which place I staid under charge of Dr. Sheldon at the Naval Hospital until Sunday morning, the 13th of July, when I left in company with Mr. Wm. P. Ewing for the Hospital at Annapolis, which is in charge of Dr. Getty of your town: and which, I will here say, could not be in better hands. When I left the Co. on Sunday, the 29th of June, Lieutenants Simpers and Jordan were both with the Co. Now I hear that some of the men have been writing home about what great things they did do, and what their officers did not do. Not a man of the 2nd Del. ever fired a single shot at a rebel. And if Lieuts. Simpers and Jordan left the Co. after I left, it is more than I heard of when I was talking with some of the men near Harrison's Landing, on Wednesday. I expect to be back with the Regiment in a short time, when I will inquire into the thing, and let you know ALL about it. But I would just say here at the close of this, that I feel confident that any one in Cecil County who is acquainted with me, KNOWS that when I left the Regiment it was because I was obliged to do so. And ANY ONE who says I left my Company when I was able to remain with it and do my duty is a LIAR. When I heard the names of some of the men who have written home in the manner you spoke of last week, I find some of them are men who SHIRKED from their duty on the Friday of the fight. Very respectfully,

Ben Ricketts,
Capt. Co. "C." 2nd Del. Vols.

Two young men of Captain Fulton's company, Purnell Legion, died: Levin Gamble, son of Charles Gamble, 9th District, succumbed to camp fever in his 19th year; Thomas Logan, son of John McCullough Logan, 5th District, died in his 22nd year. His body was brought home from Frederick City, Maryland, and re-interred at Bay View.

The *Whig* ran a long column in July headed Traders' Liquor Licenses.

The license issued under this head authorizes the sale of spirituous liquors in quantities not less than a pint. All venders of spirituous liquors under this license must have a license also trade in such articles as are generally found in stores, shops, etc., hence the name Traders' Liquor License. The following is the list of licenses issued since the 1st of May last, to the present date [July 19, 1862] in Cecil County.

    John A Craig, John H. Morgan: Cecilton
    Reed and Bro.: Bohemia Mill
    James Price, James B. Price: Pedlar's Lane
    John E. Walmsley: Price's Corner
    James Lane: Pearce's Neck
    James H. Benson, Jr.: Johnstown
    George W. Walmsley: Fredericktown
    Washington Houston, Robert McAllister, Jacob S. Hays: Warwick
        W. Murry: Concord
    Mary A. Riley: Cayott's Corner
    George C. Megill: Pond's Neck
    Charles W. Maxwell, John H. Mahoney, William McClelland, Rossell & Hines, James Denny, Victor L. Bennett: Elkton
    John Price: Lutton's Corner
    Bejamin C. Cowan: Cowantown
    George W. Denny: Bull Frog
    John Knight: Knight's Corner
    John Pennington: Bull's Mountain
    Robert Lynch: near Brick Hill
    Robert Elliot: Gridiron Fishery
    Henry Frederick, Jr.: near Principio
    A. J. Craig: Hyland's Store
    W. B. Hurry: North East
    Patrick Magee (94th Dist.): Mount Joy
    E. P. Bowens & Co., John Mears, Ballow & Griffith: Chesapeake City
        David A. Roberts: Port Herman
    S. M. C. Nesbitt, Albert Gottschalk, John Lamon, Patrick Kerwin: Port Deposit
    W. T. Richardson: Charlestown

Ordinary [tavern or hotel] Licenses issued since May 1.

Francis Little, Enoch Ferguson, Joseph S. Riale: Brick Meeting House
James Porter: Lombardville
Charles W. Kimble: Fox Chase
Samuel Gillespie Warwick
W. Manly, Mrs. Marsha Lum, Thomas M. Sturgeon, Vincent Hammond: North East
Lawrence Simmons, John W. Buchanan, Henry T. Hukill, Philip Becker, James Vance: Chesapeake City
John A. Thompson, William Grason: Rising Son
Jacob Krauss: Rock Springs
George W. Barnes: Carpenter's Point
John L. Pierce: Battle Swamp
Henry Hess: Fair Hill
W. Thompson Ramsey, Granville S. Jeffries: Bay View
Sarah A. Kirk: Blue Ball
Zimri Taylor: Hickory Grove
Geo. W. Horner, Frederick Canisius, Wm. T. Vandiver: Old Maryland Canal
Richard Dawson, Martha J. Moore: Conowingo
Bird C. West: Octoraro Locks
John A. Moore: Bald Friar
Alex H. Oldham: Back Creek
Callendar Patterson: Gurleytown
James G. Thompson, John Janney: Charlestown
Otho Nowland: Nowland's X Roads
Robert V. Trump: Trump's Corner
George A. Ewing, James Marrett, James B. Wells, Robert Walmsley, Joseph Taylor, James R. Smith, E. B. Johnson: Elkton
Mary Ann Burlin, Casper Mohrlein, Mary Ann Hughes, John R. Burlin, John Kearney, Robert Smith, Freed & Burlin, Daniel McGonegal, John Long, Owen Quinn, W. Crumpton: Port Deposit
James Cunningham, Solomon Weaver, G. W. Taylor, James Boyd, Patrick Desmond, John Burroughs, Jr., W. C. Boyd, Elisha M. Sharpless: Perryville
John Richards: Cecilton

Oyster Houses Under this license dealers are authorized to sell spirituous and fermented liquors and lager beer in quantities less than a pint.

Victor L. Bennett: Little Elk

W. P. F. Wharton: North East
Hugh Crawford, John Given, W. Falls, Christian Baker: Port Deposit
Wm. T. Emmons: Chesapeake City
Nicholas Chambers: Elkton
W. Giles, Henry Sharper: Elkton
George W. Denny: Bull Frog

The *Whig* (7/19/62) quoted three papers that described pests which attack the oatfields. The *Baltimore American* called them red weevils; the *Confederate Afflictor* described their appearance and habits in some detail and simply named them red bugs. But the *Centerville State Rights* saw an excellent chance to do a little jabbing: "These bugs vary in color, and resemble the common louse in shape. They are new visitors, and appropriately denominated Lincoln Lice." The *Whig* countered with a name of its own: Secession Lice.

The *Democrat* alerted citizens to bills that counterfeited those issued by the Farmers' Bank in Lancaster, Pennsylvania. Ten-dollar bills had been made from ones. The bills showed cattle in water and a woman on the right with a locomotive on the left. Spurious twos pictured men and girls harvesting, an ox team, boys and a sheaf on the right with a farm on the left.

Port Deposit reported the capture of three escapees from Fort Delaware.

Golden Periodical Pills
FOR FEMALES
Infallible in correcting irregularities and removing obstructions of the monthly turns, from whatever cause.

On Friday night of last week, while Constable W. Lawrence was out on patrol in Port Deposit, he came up with three men, traveling from the direction of Perryville toward Rock Run. He immediately accosted them, demanding to know who they were, and where they were going.—They seemed not disposed to give satisfactory answers, and one of the men advanced toward him. Mr. Lawrence then drew his revolver, commanding him to halt, and the party to face about and proceed where he directed. This order they obeyed with reluctance, answering his inquiries as to where they came from and whither they were going, by telling him they were from Perryville and were going to a Mr. Vandiver's, about half a mile up the street.—They said they had been directed to go to Mr. Vandiver's by a Mr. Cunningham, who kept a public house at Perryville, and who told them they would be entertained over night free, being out of money, as they alleged.

Constable Lawrence marched the party to Mr. W. Crumpton's Hotel, where free quarters were provided for them, and the next morning they were taken to Perryville and delivered into the hands of the military stationed there. The three captives proved to be part of the rebel prisoners who escaped from Fort Delaware a short time since.—Much praise is due to Constable Lawrence for his firm and decided course in capturing these three escaped prisoners, who were evidently making their way from one rebel stopping place to another. What would be the fate of Union residents in the South if they were found piloting escaped Union prisoners toward the Union lines?

It is reported that three of the escaped Fort Delaware prisoners were taken on board a schooner at Port Deposit, which conveyed them to some point down the bay.

The *Whig* published a letter from W. F. A. Torbert to quell the rumors that circulated about the 2nd Delaware. Delaware papers published contradictory reports, claimed the *Whig*, causing much bitterness between officers and men.

Headquarters, 2nd Reg. Del. Vols.
Harrison's Landing, July 21, '62
Dear Ewing:—The numerous reports that many officers of the 2nd Del. Vols. behaved badly in face of the enemy are *entirely unfounded* I would state that if such had been the case the matter before this would have been public in the shape of a court martial. I am perfectly familiar with the official report of the Regiment, made about July 4, 1862, covering the entire movement, and would assure the friends of the Regiment that no officer or man is charged with having acted cowardly or having failed to do his duty; otherwise, the Regiment in all its movements was *firm* and came into the encampment we now occupy with but few stragglers, the larger portion of whom had been taken sick upon the march. There were present with the Regiment *twenty-seven* officers during the entire series of engagements, and *eight* absent sick, with *proper authority* from the Surgeon. I do not claim to have been with the Regiment. I left Savage Station Hospital the evening before the general movement, in company with Col. Wharton, who, with myself, was upon the sick list. Two days before I left the White House Hospital where I had been down with the dysentery and fever some two weeks past, and was not yet strong enough to attempt to perform ordinary military duty.

I would add, that anyone before attempting to form an opinion from what they hear, should consider well the very trying ordeal to which a Regiment forming part of a *rear guard* to an army so vast must have been exposed. With but short rations, the Regiment was on constant duty for six days and nights. I would not trouble you with this communication, only upon the account of the officers who were so unfortunate as to fall sick during the movement. Respectfully yours, W. F. A. Torbert

---

Kollock's Dandelion Coffee
This preparation, made from the best Java Coffee, is recommended by the Physicians as a superior NUTRITIOUS BEVERAGE for General Debility, Dyspepsia, and all bilious disorders. Thousands who have been compelled to abandon the use of coffee will use this without injurious effects. One can contains the strength of two cans of ordinary coffee. Price 25 cents.

> **FRUITLAND**
> GARDEN & NURSERY
> NEWARK, DEL.
> The Proprietor of this
> Nursery is largely
> engaged in the
> cultivation of Choice Fruits for market also,
> Small Fruits,
> Strawberries,
> Raspberries,
> Blackberries.

A report from a wounded officer angered local aid societies. Upon arriving in New York, he alleged that supplies intended for soldiers never reached them: "The boat was old, weak and filthy; the load was excessive, and the fare wretched beyond anything I had ever seen. Poor soldiers! how few of the good things intended for their comfort escape the cupidity of the Doctors."

The *Whig* vouched for the integrity of the officer and offered a modest proposal to remedy the situation: "Those who have the care of the sick and wounded, and appropriate to their own appetites that which is voluntarily supplied for the nourishment and comfort of those under their charge, should be marched out and shot."

Dr. Charles M. Ellis arrived in town from Fortress Monroe via steamer to Chester, Pennsylvania. He was in charge of the hospital at the Fortress and would return shortly to resume his duties. While he was imprisoned in Richmond, Ellis saw Stephen Cameron, Elias Glenn, and William H. May. The latter was slightly wounded and confined to a hospital.

At the beginning of August, a party of ladies and gentlemen sailed down the Elk as far as Court House Point. They lunched at Welch Point before returning on their "very agreeable trip."

As Cecil Countians watched for meteor showers in August, they were treated to a brilliant display of the aurora borealis. Whenever this phenomenon coincided with a battle, the victor interpreted its appearance as an indication that the Almighty was signaling divine approval.

Thomas Jeffries of Company C, 2nd Delaware, died in camp near Harrison's Landing. His body was embalmed there and sent to Elkton for burial. Death also claimed Elizabeth Howard, the 3-month-old daughter of Col. George R. Howard of Elk Neck.

On July 26, 1862, the *Whig* ran the following account from Capt. Alonzo Snow.

SNOW'S BATTERY, Artillery Reserve, Army Potomac, HARRISON'S LANDING
    Virginia, July 10th, 1862
E. E. EWING, Editor CECIL WHIG: —Sir:—

After the first fight of our battery at New Bridge, June 5th, the promise was given that should we ever be engaged in another battle, a list of all who took part in it, and faithfully performed their duty, should be sent home for publication. Several times since then we have been under orders expecting the conflict, but the time did not arrive until Tuesday July 1st. It is but just to state that some of our men who did excellent service at New Bridge, were sick, and in advance with the trains at our last fight, but are ready and willing to render good service for their country, either sick or well, if not too weak to march.

The following is the list of those in the battle of Malvern Hills, Tuesday July 1st: Orderly Sergeant, William Trayner; Bugler, David W. Morris; Color bearer, *Daniel M. Parker*; Guidon, *George W. Roberts*; Artificers, John Russel, Stephen A. Miller, *Wm. Clayton.*

CHANGE OF HOURS.

Philadelphia, Wilmington and

BALTIMORE RAILROAD.

CARS LEAVE ELKTON

For Baltimore	For Philadelphia
1st Train, 10:20 A M	1st Train 10:50 AM
2nd " 1:18 P.M.	2nd " 3:33 PM
3rd " 12:55 night	3rd " 7:57 PM

☞ Besides which regular trains there will be a Passenger Car attached to the Through Freight train, which will pass southward at 9:30 o'clock P.M., taking passengers for Havre de Grace, and all the intermediate stations. BENJ. WELLS, Agent.

1st Piece—Serg't Wm. Pratt; Corporal and Gunner, Jacob W. McCardell; Corporal Wm. T. Coleman. Cannoniers—John T. Montgomery, Columbus S. Lawrence, Wm. Sheppard, Abraham Taylor, Wm. Haines, Charles W. Griffin, John Quigley, Wm. B. Webb. Drivers—John A. Orr, Henry H Makinson, William H. Lyle, Samuel Ortlip, George W. Conner, Wm. H. Jones.

2nd Piece—Serg't Enos T. Hall; Corporal and Gunner, Thos Murphy; Corporal, Wm. McDowell. Cannoniers—George R. Cunningham, Daniel W. Hamer, James W. Russell, Jos. Nowlin, Lewis Br....[illegible], *Wm. H. Peacock*, John H. Stephens, Jacob Cunningham.—Drivers—John J. Gray, Wm. Simpers, John S. Clarke, Samuel H. Kimball, *John Powell*, Wm. Hall.

3rd Piece—Sarg't, James Leek; Corporal and Gunner, Edward T. Thompson, Cannoniers— Wm. Dawson, *Robert Craig*, Wm. H. Wilson, Henry Wearl, *Elisha Brown*, Enos Scarborough, Wm. H. Neal, Wm. H. Barrett, JOS. C. ABRAHAMS, Wm C. Barnes. Drivers— Isaac R. Dunn, Samuel J. Barr, Wm. J. Jackson, Thos. Kirk, *Samuel M. Brickley*, W. N. Kopf.

4th Piece—Serg't, Wm. H. Cook. acting Gunner, John W. Hus...[illegible], Cannoniers, *C. H. Alexander*, Robert Schools, Henry Fisher, Wm. Rowe, Alfred B. Harris, Ellis Wault, James L. Jones. Drivers—Wm. A. Knight, *Wm. J. McLean*, David J. Heckart, Wm. M. Jones, Franklin Wire, Jas. McMinimee.

5th Piece—Serg't, *Theo. Smith*; acting Gunner, *Daniel Leary*. Cannoniers—*Thos. Duffy*, Wm. M. Lienbargh, James D. Culley, John Conner, *Edward Buffier*, John B. Garrett, *James D. Holland*, John Webber, Henry Magaw. Drivers—Samuel A. Miller, Wm. F. Cherry, *George Bishop*. John A. Ewing, John E. Killman, George Morris.

6th Piece—Serg't Walker Y. Hall; Corporal and Gunner, *Henry S. Taylor*, Corporal, John Polk. Cannoniers—Samuel Kelly, *Evan Williams*, James McDevitt, ROBERT G. RINK, John Hughes, Frederick W. Most. Drivers—Valentine Fleake, John McNamee,

Jonas A. Derr, Frederick H. Groce, Wm. P. Carr, Wm. H. Baldwin

A. SNOW, Captain.

Those in italics were wounded; those in small capitals were killed.

From Washington, Dorothea Dix requested oil cloth or oiled silk, pillows covered by material impervious to water, cotton, calico or gingham blouses or half gowns for the wounded and invalids. Adams Express shipped the items free of charge, if they were delivered to the Philadelphia office.

At this juncture President Lincoln relieved McClellan of command and appointed Maj. Gen. Henry W. Halleck in charge of the Army of the Potomac.

The first weeks in August were dry and hot. Clouds of dust swirled in the streets of Elkton, depositing a film of grit everywhere. Town Commissioners decided that the Court House bell would ring every night at ten o'clock. Within fifteen minutes all black people had to be off the streets. If they were caught breaking the curfew, they would be lodged overnight in jail and fined one dollar in the morning, unless they could give a good reason for being out. With convoluted logic, some townspeople said the law placed the blacks above whites. In their view, a white man could stay out all night with nobody to look after him, but if a black man "is found out too late, quarters are provided for him."

On August 16, Sheriff Cosgrove sold as a slave a free black named Dennis Forman, who was convicted of coming into the state contrary to law. Jacob Johnson purchased Forman for $33, but Forman "skedaddled" the same night, leaving Johnson minus his investment. The *Democrat* commented dryly: "Small profit and quick sale."

> **Phila., Wil. & Balt. Railroad**
> Trains leave North East Station as follows
> TO PHILADELPHIA   TO BALTIMORE
> Express 10:30 A.M.   Mail   10:30 P.M.
> Mail   3:15 P.M.   Night Mail 1PM.
> Night Mail 7:37 "
> Through Freight, with passenger car attached, leaves North East for Baltimore at 9:55 P.M. Stops at Charlestown, Principio, Perryville, and Havre-de-Grace
> ☞ *No train for Philadelphia on Sunday.*
> W. D. ALEXANDER,
> Agent.

In Chesapeake City John Dunning got into trouble with the law for using treasonable language. When he attempted to leave the county to evade military duty, he was confined to Fort McHenry.

Regarding the draft, the *Whig* published a long list of exempt categories. It named such persons as telegraph operators; workmen employed on arsenals or armories; ferrymen on post roads; certain state, county and federal officials; school masters; physician; ministers; conscientious objectors; disabled persons; and pilots of registered or licensed steamships. The *Whig* explained the draft:

> CECIL'S QUOTA FOR THE ARMY.—We have been informed by Assistant Adjutant General Creswell, that the quota of men which our county is liable to furnish the army, reckoning from the commencement of the war, is as near as the present inaccurate state of information will admit an approximation, 770 men. Unfortunately our county receives no

credit for any of her citizens enlisted in regiments belonging to other States. Counting those who are enlisted in the Maryland regiments, her quota falls short about one hundred. This deficiency will have to be made up, we suppose, by draft, which has been postponed till the 1st of October. Capt. Ricketts' company, the Big Elk Rangers, which was raised soon after the breaking out of the war and composed almost entirely of Cecil men, was mustered into the 2nd Del. Reg. and is consequently lost to our State and county, notwithstanding the families of the *Rangers* are recipients of the state's bounty. Cecil has numbers of her sons fighting in the regiments of other States, with whom if she were credited, would exempt her from the draft.

For Cecil County to complete enrollment, the following officers were appointed: Jas. T. McCullough, Commissioner to superintend the draft; Dr. J. Dunott, examining physician; 1st District, Thomas P. Jones; 2nd District, F. A. Crouch; 3rd District, Joseph Wells; 4th District, Wm. C. Hasson; 5th District, Benoni Cooling; 6th District, Barclay Reynolds; 7th District, John M. McClenahan; 8th District, Enoch McCullough; 9th District, J. T. Janney.

Soon deputy sheriff Janney arrested James Whitcraft, 4th District, on Wm. C. Hasson's complaint that he refused to give his name and age. Whitcraft was taken before Justice Torbert and fined $5 and costs. In the First District, Joseph C. Senneckson and Thomas R. Hays were arrested for a similar offense. A number of men left the county for Canada to avoid the draft.

James Touchstone of Port Deposit was appointed Quartermaster of the 6th Maryland Regiment. The officers expected to have a full quota of men shortly. Colonel Howard filled up his regiment.

David Boulden, accused of helping Confederate prisoners escape from Fort Delaware, was released from Old Capital Prison and no charge was brought against him, nor was a hearing held.

> Our attention was particularly called to a case of Medicines at the Fair of the Maryland Institute, viz: of STABLER'S ANODYNE CHERRY EXPECTORANT AND DIARRHOEA CORDIAL, they are most beautifully put up, and from what we have heard, they are as good as they are beautiful. Many of our physicians prescribe them with the best effect. To those suffering with Colds and its kindred diseases, we would recommend a trial of the Expectorant.

Employees of the Chesapeake and Delaware Canal Co. took the oath of allegiance. An officer from Fort Delaware administered it to John R. Price, Esq., Dr. Wm. S. Carsner, Thomas J. Cleaver, and Jos. T. Hedrick, Esq.

Enoch Cantwell of Elkton became a brakeman on the P. W. & B. Railroad; when Colonel Corcoran passed through on the train, the people turned out to "greet the Irish hero and shake his hand. The Engine was decorated with flags, which gave the train a galaday appearance."

Sad news arrived of the sinking of the *West Point*, a ship that was transporting convalescent troops. It collided with the *George Peabody* in the Potomac River and sank in ten minutes. Of the 279 persons on board 73 were lost.

A collection taken up for the Big Elk Rangers yielded a curious combination of contributions: Mrs. Davis, Mr. Wm. Pough, and Mr. Steptoe, 25 cents; Mr. Cresho, 50 cents; Mrs. E. Read, 1½ dozen eggs; Mrs. Jesse Pierson, Mrs. Thomas McNeal, and Mrs. Cornelius Danver, half bushel onions; Mrs. Dunott, Mrs. Strickland, Mrs. Fehely, and Miss Betty Hiss, onions.

The County Commissioners had to raise roughly $40,000 to pay each volunteer a bounty of $100. Those who waited to be drafted received no bounty. The *Whig* noted that there were openings in Colonel Howard's regiment. R. E. Cantwell, headquartered at Smith's Hotel in Elkton, recruited for a company of Maryland cavalry. Captain Christie's company in the 6th Maryland also needed several men. "None will ever rue serving under Christie," said the *Whig*. "His men are sure of kind treatment and good officering."

CUT AND DRIED TOBACCO, 12½ cents per lb., for sale by
WM. TORBERT.

From Camp Hoffman arrived news of Company B, 6th Maryland (*Whig* 8/23/62).

> MR. EDITOR:—We are now enjoying all the gayety of camp life—all are cheerful—and I have as yet to see one who regrets inlisting in Company B. Howard Guards. On Friday, our Adjutant Mr. Jacob B. Ash of your town, called us in line, stating that the Col. wished to speak to us.—"Soldiers of the 6th Maryland Regiment: I have called you together for the purpose of refuting a charge which has reached my ears, that is, that I am not to take charge of this Regiment, but that it is to be commanded by another." He said that it was a fabrication which was spread abroad for the purpose of injuring the 6th Md. Regiment, but he would assure us that there was not the slightest foundation for it. He also, assured us, that he had enlisted in the cause of the Union with his whole heart, that he would endure privations with us and be our leader wherever we might go. After the patriotic remarks of Col. Howard, the Regiment gave him three hearty cheers, after which it was ordered to break ranks.— The men put the greatest confidence in Col. Howard, and will follow him, if need be, to the rebel capital or treason-growing South Carolina.
>
> On Saturday evening we were called in line, to elect our Captain and Lieutenants. Lieut. J. C. Hill was elected captain of Company B. by a unanimous vote. The men fairly worship Captain Hill, and Capt. Hill appears to care more for his men's happiness than for his own. Not like some Captains that I have seen—whose aristocratic proclivities take possession of them as soon as they get in camp. He always has a smile for his men ***them where he may—and last, but not least, sees that they are well provided for.
>
> Isaac N. Benjamin was elected 1st Lieutenant. Lieut. Benjamin was a soldier in the war of Mexico, and consequently is well qualified for the position he has to fill. 2nd Lieutenant

Erastas S. Narval. Lieut. Narval has been in the service since the rebellion broke out, and is a well drilled man.—Men cannot think more of their officers than do the men of Company B.

Our non-commissioned officers are all very popular, especially Orderly Sergeant, Wm. Abercrombie, who is a ***, and one of the most jovial fellows that we ever had the plesure of meeting. His position is one of responsibility, as he has the providing of the "grub" to see too, and you may rest assured that he always has our plates groaning under the best that the camp can afford.

> **R. R. R.**
> IMPORTANT MEDICAL DISCOVERIES
> **RADWAY'S READY RELIEF,**
> Which has been used by hundreds of thousands throughout the United States, giving instant ease to all troubled with pain or sickness. Let those who are now suffering any severe pains give it a trial, for in fifteen minutes they will enjoy ease and comfort.

Mr. James Touchstone of Cecil, the unfaltering friend of the Union—who has dealt through the columns of "*The Whig*," many seething rebukes, and anihilated all the foul doctrines of the Maryland secessionists, is Quartermaster of the 6th Maryland, and arrived yesterday to take charge of his post.

The Regiment will be composed chiefly of Ceciltonians, there being four Companies partially filled up from Cecil, and a great many recruits daily arriving. Capt. Hill's Company is now full. We are to be mustered in to-day, and receive our pay. Imagine that the boys are in a remarkably good humor.

Yours, CORPORAL

Jeb Stuart's Cavalry raided Catlett's Station and captured three Cecil soldiers of Purnell's Legion: James T. Alexander, L. K. Terry, and J. Burns.

The *Democrat* reported that Captain Barr of the Second Delaware was at his father's home in Middletown. The good captain was no doubt very much encouraged to read in the article that he was "reduced to almost a skeleton by sickness. It is stated that his company musters only 25 effective men."

A federal agent arrested John C. Maxwell and William H. Smith of Port Deposit and James H. Michael of Harford County, according to the *Whig*, "for hurrahing for Jeff, and defying the government and officer in the various modes the rebels have of misbehaving." They were taken to Baltimore, where Smith and Michael took the oath and were discharged. "But Jonny not having the rum quite all worked out of him refused, and was confined in the Middle District Station. One night in this rendezvous for malefactors, predisposed him in favor of the Lincoln pill, *alias* 'the oath,' which he swallowed and was allowed to depart for his home in Port Deposit...."

Among the Elk Rangers hospitalized at Newport News are William Drew, Amos R. McNeal, Henry C. Nelson, Philip Giles, Henry Simpers, and William Sands.

The *Whig* commented upon the opening of local schools in early September.

> On Monday next the schools of Elkton will open and the juveniles who have had such a long respite from study will be mustered again under the watchful eye of the teacher, and put on the march toward the temple of knowledge. Like the famous ride to Jordan, many of them will doubtless dub it a "hard road to travel."
>
> Our town is well supplied with those classic seats of the muses—or, to drop poetry and confine our pen to common sense, with schools. And first among these institutions of learning is the Elkton Academy, under the able management of Henry W. Thorpe, A.M. Principal, Miss C.W. Thorpe, Princeptress, and Mrs. E. Duncan, Teacher of Music. The Fall quarter of this old established institution commences on Monday next, and parents who wish to send their children to a school where they may acquire a thorough practical education, combining the advantages of a healthy country, and intellectual and moral society, Elkton Academy is not surpassed by any other school of the kind that we know of.
>
> The Elkton Public School room will be opened also on that day, by the pupils' favorite teacher, Mr. Rhodes, as a private subscription school til the 1st of October, when the Public Schools throughout the county will commence. Miss Carrie H. Moore assists Mr. Rhodes in the scholastic labors of this institution.
>
> In addition to the above mentioned schools there are several others in the town which are of the infant order, more private, and of less pretending merits, nevertheless invaluable as the means of preparing the young mind for future training in the common school, and thence up through the higher walks of literature and science by the academic and collegiate courses. Those among the latter class are taught by Miss Annie Purnell, and Miss Mary Staples, on Main street, and Miss Emily Galaway, on High street.

One night in September 1862, Private Godfrey Duttenberg, Company E, 17th New Jersey, was pushed from a moving train by two drunk companions. He landed near the culvert a short distance from Elkton. His shoulder was dislocated, and nobody found him until the next morning. He was taken to Smith's Hotel, where Dr. Dunott treated his injuries.

ELKTON RESTAURANT.
If you want to find the place to get
CHEAP DINNERS, call at the
ELKTON RESTAURANT,
where you can get OYSTERS at all times
and at the shortest notice, served up in
the following ways.
FRIED,
STEWED,
ROASTED, or
RAW 12½ cts.

For those who required the services of a specialist, Prof. J. Isaacs, oculist and aurist, visited Elkton for the first two weeks in September. He took up residence at the Howard House and effected "astonishing cures for Messrs. Vikers, Crow, Shaw and Usilton."

19th-century draft dodgers drew the *Whig's* fire under the heading, "The Exempt Brigade."

The citizens of our town have been astonished the present week at the number of unfortunate among the white male population of our county, that have poured into Elkton, seeking exemption from military duty. The office of the Commissioner and Surgeon who superintend the draft, &c, have been fairly besieged by *invalids*. Bedford and Saratoga can show nothing to compare with it. It was the boast of our citizens that Cecil possessed a brave, warlike and healthy population. But the draft! that dreadful draft! has revealed to our bewildered senses that Maryland's pride and boast, Loyal Cecil, is like unto a whitened sepulchre.—Her male population between the ages of 18 and 45 groan with afflictions dire, and all the fell diseases flesh is heir to.

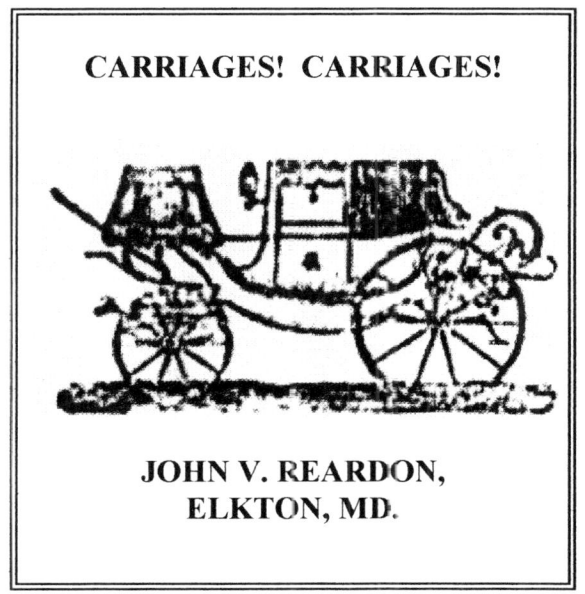

CARRIAGES! CARRIAGES!

**JOHN V. REARDON,
ELKTON, MD.**

The crowds that block up the offices of the commissioner and examining Surgeon, have been a prolific theme of remark. To see stout, young fellows, to all appearances, strong as Ajax, waiting their turn at the office doors to show their infirmities, and claim exemption from the religious duty of defending their State and country, boasting of their manhood and strength the while, and sparring, perhaps with each other, to pass away the tedious time, was both ludicrous and lamentable. Office hours did not suffice, but the seekers after exemption besieged the houses of the officers, giving them neither time to eat or repose, till they were denied admission and driven off.

Numbers who appeared as candidates for exemption were afflicted with bodily infirmities and chronic diseases that incapacitate them for military service in the field, but what shall we say in extenuation of the scores who came forward claiming exemption on the most trivial grounds, and others again, whose robust health and well known habits of manual labor, have always been the pride and admiration of neighbors and friends, presenting themselves before the Surgeon and taking advantage of some physical blemish, either feigned or real, to claim exemption from military duty? We heard of one individual who had cut his toe joint in endeavoring to maim himself. Some came with trusses, newly put on. Some borrowed the truss of a brother coward after it had served coward No. 1. Various devices were resorted to, in order to get an exemption ticket. These infirmities had all to be sworn to before the Commissioner, ere he would give the applicants a pass to the Surgeon....

For several weeks the *Whig* complained about young boys who fired shots on the causeway ostensibly to shoot birds; "but when a spirit of deviltry prompts them to discharge their guns for the purpose of frightening horses, the Town Commissioners should put a stop to their amusement. If sportsmen can't refrain from shooting while horses are on the causeway they become a nuisance and should be abated."

A train carrying troops from Philadelphia to Wilmington uncoupled, and another train crashed into the detached cars, killing or wounding several soldiers. The remaining troops were quartered in the railroad depot at Elkton, but they had no rations. Elkton citizens supplied them with food until the Government rations arrived the next night. The soldiers patrolled the railroad from Chester to Baltimore. Often convalescent troops were assigned to this duty.

Lieutenant Gideon Todd, Company I, Second Delaware, returned to the home of his father, Eli Todd. He died in his 28th year of an "affection of the bowel." Lt. Todd is mentioned in one of Lottie Ricketts' letters [See Appendix A].

In Chesapeake City, Constable Colmary arrested Joseph Edwards for selling bogus jewelry. Justice Barwick fined him $25 and costs, but when Edwards was unable to pay, he was jailed.

The county buzzed at the prospect of a visit from Gardner and Hemming's Great American Circus. For 25 cents, one could see talking horses and educated mules, not to mention "Miss Eliza Gardner, without doubt the most beautiful, chaste, and elegant Female Equestrian in the world."

How very disappointing to learn that the circus was canceled when horses and men fell into the hands of Confederates at Frederick! As for the chaste Miss Eliza, she disappeared from the pages of the newspapers in a blaze of pure glory.

The *Democrat* observed that work had begun on a railroad bridge over the Susquehanna.

Antietam. The heretofore unfamiliar name now became a household word for carnage. On September 27, the *Whig* reported:

> We have made every effort to obtain a correct list of the killed and wounded of our Cecil volunteers in the late, great battle of Antietam. The following list shows the Regiments and Companies to which they belong, and the killed, wounded and missing during the series of fights from Sunday up till Wednesday, the day of the great battle.

Agents Wanted.

To sell the best work of T. S. ARTHUR, "TEN NIGHTS IN A BAR-ROOM, AND WHAT I SAW THERE." This is a large 12 mo., of 240 pages, illustrated with a beautiful Mezzotint Engraving, by Sartain, bound in the best manner; full gilt back. ☞Specimen copies sent to any part of the United States, on receipt of the price, 75 cents. Some agents now selling this book, are making $50 per month.

Apply to
J. W. BRADLEY, Publisher.
28 North Fourth Street, Phila.

The first on our list are Companies A and I 5th Maryland Regiment, Commanded by Capt. Ford of North East, and Capt. Faehtz of Elkton, both of whom fought with the most heroic courage in the battle of Antietam, laying aside their swords and using muskets along with their men.

Company A., Captain Samuel Ford. Killed: Asa Mattox, Elkton; Oliver McCullough and Thomas Brown, North East; George McClure and John Alexander, Chesapeake City;

Wounded: John Simpers, Samuel Matthews, John West, Asbury Wilson, Wm. Price of North East; Henry Coolan, Wm. Murphy, Joseph Yeamans, and Corp. Wm. Russell of Charlestown; Charles Biddle, Philip Layman, Loftus Brotherton, George Carnser [sometimes spelled Kershner], Sgt. Geo. L Flinthan, Thomas Harmon [Harman], and Hugh Scanlan, and ___ Irwin of Chesapeake City; Gustavus Foster, and Jon. Burk, and ___ Irwin from Elk Neck.

Missing: Jacob Campbell and Jacob Lowry, Charlestown.

There were no fatalities in Company I, but the wounded included Lieut. Thomas, Corporal Geary, and William Ottley [sometimes spelled Otley; elsewhere identified as Robert Ottley], and ___ Wiley. Missing: Cor. Amor F. Dunbar, William McSorley, and Davis Geary.

Company C., Captain Ricketts, 2nd Delaware Regiment. Killed: Henry M. Bennett. Wounded: Phil Giles, Wm. Sowers, Isaac Foreacre.

> **What Soldiers Want in Warm Weather.**
> ...put into a letter a spoonful of tea or a spoonful of capsicum. [It] will invigorate digestion, and is a great antagonist of the diarrhoea, dysentery, flux and "looseness," which are great scourges of all armies.

The Purnell Legion—This body of Maryland troops was in the terrible battle of Wednesday, Sept. 17th. As company E was principally filled by volunteers from Cecil, and company H. partly composed of men from Cecil, there is much anxiety in the county to hear from them.

Company E. was commanded in the action by Lieut. Newton, and the list of casualties as reported are:—John Means, killed. Nicholas House, wounded in the hand; Jesse Anderson, wounded in the face, and Samuel Hamilton, in the leg.

By a letter from Lieut. McCauley, who had charge of Company H, we learn that they were under heavy fire for seven hours, and came off safe with the exception of John W. Miller, slightly wounded in the face and arm, by the explosion of a shell.

Gen. Green complimented the Legion very handsomely for its bravery on the field.

The October 4 issue of the *Whig* carried a letter from Antietam dated September 18, 1862.

Mr. E. E. Ewing:—Dear Sir:—As the regiment has been in the late battle and most of the members of Company C being from your town, we thought it best to write you a few lines, to publish. We are sorry, very sorry indeed, to state we have one man killed, Henry M. Bennett, who received a gunshot wound in the neck and was killed almost immediately, he was buried separately. We had beside six wounded, but none seriously: Isaac Foreacre, struck by piece of shell in calf of the leg; William Sowers, in the hand; Heaster Smith, slightly wounded in shoulder; Philip Giles, ball in the stomach; James T. Mahan, bayonet wound in leg. None of these are seriously injured, and are well taken care of. There were several others wounded slightly, but are with the company on duty. This was on the morning of the 17th, the regiment after being under heavy cannonade the day before and early that morning was ordered to move. Marching about 11½ miles we formed in line of battle and marched up and relieved French's brigade, who were fighting at the time. Our brigade, under or in command of Col. Brooks, who was acting Brig. General, halted on the ground which General French's brigade held, and commenced firing on the enemy, who were in front of us only about 50 yards, in a corn-field. Our regiment being more blood thirsty, or something else, than the other regiments of our line, to a man, let out a yell, driving the rebels pell mell before them and dropping the skedaddling "varmints" as they flew. They had the advantage of us in every respect, being behind stone fences and deep gullies to hide in. At one place there was a gully similar to a rifle pit which they had possession of and from that they annoyed French's brigade very much, picking the men and officers off. Our men alone marched over this killing and wounding great numbers and taking the rest prisoners. As we got them on the run we kept them going until there were very few to be seen. The regiment acted nobly and made a brilliant charge on the enemy, and have received great credit, of which, I assure you, Company C received a good portion and well may the fathers of the brave sons be proud now of their noble conduct. The company was in command of Lieut. Ephraim Jordan, who was always at the head of his men cheering them on, and a braver man never led a company into action than he has proved to be.

Lieut. J. G. Simpers being on detached service, Acting quartermaster, was not in the engagement. Philip Johnson, Acting Orderly Sergeant, was about as usual, kept the right of his company, cheered his men on nobly and kept them together. No braver or better disciplined man was ever in the ranks of any regiment. I would willingly say a word for all of them, but being on the battle-field the accommodations are none of the best as you

---

To Copy Ferns.
The most perfect and beautiful copies imaginable may be made by thoroughly saturating them with common porter, and then laying them flat between white sheets of paper without more pressure than the leaves of an ordinary book bear to each other, and let them dry out.

know. I must say the whole company, to a man, that were in the engagement, could not have been more noble or daring than they were as they faced the music splendidly.

Our colors were shot down three different times, and picked up and waved as suddenly as they fell. They look a little worse the ware, but that matters not as long as they stick together, and we can hold them until our *country's flag and honor* is firmly established, is all we desire to the man.   C. J. S.

> The writer may be tentatively identified as Lt. Charles J. Smith, whose parents lived a short distance from Elkton. Years later, when the survivors of the Second Delaware met on October 14, 1886, Charles J. Smith was the recording secretary.

On September 27, 1862, the *Whig* published the following from a member of the 5th Maryland.

Near Sharpsburg, September 21st, about 500 yards from the Battle Ground of Wednesday

Our regiment lost 144 killed and wounded, and 44 missing, of whom at least two-thirds may be numbered as dead; total loss 188.—Company I did not suffer so much as some others, having in all only six wounded, of whom three, Corporals Wm. McSorley, Amor Dunbar and Davis Geary are missing. Lieut. E. W. Thomas is seriously, but not dangerously wounded, a shot through the flesh above the knee, the ball penetrating the muscles, but leaving the bone uninjured. Private Willey is wounded, and Corporal Robt. Ottley, of Cherry Hill, is mortally wounded. The latter fell at the moment when the colors being in great danger, Capt. Faehtz called out "Rally, boys, to the colors!" Ottley advanced and fell. Company I did nobly especially John Tuft, who carried the colors; he and Capt. Faehtz themselves took three prisoners. The flag [the one presented by the ladies of Elkton] is pierced by sixty bullets.

Company A has suffered terribly 6 being killed and 24 wounded, also some few missing; the only one from Elkton killed being Asa Maddox, the first man shot in the regiment. The cause of their great loss is their being placed just in front of a rifle pit. The only officer killed was Lieut. Molkte of Company C, a nephew of Major Blumenberg. The Major, with Captain Bamberger were very severely wounded. Capt. Ford, though reported wounded was untouched.

Matrimonial Notice

A YOUNG GENTLEMAN of respectability, wishes to form an acquaintance with some Young Lady, in good standing, with a view to *Matrimony*. Said gentleman is of mild disposition, though in points particular; is regular in habit, and sincere in his attachment. He is of medium height, light complexion and hair, and is in moderate circumstances. None need apply unless sincere. For further information address
HARRY VERNON
Chesapeake City.

At present we are encamped on the ground which the rebels held against us on Wednesday, and although we are better off in provisions than we were during the march, yet we have many deprivations and horrors around us; for example, we slept last night amidst hundreds of dead rebels who are partially decomposed and cause an awful stench. The battle must have done terrible destruction among them, for we have counted yesterday in a straight line of no more than a mile, no less than 1,149 dead rebels, yet unburied, beside innumerable dead horses and filled graves.

We are in the second brigade, at present commanded by Col. Schley, of French's Division, Sumner's Corps. Capt. Faehtz and the Color-Bearer, John Tuft, were the last of Company I to leave the field, and then not before our reinforcements had arrived and were 200 yards ahead.

Have You Seen Them?
If not, call and look at a new lot of GROCERIES just received, and judge for yourselves whether you can buy them as low anywhere else in town as at the store in the Hollow, by
ROSSELL & HINES.

J. Polk Racine, in *Recollections of a Veteran* (1894, pp. 98-99), described John Tuft's untimely death, which occurred later during the siege of Petersburg.

...Patrick Reedy of North East, was in the act of handing a piece of fat pork to John Tuft. John yelled, "Look out, boys!" and that instant the shell struck poor John, just below the knee and mashed it terribly. Johnny Bennet and Jake Lotman went for a stretcher, and carried one of the best soldiers in the whole army to the rear, where the surgeons dressed his wound and sent him to the hospital. There his leg was amputated, above the knee, but he never recovered. As he was being carried past us, he said: "Good-bye boys; take care of yourselves. I have lost a pin. I may get a furlough—maybe a very long one. Good-bye." It was not long before we heard that the brave man had got his pass or furlough; and we hope it passed him right through the pearly gates into the kingdom of glory.

Company C of the Purnell Cavalry was mustered into service with one hundred men under the following officers: Captain Theodore Clayton, 1st Lieut. Charles W. Palmer, and 2nd Lieut. Irvill Purnell. Clayton has raised the company in 20 days, after declining the office of Assistant Assessor of the Government tax for Cecil county to enter the military.

The *Whig* ran a column of cards from various sources to verify the disability of Captain Ricketts. [Most of these notices were included with his military service records in the National Archives, Washington, D.C.] A length of red tape was required to prove he was sick at the time.

In the Delaware papers of last week appeared the following. RESIGNED:—We are informed, we believe on good authority, that Major Andrews and Captain Ricketts, of the

Second Delaware, have both resigned.—CHICKEN

The above is not quite true. The names of these officers were struck from the rolls because of their non-appearance at their posts as all officers were required to be by a certain date or furnish a sufficient excuse. The name of Major Andrews, we learn, was struck off under a misapprehension. He was reputed absent, when he should have been reported absent and sick.   DEL. GAZETTE

Which makes necessary the publication of the following facts:

On July 2nd, Capt. Ben Ricketts was, by the Assistant Surgeon of the 2nd Del. Reg., placed sick on transport at Harrison's Landing, as per following certificate:

    Camp Near Rockville, Md.   September 8th, 1862

This is to certify that Capt. Ben Ricketts, of the 2nd Del. Vol., was by me, placed on a transport at Harrison's Landing, July 2nd, 1862, he being sick at that time.
    Philip Plunkett
    Assistant Surgeon, 2nd Reg. Del. Vol.

He reported to Dr. Cuyler, Medical Director at Fortress Monroe, on July 4th—He was then sent to the Naval Hospital, at Portsmouth, and reported there same day, July 13th, he was transfered [*sic*] to Hospital at Annapolis, as per following order:

    Headquarters Middle Department
    Fortress Monroe, July 13, 1862

Captain Ben Ricketts, 2nd Del. Vols., is hereby transferred to General Hospital at Annapolis on recommendation of Medical Director at these Headquarters. By command of Major General Dix
   D.T. Van Boren Assist. Adjt. General

While at Annapolis he was, by special order of the War Department, granted sick leave of absence for thirty days, dating from July 26th, as per following order:

    Adjutant General's Office
      Washington, July 24, 1862

Leave of absence for thirty days is granted Capt. Ben. Ricketts, 2d Del. Vols. on Surgeon's certificate of disability.
  By order of Secretary of War
    E.D. Townsend
    Assistant Adjutant General

On the 21st of August, five days, or counting the grace days allowed, eight days before the expiration of his leave he joined his Regiment at Newport News. He took command at once of his company, marched with Pope arriving at Centreville, Sunday, 31st of August. The events of this, and next few days are matters of history and need not be recited here. Judge of his surprise when on the 8th of September the following order was received:

WAR DEPARTMENT
ADJUTANT GENERAL'S OFFICE
Washington, September 4, 1862

Special Orders, No. 220

By direction of the President, the following named officers are stricken from the rolls of the army for absenting themselves without authority:
******************2nd Del. Vols.

Capt. Benjamin Ricketts,
By order of the Secretary of War,
E. D. TOWNSEND, A. A. G.

He proceeded immediately to Washington, laid a statement of the case, verified by the above documentary evidence, before the Secretary of War. What proceedings were then and there had will appear by the following:

By Order of the Secretary of War
E.D. Townsend
Asst. Adjutant General

Utterly broken down in health, he was on the 13th of September, examined by Surgeon Kimberly, U.S.A., with what effect is here seen:

Washington, D.C. Sept. 13, 1862

I have this day made an examination of Capt. Ben Ricketts, Co. C. 2nd Del. Vols. and find that his left lung is considerably diseased, and I hereby certify that he requires a furlough of at least thirty days, in order to recruit his health. J. KIMBERLY, Surgeon U.S.A.

Upon this the following special order was issued.

WAR DEPARTMENT
ADJUTANT GENERAL'S OFFICE
Washington, September 13, 1862

Special Orders, No. 238

Leave of absence for thirty days is granted: Captain Ben Ricketts, 2nd Del. Vols., on Surgeon's certificate of disability.
By Order of the Secretary of War
E.D. TOWNSEND   Assist. Adjutant General

I have examined the papers herein referred to and the above statement is true in every syllable and letter. It is due to a friend who has been such since we were boys, and of whose purity of character and innate sense of honor I am as much convinced as I am of my own existence.

        W. J. JONES   Elkton, September 27, 1862

In early October, the *Whig* wagered that if Stonewall Jackson were to sweep into Cheap John's establishment, he would make the bigger haul of boots and shoes than he made when he cleared out Frederick. John agreed that his store featured the largest supply of such goods ever assembled at once in the county.

Provost Marshal Bennet set about raising a guard of ten. The cavalry was to be armed, paid by the government, and subject to the marshal in policing the county. Members furnished their own horses.

> ***Curds and Whey—Italian Method.***
> Take several of the rough coats that line the gizzards of turkeys and fowls, cleanse from the dirt, rub well with salt, and hang them up to dry; when required for use, break off some of the skin, pour boiling water on, digest for eight or nine hours, and use the same as rennet.

Two soldiers, each with the surname Bennett, were mentioned in the papers. One died at Antietam, and the other was commended for his bravery: [Henry Bennett was named above in the list from Antietam.]

BENNETT:—Killed in action at the battle of Antietam, on Wednesday 17th ultimate. HENRY M. BENNETT, of Co. C. 2nd Del. Vols., son of Henry and Ellen Bennett. In the 22nd year of his age. He fell, but he fell all covered with glory.

> No parent near him when he died
> No sister's voice to cheer;
> He spoke not, but farewell he sighed,
> To all that he held dear.

BRAVE BOY.—In the late battle of Antietam where Union valor shone so conspicuously, we have many instances of individual bravery related by comrades, but none are more deserving of commemoration by a grateful public than John Bennett, a boy of 17, the heroic son of John P. Bennett, Deputy Marshall of this county. A comrade on the battlefield says of young Bennett:—

"John was in the thickest of the fight, his Captain and all his comrades, declare no braver man ever shouldered a musket.—He was the last one of his Regiment to leave the field. He stood up and waved his hat and defied the enemy. He don't know what fear is."

In the same issue, the *Whig* noted the death of Captain Isaac Lort of Elkton in his 44th year.

Dr. Ellis's father, F. A. Ellis, Esq., remarried after losing his first wife Eliza in August 1861. His second wife was Martha A. Torbert. Groomsman was Henry R. Torbert, and the bridesmaid was Miss Hanna Torbert.

From Captain Snow's Battery near Williamsport, Maryland, came the following, dated September 22, 1862.

> CAMP SNOW'S BATTERY, near Williamsport, Md., September 22, 1862
>
> MR. EDITOR:—Permit us through the columns of your paper, to tender our sincere thanks to the citizens of Port Deposit for their kindness in presenting each of us with a handsome sword. The acknowledgement would have been made earlier, had it not been that the swords were received at Harrison's Landing on the eve of the departure of the army, since which time we have been constantly on the move, first to Alexandria and vicinity, and thence, through Western Maryland, where there was such great necessity for using the sword, that the pen had, for a season, to be laid aside.
>
> We honor and love the cause in which we are engaged, and intend that our future acts shall merit the confidence as well as the handsome gift of our friends.
>
> Our battery was engaged in the fight of Wednesday, 17th inst., until night, and in that part of the field so hotly contested by Hooker and Sumner. Our shell were freely and effectively distributed, the men holding their posts like veterans, resolved to bring no discredit on Cecil, having their ardor greatly augmented by the fact that they were fighting on Maryland soil. The hand of Providence shielded us from harm—for we had not a man either killed or wounded. Our loss was only one horse killed.
>
> Have you in Cecil *twenty-five* men good and true, who wish to strike a blow for the Union? If so, let them come to Snow's Battery, as we wish to use our *six* guns with a full complement of men to each—now we can fully man only *four*, because of loss and sickness. Truly yours, JAS. H. KIDD LEONARD S. PARKER

Address of the Battery is:—Snow's Maryland battery, Smith's division, Franklin's corps, Army of the Potomac.

WHEAT AND RYE STRAW.
WANTED

Straw in large or small quantities will be purchased at Marley Paper Mill, for which full prices will be given.
It will be required to be delivered in bales. Farmers having straw for sale are advised to protect it from the weather. For further particulars apply to WM. F. HOWARD, at Marley Paper Mill, or by letter addressed to Cherry Hill, Cecil county, Md.

The Philadelphia, Wilmington and Baltimore Railroad donated $3,000 to be divided among Cecil, Harford and Baltimore counties. The money was to the bounty funds provided for volunteers in each area.

Major Burton, commander of Fort Delaware, got provoked at those visitors who aided and abetted prisoners in their resistance to the Government. Henceforth no parties were allowed to visit the Island without written consent of the commanding officer. It seemed that ladies were in the habit of bringing presents and giving "comforts in the way of throwing kisses, waving handkerchiefs in peculiar style, and so otherwise deported themselves as to get a reprimand from the commanding officer, and finally to have a guard placed over them....Indeed so rude was the conduct of this party, that an order was issued that no she rebels should be permitted to visit the island only under certain restrictions."

> **Great Medical Achievement.**
> **Mrs. M. Cox's**
> **Indian Vegetable Decoction.**
> Composed entirely of Roots and Herbs.
> Is the Greatest Purifier of the blood ever discovered.
> One Dollar per Bottle,
> or Six bottles for Five Dollars.

From Wilmington came the disconcerting information that Captain O'Keefe of the rebel army and an accomplice named Ryan were arrested and charged as spies for visiting DuPont Powder works and making diagrams of them.

Isaac Foreacre died in a hospital near Sharpsburg from a bullet wound to the thigh. He was the son of Daniel Foreacre, who lived near North East.

William Otley heard that his son Robert, of the 5th Maryland, was wounded in that battle and went in search of him. He found him in a haystack, dirty, ragged and neglected. 18 color bearers were shot down before him, when young Otley seized the flag and was struck with a shell that tore his shoulder off. He crawled to safety and was carried to the haystack, where he lay for five days before his father found him. He remained in Frederick until he was able to stand the ride home. But in spite of his father's great effort to save him, he died on October 24 of the wounds he suffered at Antietam.

In mid-October, Big Elk wrote:

Bolivar Heights   October 15, 1862

Well, I suppose the members of Co. C, 2nd Del. Regiment—the "Big Elk Rangers"—have some friends in Cecil who are anxious to hear from us. In the first place, I would say to the parents and friends of the members of the company, do not be at all alarmed on account of not hearing from them as often as you may wish. We will use our utmost to write you a letter every week, and whenever we mention that we are all well, you can depend upon it. And if any of our men are sick I will give you their names, and tell you how sick they are,—just as well as I can. We have lost one man since the battle, Isaac Foreacre, who was wounded at the battle of Antietam. He died of his wounds at a hospital near Sharpsburg, Md., on the 30th of last month. He was wounded in the thigh by a musket ball. Those absent are: Giles at Davis Island, NY., wounded; Stretch at Frederick, Md. Wounded; Rementer, Baltimore, sick; Jones, Newark, N.J., sick; Thomas and Carr, at Hospital at Fort McHenry, sick; Campbell and Grant, at Point Lookout, Md., sick; Davis, Furguson, and Wilson were left near Alexandria, Va., at the Hospital; but they are now on their way to join us again, and are well. Boyer is in our Regimental Hospital, but he is nearly well now. Thompson has been mustered out of service, I believe.

Our Regiment arrived at this place on the 20th of last month. Our camp is well situated, on the sheltered side of the Heights.

Many of the men received by Adam's Express Co. the boxes that were sent to them the last month or so. But ...most of them were spoiled, and of no use to the men at all.

Our friends need not send us articles that are easily spoiled. But such things as canned fruits, dried beef, and a little of such medicines as we most often need, such as Essence of Peppermint, Essence of Ginger, &c. I would also say that there are but very few of us to whom a plug or two of tobacco would not be acceptable

I am very sorry to say that our Regiment has not yet been paid off. We now have due us nearly six months' pay. And it is a shame the families of the men in the Regiment cannot get their money. Our company are nearly all young men; but a great many of the men in the Regiment are married.

The 5th Maryland is in camp near us. The Cecil men of the Regiment are all well, except Theodore Gatchell, of Andora. He is quite sick at the Regimental Hospital. Mitchell Wilson, of Capt. Faehtz's Co. was buried today. I can send you the names of whole Regiments who were near the 5th in the late battle who will testify that the Regiment did their whole duty.

I yesterday saw Lieut. Ezekiel Alexander, of the 1st Delaware, who formerly lived in your town. He had command of his company during the fight, and showed by his bravery and coolness that he was fully capable of leading his Co. He deserves a great deal of praise for the manner in which he has conducted himself....Big Elk

---

GRAPE VINES
UNSURPASSED IN QUALITY; OF EVERY VARIETY, and in any numbers, for sale at VERY LOW RATES, at *Beaurepair Grape Nursery*. Send one cent stamp and obtain, post-paid, Descriptive, and Price Lists, and other particulars. Also,
PURE CATAWBA WINE
of last year's vintage, unequalled in its pure, native aroma, of dark pink color, suitable for sacramental or medicinal purposes.
Price $1.50 per bottle; $7.00 per gallon, (5 bottles.) Address
JAMES SHOBE
Upper Principio, Cecil county, Md.

Two black people were sentenced to the penitentiary. Laura Bell was convicted of petit larceny and sentenced to six months while John Allison Lee, a freeman, was convicted of manslaughter in the killing of Samuel Lee and was sentenced to five years.

From the 5th Maryland, "Impartial" struggled with the theory of loyalty and compassion for otherwise brave men who succumb to temptation. He could not excuse desertion; but neither could he bring himself to condemn soldiers who bore the brunt of battle.

> HEADQUARTERS CO. A., 5th Md. Reg.
> 3d Brigade, Camp on Bolivar Heights
> Harper's Ferry, October 27, 1862
> Mr. Editor.—I take this opportunity to enclose a few lines to your much valued

---

Notice to Tax-Payers

TAX-PAYERS of the Fifth Election District are hereby notified that I will be at NORTH EAST, on every *Saturday afternoon till the 1st of November, next*, to receive the special Tax levied for use of the Cecil Volunteers. All persons making payment on this tax on or before that day will be entitled to a deduction of five per cent on the amount of their tax.

ELI COSGROVE,
Sheriff.

---

and welcomed paper. We receive *The Whig* regularly every Monday morning, much to the delight of our boys, who have a good-natured scramble as to who shall have the first peep at the first article or letter which may interest them either personally or collectively. Since I last wrote you, many and great changes have taken place in our company. What was then a full company, the embodiment of the youth, vigor, and in fact the pride of the Regiment, is now a mere Corporal's Guard.

A campaign of fourteen months, enduring the toils and trials incident to camp life, the burning heat of the day, the chilling, cold, damp dews of night, unhealthy climate, bad water, and long marches, have told sadly upon us. And though last, not least, the battlefield has done its work. It was there that twenty-six [26] of our noble fellows bleeding and wounded in the cause of liberty; it was there that six [6] more fell slain. And it grieves me to add that two are reported to have died of their wounds, namely, John Leonard of Elkton, and John S. West of North East, thus making in all 8 killed, 21 wounded and 2 missing. Thus you see, we have suffered more as a company, than any other taken into action, taking the numerical strength of each into consideration. The cause is apparent. Every man went into the fight and remained there until every round of cartridge was exhausted. Many of them, after discharging their eightieth round, [and their last] relieved the wounded of theirs, and continued, amidst a perfect storm of bullets, to hurl shot after shot into the rebel ranks. They remained there until they performed their duty manfully and nobly. And as Cecil countians, won for themselves and their county a name, which will contribute a bright page to proud old Cecil's future history.

Having thus acquitted themselves, they recrossed the Potomac. The doing so was the occasion of a number of desertions.—This no doubt sounds bad, but allow me to modify it a little, by saying they have only absented themselves without leave. They crossed the Potomac to the Maryland side, with their arms, marched to Baltimore and reported to headquarters "for duty in the state." This course I do not approve of, and am inclined to believe that the offense will be followed by unpleasant consequences. The history of our regiment is a curious and complicated affair, and for prudential reasons, I refrain from further reference to it at present. At some more convenient season, I shall refer more particularly to the desertions from Co. A., since crossing the Potomac. I can make but one extenuating remark; the good sense of the patriotic soldier revolts at a crime so heinous as desertion, the world looks upon such as miscreants and cowards. But the most, if not all, of those men, stood in he front rank in the fight, fought the bravest, and were the last to quit the field. They were men who never shirked their duty, and always stood well in the estimation of their officers, sustaining all the virtues and requirements necessary to complete the perfect soldier.

It gives me much pleasure to state that our Orderly Sergeant, Wm. J. Morris of North East, has been, for good conduct on the battle-field, promoted to 2nd Lieutenant of Co. D. vice, Kirkwood resigned—a position which, I am satisfied, he will fill with credit to himself and to the company, to which he is assigned.

IMPARTIAL

The Best Packing Machine In Use

This Press received the First Premium at the Maryland Agricultural Exhibition, where its merits were fully tested by competent judges from New York, Pennsylvania, Ohio & Maryland, since which time some very important improvements have been added.

Dimensions of Press and Bales

From 250 to 300 pounds of loose hay can be tramped into the press room, constituting a bale in size 4 feet long, 2½ feet thick and 2½ feet wide.

In addition to being the best Hay and Straw Press now in use, this machine can be used for packing Cotton, Rags, Hemp, Broom, Corn, Hair, Moss, Husks, Wool, &c.

Big Elk wrote again from Bolivar Heights in a letter dated October 22, 1862.

Dear Ewing:—We have been looking for your paper for the last two days, to learn the news from about home. But none have yet been received.

Our division was ordered out early on last Thursday morning to make a reconnaissance in force, in order to feel the enemy in the direction of Charlestown. We had proceeded but a mile or two when we met the enemy's pickets, and driving them in, we pushed toward Charlestown, shelling the rebels whenever they made their appearance. We reached the town about 3 o'clock P.M., and being drawn up in line of battle, and having our pickets thrown out to our front, we laid down by our arms to rest. From our position we could occasionally see the rebels; but they did not attack us. We laid under arms all night on Thursday night, without tents, exposed to a cold and heavy rain. But as it cleared off again about sun up, and the sun shone quite warm, we soon dried our clothes; made our little cup of coffee, then laid down to try and get some sleep, which we could not do during the night on account of the rain and cold. We remained near the town until 10 o'clock A. M., when we were ordered to fall back again toward our present camp, the object desired by our commander being accomplished; which was to learn with what force the rebels occupied Charlestown, and to procure forage while the troops held the place, and brought it safely to Harper's Ferry. We also found several hundred wounded rebels in the hospitals of the town. The rebels found there were all paroled. After leaving the town, we fell back to within about three miles of this camp, and encamped again in line of battle for the night. On Saturday morning, after establishing our line of pickets near where we had encamped on Friday night, we fell back to our camp.

Tuesday [Wednesday] our Regiment is out to the front, as a grand reserve for the pickets, in case they are attacked. The different regiments in the Division take this position by turns.

Our Regiment was paid off last Saturday for four months, ending August 31. I believe a great many of the men of our Co. sent the greater part of their money home. It is to be hoped that the Regiment will not have to wait so long again before being paid off.

We have a new sutler for our Regiment: Mr. Gallagher, of Wilmington. He sells his goods quite reasonable; and is largely patronized by the men of the Regiment.

Our men will have, in a day or two, everything to make them comfortable, as last night requisition was made for everything they need, from a shoe-string to a rifle.

Our camp is a terribly dusty one; and being situated upon high ground we feel the wind very much.

Mutual Fire Insurance Company
OF CECIL COUNTY
The special business of this meeting will be to hear and act upon the report of a committee appointed by the last Annual Meeting to consider the policy and propriety of taking risks upon certain kinds of property heretofore rejected by the Board of Managers, viz:—Paper Mills, Cotton and Woolen Factories, Rolling Mills, Forges, &c.
A full attendance of the members is requested. By order of the Annual Meeting.
F. A. ELLIS
Secretary

If any of the friends of the men of the Co. wish to see them, now would be a good time for them to come, as the road is open from Baltimore, without any delay. And if any of our friends wish to come and see us, we promise to give them soldiers' fare and soldiers' lodgings.

Wishing to be kindly remembered by yourself and all our friends, I am very truly yours,

Big Elk

The *Whig* devoted a column to the hard economic times in the county. Hay and apples were the only crops that did well. Cutworms devastated corn; bugs, rust and dry weather combined to destroy oats; and "the quantity is as limited as the quality is inferior." Wheat suffered the same fate.

Hotel keepers complained that there had been almost an entire suspension of travel. "The war has drained the country of its floating population," opined the *Whig*, "and that busy throng which was wont to be seen on the public thorough fare has measurably diminished." Yet, in spite of bad times, proprietors sought excise licenses, hoping that better days were coming. But the paper predicted that the collector would be met empty-handed in many establishments.

> **AN INFALLIBLE MEDICINE**
> Take—One part laudanum,
>   One part camphorated spirit,
>   Two parts tincture of ginger,
>   Two parts capsicum.
> Dose—One teaspoonful in a wineglass of water.
> If the case be obstinate, repeat the dose in three or four hours.

Unscrupulous Government contractors bought up rags to make cloth called shoddy. They advertised in city papers for cast-off clothing, and in buying up all available rags, drove up the price of paper. Then they sold shoddy to the Government as good material.

Somebody slyly suggested that perhaps the scarcity of paper stock was really due to the making of shinplasters by "one-horse corporations, and if Elkton had embarked in the business there is no telling to what extremities we might have been driven for paper."

Good news! Wm. P. Price, Company A, 5th Maryland, who was reportedly fatally wounded at Antietam, had nearly recovered. Although he was shot in the face, his wounds were not nearly so serious as first supposed. He returned to his home in Cecilton but not before relieving the rebel who shot him of an Irvin revolver valued at $20.

Big Elk wrote from Warrenton, Virginia, a letter dated November 11, 1862.

Dear Ewing:—We came to this town on Sunday evening last, the 9th. And are now encamped to the south side of a hill, near a running stream of water. Our camp is about half a mile from town.

The town had a population of about twenty-five hundred before the war broke out; but now it is in a terrible condition. So many troops of both armies have been marched through the place, and there has been so much skirmishing in and around the town that the inhabitants have been nearly all frightened away, leaving their property unprotected. A good many of the dwellings are filled with wounded rebels, of which there are now a good many here.

Our men have each his own tent to carry. We use what is called "Shelter tents." They are of light cotton, each piece about six feet square. Each piece is made with buttons and button holes on three sides, and two or four of the men button their tents together, which gives them more room and makes them better shelter. When we stop near a bunch of bushes, so that the men can easily get crotches and poles, our Regiment can have all their tents pitched in about 15 or 20 minutes.—And sometimes when we are suddenly ordered to move [which we very often are] we can strike tents and be ready to march in about 5 minutes. A short time to build and tear down a house, is it not? There is a notable fact, about our Company, which is, that while some of the other companies have dwindled down to not more than 16 or 18 men, we still have 82 men.

Lieut. Jordan was left sick at Harper's Ferry. Carr our fifer, Wilson, Davis, Ferguson, Drummond, Reed, Rementer, Thomas, and Thompson [*sic*]. Giles and Stretch are away wounded.

I have heard that Thompson is dead. He was from Charlestown. Most of those away sick, are fit to return to duty, but I do not know why they are not sent back to the Regiment. Campbell and Grant were discharged [*sic*] on the 20th of October on account of general debility. They had both been sick for a long while.

> **Insoluble Cement**
> Now, at the extremity of the snail's body there is a little white bladder containing a gelatinous, fat-looking substance. If this can be extracted, and the liquid applied to the broken edges of glass or china, and time given for this natural cement to dry, the parts will hold together so firmly that they mended article is stronger at the united parts than elsewhere.

On the march from Bolivar Heights to this place, [which was rather circuitous march] we marched through a section of the country that was very stony and hilly, well watered, and the land of most excellent quality. The inhabitants are generally very poor, and appear to be in want of the necessaries of life. All the men of young or middle age, have either left the country or been pressed into the ranks of the rebel army. We generally burn fence rails for our cooking, and we can soon tear down a fence, I assure you.

We are about 40 miles from Alexandria and about the same distance from Gordonsville. There are an immense number of troops here. There was a grand review yesterday morning, ordered on account of General McClellan leaving the Army, which he formally did yesterday. On his passing the different divisions, he was received by salutes of artillery and the shouts of the men.—You have no idea how he is beloved by the old troops, who were with him on the Peninsula.

General Sumner's corps were rejoiced a few days ago at seeing him return to us again. He is an old grey-headed man, and is in truth a soldier. He shares the privations of a soldier's life with the men and is always very careful about the health and comfort of his troops. We stay but a very short time in one camp since we left Bolivar; and now we do not know what hour we may be ordered to march. Our men are all in good spirits, and willing to *go anyplace* they may be ordered. The hard fighting they did at Antietam has not cool[ed] their ardour in the least. They are now willing to take part in another battle, any hour they may be ordered.

I have lengthened my letter out more than I intended. I will try and write soon again.

We would wish to be kindly remembered by our friends at home. How is it we do not get the *Whig*? Tell our friends to direct, Co. C, 2nd Del. Vols., 3rd Brigade, Hancock's Division, Sumner's Army Corps.   Truly yours, Big Elk

AHEAD OF ALL COMPETITION!

JOB PRINTING
Of Every Description

DONE AT

THE CECIL WHIG OFFICE

Jacob Johnson, proprietor of the Howard House, died and was buried in the burial ground of the M. E. Church in Elkton. The *Whig* recalled his kindnesses to those in need of lodging, even when their cash was low. The Howard House was built by Jacob Howard and Dr. H. H. Mitchell in 1853, and was occupied ever since by Mr. Johnson. For the past few months, his son Edward ran the business.

Dr. H. H. Mitchell's name appeared for another reason. He raised on his farm near Elkton a pear that weighed 22 ounces.

Women from the Elkton Union Relief Association went to Frederick City, Maryland, and found four Cecil volunteers in the hospital there: Charles Lum, John Simpers, and Robert Otley from the 5th Maryland, and Henry Roberts from the 2nd Delaware.

Since they were well cared for in the hospital, the Association donated material to a hospital that was set up in a church. So destitute was the hospital that it had no bed linen, bandages, or a change of clothing for the patients. The women left 12 hospital shirts, 12 plain shirts, 12 sheets, 6 pillow cases, 14 towels, 12 prs. stockings, 2 wrappers, bandages and lint, 2 qts. Madeira wine, 2 doz. lemons, 4 papers gelatine, and 4 lbs. sugar.

Other donations included 3 prs. drawers, 4 pillow cases, 1 bundle each of old linen and lint, 21 towels, 3 handkerchiefs, 10 worn shirts, 2 undershirts, 3 bottles cherry syrup, 8 cups jelly, 1 bowl blackberries, 2 bottles blackberry wine, 1 bottle elderberry wine, and 1 pair of slippers.

In the last two months of 1862, war broke out in print between Quartermaster James Touchstone, the voluble blacksmith from Port Deposit, and a member of the 6th Maryland, who signed himself Cecil. An excerpt from Touchstone's long letter follows:

Port Deposit, Nov. 11, 1862

Mr. Editor:—The letter from our friend "Cecil" at Williamsport which appears in the *Whig* of Saturday last, needs some correction and qualification. This letter would make the people believe that the 6th Md. Vols. had "seen sights" and "heard thunder," when to tell the truth, we have never felt the *realities* of war. The "march to Randaltown on the 9th of Sept. and back [and no body hurt] without a crust of bread or a canteen," only a few hours job in the midst of a war in which thousands of true patriots are laying down their *lives without a murmur*, was surely a small affair, and the individual who would grumble at such a trifle, much less *publish* his weakness at such a time as this, had better be at home in the chimney corner, under the lee side of his grandmother, than in the uniform of a soldier on a hostile frontier. The want of a "crust of bread" was a *sad thing*, [and so it is to be without one's dinner] but the case is too strongly stated by "Cecil." From his statement you would think bread was scarce at camp Maffit, when in reality, it was always so plentiful that it was wasted by *the barrel* by almost all the companies.

> **Prepared Flour for Diarrhoea**
> Tie up a pint of flour very tightly in cloth and put into boiling water.
> When untied, the gluten of the flour will be found in a mass on the outside of the ball. Remove this, and the inside will prove dry powder, which is very astringent. Grate this and wet a portion of it in cold milk. Boil a pint of milk, and when it is at the boiling point, stir in as much of the wet mixture as will thicken it to the quality of palatable porridge. Stir in a little salt, and let this be the sole article of diet until the disease has disappeared. Relieve it first by toasted bread, or very delicate mutton broth; which latter is also astringent. If the disease has not progressed to the degree of inflammation, this diet will preclude the need of medicine.

At that camp we had everything in the way of provisions that a soldier or anybody else need want. We had an ample supply of the best of soft, fresh bread, the best of fresh and corned beef, the best of salt pork and bacon, beans, peas, rice, sugar, coffee, molasses, potatoes, &c., &c., furnished by the gentlemanly Commissary of Subsistence, Capt. Wells, 91 Lombard street. It is true, we had no "peaches and cream," nor "ice cream and jumbles," but these things were not down in "the Bill of Fare," at least the "Quartermast" has not been able as yet to find them in the "Regulations."

Perhaps Congress at its coming Session, [if it can spare time from other important matters] may amend the "Regulations" so as to add canvasbacks, turkeys, York oysters, mince pies, &c., to the regular rations. If so, none will hail their advent with more satisfaction than myself. But what great hardships [sore feet excepted] were endured in this great [?] march. The Regiment started out at midnight—arrived at 5 o'clock in the morning. A wagon load of fresh, soft bread [not "crust"] with other provisions was sent to the men from camp early in the morning.

Thus, they had gotten their suppers bfore they started to Randalstown, and now they had their breakfast. They were back in camp by 11 o'clock and therefore in time for dinner.

Now the tramp was tiresome no doubt, and it is likely that "Cecil" was greatly chagrined and disappointed in not meeting the "rebels under Gen. Lee," but in view of all the dreadful hardships, difficulties and extremities of this war, was it anything to complain of publicly?

But "Cecil" grosely misrepresents the truth. He says "we had not an ounce of potatoes from the 12th of September until the 27 of Oct.," whereas we had an abundance of them until we started to Monocacy, on the 21st of September. After this we hadn't them because we couldn't get them! For the same reason, which ought to be conclusive if not satisfactory, we *didn't take any* "fresh meat." Altogether, we were without potatoes about a month, and without fresh meat about six weeks. During this time, however, we had plenty of good pork and bacon. We would have been glad to have had "fresh meat," but we could not expect it in our migratory course from Camp Franklin to Williamsport. And why should we have expected it when all other troops *on the route* were without it? As soon as we arrived with our brigade at our headquarters, or as soon thereafter as our Brigade Commissary, Capt. Hathaway, could get fresh beef and potatoes for us, we were supplied....

In conclusion, let me say, if "Cecil" does not explain himself in his next letter, that I shall demand his name, after which the matter will be investigated in the proper manner.

One word or two more. Speaking of life in the army, it is not like home of course. If we have everything which we could desire, still it is not like home. The accursed rebellion, which we are trying to crush, is a big thing. We cannot expect to get through it on "flowery

DR. B. J. BING,

DENTIST,

ELKTON, MD.—All operations warranted to give satisfaction.

☞Teeth Extracted and Filled without causing pain.

Persons can rely on seeing me by calling at any time during the first three weeks of each month.

beds of ease," and it will not do to *think* too much about "fresh meat and potatoes" in the army which is much less than to hanker after them for "45 days!"

Yours very truly, James Touchstone Quartermaster 6th Reg. Md. Vols.

Cecil replied the next week, saying he did not intend to insult Touchstone, who seemed to be "excessively *touchy*, and if *touched* is very apt to fling *stones*...." Then he turned deadly serious.

> But our Q. M., in his fury, commits an error still more grave, in endeavoring to ridicule the service of a corps, in whose good name he ought to glory, and which he ought to sustain by every honorable means in his power.
>
> The exposure and service rendered by the 6th and so flippantly ridiculed by Mr. T. is substantially proven by the fact that in the "Randalstown" march 100 men, a majority of whom were physically abler men than the Q. M., were entirely broken down, and unable to keep up with the column, many of them not reaching our camp until the second day, and the whole command rendered unfit for service, for a week at least, and I fear some of them were permanently injured by that night's duty. The sneer at the labor performed upon this, and other marches of the corps comes with bad grace from one who is never called upon to share in such service, and cannot, while lying snug in his quarters, properly estimate the wear and tear upon the thews and sinews of the men performing such duty. His efforts to turn into ridicule the complaints made of the quality of the provisions is in still worse taste, from the fact, that no one knows as well as the Q. M. that a large proportion of the rations forwarded for the use of this Regiment were unsound and totally unfit for use, and that no one has complained more loudly than he has on the subject.
>
> Amongst the articles, were stinking beef, pork, do., mouldy and wormeaten bread, rotten beans, and ground coffee, [misnamed such] which tasted as if manufactured of said beans. Suffice it to say that this regiment, numbering at most 800 men, have had within the last two months, 400 men sick with jaundice, to say nothing of those affected by rheumatism, typhoid fever, and other disorders, which, our Surgeon believes, were caused by extreme exposure and bad rations. The same low estimate of the service and exposure of our men in the calling a large portion of them out night after night, of the last week, after they had retired for the night, and on one of these nights marching them through rain to

---

FOR RENT

MY HOUSE and Garden, Shop, Stable and Lot, all the same property, in the village of Cecilton, for the ensuing year.—It would be a good stand for a good Shoemaker. For Terms, apply to J. J. Pearce, Chestertown, Md., or to Mrs. Sarah Pearce, Cecilton.

J. J. Pearce.

Hagerstown and back, would only have the effect to bring down the contemptuous derision of our worthy Q. M. So I shall not attempt to sketch it. Pardon the liberty I have taken in the matter, and the storm I have innocently let loose, giving you trouble, and I doubt not, [at least in the estimation of our Q. M.] demolished entirely poor "Cecil."

CECIL

On a happier note, the papers observed that Capt. Ben Ricketts was promoted to Major of the Regiment. At the same time in mid-November, Dr. T. J. Dunott, examining surgeon at Camp Bradford, visited Elkton for a short time.

Dr. Gilpin named his Elkton hotel Felton House in honor of the president of the P. W. & B. Railroad, noted the *Delaware Republican.*

A new schoolhouse was built on the road from Elkton to Newark. It was near Cat Swamp, once inhabited by a nefarious lot; in the recent past, the area was settled by a "better class of people." Few people, said the *Whig*, would recognize Cat Swamp of twenty years ago, when the natives were known for drunkenness, riot and even murder.

Shriner's Indian Vermifuge,
Since the introduction of this beautiful preparation, it has been steadily advancing into public favor. Its astonishing efficacy in expelling Worms has won for it many friends wherever it is known .... To make it still more worthy the Proprietor is putting it up in a much handsomer style than formerly. It is now prepared with the greatest care of uniform strength with plain directions, so that any one can administer it. It is entirely Vegetable—Perfectly Safe and Harmless.

Big Elk wrote two letters from Falmouth, Virginia. The first was dated November 18, 1862.

Dear Ewing:—We came here yesterday evening—I believe I last wrote to you from Warrenton. The day before we left that place our Regt. was ordered out on picket duty, and remained out until the next morning. We left Warrenton on Saturday morning about 8 o'clock A.M., furnished with three days rations. We passed over some of the worn out land of "Old Virginia" on our march here. About two miles from this place part of our regiment were sent out as skirmishers and to protect some of our artillery officers who were looking for a good position to plant their batteries so that they could shell the rebels who were on the opposite side of the river. Falmouth is a small town directly opposite the city of Fredericksburg. Our batteries had scarcely been placed in position when a very sharp artillery fight commenced at a range of about two miles.—Our regiment or rather eight companies of the regiment were acting as a support of the batteries The rebel firing was very accurate and very rapid. A number of shells exploded over and around our regiment, and for 15 or 20 minutes, [while we were being placed in position] pieces of shell were cutting the trees and branches all around us. To the surprise of all the regiment not a single man was hurt. We soon were placed under the brow of a hill where we were less exposed, and remained there until the firing ceased, which was about dark. The firing of the rebels was from a battery on the opposite side of the river, but which was silenced by our artillery; and since they first ceased to fire, we have heard nothing from them.

The bridges at this place were destroyed by the rebels some time ago. Part of our brigade was the only infantry that came here. The rest of the corps stopped about three miles back. We laid in line of battle all last night, and now we do not know what hour we will have to march. Gen. Bayard's cavalry is on our flank, scouring the country.

We are all well, and although it is cold and very disagreeable none of the men complain.

I am writing this on a little piece of board for a table, and using a lead pencil for a pen. I can do no better to-day. I will write soon again, if I have an opportunity.

Yours truly, Big Elk

The next letter was dated November 22, 1862.

Dear Ewing:—Although I wrote you a letter a few days ago, I thought to-night I would try and write you another, and tell you something of our whereabouts and of our surroundings. The town of Falmouth is on the north bank of the Rappahannock river, 110 miles from its mouth. It is directly opposite the city of Fredericksburg. The latter place has a population of about 7,500. The river is navigable to this place. Falmouth is in Stafford county, and Fredericksburg is in Spotsylvania county. From the bluffs on which we are encamped we have an excellent view of Fredericksburg. It is a city of very extensive manufactures, the principal of which are, flour, cotton, woolen and paper mills. The power used is water, and about one mile above the city is a splendid dam said to be the finest piece of work of the kind in Virginia. It was built by a New York contractor, belongs to the city of Fredericksburg. The river at the point where the dam crosses, is nearly five hundred yards wide, and the fall is thirty-two feet. The city of Fredericksburg is 70 miles from Washington and 65 miles from Richmond connected with either capital by the Richmond, Fredericksburg and Potomac R. R. The great Southern Mail route previous to the breaking out of the rebellion. The Masons, Montorns, Fitzhughs and other families of the F. F. V., live in this neighborhood. General Ashby, [of the famous Ashby cavalry] who was killed at Luray, came from near this place. The last rebel troops that held this place was Ball's Va. Cavalry. The last U.S. troops here were Burnside's. The U.S. troops left here the 31st of last August; and the rebels left here last Monday; and from what I can learn they left here in very much of a hurry. The river at this place is not more than 200 yards wide I think. Our pickets are on the banks of the river, and immediately opposite on the Fredericksburg side, are the rebel

> **NOTICE**
> My wife, Harriet Moluck, having left my bed and board, without sufficient cause, I hereby warn all persons against harboring or trusting her on my account in Cecil county or elsewhere.
> SAMUEL MOLUCK

pickets. We can see each other very plainly. The clothing of the greater part of the rebel pickets appear to be U.S. uniforms. The rest, the real dirty "butternuts." The pickets often hold conversation with each other, but it is not allowed. As picket firing is not allowed on either side, the pickets take no pains to hide themselves.

We can plainly see several rebel batteries in position on the opposite side of the river; and last night they threw up slight earthworks in front of some of their pieces.

You have often heard of the Richmond prices for the necessaries of life. Well, I will give you the prices at this place, and although some of them may seem to be *rather high.*—Still it is an actual fact, for I have a list of the prices from one of the most reliable citizens of the place: —Coffee, $8.00 per lb.; sugar .75 to $1.50; tea $5.00; bacon, 60 cts; salt $80.00 a sack of three bushels; whisky, $15 and $20 a gallon; flour, $25 per bbl.; potatoes, $4 per bushel; apples, $3; turnips, $3; corn $1.50; oats, $1.25; wheat, $3; boots, $25 per pair; cider, $40 per bbl.; calico that used to bring 12½ cts. is worth $1.25 per yard, and men's clothing, it is almost impossible to get at any price.

> **$3,000 to $5,000 WANTED**
> The advertiser wants a partner with the above named sum to join him in a safe and profitable business in a Western town.
>
> ☞ For particulars, apply at
> *The Whig* Office.

Our regiment was ordered out on picket duty yesterday morning at 9 o'clock, and remained out until about 5 o'clock this evening. It rained all day yesterday, which made it very disagreeable indeed. Our line extended up the river for about 2½ miles above the town. During the heaviest of the raid I, in company with Col. Baily, the colonel of our Regiment, rode up to a farmhouse very close to our picket lines, and asked shelter from the storm. We were warmly welcomed inside, and you may judge of my great surprise, when I found that the owner was an old friend of mine, and an acquaintance of hundreds of my Cecil county friends.—It was none other than Mr. Richard H. Bryan, formerly of Chesapeake City. Although he has suffered considerably on account of the war, he is very comfortably fixed and is surrounded with full and plenty of the comforts of life. His estimable and worthy lady very soon had prepared for the colonel and myself an excellent meal. And I tell you what it is it would have done your heart good to have seen us at the table. We came in cold, wet and hungry. We were soon warm, dry and fed.—What more could we have asked? You may rest assured we spent the evening very differently from the way we expected to have done, when we went out on picket. After supper we were treated with excellent apples and cider; and talking of Cecil and our Cecil friends, the evening passed away very pleasantly I assure you. Mr. Bryan owns a large and valuable farm, on which is a large apple and peach orchard. From his residence he has a beautiful view of both towns, the river and valley.

I will write to you again very soon if I have an opportunity to do so.

Before you hear from us again, you will most probably hear of some "HOT work" being done in these whereabouts.

The men of Company "C" the "Big Elk Rangers" are all well. We do not hear from home very often now, and have received no copies of The Whig for some time Hoping our Cecil friends are well. I am truly yours,

Big Elk

In mid-December, the *Democrat* reported that six pickets froze to death in a camp of the Army of the Potomac.

The Christmas season brought ads for a variety of items. In advance of the holidays the *Democrat* announced: "There's no use in talking. Cheap John does undersell his neighbors. Somehow or other he will buy bargains, and what is better still, he will sell them to his customers who come from far and near to deal with him. Just cast a glance toward his store, any fine day, and see the carriages, wagons, etc., hitched opposite. That tells the tale. People will buy where they can buy cheapest, and John is bound to sell bargains to all who call on him. He is now getting ready for Christmas and will have all sorts of good things for customers during the holidays."

A curious notice advertised secret symbols. If readers sent $1.05 to Lackland Janney in Bay View, they received a copy of the symbols with instructions. Perhaps they were the same symbols that Jubal Early noticed six months later when he neared Gettysburg: "As we moved through the country, a number of people made mysterious signs to us....Some enterprising Yankees had passed along a short time before, initiating the people into certain signs—for a consideration—which they were told would prevent the 'rebels' from molesting them or their property....These things were all new to us, and the purchasers of the mysteries had been badly *sold*. The...signs...were supposed by the Confederates to be made by the Knights of the Golden Circle, a secret organization said to sympathize with the South, but of which our soldiers knew nothing." (Quoted by Richard Wheeler in *Witness to Gettysburg*, 1987, p. 82).

COOK'S IMPROVED
Portable Sugar Evaporator.

The subscriber has received from the proprietor the sole Agency for the sale of Cook's Improved Portable Sugar Evaporator, in the counties of Chester, Delaware, and Montgomery, in Pennsylvania; Burlington, Camden and Gloucester in New Jersey; New Castle and Kent, in Delaware; Cecil, Harford and Baltimore counties in Maryland.
Also, an Agency for the sale of the most important
CANE CRUSHERS,
for horse and water power.
A limited quantity of Cane Seed on hand for sale.

☞ For Information about the *cultivation* of the cane and its *manufacture*, send for circular.
MILTON CONARD
West Grove, Chester co., Pa.

In the Hollow, William McClelland had a sale on black dresses, while at the east end of Elkton, George Earle and Enoch Crouch planted a row of horse chestnut trees from Mill Lane to the race. These alternated with sugar maples, which were planted in the spring. Sidewalks were graded and the townsfolk envisioned a "beautiful promenade."

The *Democrat* offered suggestions for those who did not know what to give for Christmas: "To an enemy, forgiveness; to an opponent, tolerance; to a friend, your heart; to a child, good example; to a father, deference; to a mother, good conduct; to yourself, respect; to all people, charity."

The *Delaware Republican* [12/11/62] reprinted an unsigned letter from the 2nd Delaware.

> On account of the brave and reckless fighting our regiment did at Antietam, and at other battles the regiment has been engaged in, we are now called by the—not very euphonious—name of "The crazy 2nd Delaware." on account of the terrible ordeals through which we have passed, we have dwindled down by sickness and the ball, to but about 400 men present. We have 186 men away at the different hospitals, nearly all of whom are able to be, and should be with their regiment. But rest assured the men we now have are of the right material, and are just as able, just as brave and just as willing a set of fellows as ever shouldered a musket or marched to the battlefield....
>
> As a proof of the high esteem, and as a just appreciation of the standing that Capt. Ricketts has always held among his brother officers, he has been selected as Major of the Regiment, and now holds that position. He is from Elkton, Cecil county, Md., and commanded Company C.

IOWA LANDS FOR SALE
The following Lands will be disposed of at low prices for Cash or trade. To a speculator or settler, they are richly worth the price asked:
160 acres in Iowa county, Iowa
160 acres in Poweshick county, Iowa
80 acres in Johnston county, Iowa
210 acres in Worth county, Iowa
1 Lot 80 x 160 feet in Iowa City, Iowa

☞For particulars, apply to
S. DREW THOMAS

From Falmouth, Virginia, Big Elk wrote on December 8, 1862, his last letter to the *Whig* before being wounded at Fredericksburg.

> Dear Ewing:—I am commencing to write you a letter, and am sitting in our Sibley tent, with the door closely tied up, and the stove just about as warm as burning wood will make it. Snow fell all day on Friday, and the ground is now covered. It is very cold this morning and the wind is fairly howling over the hills that bind the old Rappahannock. The men are still quartered in their little shelter tents but they have built up little log huts from three to five feet high, plastered up the cracks with mud and covered them with their little tents,

making them much more comfortable, and giving themselves much more room. A number of the men have fitted in their tents a kind of underground stove, made by digging a trench from the inside to the outside of the tent, covering the trench with flat stone, and making a chimney out of an old barrel. The continuance makes an excellent substitute for a stove.

The officers are quartered in tents also, some in Sibley some in Wall tents, and some in common tents, and manage to keep themselves quite comfortable. You know the men are allowed a certain quantity of provision for each day; but during our last march it was impossible for the Quartermaster to furnish them with the full supply, owing to the want of transportation. Well, the Regiment is entitled to the full allowance of rations; and will be paid the value of the rations now drawn, in cash; which amount is placed in the hands of the commissioned officers, and is called "The Company Fund." This fund is used in such a manner as the men of the company together with the officers, think best.

Potatoes and onions have been ordered to be distributed to the soldiers; which is an excellent arrangement, as the men need all the vegetables they can get.

A number of the men who have been away from the regiment, at the different hospitals, came back last Friday, looking better as a general thing, than the men who have been with us. The recruiting party who have been in Wilmington since last July, came back also; and strange to say, they brought back *not a single recruit*. Why I cannot tell; certainly it cannot be on account of the Regiment needing a reputation for discipline and bravery.—Maybe the men who were sent on that service did not bestir themselves as much as they might have done. I hear that the pleasant little city of Wilmington is a very good place to be quartered in. *Pity* they were disturbed, and ordered back to their Regiment, where they may have a chance to do duty of another kind.

Our mails come much more regularly than they did, and I suppose our friends get letters from us regularly now, as the mail is sent away from here every morning, by way of Aquia creek and Washington.

As Winter has come now in real earnest, and we have a great deal of picket and fatigue duty to do, and as it is very cold handling guns, axes, spades, &c., these cold mornings, I

CONCERT!

A GRAND UNIQUE
ENTERTAINMENT
will be given in the room over
Mr. C. W. Maxwell's store,
on SATURDAY EVENING,
the 10th inst., that will pay any one
who has a taste for Music to visit.
Wm. J. T. MURPHY
is the greatest Banjoist
in the United States.
J. T. EMMART is also the finest
Darkey alive,
and HARRY D. EBEN
never had an equal at imitating
Birds, Ducks, Geese, Pigs, or Pups.
Go and see them.

wonder if some of our kind and good Cecil ladies could not send us down some warm mittens, like those they sent us last Winter while we were at Drummondtown. There are about seventy men in company C, and to furnish each man of the company with a pair of mittens would only take about *half a dozen dozen*. If our kind friends should be suddenly taken with such a pious notion, tell them that if they pack that many in as small a box as they can, and direct the box [with contents marked.] to Major Ben Ricketts, 2nd Del. Vols. 3d Brigade, Hancock's Division, Sumner's Corps, that the Big Elk Rangers will have their hands in it, in about five days after the box leaves the Elkton depot.

Sergeant Johnson of Company "C." has been appointed Commissary Sergeant in place of Henry Nelson, who has been promoted to Quartermaster Sergeant. Both are fine, steady young men.

Big Elk

Ben Ricketts' name next appeared in the list of wounded. As he climbed over a fence, a shell exploded against a post, wounding him in the groin. His injury was judged not to be life-threatening, but he was not able to walk. He returned to Elkton via train on Wednesday, December 17. From the station, he was carried on a litter to the home of his boyhood friend, W. J. Jones, where he remained overnight. The next day, he was conveyed to his mother's residence outside town.

MADAME SCHWEND'S INFALLIBLE POWDERS
For the speedy and effectual Cure of all Inflammations, Fevers, Rheumatism, Dyspepsia and Liver Complaint, Piles, Gravel, and all Acute and Chronic Diseases of ADULTS and CHILDREN.
Send 3 cent Stamp to her Agent,
G. B. Jones
Box 2070, Philadelphia, P.O.
Agency, S.W. cor. Third and Arch Sts.
Hundreds of testimonials.

The account of other casualties, as published by the *Whig*, was somewhat unclear:

> The following members of company C, 2nd Del. Vols., [Big Elk Rangers] who were enlisted by Captain, now Major Ben. Ricketts, in this county were killed and wounded in the battle of Fredericksburg. Major Ricketts being among the number.
> Major Ben Ricketts, contusion in the groin; Private Geo. McNeal; Corporal W. Kingston, mortally wounded in the groin; Serg. H. Bennett, cut over the left eye with a ball; Private Philip A. Johnson, killed; Private Robt. McClure, wounded in right side; Private G. Ferguson. Col. Baily, of the Regiment was wounded in the breast.

The *Whig* published a summary of the amount paid and still due to the Volunteer Fund by district. Some people were slow in giving, and the paper chided them: "A few instances have come to our notice, in which parties have demurred somewhat at paying this small demand upon their resources, which goes to cheer and support the wives and children of those brave men who have periled life and limb, that we may remain comfortably in our homes, safe from the horrors that no language can portray, which is being poured out on wasted Virginia and other border states. We intend to obtain the names of those who refuse willingly to pay this bounty appropriation, and publish them for the children of those brave men who are in the tented field, many of them to perish there—to read and hold up as a reproach and a mocking to them...through all time to come."

There followed, probably not by coincidence, the names of the wounded and dead at the Battle of Fredericksburg.

On Christmas Eve, the women of Trinity Church sponsored a supper from 7 to 10. Admission was ten cents, supper extra.

A Christmas concert was presented in the M. E. Church by the choir, assisted by amateur singers in Elkton and by ladies and gentlemen from Philadelphia. The program was presented on Christmas night at 7 o'clock in the church. Admission was 25 cents; children under 10 years of age, 15 cents.

On Christmas Day those serving at Harper's Ferry received a reminder of home. The *Whig* [1/10/63] quoted the *Baltimore American*, which noted that Quartermaster Touchstone spoke on behalf of the ladies of Cecil County and Col. Howard for the 6th Maryland.

A very interesting ceremony came off here on Christmas day, in the presentation of a beautiful flag to the 6th Maryland Volunteers, commanded by Col. George R. Howard. The flag is one of rare beauty and workmanship, and reflects imperishable credit on the fair Ladies of Elkton and Cecil county who contributed to it. It is not intended to lessent the claims of any of these fair ones to our thanks that we mention the names of the good and patriotic lady of our distinguished Comptroller, Mrs. S. S. Maffitt. She was the head and front of the movement, and like her honored husband, who is a statesman and a patriot of the first water, she never does anything half way. The following inscription is tastefuly set in gold letters in a circle within the field: "From the loyal citizens of Elkton, Md , to the 6th Regiment Maryland Volunteers."

The flag was presented to the Colonel of the Regiment during dress parade, by Quartermaster James Touchstone, on behalf of the ladies—the Regiment being formed in a square, the parties performing the ceremonies taking position in the center thereof.

At year's end a letter arrived at the *Whig* from the 5th Maryland, Company I.

Harper's Ferry, Va., Dec. 16, 1862
MR. EDITOR:—As it has been some time since there has been a letter in *The Whig*, from our regiment, I concluded

---

MILLINERY

Mrs. M. E. JOHNSON and M. J. LEE have opened a MILLINERY establishment at the residence of Mr. John Matthews, in the village of NORTH EAST, where they are prepared to furnish their friends and the public generally with BONNETS, SHAKERS, HATS, RIBBONS, &c., &c., at reasonable rates.

☞ Bonnets repaired at short notice, in the most fashionable manner.

that a few lines from an Elkton boy would be read with interest by our friends in Cecil. On the 9th we received orders to pack up ready to march and in the evening of the same day we left our encampment on Maryland Heights, where we have been engaged working on the fortifications for the last four weeks. The works on the Heights, which are nearly completed, are of quite a formidable nature, and render the continued occupation of Harper's Ferry, by our troops, a sure thing for all time to come. We are now quartered in Harper's Ferry. Col. Schley is in command of the place, and the regiment is situated in different parts of the town, part of the men guarding the government stores, and part under command of Lieuts. Carrol and Benjamin, acting as Provost Marshal's Guard. The 6th Md. Regiment came down from Williamsport, on Saturday, and are now encamped on Bolivar Heights. The Regiment presents a fine appearance, and we were happy to see all the Cecil boys in good health and spirits. On Sunday a body of Major White's rebel cavalry, about 200 in number, made a dash into the old camp of Kane's Brigade, in Loudon Valley. A number of convalescent men had been left in the camp, and a quantity of stores and camp equipage. The rebs proceeded to capture and parole them, and then set about destroying the stores. In the meantime word was brought to Col. Schley of what was going on, and in a very short time he was on the road to Loudon Valley with five companies of the 5th, five of the 6th Md., two pieces of artillery, and a company of cavalry. They pursued the rebs for five or six miles, took some prisoners, and then returned to camp without any accident, except the loss of the Colonel's horse, a splendid animal that was shot by the accidental discharge of a pistol.

There have been several changes in our company lately. Capt. Faehtz has resigned and been succeeded by Capt. Edward Koch, formerly first Lieutenant of Company C. He is a fine officer and very much thought of by the men. Lieut. Carrol has been promoted to 1st Lieutenant of Company C, and Orderly Serg't. Purnell, to 2nd Lieut. of Company G.

As Christmas is drawing near the boys begin to talk a good deal about old Cecil and the good times they would have if they could only get a furlough.

COAL OIL FOR BED-BUGS
Coal oil is said to be a sure destroyer of bed-bugs. Apply plentifully with a small brush or feather to the places where they most do congregate. The cure is effectual and permanent. Gilt frames, chandeliers, &c., rubbed slightly over with coal oil will not be disturbed with flies.

The health of the men, generally is good, only one man [John Simpers] being in the hospital.

Wishing all our friends a merry Christmas, and hoping that when the next one comes round, we may be with them to enjoy it.—We remain yours, &c., Co. I.

In late December, Captain Foard's vessel that sank a short distance from the wharf at Frenchtown two weeks previous was raised. "She was loaded below with grain, and on deck with hay and staves.

The grain was all saved, but in a damaged condition. She was cut through by ice."

1862 ended with a New Year's supper given by the United American Mechanics of Elkton at J. R. Smith's hotel. Only a few tickets were sold outside the order, and those who wished to partake of a good supper could do so by contacting a member.

GLOSSING LINEN

The linen to be glazed receives as much strong starch as it is possible to charge it with, then it is dried. To each pound of starch, a piece of sperm, paraline, or white wax, about the size of a walnut, is usually added. When ready to be ironed, the linen is laid upon the table and moistened very slightly on the surface with a clean wet cloth. It is then ironed in the usual way with a flat-iron, and is ready for the glossing operation. For this purpose, a peculiar heavy flat-iron, rounded at the bottom and polished as bright as a mirror, is used. It is pressed firmly upon the linen and rubbed with much force, and this frictional action puts on the gloss.

4
Cecil County

1863

The year opened with the controversial Emancipation Proclamation. The *Democrat* quoted three papers that stood against it: The *Boston Courier* called it a "stupendous folly," the *Baltimore Gazette* named it the "gravest and ghastliest act of this terrible civil war," while the *Philadelphia Journal* viewed it as "unconstitutional." The 1861 census, continued the *Democrat*, revealed that 50% of the colored in free states were mulattoes, but only 11% of the colored were mulattoes in slave states. The obvious conclusion was that unless the country wanted a high percentage of mulattoes numbered among its populace, it had well nigh preserve that "peculiar institution."

A change occurred on Elkton's Main Street. After Cheap John consolidated his Wilmington and Elkton stores in the former city, his old site was occupied by Robert C. Levis and Thomas Merritt, dealers in groceries and dry goods.

Diarist McCauley's dislike for John was not so great that it prevented him from taking advantage of a bargain when he saw one. He wrote on February 14: "Cheap John is preparing to leave town where he has been for a year past puffing himself as the poor man's friend. I bought a carpenter's level."

On the outskirts of Port Deposit, John J. Smith decided to give up farming and go to hotel keeping. His entire farm stock was up for auction and he planned to manage the Washington House in Port Deposit, formerly occupied by Mr. Crampton.

McCauley commented about a street fight between editors Ewing [*Whig*] and Crow [*Democrat*] over an article that appeared in the *Whig*.

Manufacturers and butchers were reminded to fill in and return the blanks for their monthly returns to the Assistant Assessor in Elkton. If millers sold more than $1,000 worth of flour or meal, they, too, must be licensed as retailers or be subject to stiff fines. Sellers of spirituous liquors who did not apply for licenses must cease selling or suffer the consequences.

The *Whig* quoted West Chester's *Village Record* for Colonel McIntire's obituary, which it ran on January 31, 1863.

> Colonel McIntire was a native of Cecil county, Maryland. After graduating at Yale College, he commenced his legal studies at the Law College, New Haven, and finished with J. J. Lewis, Esq., at West Chester. After a thorough course of studies, he was admitted

to the bar of Chester county, and opened an office as an attorney at law. After the Rebellion broke out, he joined the Brandywine Guards, a volunteer corps which was formed in West Chester, and by common consent was called to the command of the company. The Guards was the first company from Chester county to join the Pennsylvania Reserves—two Regiments of which were encamped at West Chester. The company entered Camp Wayne, and Col. McIntire had command of the Encampment until the 1st Regiment was formed, and Col. Roberts of Pittsburg, arrived and took charge of it; when Capt. McIntire was elected Lieut. Col. of the Regiment. After the Regiment left Camp Wayne it joined the Pennsylvania Reserve Corps, under the command of General McCall. The history of this corps is well known—its gallantry is well attested—its renown will ever shed a luster upon the Keystone State; it was before Washington when the Capitol was in danger—and on the Peninsula in the ever memorable seven day's contest; and Col. McIntire shared in all its trials, perils, and sacrifices. He was wounded in the battle before Richmond—lost a limb—was taken prisoner—exchanged, and sent to New York. Before he returned to his home he was elected to the office of the District Attorney for Chester county.

> **Cold Slaw**
> Yolks of two eggs, a tablespoonful of cream; a small teaspoonful of mustard; a little salt; two tablespoonfuls of vinegar. If cream is not used, put in a small lump of butter, rubbed in a little flour. Cut the cabbage very fine; heat the mixture and pour it on hot.

REMAINS OF COL. ROBERTS.—The remains of Col. Roberts, were interred at Oakland Cemetery, at West Chester, yesterday Monday, the 19th instant—from his father's residence in East Goshen. They were followed the same day by the remains of his bosom friend Col. McIntire, which were buried by his side. The careers of these lamented and gallant men were singularly coincident. Both were young—they were members of the same class at college—students in the same office—members of the same bar; of similar stamp of politics—both were nominated by their political friends as candidates for the same office; both by a similar impulse joined the army of the Republic—both were brave and rose to distinction in the profession of arms—and both fell victims of the unhallowed rebellion, within a few days of each other—they were buried on the same day, and now lie side by side in the same graveyard! A more gallant man than Col. Roberts never lived.

[Later, on June 4, 1864, the *Whig* editor wrote that he passed through Oakland Cemetery during the previous week and saw the monument on Lt. Col. McIntire's grave. "On one side is engraved his birth, age, &c.; on the opposite some very appropriate remarks of his talents; on another his graduation at Yale college in 1856, his admission to the Bar of Chester county, in 1858, and his election as District Attorney in 1862. On the fourth was the list of battles that he had been engaged in.—The last was the battle of New Market Cross Roads, on the 30th of June, 1862, in which he was wounded, and from the wounds of which he died."]

That same issue carried a pair of letters that reveal the war from two very different vantage points. Rev. Joseph T. Brown of Cherry Hill gave a poetic description of Harper's Ferry before noting. "The Shenandoah river, running down between Loudon and Jefferson counties empties its troubled waters in the bosom of the Potomac. The pontoon bridge across the Shenandoah, over which the 2nd Del. Regiment marched when on their way from this place to join Burnside's army, has been removed, and a wire bridge built, which connects Loudon and Bolivar Heights. There is still remaining here some evidence of John Brown's folly."

Then the writer praised the clean living and high thinking of the 6th Maryland. "I have yet to see the first officer, commissioned or non-commissioned, indulgeing in 'card playing.' The vile practice of profanity, vulgarity, and 'card playing,' prevails to an alarming extent in the army; ....and yet there is a disposition on the part of a majority of our men to be cautious in the presence of those whose proclivities run in an opposite direction."

> DR. WM. B. HURD'S
> **NEURALGIA PLASTERS.**
> FOR THE CURE OF
> NEURALGIA OR TOOTHACHE.
> They act like a charm, and are perfectly harmless in their nature; do not produce a blister, and leave no unpleasant results.

Rev. Brown circulated 800 copies of the New Testament and organized prayer meetings and Sunday school. He asked that anyone with extra religious tracts send them to the Soldiers' Aid Society in Elkton, which would forward them to the Regiment. These tracts, the preacher hoped, would "take the place of cards, at least for the time, and thus avert the mind form a practice that threatens ruin and destruction to the young men of our army."

Presumably, some soldiers did not fall under the benevolent influence of the spiritual tracts. They were participants in General Burnside's infamous "mud march," and Bucktail—a correspondent from the Bucktail Rifles—wrote from near Bell Plains, Va., January 25, 1863.

The writer may be tentatively identified as Joseph A. Roman, Co. H., 190th Pennsylvania. He became 1st Lieutenant in Company K of the 203rd Pennsylvania, according to information in the Historical Society of Cecil County. He was discharged 6/22/65 and farmed land in Colora. After the war, he was a member of the U.S. Grant Post #10. Roman died 11/10/1921 at the age of 83 and was buried in Oregon City, Oregon.

> MR. EDITOR:—We received marching orders on the morning of the 18th, but did not move until noon, the 19th. We marched about a mile above Falmouth, where we encamped for the night; it commenced raining about dark, and continued all night. The next day we again took up line of march at 6 o'clock, marched up the river about 8 miles, where we again encamped for the night; it still continued to rain, making the roads very muddy and

marching very disagreeable. The 22nd we were ordered to hold ourselves in readiness to move at a moment's notice. We did not move that day, but were out in all the rain. At dark we were ordered to put up our tents. The next morning we took up our line of march at 8 o'clock, and were much surprised when we came out on the road that, instead of going towards the river, we were marching back on the road we came, but soon saw the cause of our going back. We soon came on a battery sticking in the mud, the officers ordering this one, and that one, the men swearing, some of the horses lying down in the mud, and a general confusion among all hands. All along the road were pontoon wagons and supply trains, sticking fast in the sacred soil about hub deep. We arrived in camp about dark completely worn out; but soon had rations drawn, and our suppers cooked; and such grand suppers! hard tack, salt horse and coffee.

We do not blame General Burnside in the least for failing to cross the river, but still think him just the man to command this army, and are always ready and willing to go wherever he orders us. Our Regiment now numbers about 150 men; the most of them new recruits, and is commanded by Capt. Taylor, of Kennett Square, who is a splendid officer and a perfect gentleman; and an officer that is not afraid to lead his Regiment in a fight though the missiles of death fly thick as hail. We have comfortable quarters, plenty to eat, but little duty to do, so our friends need not be uneasy about us, but if any of the ladies of Cecil county have any delicacies that they would like to send some old veterans, they can direct the box to Company H, Bucktail Rifles, Penna Reserve Corps, Belle Plains, Va., and they will be thankfully received by   BUCKTAIL.

> **Loaf of Cake**
> Two teacupfuls each of sugar and butter, mashed together; 2 eggs well beaten and mixed with the sugar and butter; 2 teacupfuls sweet milk; a heaped teaspoonful of cream of tartar; 1 even teaspoonful of saleratus, mixed in 2 teacupfuls of wheat flour, and 2 teacupfuls of Indian meal; the whole to be mixed well together and baked 1 hour.

Dr. Charles Ellis demonstrated the overwhelming, if sometimes irrational joy of a returning soldier at the sight of his home town. After his release from prison, he inadvertently boarded a train that did not stop at Elkton. No matter that the locomotive was traveling at full speed, Ellis could not bear the prospects of passing by home. He jumped off at Elkton and was severely bruised. Surely a surgeon realized better than most the likelihood of sustaining crippling or fatal wounds in such an action. Evidently a stint in Libby Prison made even a doctor throw caution to the winds when the hills of home came into view. Shortly thereafter, Ellis practiced on Bow Street, next door to the office of his father, F. A. Ellis.

A new correspondent from Company C, Second Delaware, wrote from Falmouth, Virginia, a letter dated January 29, 1863.

Mr. Editor:—Dear Sir:—The mails having been so irregular for weeks past, the men receiving few or no letters at all, but as they are now supposed to be regular once more, I thought a few lines from an old member of Company "C," Big Elk Rangers, would be acceptable and interesting to the families and friends of the Company. The reason for the irregularity of mails is simply this:—Through neglect or mistake our bag for weeks has been sent to Howard's Division headquarters, and allowed to remain for some days, and then sent back to Washington to be placed in the dead letter or some other office, instead of being sent to Hancock's.

The paymaster visited us on the 24th inst., and a welcome visitor he was, too; yet he only paid the regiment of two months [September and October]. There is now nearly, or quite three months due us. We have no cause to complain, yet the wants of many of the soldiers' families are what we look at.—You know if a regiment has anything like a suttler every soldier owes him more or less, consequently if he draws on the suttler for three months and only gets paid for two the suttler presents each man his bill in full, spoiling the calculations of the soldier, and he falls short of money and possibly has to wait two to four months before getting paid.

HERRING to Suit the Times!
Just received 125 Barrels of Labrador HERRING at $2.50 pr barrel by WM. P. MORGAN, Provision Dealer

There was another movement on foot some time ago [an advance] but owing to a heavy rain, falling the night before, the whole thing was abandoned, the roads being in such a dreadfull condition, knee deep with mud; notwithstanding the artillery and infantry were all in position before day break. The Pontoons, of course, stuck again, but in the mud this time. Yesterday we had quite a snow storm which continued all night. There is now some 8 inches of snow on the ground; today is most beautiful, the sun shining brightly, with a clear sky, yet sloppy underfoot. The soldiers are all very well shod with Uncle Sam's brogans.

There is little or no excitement hereabouts; everything is quiet along the lines. There are comparatively few sick in the regiment, none seriously ill; one man of Company "F" died and was buried on Sunday, with military honors. His name was Carr. The hospital is now empty, Company "C" only having one man on the sick list, and he is able to be about. We have some 30 men doing Provost Duty at the neighboring farm house and barns. Company "C" has a large number on that duty, it being yet the largest company in the regiment. They all live high and are comfortably fixed, yet singular it may seem some of those houses are owned by, in fact some rampant secessionists live in some of those we are guarding, yet we try to do the fair thing and will allow no wanton destruction of property. It was laughable to see the Jew pedlers coming into camp on Sunday after pay day, with all sorts of notions, catch pennies &c. Mind they would not come in before the men were paid off, but now they meet with very little success, as our Lieutenant Colonel calls them "blood suckers" and drives them off by saying he will confiscate all if they do not leave soon. They take the hint before receiving a kick, and skedaddle.

Our Brigade has been relieved by Acting Brig. Gen. Brooks', consequently we will have to go to the rear. The new camp ground is situated about two and a half miles northeast of Falmouth. We have sent details out to clear the ground, which is a most beautiful place. Bordering all sides of the Brigade will be left standing a neat fringe of pine trees, but the men do not like the idea of leaving their old quarters, as they have to build new ones, the plans for which are all drawn. Each cabin or hut, as the soldiers call their quarters, will be 8 by 16 feet, all of uniform size in every respect with company parade ground 16 feet in width, kitchens 15 feet to the rear of men's quarters; line officers 15 feet to the rear of kitchens; Field and Staff 15 feet to the rear of line officers', which, when completed, if we are allowed the time by Hooker, will be a good camp and a neat one. The officers are slim in the regiment, and you can see them drooping their way through the camp as if they were lost, owing to so many of the officers being absent, wounded and sick. Those that are present pass their time very drearily, and they are in hopes of them all rejoining the regiment soon. There is little or no amusement going on, the men are all very quiet and settled down like old age; in fact camp life in this section of the country is dreary enough at the best of times. I will not intrude any longer. All the men from Big Elk and its vicinity heartily join in sending their best respects to their families and friends. C. J.

A New and Splendid Assortment
of
Buffalo Robes and Horse Covers
SELLING LOW, BY
JOHN PERKINS, JR.
ELKTON, MD.

In mid-February the *Whig* noted that William Kingston, 23, had died on January 4, 1863, at Fredericksburg. His death resulted from the accidental discharge of a comrade's rifle. Bereaved friends escorted the remains to Elkton, and interred the body in the cemetery of Union M.E. Church.

Since the Emancipation Proclamation freed slaves only in those states which seceded from the Union, slaves were still held and sold in the county, and free blacks were sold into slavery as punishment. On February 2, 1863, for example, the *Whig*'s list of court proceedings included: State vs. Emeline Henry [free negress] arraigned for petty larceny. Verdict not guilty.

State vs. Jas. Bayard [col'd.] trial for stealing horses of W. H. Harrison. Guilty and sentenced to receive 25 lashes. Within the month, the paper reported that Sheriff Cosgrove carried out the sentence in the jail yard.

Samuel Hawkens [free negro] found guilty of stealing beef, the property of Jas. G. Burlin, sentenced to be sold for one year in the state.

Another case involving a white tavern keeper was also tried that February. The *Whig* continued:

> State vs. Patrick Desmond, for committing an assault with intent to murder, upon Joel Burdick, a private in the 18th Connecticut Regiment, stationed at Havre de Grace and Perryville. Jones for State, F. Stump and J. T. McCullough for defense.
>
> The assault was committed on the soldier while on guard at Perryville, on the night of the 27th of January by two men, who approached him stealthily from behind, while two others in front attracted his attention.
>
> The parties in front were hailed, but refused to answer, the sentinel brought his gun up, but was at the moment seized by the throat from behind, disarmed, and left senseless. When he recovered, he managed to reach his comrades and make known his case by signs, the injury having deprived him of the power of speech, which he has not yet regained. Pat Desmond keeps a low grogery at Perryville, which is such a nuisance that the officers threatened to tear his establishment down, and one of the men having expressed himself as ready to volunteer in that service, Pat, the proprietor, threatened to have his heart's blood in revenge for the offense. Desmond, by inquiry, learned that this soldier, whose blood he had thirsted for, was to be on duty that night, and summoning to his aid three other of his confederates, the party set out to accomplish the threatened deed.
>
> The evidence was mainly circumstantial, but consisted of a chain which strongly connected the parties implicated, with the deed. The reason assigned for leaving their foul purpose but partially executed, was their discovering they had got hold of the wrong man, Burdick not being the person against whom the threats were made. The jury rendered a verdict of guilty on the second count or for assault and battery.—
>
> The Court sentenced Pat Desmond to eight months in the county jail and a fine of $1.00 and costs, which will amount to about $100.

STEEL SPRING HORSE RAKES.
Wheeled Rakes of best Spring Temper, and of the best Cast steel. Warranted. For sale by
John Partridge

General Rosecrans published a roll of honor that included the names of J. Torbert, son of W. Torbert, Esq., of Elkton, and H. J. Chilton, known to many in town. Both were members of Company L. James Conway, Company E, formerly of Elkton and brother of Mrs. James Denney, was also honored as "the bravest of the brave."

Captain E. F. M. Faehtz, formerly of 5th Maryland, Company I, and recently an aide on General Shriver's staff, was appointed Major of the 8th Maryland. An ad ran in the *Whig* under the heading For Rent: "The house lately occupied by Captain Faehtz, nearly opposite Col. Groome's, will be rented until the 25th of March, [Moving Day] on reasonable term. Apply to W. P. Ewing."

An agent of a portable gas company visited Elkton to obtain names of those who wanted to have their homes or business establishments lighted by gas. At least 100 had to sign if the company was to install the new system. The *Whig* pointed out that one town on the Eastern Shore was so lighted and was satisfied with the results.

In February 1863, E. E. Ewing, *Whig* editor, married Clara Vaughan of Camden, New Jersey; S. Drew Thomas married Martha Elsie Finley of Philadelphia; and the Howard House was the scene of the wedding between Jonathan Montgomery Scudder and Isabella Gilbert, both of Elkton.

> The Thomas-Finley marriage is probably surprising to local 20th-century history buffs because many are under the impression that the author of the Elsie Dinsmore books never married. Margaret Leech, in *Reveille in Washington*, wrote: "In Philadelphia, he [Dr. Clement A. Finley] had an old-maid niece called Martha, a female who tried her hand at writing stories. Before he died, he would see Martha Finley make a success with her *Elsie Dinsmore* books." If the marriage notice refers to the same Martha Finley, it is news indeed.

Howard I. Guy of Brick Meeting House advertised an extensive carriage sale on March 21. Persons wishing to buy a new carriage would find "every variety of style for country use and finished in a superior manner."

McCauley wrote that John Wood was ordered to return to his regiment; Dean Clark started back to his regiment at Frederick, "from which he had taken French leave some two weeks ago."

The papers ran accounts of alleged misdeeds involving a pair of Cecil soldiers: Capt. Samuel Ford and Lt. G. W. Benjamin. Ironically, the latter's wedding was announced on May 7, 1863, in the *Whig*. "Benjamin – Mercer.—At the M. E. parsonage in this town, by Rev. W. H. Elliott, on Wednesday evening last, Lieut. GEORGE W. BENJAMIN, of Company A, 5th Md. Regiment, and Miss AMELIA MERCER, of North East."

> **M. E. CHURCH LECTURES**
> Rev. H. F. Hurn's Lecture
> ON
> **"ATTILLA—THE HUN,"**
> unavoidably postponed on Wednesday night last, will be delivered in the Elkton M. E. Church on WEDNESDAY NIGHT, next, the 5th inst.,
> at 7½ o'clock.

THE PROVOST MARSHAL OF BERLIN IN THE OLD CAPITOL.—For some time frequent complaints have been made that those in charge of the Government ferry at Berlin, Maryland, were prostituting their positions to line their pockets with the funds of those who desired to cross the Potomac, either with good or bad purpose. Colonel Baker, Provost Marshal of the War Department, took the matter in hand, and on Friday arrested Captain Samuel Ford, Provost Marshal of Berlin, and Lieutenant G. W. Benjamin, his assistant, and also Mrs. Frances Able, a Government detective, employed by the military authorities at Baltimore.

The officers are charged with selling passes to all those who were able to purchase, and of requiring a liberal division of the funds of persons coming North of going South. We understand that they were confronted in this city by a couple of ladies who were forced to divide. They were sent to the Old Capitol.

Mrs. Able was sent to Berlin to aid the Government by searching females crossing the river either way, and to keep an eye open for the interests of the Government generally. Instead of doing so, she looked exclusively after her own interest, and sacrificed that of the Government and those who sent her there.

If the facts should be proved as charged it is to be hoped that the Government will make an example of them. Of course, it is impossible to deprive the South of the information and contraband goods, if the crossings of the Potomac are not guarded by the parties whose love of country is stronger than their love of gold or green backs.
Washington Chronicle

The two officers referred to in the above article from *The Chronicle*—Captain Ford and Lieutenant Benjamin— are from North East, and belonged to Company A, 5th Maryland Regiment. Our citizens will be grieved to hear of the arrest of these officers from Cecil, and we hope the charges against them may prove unfounded, but if guilty, no man who trades in the blood of his country should escape the utmost rigor of the law. All such are worse than openly armed rebels.

The enterprising Proprietor of Chestnut Grove Whiskey, (the Purest Medicinal Agent ever known.) has furnished the community a Stimulant, Pure, Healthful and Invigorating, at the same time a mild beverage. It is calculated to do away with the vile drugged stuff that is palmed off on the community, and which is injurious to body and mind. In addition to the certificates beneath, he has received a Diploma from the State Agricultural Society, and additional testimony from DR. JACKSON of Boston, who testifies under oath to its absolute purity. For sale by C. WHARTON, JR.

On March 26, the *Whig* reported the death of Lieutenant Benjamin.

Lieutenant Benjamin, of Company A, 5th Md. Vols., died of smallpox, on the 16th inst., at the small pox hospital, in Washington. It will be remembered that his arrest by the Government for selling passes to blockade runners to cross the Potomac was announced in *The Whig* of the 14th inst. He was married the day before his arrest, and was taken from the cars and from the side of his young and beautiful bride when on his way to join his regiment.

The Lieutenant declared with his dying words his innocence of the charges preferred against him, and accused the female detective who brought the accusation, of malice, and a design to conceal her own guilt of retaining money and valuables which she had acquired by searching lady blockade runners, and which should have been turned over to the use of the Government. This statement is published on the authority of the doctor who attended the Lieutenant, during his last illness.

Meanwhile Captain Ford was confined to the Capitol Prison in Washington, awaiting trial. On October 3, the *Whig* noted that "the case of Captain Ford is still on Trial before General Slugh's court-martial, the examination of witnesses for the defense having been commenced on Tuesday." The matter was not finally settled until mid-October.

C. J. wrote again from the camp near Falmouth, Virginia, on March 9, 1863.

TO THE EDITOR OF THE CECIL WHIG: SIR:—For want of something to do I will now undertake to write you a few lines, to let you know that the 2nd Reg. Del. Vols. is yet alive in good health and spirits, awaiting for some new excitement, as you know there is little or none here. The Regiment never was in better health and spirits than it is at present; but these cold nights of late have been rather severe on our men, some of them were badly frost bitten while on picket duty, yet they had good brogans on. They are now to be seen hobbling around camp doing well, not a murmur is to be heard from them, as they know such duty has to be done, and they do a good share of it too. We have now regular March weather, which of late has been raging furiously, making our canvas houses quiver and shake to stand the pressure. This day is a most beautiful one, more like the month of June, the sun shining brightly, and the ground drying nicely. Colonel Wm. P. Baily, Captain Thomas M. W*** [illegible], and Lieutenant Charles Reynolds, who were wounded at the battle of Fredericksburg, have returned to the Regiment, and welcome they were. It revived the officers and men considerably to see them once more. Their wounds have not yet healed properly; Colonel Baily's arm hangs useless by his side, it being paralysed.

Company "C" Big Elk Rangers are getting along remarkably well, officers and men, *** [illegible]—yet there is plenty of muscle remaining for another brush. No ways anxious but will do their share of fight, honestly too, if called upon. No better spirited men can be

Poor Richard's Eye Water.
CURES ALL DISEASES OF THE EYES: Cataract, Pterygium, Film, Inflammation of every kind, no matter how long standing, Weak Eyes, Sick and Nervous Headache, and Sore Throat are quickly relieved.
Price, 25 Cents per Bottle.

scared up in the army. On the 28th, the last day of February, we "mustered for pay," and the Regiment made a neat soldierly appearance. The rolls were made on promptly for four months, and forwarded to Washington. The men are now anxiously awaiting the arrival of the pay master, to receive Uncle Sam's green backs, which would be very acceptable, the sooner the better as the families of some want.

> **NOTICE**
> *In the Circuit Court for Cecil county. In Chancery. May 27, 1863.*
>
> ORDERED, that the sale made and reported by James T. McCullough, Trustee for the sale of the Real Estate of Excelsior Lodge, No. 67, of the Independent order of Odd Fellows of Maryland, be ratified and confirmed, unless cause to the contrary thereof be shown on or before the third day of August next; provided a copy of this order be inserted in some newspaper printed in Cecil county, once a week for one month before the first day of July next.
> The report states the amount of sales to be $870.
> W. H. RICKETTS, Clerk.

Our Corps was reviewed by Gen. Joseph Hooker last Thursday morning. The troops made a fine appearance drawn up in close column by brigades. The General with his brilliant staff rode to the front, and after receiving the customary salute, commencing on the right, dashed at a furious gallop to review the troops, the colors dipping, the officers and men saluting, and the drums rolling as he passed each brigade. General Hooker then having taken up his position in front and center of the Corps, the several regiments passed in review in companies by column. The sight was a most imposing one, and would have made you civilians open your eyes to have seen the steady tread of these warworn veterans. General Hooker with his smiling countenance, and betattered flags flying which the troops so long have fought under, seemed to put a new spirit in everyone's heart who witnessed the review.

Hoping I am not intruding on your valuable moments with the Big Elk Rangers, to families and friends,

I am respectfully,　　yours &c.,　　C. J.

That spring a house partially collapsed, but one person inside was not all that troubled. McCauley wrote, "John Spence was in the house and tolerably drunk. Said that he was not afraid—that he was tickled to death at hearing it tumbling out as he lay in bed."

It was Moving Day again, and although the *Whig* was not happy with the practice, it printed:

> Moving Day, clear the way,
> Baskets—barrows —bundles,
> Take good care, mind the ware, Betty, where's the bundles?
> Pots and kettles, Broken victuals,
> Feather beds,
> Plaster heads,
> Tow mattresses
> Looking glasses,
> Spoons and ladles,
> Babies' cradles,
> Cups and saucers,
> Salts and casters,
> Hurry, scurry, grave and bay,
> All must trudge on Moving Day.

Lest anyone presume that bureaucracy and potholes are 20th-century scourges, the *Whig* published two articles that attested to their unwelcome presence in the 1800s. The first ran under the heading RED TAPE AT HARPER'S FERRY.

> The following extract from a letter by Corporal A. stationed at Maryland Heights, where the Sixth New York Artillery is now encamped, shows what a beautiful arrangement, "the channel" in which Red Tape runs, is supposed to be:— "A young man was quite ill with typhoid fever, and it was regarded as important that he should be sent North, for a change of air and also to get home-nursing. An application on the 'prescribed blank' was filled up according to the present arrangements, and the surgeon's certificate with the customary Latin appended. This was forwarded by the Captain to the Colonel, and by the Colonel to Gen. Kenly, who forwarded it to Gen. Kelly, who forwarded it to Gen. Schenck, who has a staff officer for attending to such routine business. This staff officer referred the application to the medical director, who considered the matter profoundly, and concluded that the Latin was not quite satisfactory; so he returned it to said staff officer. remarking that the surgeon should be more explicit, etc. The staff officer returned the paper to Gen. Kelly, calling attention to the endorsement of the medical director. General Kelly's Assistant Adjutant General returned it to General Kenly, calling attention to the above endorsement; General Kenly's Assistant Adjutant-General returned it to the Colonel calling attention to the preceding endorsement; the Colonel's Adjutant sent it to the Captain; the Captain sent it to the surgeon. The surgeon, in reply, stated that 'the man was dead.'"

At home, B. Myers, who once kept a scouring and repairing shop in Elkton before he enlisted, came home and experienced his own problems with red tape. Marshal Bennet arrested him as a deserter, lodging him in jail until the next morning, when he learned Myer's discharge was in order.

As for the potholes, the road to Newark had such large craters that it took six loads of cinder and gravel to fill some of them. The paper pointed a finger at the large wagons of the iron mills located farther up on the Big Elk. If such craters were not enough to daunt the dauntless, there were worse obstacles on the "new" section of Marley road. Stumps, six to eight inches high, tried one's patience and threatened one's life, especially if one was so rash as to travel that road by night.

The *Whig* noted the death of Joe Pudd, a former slave. He was owned by Colonel Richardson but had been free for many years. He remembered the burning of Frenchtown by the British and their visit to Cedar Point. He helped haul gravel for the causeway and made bricks for the old bank.

On July 4, Pudd customarily dressed in an old State uniform, with a plumed military hat. He was a one-man band, beating a drum and whistling in imitation of a fife. Boys followed him as he made his way about Elkton on the holiday.

The P. W. & B. Railroad added Arctic cars to its line for the transportation of perishable freight. "They are nothing more nor less," said the *Whig*, quoting the *Baltimore Sun*, "than great refrigerators, constructed in the shape of eight-wheeled freight cars. The top, sides, ends and doors are all double, and between the inner and outer surface, core, shavings, and other non-conductors of heat, are introduced. The whole interior is lined with zinc, and at each end of the car is a large compartment for the reception of ice, by means of which the atmosphere within will always be kept at a low temperature."

The Methodists in Elkton planted a hedge of Osage Orange around their cemetery. It was hoped that within three or four years a live fence would enclose the area, adding to the serenity of the setting. Gary Wills pointed out in *Lincoln at Gettysburg*: "The cemetery was the supreme locus of liminality in the nineteenth century. It was the borderland between life and death, time and eternity, past and future."

19th-century writers, including Cecil penmen, reflected a fascination with melancholy that modern readers may initially find cloying or bizarre. However, when viewed against the backdrop

---

Scrofula, or King's Evil,
is a constitutional disease of the blood, by which this fluid becomes vitiated, weak and poor. Being in the circulation, it pervades the whole body and may burst out on any part of it. No organ is free from its attacks, nor is there one which it may not destroy. The scrofulous taint is variously caused by mercurial disease, low living, disordered or unhealthy food, impure air, filth and filthy habits, the depressing vices, and, above all, by the venereal infection....

One quarter of all our people are scrofulous; their persons are invaded by this lurking infection, and their health is undermined by it. To cleanse it from the system we must renovate the blood by an alternative medicine, and invigorate it by healthy food and exercise. Such a medicine we supply in

**Ayer's
Compound Extract of
Sarsaparilla**

of Transcendentalism, the absorption with things eschatological becomes at least comprehensible to the 20th-century reader.

Col. George R. Howard, 6th Maryland, resigned and the position was filled by Lt. Col. John W. Horn of Baltimore.

News dated April 23, 1863, from the 2nd Delaware arrived from camp near Falmouth, Virginia.

> MR. EDITOR:—It is now raining very hard, and very muddy under foot, which makes it anything but agreeable to us soldiers. Nevertheless, I welcome it to-day, as it gives me an excellent opportunity of writing you a few lines.
>
> We were visited yesterday by his Excellency Governor Cannon, of Delaware, accompanied by Adjutant-General Samuel Harrington, Judge Houston, Professor Porter, Colonel Curtis and Doctor Nolen. Father-like, they came to visit the troops of the Diamond State, and were welcomed, I assure you. They arrived at Falmouth Station at 1 ½ o'clock P.M., and were met by the Officers of the First and Second Delaware Vols., who were mounted on all sized and colored horses. After the Officers being presented to them, they mounted the choice steeds which were waiting for them, as they refused Uncle Sam's omnibus. After seeing our officers mounted, they preferred the same. The Governor mounted the beautiful arched-necked, white steed of Lieut. Colonel Stricker, and took the lead, with the Colonel of the First and Lieut. Colonel of the Second on either side.
>
> They moved on, followed by the Officers, forming a neat and brilliant staff for the occasion. They halted at the peak of a high hill to give them an opportunity of viewing the city of Fredericksburg and the battle-field. Several batteries and camps of the enemy were to be seen, their timber now being slim, like our own. In a few minutes they arrived at General Hancock's Headquarters. The Governor and suit were kindly received by Col. Brooks commanding [now ours] the Fourth Brigade. Leaving the Governor to dine with him, we proceeded to camp, to prepare for the Brigade Drill and Review, which he apparently was much pleased with.
>
> At sundown we formed for Dress Parade, when Judge Houston delivered a short patriotic speech on the behalf of the Governor, which was to the point in ever particular and suited to the times. After the close, three time three hearty cheers were given for the Governor, Judge Houston, our Commanding Officer and others.
>
> The army of the Potomac has nearly or quite been paid off in full to Feb. 28, and no

---

MR. AND MRS. ASCHERFELD, Professors of Music, beg leave to give notice to the citizens of Elkton and vicinity that they will be ready to receive applications for pupils, after Thursday, April 2, at the former residence of Captain Faehtz.

doubt there has been many a heart gladdened by the receipt of some of the green backs. Our Chaplain on the 21st inst., took some $10,000 to Aquia creek and placed it in the hands of the Adams Express Co., to be delivered to the men's families and acquaintances. There is much more to be sent.

The army is now in a splendid condition, well disciplined and in good health, not lying in idleness, but good naturedly awaiting for good weather, knowing that all dependence can be placed in our Commanding General, Joe Hooker.

You will excuse this short epistle, as everything is quiet along our front, and other news scarce. With the promise that you will hear well of the 2nd Delaware throughout their term, I am yours,

C. J.

In the midst of [1] noting that Lawrance Simmons of Chesapeake City was arrested and taken to Baltimore for cheering for Jeff Davis and [2] grumbling about the impassable conditions of the "much lawed" Ash's Bridge north of Elkton, the *Whig* took a lighthearted look at a chase around town when the prosecuting attorney's [W. Jones'] canary got loose. "The yellow plumed minstrel mounted a maple near the house and began a morning hymn to the god of day, but was soon frightened from his perch by a crab net and other like contrivances for the capture of small game being thrust at him, which induced the little aerial stranger to 'change his base.' Sheriff Cosgrove, through the aid of that peculiar skill, known only to the detective craft, succeeded eventually, in arresting the fugitive and remanding him again to his wire prison."

Sympathy for the Confederacy, never far from the surface, erupted again, for McCauley wrote on May 1: "Charles Cochran of Middletown, Del., arrested by Lieut. of Guard at Elkton for disloyalty to the Government and sent to jail. There was considerable excitement and some threats of taking him out.—More force is telegraphed for and 20 soldiers arrive from Havre de Grace. The jail is guarded."

Apparently not all was fair in war, for in the Union view the rebels violated the norms of "civilized warfare." On May 9, 1863, the *Whig* reported:

> Surgeon Thos. A. Getty, U.S.A., Medical Director of the 4th Army Corps, and whose mother and sisters reside in this town, came very near being captured by the rebels recently at Williamsburg, Va. The Doctor's absence from the insane Asylum, which institution he had under his charge, at the time the raid was committed, saved him from the clutches of these wretches.

TO FARMERS,
THE HIGHEST CASH PRICES PAID
FOR
Cattle, Calves and Sheep,
delivered at Smith's Hotel, Elkton, Md.
MAHANEY & WELLS

General Dix has determined to put an end to these raids. He has written a very plain letter to Henry A. Wise, commanding the rebels near Williamsburg concerning the matter. It says notwithstanding General Wise's professions of kindness to the insane at Williamsburg, and his charitable petition to Gen. Dix for their relief, in default of his own ability, the rebels have been permitted to make raids upon this sacred ground, and recently stole off several colored servants and nurses from the Asylum for the Insane. These raids have been repeated and assisted by the town inhabitants.

Gen. Dix therefore threatens, in case the aggressions continue, to send the insane to Richmond. He will also destroy any house from which our soldiers may be fired upon, and put to death, as a violation of civilized warfare, any private citizen who co-operates in these attacks.

T. S. & J. A. YOST,
(SUCCESSORS TO BUSHNELL & TULL)
Manufacturers of all kinds of
CHILDREN'S CARRIAGES,
PERAMBULATORS
GIGS, WAGONS
with or without springs,
VELOCIPEDES
WHEELBARROWS,
SLEIGHS,
SLEDS &c., &c. Also,
Steel Skates and Brass Grainers,
MANUFACTORY:
Cor. of Third Street & Girard Avenue, Philadelphia

A correspondent from Snow's Battery wrote from Acquia Creek on April 20, 1863. The letter ran in the *Whig* on May 9.

MR. EDITOR:—Thinking our friends in Cecil take as much interest in us to desire to know of our whereabouts and doings has induced me through the medium of *The Whig* to try and inform them.

We left our winter-quarters, near White Oaks church on the morning of the tenth of this month, and on the evening of the same day pitched tents near Hunt's Reserve. We remained there two days; then resumed our march, and in eight hours arrived here. Nothing of any interest varying the monotony of our change of base

We are now camped within one mile of the Potomac, of which we have a magnificent view, presenting an exhilarating contrast with its panorama of sailed and steamers, to that of the dull, dreary pine forests we have just emerged from, especially to us who have spent the most of our lives upon one of the most poetical rivers in North America.

Our present camping ground is an excellent selection, being upon an almost level field, near one hundred feet above the level of the river, and bounded on all sides by deep ravines, whose precipitate sides at the outbreak of the war were covered by dense woods and underbrush, which have been cut down in order that our gunboats can the better throw their iron moral persuasions.

On [our?] guns, in battery, face westward and command one of the principal roads to the landing at the terminus of the Fredericksburg and Potomac railroad.

We now constitute part of the force detailed for the protection of Hooker's base. On several of the most prominent hills earth fortifications have been thrown up one of which it is said we will occupy. But this is doubtful, as their erection is only a precautionary measure, to be take [n] advantage of in case of extreme necessity. Should the rebel cavalry make a lengthy dash this far, the Battery is confident that outside of the forts they will be more than a match for them.

All the men, but two or three, are fit for duty. The sanitary condition of the company has been exceeding good the last three or four months, the mortality being but one, whose disease was contracted during our fall campaign.

Should the Battery remain here during the summer months, we promise ourselves to forget our experiences of the most disagreeable and darkest features of the war in the enjoyment of some of the pleasures our change of scene and circumstances permit. Fish lines, eel barrels and other apparatus of the piscatorial art are in prospective or already bought or being made.

We drill three times a day, so it will be difficult to forget powder, cannon and war, in the intervals, no matter how exciting the sport we may engage in. No doubt Cecil friends heard we did not pass inspection. This was owing to the lack of discipline in the absence of the Captain on sick furlough. We venture to assert that we have a Lieutenant who is one of the best shots in either the Volunteer or Regular service. Yet our not passing inspection was in part due to a wild shot made by him. Colonel Tompkins [our inspector] placed a target one mile off, and told the Lieutenant to try his hand, or rather head, at a shot, which he did, but the ball struck about 60 yards off the mark. The Colonel did not give him another trial, but was evidently unfavorably impressed with our officer's gunnery.—There certainly was a defect in that ball, for, as I said before, our Lieutenant is a crack shot.—We have had another inspection since, and now stand among the number ones again.

Yours respectfully, ACQUIA

> COAL.—The celebrated Baltimore Company's Coal for Family Use on hand and for sale.
> **D. SCOTT & BRO.**

The 5th Maryland noted Christmas in May, according to the description of the decorations.

POINT OF ROCKS, Md., May 4, 1863.

MR. EDITOR:—It would be a favor, which will be appreciated and which would only be adding another to the many obligations the 5th Maryland is indebted to you for, by publishing the following:

On Friday, the 1st day of May, arrangements had been made by the members of Co. C., Capt. John Carroll: Co. D., 1st Lieut. Wm. G. Purnell, commanding, and Co. F., Capt. Salome Marsh, to celebrate the occasion, by a display of fireworks and a general illumination throughout the camp. The exertions of the men were actively seconded by the countenance and support of their officers. Invitations were given to all the citizens of the surrounding villages, a larger number of whom gratefully accepted the invitation—the majority being ladies. In speaking of the latter, I am happy to have it in my power to bear testimony to the grace and beauty which abounds in this portion of Frederick county. They were a decided acquisition, and added considerably to the enchantment of the occasion. The different avenues were artistically ornamented with evergreens, as were also the officers' quarters, and principal entrance to the camp. Arches were formed, and an illuminated inscription of *"Hail to our Colonel, Wm. Louis Schley!" "Death to Traitors!" "Down with Copperhead Democracy!" "Welcome to General Morris, commanding the 2nd Brigade!"* &c., &c. The national colors, with the Irish and Dutch flags, adorned each archway, the regimental flags being displayed at the entrance. In fact the whole arrangements were most beautiful, and created quite a grateful surprise. ...

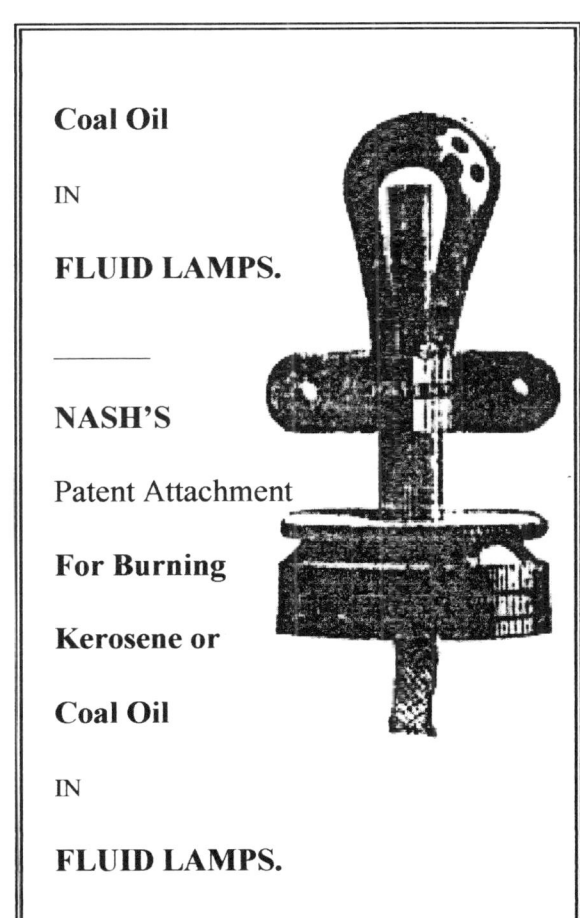

Coal Oil

IN

FLUID LAMPS.

NASH'S

Patent Attachment

For Burning

Kerosene or

Coal Oil

IN

FLUID LAMPS.

The worthy master of ceremonies, Capt. John Carroll, introduced *"The Guest of the Evening,"* Col. Wm. Louis Schley, in a beautiful address, appropriate to the occasion, wherein he evinced much feeling. He pointed out the many obligations that both officers and men were under to Col. Schley, and from the repeated cheers with which he was greeted, the sentiments were endorsed and approved by the whole command. The Colonel in reply, modestly thanked the officers and men of his command for the unexpected compliment which was paid him, expressing his determination to stand by them, and by the Administration, as long as this war lasted; that the present occasion was one he should never forget; concluding with a toast for Abraham Lincoln and the administration, which was received with tremendous cheers, frequently repeated. Songs, speeches and toasts were the order of the night; when at a late hour the happy party broke up....

The following promotions have been made in the 5th Maryland: Joseph Rothrock, Co. D. to be 1st Lieutenant of Co. A., vice Benjamin, deceased; 2nd Lieutenant, John B. Wilson, Co. D. to be First Lieut. and Adjutant, vice Stephens, discharged; John D. Babb, Commissary Sergeant to be 2nd Lieut. Co. D., vice Wilson, promoted; Sergeant Isaac D. Davis, Co. I, to Commissary Sergeant, vice Babb, promoted. I am yours truly,

J. B. W.

[Presumably, the writer was John B. Wilson, mentioned in the lists of promotions above.]

The *Whig* devoted considerable coverage to a serious railroad accident in Elkton. The excerpt showed people of a community pulling together in a crisis.

On Thursday afternoon last the 1:20 P.M. express train from Philadelphia, met with a serious accident. A piece out of one of the rails about three hundred yards above the Elkton depot threw one of the middle cars off the track, and the train being under rapid headway, at the time, it was impossible to stop it until it had passed the depot, ran afoul of a lime car standing on the sideling and upset the car which was running diagonally on the track, one pair of trucks being thrown astride of the rail by the first occurrence of the accident. Three of the cars were more or less broken, and several persons injured—five of them severely. John R. Hogg, Jr., who is employed as a brakesman on the road, but who was not on duty at the time of the accident, was standing by the Felton House on the corner of Bow street when the train passed, and approached the cars to pick up a newspaper which was thrown from the train, without perceiving that one of the cars was running, or rather, being pushed diagonally by the force of the train, was struck on the head by the car, and knocked sixty feet. He was picked up senseless, but soon recovered, and was taken to his residence a short distance from the scene of the accident. His head is seriously injured, but it is believed not fatally.

The car that was thrown diagonally on the track by the broken rail, came in contact with

---

SLATE

To Builders and the Public,

WE are Agents for the sale of the Peach Bottom, York county SLATE, of all kinds: Best Blue Gauged, 2d Quality and Small, and can furnish Slate, at short notice, either put them on or sell them by the square. They cost less than Shingles.

J. A. DAVIS & CO.
Port Deposit

a lime car on the sideling a short distance below the depot, which upset it, very severely wounding two ladies and a gentleman.

Mr. J. C. Kimball, wife of Captain Kimball, a Regimental Quartermaster stationed at Suffolk, with her son about eight years old, on her way to visit her husband, received very severe injuries about the head and face, and was carried to the Felton House where she remains at present. Her son also received some slight injuries about the face. Mrs. Kimball is a citizen of New Haven, Connecticut. A gentleman, a citizen of Philadelphia, was injured in the collar bone, but not dangerously. Mrs. O. D. Jenkins, wife of Lieut. Jenkins, of the 1st Pennsylvania Rifles was wounded in the head very badly, and also injured in the back. She was conveyed to the residence of J. P. Bradbury, Esq.

> **Peach Growers, Take Notice.**
> WANTED, to engage for the Peach Season, two good BUDDERS. Address, with terms,
> A. F. CONARD & BRO.

Gustavus Smith, of this county, who was brakesman on the train received some severe cuts and bruises about the head and face. He was taken to the house of Mr. Alexander. Some of the other passengers received slight bruises, but none so serious as to incapacitate them from proceeding on in the train. The engine and front cars not being injured proceeded, after a short delay, on to Baltimore. The wounded were attended by doctors Dunott and Ellis who were promptly on the ground, and rendered surgical aid. The citizens vied with each other in rendering every assistance in their power to alleviate the sufferings of the wounded. At present writing [Friday afternoon] the parties are doing well.

According to the *Democrat*, Jere Bell, a free black from Cecil, was sentenced in Kent County for enticing slaves away from their owners. He was sentenced to six years in the penitentiary, with another year added for larceny.

In that same issue, 5/9/63, the *Democrat* reported that Quartermaster R. F. May notified the father of Lt. Ephraim Jordan that his son was wounded in the shoulder by a Minié ball at Chancellorsville. He died on the next day in a nearby hospital.

The *Whig* added:

> The following is all the information we could gather of the 2d Del. Vols., who participated in the desperate and bloody contest at the battles of Chancellorsville. Company C. of that Regiment...were principally composed of men from this neighborhood. Lieut. Jordan, 3d officer of the company, wounded in the fight on Saturday, the 3d, in the left breast, by a rifle ball, which inclined downwards, and remained in his body, died on Monday the 4th. His remains were embalmed, and brought home on Friday last. His funeral will take place from the residence of his father tomorrow [Sunday] morning at 10 o'clock.

Sergeant Ebenezer A. Alexander of Co. C. 2nd Del. Reg. writes from camp that Lieutenant Jordan and 25 men were detailed to hold some rifle-pits and that only 6 of them returned. The Lieutenant was mortally wounded and Henderson Scott and J. H. Smith, each lost a leg. The remaining 17 are prisoners, viz:

M. Whitcraft, Robert McCullen, Asbury McDonald, William Founds, Washington Heath, Joel Lacy, Jethro McCullough, Amos McNeal, George McNeal, John Pidgeon, Charles Reed, S. Stretch, A. Snyder, Martin Anderson, Thomas Miller, Geo. Davis, Robert Davidson.

Mr. John Bennett's son Harrison, a member of Company C, 2d Del. Reg., who has been promoted for gallant and meritorious conduct on the battlefield, in writing to his parents after the battle, said: "It was the hardest eight days the 2nd Del. ever put in, marching and maneuvering all day, and throwing up breastworks and rifle pits all night. Our loss was very severe in our regiment, our company suffering more than any other; in fact nearly one-half—twenty in all—being killed, wounded and missing, and three or four of the missing, were to my certain knowledge badly wounded. I do not think we were ever in such a trap before. They [the enemy] had a fire on us from three different points. The regiment fired, on an average, one hundred and fifty rounds to the man."

On May 17, McCauley attended the funeral of Lt. Ephraim Jordan, Company C, 2nd Delaware. "Killed at Chancellorsville, Va. Sermon by Tos. Miller. Large funeral. Buried at St. John's."

A week later Hannah Terry, widow of Eli Terry, petitioned for a pension. McCauley was reminded of her husband and wrote: "Whatever instructions I had in smithing or wheelwriting I learned from Eli Terry. He was a lively fellow of some learning and much ready wit, but his besetting sin was a fondness for whisky. He had a helpless, idiot child— he would play the fife to divert the child and give it a dram, then he said it was happy as a lord. His intemperance brought on disease and he died in great destitution about the year 1834."

Garner & Hemming's GREAT American Circus.
Great Troupe of European & American **Male and Female Artists,** and the most Magnificent collection of wonderfully trained Horses and Ponies, ever brought together, affording facilities for the presentation of more Novel and Varied Performances than have ever been given in a traveling exhibition.

The *Delaware Republican* [5/25/63] presented a harrowing description of a hospital fire.

> Headquarters of 2nd Del. Vols.   May 11th, 1863
>
> Our regiment has again been in action, and I will give a brief sketch of their doings. We left quarters the 28th of April, and camped at night three miles off, marching the next day to United States Ford, where we again rested for the night. Here the river cannot be waded, but three very steep roads bind [wind?] down the otherwise precipitous banks to its edge, and down these roads the huge pontoons had to be taken entirely by men; following them the artillery trains were driven down, long lines of men remaining in the rear to hold back each piece as it made its perilous descent, and thus a whole day was consumed.
>
> At sunset, the infantry commenced crossing in two columns, and on reaching the other side took up a line of march due South, through the woods, passing several deserted rebel encampments and a large bakery on the way, and halting for the night on an open plain near a white house. Up to this time we had met with no signs of the enemy, except a large number of prisoners sent to the rear by our cavalry.
>
> At 10 A. M., on the 1st, our Division marched up the road to Chancellorsville, there took the plank road toward Fredericksburg, and on reaching a white house owned and occupied by the Rev. Mr. Chancellor [a Baptist minister] found evidence of a contest, several of our men having been killed and wounded. Our Regiment, not yet under fire, marched to the left of the road, and, forming column, closed in mass, and, detaching two companies as skirmishers, lay down to wait the attack. In a few minutes the enemy opened fire from the adjoining woods, and the shells began to whiz and burst around us, but, as it was evidently not the policy of our general to fight here, our forces fell back to the woods, and commenced throwing up earthworks with a rapidity that seemed like magic. All night parties of men were chopping at the trees, occasionally cutting one down and running limber bones drawn by six horses up and down the roads. Just before daybreak when the earthworks were finished, the whole force fell back to the woods, evidently to give the rebels the idea that we had skedaddled.
>
> Our Division now took position in the woods at the left of Chancellorville with other Divisions on either flank, and so remained quiet until about 2 P. M., when artillery firing began, followed by musketry, the shells and round shot flying briskly around us as we lay in the front line of battle, with our pickets in rifle pits about two hundred yards in advance. In these rifle pits the fiercest fighting of the battle took place, for the rebels coming upon

---

A Hint or Two:—To keep ice from windows, take an ordinary paint-brush or sponge, and rub over the glass once or twice a day a little alcohol, and it will keep the glass as free from ice as in the middle of Summer; and it will also give as good a polish as can be got in any other way.

them unawares and finding themselves at bay, struggled desperately to escape. Here Lieutenant E. Jordan, Company C, received his fatal wound, the ball entering his neck and glancing downward. Captain McCullough and Lieut. Reynolds, than whom no braver or more generous men ever buckled on a sword, were also wounded at this time, and from this pit but few of our men ever returned, though we fondly hope the missing ones are prisoners. During the battle the large brick house at Chancellorville, filled with wounded, took fire from the shells of the rebels. Instantly a party of our regiment, among whom was Sergeant-Major Smith, rushed to the building and removed the wounded from the lower floor, but were unable to reach the upper story on account of the flames. Too much praise cannot be bestowed upon this heroic band who performed their task while shot and shell were riddling the building. Indeed all our boys expressed themselves bravely and bore their wounds cheerfully.

> *Cup-Cake, the Nicest Kind.*—1 cup of butter, 2 of sugar, 3 of flour, the whites of 8 eggs, 1 cup of sweet milk, 2 teaspoonfuls cream of tartar, 1 [small] of soda. The cream of tartar to be put in the flour, and soda in the milk. Stir in the milk and flour the last thing, alternately. For cocoa-nut cake grate one cocoa-nut and add to it.—or a pound of blanched almonds; and extract of bitter almonds and a glass of brandy, will make delicious almond cake.

No place in the whole field was safe. Sergeant Smith, Co. H., being killed in our very hospital, which was several times shelled out. During the battle, the Regiment was under the command of Lieutenant-Colonel Striker, who received much praise from his superior officers for his coolness and bravery in the field.

We are now back in our old quarters and the enemy are exalting at what they call their victory, but their loss was immense, and a few more such victories would destroy their army and Confederacy.

BRUMLEY

Notice of Maj. Ben Ricketts' honorable discharge appeared in mid-May. The *Whig* editor's disenchantment with the powers that be slipped into the article.

Their [the Big Elk Rangers] first experience in battle was in the memorable Seven Days' fight on the Peninsula. On the retirement of the army from there they landed at Alexandria, and in company with Sumner's corps they marched out to support Pope. But as the blundering had done its work before they could arrive, they were ordered back, and, we believe, covered Pope's retreat. They then went with McClellan to drive the rebels from Maryland, and in the battle of Antietam, which followed, acted in the bravest manner, and lost several men killed and wounded. We next find them storming those impregnable works at Fredericksburg, on Saturday, December the 13th, 1862, where the Major—having been promoted int he meantime—was wounded at the head of his men. Since that time the major has been unfit for duty and seeing no prospect of a speedy recovery he has resigned.

At the beginning of the war, John Hasson left Elkton to join the Confederate Army. His father, Jas. Hasson, Esq., was a dyed-in-the-wood Union man. How to account for a son's waywardness? Well, he did work for the *Baltimore Sun*, the *Whig* reminded its readers, and "evil communications corrupt good manners."

Near North East and at Stites' Mill, somebody put obstacles across the tracks at night to derail the trains. Lanterns revealed the danger in both cases in time for the engineers to avert tragedy.

A diving bell was lowered into the Susquehanna in preparation for the building of a bridge. It was reported that the river bottom was thickly covered with eels.

Lt. Charles J. Smith, signer of the C. J. S. letters, wrote to his parents who lived near Elkton to tell them of his capture during the recent battle of Chancellorsville. Smith was put on board the steamer *Spalding* in the company of six men from Company C, 2nd Delaware: Amos McNeal, Washington Heath, Charles Reed, Thomas Miller, Robert McCullen, and Jethro McCullough.

Left behind were William Founds, Azarias Snyder, Marcus Whitlock, Robt. Davidson, Martin Anderson, Asbury McDonald, S. C. Stretch, Joel Lacy, George Davis, George McNeal, and John Pidgeon. Nobody knew why some captives were released while others remained in Confederate custody.

The *Delaware Republican* quoted a similar letter from "Lt. Charles J. Smith, Company K, 2nd Reg't Del. Vols., addressed to his brother, Sergeant Major 2nd Delaware Volunteers." The Smiths of near Elkton, then, had two sons in the 2nd Delaware.

The next week, in the issue of May 30, 1863, Lt. C. J. Smith wrote a long letter to the *Whig* entitled "Experiences of a Prisoner of War."

Runaway Negroes Arrested,

TWO Negroes, calling themselves respectively Joseph Stewart and Isaac Johnson, were arrested as runaways and confined in the Jail of Cecil county, on Tuesday, the 1st instant. Johnson is about 35 or 40 years of age, slightly gray, about 5 feet 10 inches high, dark copper color, and has on a suit of heavy drab kersey or home-made cloth.

Stewart is about 25 years of age, 5 feet 6 or 8 inches high, dark copper color, has a coat of same material as Johnson and blue striped pantaloons. These negroes are supposed to have come from the neighborhood of Winchester, Virginia.

ELI COSGROVE

American House, Annapolis, Maryland   May 25, 1863

Mr. Editor:—I thought a few lines from the 2nd Delaware would be very acceptable, so I think my duty to let you know our whereabouts, with a few items of our doings &c., prior to our capture. The regiment left camp near Falmouth, April 28, at 6 a.m., for the right; marched some two hours, then we supposed we would encamp for the night; raining all the afternoon, left camp at 9 p.m. for fatigue duty; a thousand men threw up six breastworks opposite the Rebels' batteries which were in sight; almost finished our part when relieved at 10 p.m.; arrived at old camp grounds at 12 M.

29th—Left camp at 8 a.m., marched three miles through the mud; the regiment was then detailed to dig the pontoons out of the mud, assist in laying them &c; The first bridge was completed by 12 M, without our forces being molested; after all the troops having crossed our Regiment working hard, it was ordered across at 8 p.m., marched until 11 p.m., when we arrived up to our new lines; many prisoners were captured and conducted to the rear, which gratified us all.

May 1—remained in camp in quietness until 12 M., when heavy cannonading commenced in our front; already, waiting for orders, received orders at 1 p.m. to go to the front; did not get engaged; after remaining there for some two hours we were sent to the rear, for purposes not known. Infantry were engaged and many wounded on both sides; at dusk our brigade was ordered to the front; We supported the pickets and skirmishers all night; the Rebels shelled us from 8 until 9 p.m., and though they had good range on us, not a man was hit; We were relieved at daybreak, but only to make a flank movement.

2nd—Made the move in the woods, to the left, formed in line of battle, awaiting the enemy's approach; 7½ a.m., heavy cannonading commenced on our right; our Brigade and Division batteries were engaged; we immediately threw up breastwork, dug rifle pits &c., all along our lines; at 12 M. most of the regiment was sent out on picket. Pickets and skirmishers firing all the afternoon; the Rebels shelled our breastworks but did us no damage; remaining portion of our Regiment lying in the works, awaiting the enemy to advance; our pickets were engaged off and on all day; the enemy advanced in force, trying to carry our works but were repulsed every time; our Regiment lost two men wounded.

3rd—Sunday morning—Shortly after daybreak I was ordered on picket, with Lieuts.

To Be Sold at Private Sale,
BECAUSE not needed any longer, a very safe, gentle and large MARE. Works in single or double harness, on the farm or under the saddle. Also, a single-seated Rockaway, with front seat for children, was new last spring, and is in good repair.
Terms accommodating. Apply to Mr. James Gifford, Upper Principio, Cecil co., Md.   JOSEPH COOK.

Jordan and Jones and 75 men; I had command of the detail; after reporting and forming on the left of the 145th Reg. Pa. Vols. by order of Major Scott, I was informed by the Lieutenant Colonel commanding the regiment that we were the reserve; but in a few minutes firing commenced on our right, and I was ordered to send one-third of my detail in; I immediately did so, in command of Lieutenant Jones; in about ten minutes after firing commenced in my front; I was then ordered in by Lieutenant Colonel commanding; I advanced my men in line, and before coming to the rifle pits deployed them. The sharpshooters firing close and quick on us, here Lt. Jordan Co. C. was shot in the breast while in the act of sitting down; he walked off the field, at or about noon; there was heavy fighting on our right; our detail was under a fierce fire of shell and bullets for, I should judge, an hour or more; the sharpshooters hit several of my men, one of Company G and one Company B; when suddenly some men were seen running from our right to the rear; my men wanted to do the same, but I drew a bead on the leader and threatened to shoot him if he did not return; which he did; I had no order to fall back and therefore told them it was when I said so; the 66th New York officers then told their men to fall back; my men being mixed with them also fell back; no doubt many of them reached our line safe, but Lieutenant Jones, 36 men and myself, to my knowledge were taken prisoners together with many officers and men of other commands; Brigadier General Hayes and staff, Colonels, Lieutenant Colonels, Majors, Captains, First and Second Lieutenants to the number of 136; my sword I surrendered to a Lieutenant of the 4th Ga.; a Captain of the 66th New York by that time came up, when a private stepped out to him and said he wanted his sword; the captain told him he could not have it, but that he would give it to his Captain, at which the private took hold of him with his left hand and struck him a stunning blow with his right hand, felling him to the ground; all this was done in front of his regiment; officers and men looking at the brute without saying a word and the poor fellow without anything or anybody to defend him.

We then took up our line of march for Richmond, with the disagreeable Rebels at our side in the shape of guards—but blackguards they were; reaching the plank road. We were hurried up and greeted by, "Here Comes the D--n Yankees!" "Kill them," &c.&c. "How's Fighting Joe?" "Has he crossed the river?" marched some five miles and encamped for the night; we passed over the battle ground which our forces had an hour or two previous, and such a sight I never before witnessed; the killed and wounded actually were lying in heaps, the Rebs two to our one; our grape and canister had done their work.

NOTICE

THE Annual Election of Nine Directors of the Cecil Bank, to serve for the ensuing year, will be held at the Banking House, the 1st MONDAY IN MAY, (5th proximo,) at 12 o'clock M.

THOS. C. BOND,   Cashier

4th—Started at daybreak, via plank road, for Richmond; did not walk fast, owing to some being sick and wounded; encamped early, to start again at dusk; started and marched about two miles, cavalry guarding us; they sent scouts out; one in a short time came flying back, and spoke in secret to the officer; we were halted and turned back; the reasons for their doing this was that they came across some of our cavalry; had they kept on, I have no doubt we could have been recaptured; nothing to eat; the "Confeds" striped [sic] our men of nearly everything.

5th—Started about 9 A. M. for Guinea Station; nothing to eat; brought some gingernuts at $1.50 per pint; arrived at Spottsylvania Court House about dusk; officers and men were confined inside the yard, with the guard on the outside; we were subject to snarls and yells of the rebs until bedtime.

6th—Was awakened early for another start; officers were treated well by those in charge of them; furnished us gratis with a drink of peach brandy; Captain Beck of the 4th Ga. had us in charge; arrived at Guinea station at 2 p.m.; nothing to eat; our men suffering for food, God knows how the Rebs stand it, as they had nothing for some time; The roads were lined with confederate wounded—never saw so many; the ambulances, wagons &c. were going to and from hospitals continually; commenced raining in torrents shortly after our arrival; we poor d--s is without any shelter and full of dust; very few had any shelter at all at night; twenty of us with one guard and the liberty to leave camp to hunt shelter; all succeeded except another and myself; had we known the road we could have made our escape; at last we went into a hospital, sat up out of the rain, drank a canteen of whiskey a steward stole for us, and returned to camp early.

> *To Clean a Carpet.*— To clean a carpet, shake and beat it well; lay it upon the floor and tack it firmly; then with a clean flannel wash it over with one quart of bullock's gall, mixed with three quarts of soft, cold water, and rub it off with a clean flannel or house cloth. Any particularly dirty spot should be rubbed with pure gall.

7th—Were told we would start early in the cars for Richmond, but they were loaded with wounded; stormed nearly all day, and was bitter cold; at 4 p.m. the officers were ordered to fall in for the cars to Richmond; raining very heavy; stood waiting at the cars to get in until 11 P.M., when "all aboard" was cried; one-half then returned to camp to stand in water ankle and waist deep in places; we received that afternoon, I forgot to mention, one pint of flour, and about ¼ lb. salt horse; made lead cakes, and had a meal for the first time since our capture.

8th—Officers aboard the cars for Richmond; the poor men had to foot it, notwithstanding many of them could have ridden; arrived in Richmond at 5 p.m.; streets crowded with Confeds., who threw many insulting remarks at us, such as, "D--n Yankees!" "Got to Richmond at last!" &c, &c; was conducted into the Libby Warehouse, and by 8

> SOMETHING NEW!
> **A LIVING HOME!**
> Built and arranged by the Proprietor with the intention of making it emphatically what its name indicates, a Home not exclusively for any particular Medical system, but where all persons can choose such treatment and mode of living as they prefer, at reasonable charges.
> Opportunity for various kind of light labor, combined with a variety of recreation, and a wholesome system of dietetics, will form the basis of the establishment. The institution will be arranged in five different departments....
> The Institution has a front of 136 feet towards the city of Wilmington and Delaware River, three and four stories with piazzas, presenting a variety of scenery not surpassed by any in the United States.

p.m. all hands were searched; such as coffee and sugar they confiscated, all money over $10 was also taken; names registered once more, making the sixth time, and then consigned to different rooms [floors]; nothing to eat, as usual; it was pretty clean considering, with bunks for two, here and there.

9th—Slept tolerably well; 9 a.m. half allowance of fresh bread for two meals, was brought us with some flitch; many Confeds. visited us during the day, a Captain [a minister] had prayer at 5 p.m., which was a very appropriate one for us as prisoners of war, our rights, country, Union, &c ; some visitors garbed in brilliant Confed uniforms, through ignorance or contempt, talked aloud.

10th—Sunday—all well; the same rations as usual, which was really barely enough for one meal; we slept the greater part of the time to forget hunger; one officer remarked, "Oh, that I only had an end of my mother's dishcloth to suck at! How much better I would feel!" Had Divine service at 10 a.m., full attendance, without being disturbed; sang Union hymns and after that was over, looked at the ladies; I was looking out when an officer below cried out, "Keep your d--d Yankee head in there if you do not want a ball put through it;" I complied with his ungrateful request, giving him a hateful smile; not having half enough to eat, sent out for bread, coffee, eggs, &c., at outlandish prices; ground parched corn labeled "Family Coffee" $1, eggs $2 per dozen, one-half rotten; evening, our men arrived afoot, and a war-warn, dirty looking set they were, but not half as hard as the Confeds; and nevertheless I saw them with my own eyes those sneaking butternuts take the clothing from our dead men's bodies and their shoes before they were actually done kicking.

11th—All well; received eggs and sugar $1.50 per pound and black at that; Confeds visited us during the day; in the evening had prayer, singing of patriotic hymns, &c.; during the morning received the Reb papers, half sheet, 20 cents, "Jackson's Death," the paper ordered and lined with heavy deep black.

12th—Rose early, quite refreshed; received the morning papers denouncing the Yanks, resolutions on the death of Stonewall, stores to be closed, Confed. Home guards and strangers invited to join in the procession from place to place; the Yankees will not have the chance of seeing him go to ___; received half a loaf, three cents worth of bread for the day, half a pound of liver to be divided between four hearty men; potatoes selling at $16 per bush., flour 20 cents per pound; nothing of interest transpired during the day; bought three-cent loaves of bread, three mouthfuls, at 15 cents each; shaving, with a wash yourself, 23 cents. Prayer in the evening; retired about 9 p.m.; all hands awakened at one by a Confederate Sergeant and told to prepare as we would start for City Point at 3 a.m., coffee was cooked and the last meal eaten, we supposed, at 3 a.m.; no one came with the good new of "Fall in," so we took another nap; slept until 9 a.m. and no signs of a move; started at 3 p.m.; marched three hours in pitch darkness, mud, rain, thunder and lightning, encamped after marching some ten miles but only for a rest, as all were much fatigued.

> **Delaware Home for the Insane.**
> This Institution will be conducted n the same general principles as the Living Home, and managed by kind and experienced nurses. The building has been arranged for the safety and comfort of its inmates, while it is free from most of the prison-like bolts and bars that have such an unpleasant appearance in other institutions. The Proprietor will take the general superintendence of both the Living Home and the Home for the Insane, and by combining a judicious system of light labor, will be enabled to make the charges considerably less than any other institution in the country.
> **Boarding and Nursing**
> Will be from Three to Twelve Dollars per Week, including Medical attendance or not, as may be agreed upon.
> **Dr. J. A. Brown,**

14th—We started early; ate a good meal at Petersburg, Virginia, treated tolerable; citizens quiet, except one old man who was in second childhood or something else, and urged his little one to strike every officer who passed, with a Secesh rag, arrived at City Point, distance 32 miles in 15 hours; 7 flag of truce boats were there awaiting us, also some 500 Confeds. exchanged; got on board the *S. R. Spaulding* at 3 p.m.; nothing of note; good accommodations; plenty of food, with champagne to rense it down; breakfast at 8 a.m.; more for 60 cents than in Richmond for $10; stopped at Fortress Monroe an hour or more for orders; passed several of our own and English men of war, and two of what are called 'Devils'; passed a prize schooner loaded with cotton, in tow of a gunboat.

16th—Arrived in Annapolis, Md., at 6 p.m.; officers boarding at the hotels, awaiting accommodations at Camp Parole; ordered to report daily at 9 a.m. The men are at camp; some eleven of the Big Elk Rangers, who were unfortunately captured with me, are here; all are well and hearty, and join in sending their respects. I am very sorry, indeed, that Lieutenant Jordan met his death there, as he was one of the bravest in his country's cause, and always did his duty without flinching. Respectfully yours,   C. J. S.

The summer of 1863 saw the usual number of strawberry festivals and Sunday school picnics. Members of a newly formed chess club met on the third floor of the Farmers and Merchants Bank in the evenings to pursue their hobby. Young ladies raised funds to hold a dance at Buchanan Hall in Frenchtown. So full was the social calendar that two other dances were held in Elkton during the same week.

After a dry beginning, June ended with refreshing showers that restored the oats and grass, but the town ordinance against allowing pigs to run loose in the streets of Elkton was violated daily.

Evidently the *Democrat* suffered for making such negative comments about the county seat, for the next week it described Elkton as a "pleasant summer resort." A two-hour train ride delivered a passenger to either Baltimore or Philadelphia. Trains ran three times a day. The town was free of mosquitoes and board was cheap. Hotel accommodations were adequate, there was a good livery stable, and sportsmen enjoyed fishing and gunning. If only somebody would round up those pigs....

Some members of the 6th Maryland were captured by guerrillas while guarding a train; Wm. Thompson, Jas. Beers, William Hodge Bennett, Company B; Wm. H. Dickinson, Company E; Thomas P. Mace, Company G. The next week, the *Democrat* reported that the first three were safe in Camp Parole, Annapolis.

After being wounded in a fight on the Rappahannock with Stuart's Cavalry, Adjutant Rudolph Ellis of Rush's cavalry [6th Pennsylvania] returned to his father's home to recuperate. According to McCauley, he was struck on the shins by a bullet during a cavalry fight at Beverly Ford, Virginia.

TO FARMERS AND THRASHERS.

WHEELER'S PATENT
HORSE POWER, &C.
Single and Double Horse Power
AND COMBINED
Thrasher and Winnower
as also, CLOVER HULLERS, FEED CUTTERS, Circular and cross-cut Saws, horse rakes, and a greatly improved LEVER POWER, for two, four or six horses, which runs easier and better than any lever power now in use.
JOHN D. MICHENER
WEST NOTTINGHAM,
Cecil county, Md.

Frederick Newhall, General Plesonton's aide, reported (Wheeler 1987, p. 31): "I found myself with ...the 6th Pennsylvania Cavalry, and at that moment the adjutant, Lieutenant Rudolph Ellis, was severely wounded....I said a word to him and was then immediately confronted by Captain Wesley Merritt, commanding the 2nd regulars, who was dashing through the wood without a hat, having just lost it by a saber cut."

Not all the action took place on the front. Two farmers, David M. Sherer and James Smith, shot each other is a dispute about the boundary between their Blue Ball farms.

As the rebel army continued on its way toward eventual confrontation with the Union forces at Gettysburg, people fled from the area into Lancaster and Cecil counties. Conowingo Bridge was thronged as carriages, wagons and livestock press across the river. A number of people stopped around Brick Meeting House and Rising Sun with droves of mules, cattle and horses. Here they hoped to be safe from the rebels, who exhibited a "warm attachment" to livestock.

> Children's cotton Hose in great variety, at E. BROWN, JR.

Troubled about the safety of their loved ones, Cecil Countians were unable to enter into Fourth of July festivities in 1863. Then as if to confirm their worst fears, news arrived from Gettysburg via the papers.

The *Whig* noted that from the 2nd Delaware 26 participated in the battle. 12 were wounded, but none killed. The 176 who had been captured at Chancellorsville were still being held by the Confederates. Those who came home to recuperate supplied the papers with the names of the wounded: Capt. John G. Simpers, Serg. Wm. Davidson [who died from a head wound, his body returned to Elkton for burial], Corp. Wm. Souers, Corp. Marcus Whitcraft, Corp. Samuel Biddle, Corp. Thos. Kelly, David Lily, Charles Hayes, George Pierson, Aquilla Mahon, and James Leonard. Among the missing were George Maffit, Geo. Wright, James H. Mahon, Chas. Basketer.

Lt. Wm. Smith, Company F, 2nd Delaware, whose father lived a few miles from Elkton, was wounded in the arm. Capt. Ezekiel C. Alexander, 1st Delaware, was missing, too.

Smith, no first name given and identified only as "the razor strop man," fought at Gettysburg with the 140th New York. He sustained a serious leg wound and had "just one more left."

As if unable to bear any more grief, the county turned momentarily from its losses and exulted in the fall of Vicksburg by ringing bells and firing guns.

On July 11, the *Whig* noted that local citizens traveled to Gettysburg to assist the wounded.

> Three large boxes well filled with articles for the hospital department, comprising wines, jellies, and other delicacies were sent by our citizens to the battle-field of Gettysburg early the present week. W. J. Jones and J. A. J. Creswell, Esqs., left Elkton on Monday afternoon for the battle-field, in a two horse Jersey wagon, with a quantity of necessaries for the wounded. Other parties also left our town for the scene of carnage. They all went towards Gettysburg *after* the battle, some on errands of mercy, others out of curiosity.

The following appeared the next week, July 18.

> The "good Samaritans" have been at work this week, providing things of comfort for the wounded soldiers. We are only surprised that more has not been done. We have seen a number of persons who have visited the battle-field, and they all agreed that there is great need of nurses. The wounded Rebels having been deserted by their companions, makes the number to be attended very large. There are many men who are loafing about—a large part of them great preachers of peace. Why have they not gone to relieve their fellow-men—and their friends—who are suffering for the most common attentions? Where is their boasted chivalry! If they have not the courage to take up arms to help their friends, one would suppose there was manhood enough located somewhere in them to go to their relief when they are wounded and in need of every attention.

Winchester, Virginia, changed hands 72 times during the war. During one of the times it was in Confederate hands, a wagon train retreated from Berryville, Virginia, to Harrisburg, Pennsylvania. On its way to rejoin the army, 126 wagons, drawn by 4 horses each, passed through Fair Hill, Blue Ball, and intermediate points to Conowingo.

Patrick Kelly and Richard Johnson were arrested at Conowingo Bridge and charged with trying to ferry deserters across the Susquehanna at Havre de Grace and cheering for Jeff Davis. They were taken to Baltimore and held for a hearing before colonel Fish. Thomas Nash was arrested on a charge of giving aid to Confederate prisoners. He, too, was held for a hearing.

> To Destroy Flies.—To one pint of milk add a quarter of a pound of raw sugar and two ounces of ground pepper; simmer them together eight or ten minutes, and place it about in shallow dishes. The flies attack it greedily, and are soon suffocated. By this method kitchens, &c., may be kept clear of flies all Summer, without the danger attending poison.

Conowingo got into the papers again when a horseman represented himself as a courier direct from General Meade with instructions to mine and prepare the bridge for destruction. Jeb Stuart's cavalry were reported in the area. The commanding officer knew the fishy smell was not coming from anything swimming in the Susquehanna. Under questioning, the courier gave conflicting stories. "They were going to shoot him on the spot but sent him to Philadelphia instead," reported the *Democrat*.

Railroads must be guarded and the guards must be fed. John W. Pentz of Baltimore was awarded the contract for supplying the troops stationed along the Philadelphia, Wilmington and Baltimore Railroad, between Baltimore and Havre de Grace, with fresh beef at $6.80 per hundred pounds.

Confederate John Hasson, who was exchanged two months ago, was again captured at Harper's Ferry and taken to Baltimore.

In the issue of July 25, 1863, the *Democrat* reported on conditions at Fort Delaware in an article quoted from the *Delaware Republican*. In addition to the problems with the water, 150 cases of smallpox were reported on the island in October.

There are now several thousand prisoners at Fort Delaware, their number having been greatly increased this present week. The rebels suffer immensely, many of them sick, and some of them give up the ghost almost every day. On Thursday last no less than 17 were interred, having been conveyed to the adjacent shore of New Jersey for that purpose. By the addition to the number of prisoners, the mortality will be proportionately increased. It would be a good thing if they could be quartered where better water could be obtained.

John Rowan, commander of the 3rd Maryland [CSA] Battery was captured at Vicksburg.

A horse thief named Foster shot himself in the foot when he "sold" a bay horse to Charles Cooper of Charlestown for $80. Cooper put $30 down with the agreement to pay the balance when Foster returned with the horse. People began to suspect that Foster was not all he appeared to be. Unfortunately, he roused one Thomas Cooper late at night and offered $3 for a ride to Elkton. The latter cheerfully conveyed his passenger straight to the jail, where he remained "in default of $50 to fee some friendly lawyer to procure his release."

The county sweltered in August of '63. The temperature hit 106 degrees. Diarrhea was prevalent among children; the *Democrat* advised "wholesome restraint in regard to fruit."

A draft club formed in Cherry Hill. Twenty-four members paid $50 each toward the exemption of any of its members who were drafted. Joseph Miller, Esq., was treasurer. A similar club formed in Elkton. Some men used other methods to evade the draft. James Young, for example, was brought from Philadelphia on board a ship with the first detachment of draftees under Major Sellers. On his third attempt to escape, he was shot to death on the Chesapeake and Delaware Canal. Others on board cut through a 3-inch bulkhead with a penknife in a frantic attempt to escape.

The *Democrat* quoted the *Philadelphia Transcript* on August 15, 1863.

> The lock tender and one of the soldiers brought the body from the engine room and searched the pockets. There was nothing found therein besides the money that the unfortunate young man had received in pay for becoming a substitute. His body was taken

---

West Nottingham Academy

THE WINTER SESSION of this well-known Institution for Young Men and Boys, will commence on Monday, November 2nd, 1863.
Tuition in ordinary English Branches, Higher Mathematics and the Classics. Students prepared for any of the College Classes, or for the Counting Room.
Tuition for boarders $75, per session of 5 months. Day Scholars, $6 to 10.
☞ For Circulars and other information, address
GEORGE K. BECHTEL, A.M.
WEST NOTTINGHAM
Cecil county, Md.

to Chesapeake City, about 9 miles distant, when it was thrown ashore and left. Some of the inhabitants took charge of the remains and buried them. There was no inquest held, nor was there any officer, Municipal, State or National, to take any legal notice of the affair. News of his death, having been sent to Philadelphia, a few of his friends proceeded to Chesapeake City, brought the body to this city, and was decently buried yesterday

Emma, a servant of Dr. Wallace, left Elkton, taking her small child with her. "She and her child must be fortunate indeed, if they fare as well in the future as they have in the past, under the roof of a kind and humane master," speculated the *Democrat*.

In Bohemia Manor, B. F. Sluyter and Joshua F. Biddle, Esqs., were arrested and sent to Baltimore in the custody of Provost Marshal Bennett, charged with hurrahing for Jeff Davis.

McCauley attended the funeral of Davidson D. Pearce, whom he identified as a "Secessionist sympathizer."

Simmons & Co., wholesale coal dealers, built extensive wharves at Locust Point. Water was deep enough there to accommodate large vessels. Coal was stored in great quantities on the new wharves until it was loaded onto ships.

Baker and Company nearly completed the gas house in Elkton. Fitters worked on pipes and chandeliers, and the street lamps were put in place upon the posts. The project was expected to be finished by the end of September.

The *Democrat* quoted the Philadelphia *Inquirer* regarding an incident involving George Biddle of Cecil County as he pursued a former slave.

Mr. George Biddle of Cecil County, Md., recently drove out to Camp Wm. Penn in a carriage to seize a colored soldier named John Price, a private in Company I, Sixth Regiment. He claims Price as his slave. Price was enlisted in Delaware and was home the week before last on a furlough. He said his master followed him to camp.

When Mr. Biddle's errand became known, the men became excited, and, in a threatening manner surrounded him, when he beat a hasty retreat. He afterwards found Col. Wagner at a neighboring house, who informed him he could not take the man. On returning to his carriage, Mr. Biddle was again surrounded and would have met with rough treatment but for the timely arrival of Col. Wagner, who assured the men that the alleged should not have to be taken back, when they became pacified.

Wanted Immediately,

A GOOD SALESMAN or SALESWOMAN; one that is acquainted with the business, and can come recommended; no other need apply.

Phillip Ellis of the 6th Pennsylvania Cavalry visited home and spoke well of the military. In one raid, he was within four miles of Richmond.

Rains washed out the underdrain, which was newly built by the Town Authorities, and which ran from Main Street down Soap House Lane into the marsh.

The *Whig* simply reported the death of Rachel May, wife of Benjamin F. May. But on September 24, 1863, McCauley added the following notation:

> Went to Elkton this morning—heard of the death of Mrs. Rachel May, wife of Ben. F. May, by suicide.
>
> Her son William left sometime ago for the Confederate Army, which had give her much trouble, and the late decease of her sister Mrs. Ellis is said to have borne heavily on her mind—the family was predisposed to insanity, her sister Mary having hung herself and Hannah having been deranged for many years. Mrs. May was suspended to the bed post by a ribbon, having got up early in the morning and committed the act before the rest of the family had arisen.

C. J. Wrote to inform the *Whig* of activities of the *Second Delaware*.

Near RAPIDAN STATION, VA., Sept. 19, 1863.

DEAR SIR:—Our Regiment took up the line of march with the Corps on the 12th inst; marched to near Rappahannock Station, and encamped in a drenching rain for the night. 13th took up the line of march; heard cannonading distinctly, which proved to be a fight between our's and the rebel cavalry. The Rebels fired as they retreated, and disputed every inch of ground; but our noble cavalry proved to be too much for the Rebels, as they were driven eight miles, that night, beyond Culpepper. We passed 8 pieces of artillery, 2 rifle guns, and one howitzer, with some thirty prisoners, captured by our cavalry. We encamped for the night within a stone's throw of Orange and Alexandria Railroad, and a mile off Culpepper; the day was exceedingly warm and hard on the men, owing to the scarcity of water, which was miserable.

14th our young, gallant Lt. Colonel, in command of the 145th Penna. and 2d Del., was ordered out on picket, on the flank. All quiet up to 12 o'clock M., when heavy cannonading commenced at a distance; nothing further during the day.

15th still on picket, every thing quiet.

16th all quiet, being short of grub for the first time; a couple of our officers on picket, started out to hunt up something; went to a farm-house, bought some tomatoes, and ordered a large corn cake to be baked by the time they returned; seeing another farm-house

---

To Preserve Strawberries in Wine.—Put a quantity of the finest largest strawberries into a gooseberry-bottle, and strew over them three large spoonfuls of fine sugar, fill up with Madeira wine or sherry.

at a distance, they concluded to go to it, to see what was to be seen—distance about two miles or more outside of our lines. The first thing that drew their attention was civilian dressed in drab clothes, a genuine looking Reb, coming from his house on the double quick, saddling up his horse, and on surveying the vicinity, small squads of horsemen were plainly to be seen 200 or 300 yards distant, which looked to them very suspicious, and as if there was a trap set for them; when all of a sudden eight fleet horsemen were seen coming after them in full run—they turned their horses, put the spurs to them, and into our lines they flew as if all rebeldom was after them. Our pickets saw the cavalry men chasing our men, but their horses being fleet ones gained ground on the supposed Rebs; the facts were reported to the commanding officer of the picket, who sent out a detachment of one Capt., one Lieut., and 42 men in pursuit of them, which was planned exceedingly well; advancing cautiously, they came on to the horsemen, which proved to be general French's staff—he having sent his Staff after the two as being guerillas, and the two run from them fearing they were rebels, as they wore corduroy breeches.

A good joke but well paid for, for the corn cake was lost—and while the detachment was out, orders came for us to move to the front, but not wanting to leave them in the lurch, two-thirds of the officers and men awaited their return, to see if all was right; the rest marching on—we lost the brigade, and encamped in the woods for the night.

Next morning 7 o'clock 17th inst., the Regiment passed up; we fell in, and were informed that three day's rations had been given out, marched until 1 o'clock, P.M.—eighty men sent on picket—we are now lying in the same place, about a mile and a half from the Rapidan; the rebel pickets were close to us, and they would fire on officers and men; our men not being allowed to fire at them.

Your favor [issue of the 12th inst.,] duly came to hand last evening, and I assure you was duly appreciated by officers and men of Cecil county; at the words *Cecil Whig* being spoken, the boys flocked to hear the news from the neighborhood of Big Elk. They are all enjoying excellent health with but few exceptions, and wish to be kindly remembered to relatives and friends.

The *ticket* pleases all, and we trust that all loyal men will look to their own interest and their noble sons, relatives and friends who are now in the field shedding their last drop of blood for the Union, to keep a bright look out, and not allow their eyes to be closed by a Copperhead. The Unconditional Union Ticket is the one we want and no other—beware, as much depends on it.

We are expecting to advance in a day or two, and the army is in a splendid condition;

DAIRYMEN TAKE NOTICE.—Spain's premium Atmospheric Churn, received this week, and for sale at the mammoth Tin and Stove warehouse of CANTWELL & EDER.

plenty of bone and sinew left, and we are in hopes of doing our work well. Hoping that you will attend to other affairs, adieu.

Respectfully yours, &c.,
C. J.

In early October the 5th Maryland was ordered to Wilmington. Afterward it was assigned to provost duty. It will probably never again be assigned to field service, said the *Democrat*, for it is almost entirely devastated by battle and disease.

In the days before the *Guiness Book of World Records*, newspapers printed unusual examples of one-upsmanship as fillers. The *Democrat* noted that Mrs. Wannamaker from New York State weighed 700 pounds. To maintain her considerable avoirdupois, she ate 24 ears of corn...at the last meal before she died.

In Elkton, gaslights illuminated the town for the first time on October 1, 1863. Pranksters, however, anticipated Halloween and used the occasion to move carriages and farm equipment to the doors of houses, change signs, and play other tricks. Feeling that "such fellows should be paid for their trouble," the commissioners offered a reward.

James Welsh, a member of the 26th Pennsylvania Volunteers, was wounded at Chancellorsville by a ball passing around his ribs and out the front of his body. He was taken to Chester Hospital, where he did well and was assigned to duty in Philadelphia. He returned to Chester, apparently for a check-up, but meanwhile, his surgeon had been changed. The new doctor, said the *Whig*, "probed the wound, which was almost healed and the unfortunate victim of surgical blundering sank beneath the torture and soon after expired." Welsh was buried at Zion Presbyterian Cemetery.

Wm. Sowers, 2nd Delaware, Company C, was admitted to Tilton Hospital in Wilmington, Delaware.

Sporadically, the papers reported that prize fights took place illegally in the county. In October of 1863, the *Whig* said that a match was broken up in Charlestown between Charley Lynch, a well known English prize fighter, and William S. Toal, alias the Dublin Youth. The paper offered the hope that New York "pugs" will no longer disgrace the soil of Cecil.

The *Democrat* reported on October 24: "Captain Samuel Ford of the 5th Maryland regiment, who

---

LIST OF LETTERS

REMAINING in the Post Office, Elkton, Md., on December 12, 1863.

Bedwell John	Smith Mrs. Mary
Ruler Miss Julia L	Simpers Mrs. Eden
Johnson Robert	Tayler Miss Ellen
Johnson Wm M	Wilson Master Jas
Moore Miss C M	Wroth John
O'Connor John	

☞Persons calling for the above will please say they are advertised.
JAMES McKINSEY, P. M.

was arrested in March last on charge of having, while acting as Provost Marshal at Berlin, Maryland, connived at the robbing of Mrs. Padgett and Miss Adams by some of his detectives, has been honorably acquitted and restored to his regiment."

The *Whig* ran the following letter and added comments of its own.

WASHINGTON, D.C., Oct. 13, 1863.

Dear Ewing;—In the absence of local news that would be of much interest to you, I will write you of a matter that has been exciting considerable interest here, and relates to a citizen of your county; I mean the case of Capt. Ford, 5th Md. Vols.

You remember about seven months ago you noticed in your paper the arrest of Capt. Ford, he being charged with allowing, and profiting by, a contraband trade across the lines at the point where he was stationed—Berlin, Maryland. Being committed to the old Capitol Prison he was closely confined, and allowed no hearing by any of the authorities. Six months and six days after his imprisonment the officer in charge of him received a note from the President, ordering Capt. Ford to be brought before him for an interview.

The conversation between the President and Capt. Ford caused his trial to be brought up immediately before a court held here for the hearing of such cases; and before that court Colonel Baker—the Government detective—Col. Schley, Col. Fish, Col. Holland, Capt. Neans, of Va. Cavalry, Capt. Tall and other officers who knew Capt. Ford as an officer, and who knew the position Capt. Ford held as provost marshal at Berlin, testified, that his character as a man was upright, and that he was incorruptible to bribery. Col. Fish, Provost Marshal of the Middle Department, [in which Department Capt. F. was acting] testified that, prior to Capt. Ford being placed in command of that post, *millions* of dollars worth of goods had passed the lines, and that it seemed almost impossible to stop the illegal trade. And that on account of the character of Capt. Ford for honesty and attention to his duties, he was placed in that position.

Col. Fish also testified that he believed, as nearly as possible, with the force Capt. Ford had at his command, that trade was stopped. THESE ARE THE FACTS. *It is in evidence* that if Capt. Ford would pay certain parties money, that he would be released; and when such an offer was made to Capt. Ford he endeavored to spit in the face of the person who made the offer, saying he "would rather die and rot in prison than allow such a thing to be done." *It is in evidence* that during his confinement he always expressed the deepest and

---

TO SPORTSMEN!!

SHOT by the Bag or Pound, Powder by the keg, ½ keg, ¼ keg, or Pound, Water proof and common Caps by the 1,000 or Box, Elys and Baldwin's Wads, Shot Pouches and Powder Flasks; also a fine article of English Cord for suits, for sale at the Cheap Store at low prices for Cash.

WM. T. MCCAULEY

truest loyalty to the government, while many of the officers in the prison with him cursed and abused the government and military authorities. *It is in evidence* that he was offered first $1200 and then $1700 if he would allow a person he had arrested for smuggling, to escape; and that he only confined the prisoner the closer. *It is in evidence* that some of the witnesses believed Capt. Ford was the victim of a conspiracy.

It is in evidence that while doing provost duty at Berlin, Md., Capt. Ford was a sober, energetic and useful officer. The character given him by some of his acquaintances from Cecil was that of an honest, upright man, and worthy of any trust that might be placed in his keeping. I think the garbled and detached statements that have been published concerning him, do him the greatest injustice. I will urge him to publish the testimony in his case; and hope Cecil county will suspend an expression of opinion concerning the case until then.

CECIL

CHRISTMAS CONCERT.

THE Sabbath School of the Elkton Methodist Episcopal Church, assisted by the Choir, will give a **Concert of Vocal Music.**
☞Admittance 20 cents.
Children under 10 years of age
10 cts.

Since the above letter was written, Capt. Ford has been honorably acquitted and restored to his regiment, which is now stationed at Wilmington, Del. The *Baltimore Clipper* says: The court martial which has been investigating his case not only pronounced him entirely guiltless of the charge, but commended him for the correct manner in which he had performed his duties; recommended that he receive his pay for the six months during which he was confined to the Old Capital Prison; that he be immediately returned to his regiment, and that a liberal furlough be allowed him in view of the great wrong that had been done him. The decisions and recommendations of the court were immediately approved by the Secretary of War, and Captain Ford will soon resume the command of his company.

All the evidence of Col. Baker, Provost Marshal of the War Department, of Col. Fish, of Baltimore, of Col. Schley, of the 5th Maryland Regiment, Captain Tall, Lieutenant Silesky, and all others, both for the prosecution and the defense, went to exculpate Captain Ford from all blame. He will have the evidence and findings published and forwarded to his friends for their perusal.

Rising Sun residents were saddened by the death of Lt. John Selfridge of the 6th Maryland, who died in a camp hospital near Culpepper, Virginia, on September 30, 1863. He had been in the army for little over a year, when he became ill. In that time he rose through the ranks to Lieutenant. His widow survived him. The funeral was held in Rising Sun M. E. Church, and he was buried at House's M. E. Church on October 8.

In Elkton, P. C. Strickland built a new Odd Fellows Hall on North Street. The three-story brick building measured 45 by 70 feet. Farmers and Merchants Bank of Cecil occupied two of the six ground floor apartments. Mutual Fire Insurance took the third, while the other three were rented for offices. The second floor was used as a town hall, and the third divided into lodge rooms. The new facility was heated by hot air and lighted with gas.

John S. Rossell fenced a lot in the rear of his Elkton store, where he planned to put a wood depot. This project was a great convenience to the people, for they could easily procure dry wood at any time. That fence inspired the *Whig* to indulge in a little wishful thinking: "A few more men of Mr. Rossell's enterprise, and Elkton will throw off her lethargy, and rival some of the western towns in industry."

A soldier was shot and wounded in Chesapeake City, but the incident was not particularly related to the war. William Russum, 5th Maryland, was home presumably to vote in the election. Somehow, he got his thigh broken by a pistol shot fired by "one of his comrades."

And that was not the only activity in town on Election Day. Christopher P. Ward, "a notorious rebel sympathizer," was arrested by Colonel Fish and sent to Fort McHenry to await trial.

The *Whig* on November 7, offered a tantalizing view of Morris Cummings' store. He sold a variety of candy: mint, sassafras, vanilla, anise seed, wintergreen, teaberry, clove, horehound, lemon—round and flat, almonds—burnt and rose, stick and drop candies.

"Among his family of cakes are cup cake, drop cake, sponge cake, wafer cake, shrewsbury cake, pound cake strips, lady fingers, plain and almond macaroni, fancy diamond Spanish macaronies; federal cake ornamented, pound cake; also taffies of all descriptions, comprising butter, solferino, cocoanut, tea, berry, etc., etc."

CUSHINGS & BAILEY
WHOLESALE
Bookseller and Stationers
No. 262 Baltimore Street
opposite Hanover

The Battle of Missionary Ridge raged on November 25, 1863. According to information in the Historical Society of Cecil County, David C. White, a Confederate soldier from Port Deposit, participated in that engagement.

White had attended West Point until war broke out in 1861. He, along with other cadets, resigned and joined the Confederacy. General William Hardee appointed White to a position on his staff with rank of captain. He quickly advanced to major, lieutenant-colonel and colonel.

At the Battle of Missionary Ridge, Hardee directed Colonel White to capture the "Glass House" below the tunnel from which Union sharpshooters were picking off Confederate officers. White, 23 years old at the time, led 300 men down the incline and burned the house. General Cleburne called him "the personification of a soldier." White is buried in North East Cemetery.

Two young Cecil women died in December: Charlotte Ricketts at the home of her mother-in-law on the Big Elk Creek; and Clara V. Ewing, wife of the *Whig* editor, E. E. Ewing. The latter was in her 27th year; the obituary said simply: "She was love."

On December 12, 1863, the *Whig* listed the killed and wounded belonging to Companies B, E, and G, 6th Maryland Volunteers, in the recent advance of the Army of the Potomac.

Company B.—Killed—John B. Pratt.—Wounded—Sergeant Mansel B. Moore, hand, severely; Color Corporal John D. Hall, arm, severely; Corporal Wm. Biggs, leg, severely; Private Francis Moore, arm and side, severely; Alexander Burley, face, slight; Wm. Davis, arm, severely; Wm. Alexander, hand, slight.

Company E.—Killed—Sergeant Ebenezer N. Watts and Private Alexander McCrey; Corporal Thos. Murray, slightly wounded in the head.

Company G.—Wounded—Privates John Cantwell, George Spence, Albert Gregg, Moses Temple, John Himberly.

Someone with a wry sense of humor and a penchant for understatement in the midst of trouble wrote to the *Whig* from the Methodist Church Hospital in Alexandria Virginia. The letter was dated December 11, 1863.

> FRIEND EWING:—Presuming you would like to hear of the trials and tribulations of the Boys of My Maryland, who are trying to find the road to Richmond with the army of the Potomac, I drop you a few lines. There are a number of the 6th Md. at present in the hospital, suffering from their wounds received in that skirmish, as the press called it, on the 27th ult. Now if that was a skirmish, I hope never to see a battle; by-the-by I believe a fight which does not last for four or five days is not termed anything but a skirmish; but such as it was, it has caused many a happy fireside a mournful Christmas, and left many a gallant youth a cripple for life.

> But I am digressing. On Thanksgiving Day, while our friends were enjoying the dainties of life, we were nibbling hard tack, and marching to pay our respects to the Johneys. At night we crossed at what is called Jacob's Mills, five miles above Germania Ford. On Friday, the second division of our corps took the advance; we did not expect we would meet much opposition, but soon skirmishing commenced, and we knew that some of our misguided brothers were in the vicinity. The firing grew faster, and we took up our line of march to take a hand at the game in which death was the dealer; we did not have long to wait, for a few minutes walk soon brought us to within 300 yards of the Butternuts.

APPOINTMENTS
BY THE
COUNTY COMMISSIONERS
FOR TAX COLLECTORS.

1st District,	W. Scott Price
2nd "	A. P. Barwick
3rd "	William Rutter
4th "	Alban H. Brinton
5th "	Dr. N. B. Morrison
6th "	Jas. A. Coulson
7th "	John Craig
8th "	James Cummings
9th "	Samuel J. Brown

FOR FISH POT CONSTABLE,
Richard Warner, 8th District
By Order
J. S. CRAWFORD

Nothing but a small clearing intervened between the enemy and ourselves. The woods were so thick that artillery could not be brought in to advantage, but a section of the 6th R. I. battery soon began to talk and the Johneys not to be outdone in exchanging iron compliments, brought on a section also, and the way the canister flew among the trees was a caution to the gray squirrels; here and there a comrade would drop, some would crawl to the rear, while others had fought their last fight, and their proud spirits took their upward flight to appear before the Great Chieftain of us all.—Peace to their remains; memory will drop a tear on their rude graves in the wilderness.

Night soon drew her sable robe over the scene, and friend and foe rested. Now came strategy, which as a writer says, is a fine thing when one does not understand it. The Johneys tried to flank us, but not succeeding in that, they fell back; when morning broke, the bird had flown, and we left the field to join the main body of our army. The rebel dead and wounded were left, as we had not enough transportation for our own. At 4 P. M., on Saturday, the army came up to Lee, who had fell back to Mine Run, a small stream some five miles from Orange Court House, there they worked like beavers, throwing up intrenchments. A flank movement was in contemplation, when an order came to fall back; and on Tuesday, after having escaped nearly freezing to death, we recrossed the Rapidan at Culpepper, mine-Ford, reaching Brandy Station on Thursday; and then after escaping starvation and being jolted to death in the ambulances, we took the cars for Alexandria, and here our trouble for a time ended.—The deed was done. Lee was scared; and the army has gone into Winter quarters; and now the old telegram will be: "all quiet along the line."

But, I fear, I am trespassing on your valuable columns, and as the Surgeon is coming, I will, for the present, close

All honors to old Cecil; her sturdy sons have been tested, and their wounds show it today. The 6th Regt. Md. Vols. has won its place in the pages of history; long may it stand an emblem of its country's rights. The noble Flag, the presentation of the loyal ladies of Elkton, floated over us while we met the traitors and put them to flight.

CRIPPLE FROM CECIL COUNTY

MANHOOD;
HOW LOST! HOW RESTORED!
Just published, in a Sealed Envelope. Price Six Cents. A LECTURE ON THE NATURE, TREATMENT and RADICAL CURE of Spermatorrhea or Seminal Weakness, Involuntary Emissions, Sexual Debility, and Impediments to Marriage generally, Nervousness, Consumption, Epilepsy and Fits; Mental and Physical Incapacity, resulting from Self-Abuse &c.—By ROBERT J. CULVERWELL, M.D., Author of the "Green book," &c.

The *Whig* ran a letter from Rev. Joseph T. Brown on December 19, 1863.

Camp of the 6th Reg. Md. Volunteers
Near Brandy station, Va.,   December 10, 1863

MR. EDITOR—Our facilities for writing are anything else but favorable, nevertheless they are more to be desired than the facilities of Libby Prison.

On the 26th ult., it being our national fast day, the Army of the Potomac moved in grand array; the 3d and 6th Corps crossed the Rapidan on Pontoon bridges at Jacob's Mill, between sunset and dark; the 1st, 2nd, and 3d Corps crossing at other points. We encamped for the night half a mile on the South side of the Rapidan. Early on the morning of the 27th we were called into line, and with a spirit characteristic of our noble men, we moved off, expecting to have work to do before night. With slow and quiet steps, feeling our way through a dense forest, seeking the whereabouts of the enemy we were pursing, when about 11 o'clock the booming of cannon on our right gave the evidence that we were already engaging the enemy's skirmishers. About 8 o'clock the fighting began to assume the character of a real fight. Soon the 2nd Brigade, commanded by Col. Knifer, to which the 6th Md. attached, moved into line in double quick.

The First Spring Exhibition
And Agricultural Fair of the New Castle County Agricultural Society,
Will be held on their Grounds near the City of Wilmington, on
Wednesday, the 21st of May, 1862.

Feeling a deep interest in the fate of our boys, I rode into the line, and only left my position when ordered back by the Major.—Suiting the action to the command I came out at double quick. Scarcely had I reached the rear when the wounded were being carried back. The work of death had already commenced. For 2½ hours it was one continual roar of musketry; surely, thought I, no man can come out of that fight without being killed or wounded. But the God of battles was with us. He who holds the whirlwind in the hollow of his hand, and for his own glory defends the right, was gracious unto us; though we lost in killed or wounded, perhaps a 1,000 men,—our enemies lost two for our one. Heaps upon heaps they were piled on the battlefield, and left by their merciless leaders without a burial and without care. The 6th Md. lost in battle 10 killed and forty-one wounded, making in all fifty-one men. They were in the hottest of the fight, led on by Col. Horn, the bravest of the brave, and the calm, deliberate Major

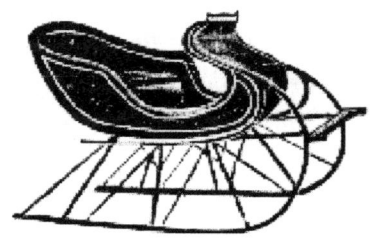

Hill—they entered into the awful conflict with a will to do their duty if death should be the result. Gen. French, who commanded the 3d Corps, could be seen mounted on his sorrel horse, as calm to all human appearance, as a Summer eve; while his aids were busy riding to and fro, amongst them Capt. Frank Torbert, formerly of your town. I shook hands with the captain while the fight was raging. I never saw him looking better. Our Colonel's horse received a shot, and a ball passed through the Major's coat, hitting his saddle, but doing him no harm.

I spent the night at the hospital, doing what I could for the wounded. The 128th unpleasant and raining—moved our wounded to the front—arrived at Rolison's Farm about 1 o'clock, where there had been some skirmishing in the morning—encamped about 8 o'clock at night, three miles from Rolison's Farm—woke up on Sabbath morning in full view of the Rebel army and their fortifications. This was to have been the grand battle ground, but in this we were disappointed, as there was no righting on the Sabbath, save some little skirmishing. This night was extremely cold. We made ourselves as comfortable as we could by building a brush arbour and making a log fire. At 2 o'clock Monday morning we were aroused from sleep with the order: "get ready to march." A cup of coffee was soon made, and again we were on the march; striking for the plank road from Fredericksburg to Gordonsville. By day-light we were in the line of battle on the South side of Mine Run. The Rebels and their fortifications still in our front. At 8 o'clock heavy cannonading on our right and left, and some skirmishing in our front. Everything indicated a general fight all along the line.

> WARTS ON COWS TEATS.—In answer to an inquiry in No. 23 of the "Dollar Newspaper" how to cure warts on cows teats, I answer soft grease, of any kind, used free at every milking will prove a remedy; they will disappear in a month.

The Surgeons and Chaplains, assisted by the Pioneer Corps, set to work falling trees and clearing the ground for a hospital. Already the wounded are being brought in and cared for.

At 1 o'clock our brigade received orders to return to the place we left in the morning; the 2d Del. coming in as we were moving out. Tuesday morning our Reg. was ordered to the support of a Maine battery. At 7 o'clock in the evening the whole army was on a retrograde movement; 5 o'clock on Wednesday morning found us on the north side of the Rapidan, having marched all night—we encamped and threw ourselves upon the ground, if possible to snatch an hour or two of sleep. In this we were successful. Soon after sun rise we received orders to prepare for a march; and after having drank some coffee, we moved off; the Rebels pursuing and throwing their shells in our rear, but without effect. At 5 o'clock in the evening we encamped, expecting to get a good night's rest and sleep, but in this we were disappointed. At 2 o'clock on Thursday morning, without getting our coffee, we moved off, arriving at Brandy Station a little after sunrise.

Thus Mr. Editor, I have given your readers a running sketch of our seven days' and nights' marching and fighting. I look upon our falling back to the North side of the Rapidan as a wise and prudent move.

Artillery, wagon trains and ambulances stuck fast in the mud, so that it would sometimes require two teams to draw one; such was the condition of the roads. Our officers—*noble men*—offered the Rebels every inducement to come out and fight; but all to no purpose. To have attempted to storm his works and drive him from his stronghold would have resulted in the loss of many a brave and good man; but our men were ready even for that. *Bold as would have been the experiment*, they were ready with bayonet in hand, to charge upon, and, if possible, drive him from his works; but wisdom, dictated another, and, we think, a better course, namely,—falling back to the North side of the Rapidan.

I believe that Lee is afraid of Gen. Meade, and his army, otherwise he would have tried, at least, to have driven us from the Wilderness. Let Lee cross the Potomac, and how soon is our army on his trail, and gives not up the chase until he is whipped or driven back. If he wants to drive us, as invaders of his soil, why does he not do it? The reason is plain,—he is afraid to attack Gen. Meade and his army in an open fight.

> *Yorkshire Pudding.*—Beat up two eggs in a basin, add to them three good tablespoonfuls of flour, with a pint of milk, by degrees, and a little salt; butter the pan, bake half an hour, or bake under the meat; cut it in four, turn it, and when set on both sides it is done. A tin dish, one inch and a half deep and eight inches wide, is the most suitable for such proportion.—*Soyer.*

JOSEPH T. BROWN

In the last issue of 1863, the *Whig* ran another letter from the 6th Maryland that depicted a welcome change of pace in camp.

BRANDY STATION, VA.
Camp 6th Md., Vols., Infantry
December 16th, 1863

DEAR EDITOR:—The dull monotony of camp life with us was relieved last Sunday by one of those pleasant little incidents which have rarely occurred in our regiment, viz,—the presentation of a standard of colours; that gift which is so highly prized by a true soldier. The occasion was one of interest to all; the members all out in holiday attire, formed on the parade ground "in close column by division." The colors are of a very fine texture, and the gift of a few of the loyal men of Maryland; and presented to us on behalf of the donors, by our late worthy Lt. Col. Wm. A. McCaleb. In presenting them the Col. said that in taking leave of the Regiment with which he had been so long connected, he could not possibly leave to our keeping anything over which we would guard with a more jealous eye, than the emblem of our nationality as a people, linked with that of the little, though loyal State, from whence we came. He said it was unnecessary to tell us what our duty to those flags was; for he felt assured from our actions in the past, that as long as one man lived to defend them, they would not be trailed in the dust, or stained with dishonor.—In concluding, he only asked us to do in regard to those colours, as loyal Marylanders had ever done; namely,—bear them in honor, or die in defending them from the ruthless grasp of a traitorous enemy.

In the absence of Col. Horn, Major Jos. C. Hill accepted them in behalf of the regiment in a few appropriate remarks, thanking the kind donors, and referring them to the record of the past, as a sufficient assurance that they should only be carried in honor on every battlefield of the future as the old one had been in the past.

The occasion is one that will be referred to in the future as one of the most pleasant reminiscences of our volunteer service; and closed with three times three cheers for the Union, the Flag, and the kind donors; who were Messrs. L. Seldnor & Co., J. Harris, H. C. Comegys & Lt. Col. McCaleb.

The health of our regiment is better than it has ever been—all in the spirits, and ready for any work we may be called upon to perform.

CARROLL

RICE MERINGUE.—Swell gently four ounces of rice in a pint of milk, let it cool a little, and stir one and a half ounces of fresh butter, three ounces of pounded white sugar, the rind of a lemon, and the yolks of five eggs. Pour the mixture into a well-buttered dish, and lay lightly and evenly over the top the whites of four eggs beaten to snow. Bake the pudding for ten minutes in a gentle oven. The peel of the lemon should be first soaked in a wine-glass of white wine before it is added to the other ingredients.

Arthur's Home Magazine

5

Cecil County

1864

Snow's Battery was stationed at Maryland Heights, and the *Whig* ran a letter on January 9 from "Potomac." After a poetic description of winter winds, the writer closed with a few pungent remarks about Copperheads.

> Before I close, Mr. Editor, let me inform you how we discover Copperheads. We catch hold of the old rotting stump slavery and shake it. Out comes the Copperheads, if near, from the McClellandye to the real treason color. Also any man that advocates McClellan, advocates Woodward, Seymour and Vallandigham, and has the seed of treason within him.

The *Democrat* reported on January 9, that the 5th Maryland was reenlisting as the 1st Regiment Maryland Volunteers. Greatly reduced in number, it was presently in Delaware under the command of Col. Wm. L. Schley.

"Old John" Carroll froze to death in his cabin in a woods near Newark. On January 16, 1864, the *Whig* noted that he was a bone gatherer, who in former days carried on a respectable business. Of late, he paced the streets of Elkton and nearby towns with a sack on his back, seeking to obtain a livelihood by following up his old occupation. Storekeepers knew his familiar order of "a cent's worth of crackers and a bit of chase," while from rum sellers he'd request a "glass of whisky."

According to the *Democrat*, 120 black soldiers under the command of white officers passed by from lower Cecil en route for the camp at Benedict.

County citizens were inconvenienced when train service was slashed further. Fewer trains stopped at Elkton, but the *Whig* hoped that if the town's prominent citizens presented their case to the railroad company, the matter could be rectified.

Captain Bennett arrested three deserters: Wm. Foreacre, Co. A, 8th Maryland; Hugh N. Armstrong, 3d Delaware; and Lewis Barber, Co. G., 6th Maryland.

John McAllister landed in jail for "riding his horse on the pavement and galloping through town in a general unruly manner. Too much of the 'over Joyful' was the cause."

A letter writer to the *Whig* complained about crowds of boys who congregated in front of Levis and Marrett's store to "bawl at" and insult passers-by.

Cheap John made the paper again, this time for his store in Wilmington. The *Whig* of January 30, 1864, carried the following:

> A squad of soldiers belonging to the 5th Md. Reg., who took a lot of prisoners from Fort Delaware to Wilmington, bound for Washington, having turned over their prisoners to a squad awaiting them at the former city, proceeded to exchange for whisky the money they lately received from the paymaster. The Purnell Cavalry were ordered to arrest them, but experienced some difficulty in obeying the order, as they seized every chance to escape or resist. In the evening, the balls flying after fugitives made it both unsafe and unpleasant to be walking in the streets. A ball fired at one man was imbedded in the door of the Milliner store of Mrs. Dennis, creating quite an excitement amongst the occupants. Another ball struck an iron awning post and glanced through one of the splendid plate glass windows of the famous Cheap John. We believe they succeeded in arresting nearly all of them. Whisky, as usual, was the cause of the whole disturbance. The only person seriously hurt was a small jackass in Cheap John's window, which, we believe, lost its tail.

The *Democrat* noted on January 30 that after boarding the train in New Port, Delaware, the 5th Maryland had traveled from Brandywine Springs to Baltimore.

In the following issue, February 2, the same paper reported the death of Lt. Wm. T. Patton, CSA, son of John P. Patton, Esq., of near Port Deposit. Patton was killed when the gunboat, *Queen of the West*, was destroyed on the Mississippi in April. Even though Patton grew up near the water, he had never learned to swim. When the Union attacked the *Queen of the West*, Patton threw a bale of cotton overboard with the intention of clinging to it and thereby keeping afloat. But the bale capsized and he drowned.

Lord's factory, which had been shut down for lack of cotton, was shortly to resume the manufacture of counterpanes and tablecloths.

Oysters, Ice Cream
AND
CONFECTIONERY,
FOR
LADIES AND GENTLEMEN,
AT THE NEW SALOON on North street, next door to the bank. All kinds of Candies, Taffies, Cakes, Pies, Oranges, Apples, Nuts, Raisins, Ice Cream, &c., are always kept on hand. Fresh supplies received from the city weekly.
Also, OYSTERS served in any style called for; or for sale in the shell by the bushel, or opened by the gallon, quart, and pint.
Feeling confident of giving entire satisfaction to all who may patronize her new Confectionery, Fruit, Oyster, and Ice Cream Saloon, public patronage is earnestly solicited.
MRS. EMMA E. GILES

The *Whig* poked good-natured fun at Charles L. Boulden and E. J. Torbert when they claimed to have bagged a larger-than-usual otter. The paper said that since the 19½-pound monster had no wounds, he died from over-exertion in chasing the men. Besides, "reputable witnesses" saw them in rapid retreat with the otter gaining at every step.

Two "bad boys," Sam Loman and George Buchanan, were brought before Justice Torbert for insulting people on the street. Said the *Whig:* "They were released with a reprimand and on giving their promise of better behaviour in future. We have a bad set of boys in Elkton, and they should be dealt with more sharply."

The *Whig* published a "cure" for warts. No doubt some people chose to keep their warts.

Lay on the wart a piece of roll brimstone about the size of a small grain of wheat, and set fire to it, letting it burn up the brimstone if the patient can bear it; if thoroughly done, the wart will soon come off. I lately saw the experiment tried upon a wart on the hand, and the wart came off smoothly in the course of a few hours.

REMARKS:—We have a much better cure for warts than the above, which we know to be both cheap, simple and efficacious. It is to apply to the wart, with the end of a knitting-needle, a little *fuming nitric acid* to be had at the apothecaries. repeat the application once or twice, and in two or three days the excrescence will come off, without leaving any mark. A few cents' worth will remove a thousand warts. It is a liquid that should be used with care.

CHAS. PEACOCK   R. C. CARTER.
SPRING
1864   1864
PEACOCK & CARTER
CHERRY HILL, MD.

HAVE now in store one of the Largest, Prettiest and Cheapest stocks of
SPRING GOODS
in Cecil county, to which they invite the attention of the Public.
LADIES' DRESS GOODS
from 12½ cents up; Good spool
COTTON at 8c, and everything else in proportion, at the
Cherry Hill Store.

In the same issue [2/20/64], the *Whig* recalled a notorious murder of the past.

Margaret Arelia. This old lady, so well known in the county of Cecil, with her land trials, twenty years ago, has left the county, and moved with her family, to the Tuscarora Valley, in Pennsylvania, to a tract of land which her father, Stephen Porter, had obtained by a claim of preemption. Many years ago, when the courts of Cecil were held in Charlestown, Stephen Porter was tried on a charge of homicide. This was a noted case, and was long talked of by the people of the county. Stephen was acquitted. He was defended by Litherbury, a distinguished lawyer of that day, usually called Leatherbury.

Stephen Porter furnished flour or wheat to the army, which rested some weeks in his neighborhood, on its march to Yorktown, and which Margaret alleged, was never paid for, and that she still had a just claim for it against the Government.

During her surveys about the Octoraro there was considerable excitement in the neighborhood, and numbers of witnesses in attendance. David Moore, John Troy, and Hart, with several others, were usually summoned.

Margaret attended on the ground and gave direction for the location of "Dividing," "Steeles," "Bourn's Forest," "Bell Vale," "Long Lane," "The Biter Bit," and "Crawford's Last Shift." Belle Vale was the beautiful valley for which Margaret had obtained a patent, but there was no birth for it without swinging Dividing around to the left; but that old track had got too firm a hold to be moved, and Belle Vale, though it had a name, had no local habitation.

Margaret Arelia had instructed her colored man Alfred, in the art and mystery of surveying, but she alleged that Dr. Lewis broke his spirits, when he told him, "that no d--d negro would look through his compass," and that Alfred surveyed no more, but turned his attention to millwrighting.

Margaret prided herself in treating her guest with politeness and hospitality, though in rather a rough way.

She had a painting of her mother, which had, one day, been a handsome picture. She said it was executed by Mr. Peale while on a visit to their family, many years ago....

A state fair was to be held in Baltimore during the week of April 18. Women of the various counties were strongly urged to send money to Mrs. P. Hopkins, Treasurer, or goods to Mrs. J. Tome, President. The note was signed by the corresponding secretary, Miss M. Ramsay, Port Deposit.

Also from Port Deposit came the news that the steamer *John F. Rodman* ran regularly between that city, Havre de Grace, and Bell's Ferry. It connected with trains from Philadelphia and Baltimore. The stage for Rising Sun, Oxford and Philadelphia Central Railroad connected at Port Deposit every day. Passengers for either stage took the 8:15 a.m. train from Philadelphia, or the 8:40 or 10:00 a.m. train from Baltimore.

Recruitment continued. Captain Christman, 2nd Delaware, was detached to enlist men in the 5th Maryland. His headquarters were in Elkton. Lt. H. Bennett, 2nd Delaware, recruited for his regiment from headquarters in Newark, Delaware.

Mary A. Jones took over the millinery store formerly operated by Mrs. Leffmann. The Presbyterian Sabbath School of Chesapeake City held an exhibition, while the Enterprising Juniors of North East raised funds in the Temperance Hall for a library.

IMPROVED Skeins and Boxes for road wagons, from the celebrated "Carbon Poco Iron," unequalled by anything in the market. In order to avoid getting a spurious article, get them from
E. W. STAPLES

E. A. Harvey's team stood on North Street with the wagons loaded with coal, "and drivers absent as usual," said the *Whig*. Some boys threw snowballs and frightened the team. One animal turned short and broke the wagon tongue, starting up the Main Street sidewalk, dragging one of the horses, which was thrown when the team broke loose. The harness on that horse gave way and the horse freed itself. The other horses ran into Mrs. Jones' house above the Union Hotel and were knocked down. One was severely injured.

"Professor Wright," arrived in town and posted notices that he would deliver a lecture on the occult sciences. A small crowd gathered at the appointed time and soon discovered the professor was a hoax. The "boys," seeing an opportunity for a little revenge, snowballed the professor, who hid himself in the Court House until Sheriff Janney escorted him out of the line of fire.

Wm. P. Baily, Colonel of the Second Delaware Volunteer Infantry, wrote to Mrs. Elizabeth Hiss from Sheppard's Grove, Virginia, to thank her for the regimental flag her organization sent. "Another reason," said Baily, "why we highly prize your gift is that the Flag we took with us from home nearly three years since, is now so war worn and tattered as no longer to serve the purpose of a Flag, many of its bearers have fallen while carrying it aloft amid the crash of battle. Its staff is broken and the pieces cling like an ivy to a ruin, a few stained and rotten threads, but to us it is still the dear old Flag...."

> SODA CRACKERS.—Seven teacups flour, one half teacup butter, two teaspoonfulls cream tartar, one teaspoonfull soda; rub these thoroughly into flour; add one and a half cups of water; work thoroughly; pound the dough till it snaps. Bake quickly.

The 6th Maryland wrote from near Brandy Station in a letter dated March 8, 1864. The *Whig* published it on March 19.

> Mr. Editor....Our Regiment is encamped about two miles south-west of Brandy Station, on the property of John Minor Botts, being quartered in huts, built by the rebs before the advance of our army across the Rappahannock on the 8th of November last. Though our quarters are not very grand in either architecture or building, they are nevertheless very comfortable; and we feel rather under obligation to the johnnies, for furnishing us with such comfortable quarters.
>
> Wm. H. Bennett, Drummer of Co. B., son of Mrs. Rudolph Bennett, of your town, has been promoted to Drum-Major of the Regiment. This is a well-deserved compliment. Though he is only seventeen years of age, he has never faltered; but has stood with the Reg. through thick and thin, and has endured the hardships of a march to Richmond; and been held in durance vile for some time in Libby Prison.
>
> While in Cecil county, some time since, I was told that two-thirds of the Army of the Potomac would support Gen. McClellan for President, at the next Presidential election. As an illustration of the sentiment of our Reg., I will give you the result of a vote polled in it

a few days ago. There were present 400 voters; A. Lincoln receiving 395, McClellan 5; scattering 3; blank 1. This fully demonstrates that the 6th Md. Reg. is entirely satisfied with the Administration, and are willing, and even anxious, that the present incumbent shall hold the reins of Government for four years longer.

Sixteen months ago, this Reg. fairly idolized Gen. McClellan—thought that he was the only man to lead the Army of the Potomac to victory, and crush the Rebellion.—Now, among all the officers of the Regiment he has but *one* champion to espouse his cause, and I am sorry to say he hails from Cecil. During the travels of the Regiment through Virginia, they have had their eyes opened, and have seen the evils of the everlasting curse of slavery, and, like true Marylanders, when convinced of wrong, try to get right; and when George B. McClellan promulgated his pro-slavery opinions, they repudiated him. How any man who has traveled through the Free State and seen their thrifty condition, seen the towns rise as if by magic, seen the man who depends on the neat cottage and everything cheerful around him; then visit this wasted country, where you may travel for miles without as much as seeing a village of a dozen houses—hear the women and men using the same dialect as the negro—see nothing but a wilderness, and hear nothing but ignorance—how a man can, with all these things staring him vividly in the face, exclaim "I am a Constitutional Union McClellan man," I am unable to say.

> SUPERIOR GRAHAM BREAD.—One quart of warm water, and one tablespoonful of yeast powder, with unbolted wheat flour, sufficient to make a stiff paste.—Knead well, and let it stand fifteen minutes in a warm place. Then bake in a moderately hot oven; and you will have bread fit for a king.

How we would like to be home in April next, to have the opportunity of helping to blot from Maryland the pollution which has so long retarded her prosperity, and help set her beside her sister states of the North; but though we can't be there, we feel assured that all will be well, and that the sun will rise on the 7th of November to see Maryland regenerated from the loathsome institution of slavery, which has been so long knawing at her vitals

Yours,
COMPANY B

County Commissioners received from Governor Bradford the names of four black Cecil Countians who volunteered for the army and were mustered into Company C, 30th U.S. Colored Troops, with authority to draw on the Treasure of the State for the State Bounty.

The *Democrat* [4/2/64] reported that "25 negroes enlisted at Port Deposit and credited toward Philadelphia's quota."

A tableau held at the Court House for the sick and wounded soldiers was largely attended.

Captain Alexander of the 1st Delaware and Lt. W. G. Purnell arrived in Elkton after being released from Libby Prison.

Another new side-wheel steamer, *General Grant*, plied the waters of the Bay in place of the old steamer, *Port Deposit*.

B. F. May sold at auction the remaining stock in his store. He planned to depart for Baltimore shortly.

A picturesque scene was played out in Elkton with the arrival of the 3d New Jersey. The *Democrat* reported:

> 3rd New Jersey Cavalry, Col. A . J. Morrison, about 1200 strong, arrived here between 3 and 4 p.m. and encamped east of town. A band of 16 buglers preceded the cavalcade, at the head of which, with the principal officers, rode a young lady with flowing curls, understood to be the wife of the Adjutant. They took up their line of march on Monday morning, proceeding to Perryville, where steamers waited to convey them to Annapolis.

McCauley saw the 3rd New Jersey and to the above information he added: "This is the largest body of horsemen that I have seen—they are mostly foreigners—new recruits."

The *Democrat* found itself perturbed when the postmaster put Abolitionist pamphlets in the April 2 issue. "He inserted in the paper...an electioneering abolition pamphlet....The trick was at once understood by our subscribers as soon as they discovered the obnoxious document. We leave our readers to form their own estimate of an official who has shown himself capable of conduct like this."

The *Whig* [4/16/64] related that notes from donors appeared on some items sent to soldiers.

> Some of the marks which are fastened on the blankets, shirts, &c., sent to the Sanitary Commission for the soldiers, show the thought and feeling at home. Thus—on a homespun blanket, worn, but washed as clean as snow, was pinned a bit of paper which said,: "This blanket was carried by Milly Aldrich, who is ninety-three years old, down hill and up hill one and a half miles, to be given to some soldier."
>
> On a bed-quilt was pinned a card saying: "My son is in the army. Whoever is made warm by this quilt, which I have worked on for six days and most of six nights, let him remember his own mother's love."
>
> On another blanket was this: "This blanket was used by a soldier in the war of 1812—may it keep some soldier warm in this war against traitors."
>
> On a pillow was written: "This pillow belonged to my little by, who died resting on it; it is a precious treasure to me, but I give it for the soldiers."
>
> On a pair of woolen socks was written:—These stockings were knit by a little girl five years old, and she is going to knit some more, for mother says it will help some poor soldier."
>
> On a box of beautiful lint was this mark: "Made in a sick room, where the sunlight has

not entered for nine years, but where God has entered, and where two sons have bid their mother good-by as they have gone out to the war."

On a bundle containing bandages was written: "This is a poor gift, but it is all I had; I have given my husband and my boy, and only wish I had more to give, but I haven't."

On some eye-shades were marked: "Made by one who is blind. Oh, how I long to see the *dear Old Flag* that you are all fighting under."

A spokesman for Company B, 6th Maryland, wrote a letter on April 10 in which he expressed annoyance that his company did not get home to participate in elections. After learning that the county voted as he would have it do, he added: "One thing that we wish to impress is, that you urge, through your columns, the necessity of the Convention in forming the new Constitution, in having a proviso allowing the soldiers to vote in the field. Then we can charge to the front with the bayonet, and thrust to the rear with the ballot."

Then he told of an occurrence on the picket line when a starving woman was found, who said she had nothing to eat for weeks except what she received from the U.S. Government. Officers asked her if she would take the oath of allegiance and she replied that she would sooner eat leaves.

> **CARD**
>
> I HAVE associated this day HENRY HINLEIN and SIMON HEINEMAN in partnership with me, under the firm of A. GOTTSCHALK & CO., to carry on the clothing Business at my old stand, the *Granite Post Clothing Hall.*
> A. GOTTSCHALK.

The writer concluded: "Yet how many are there in the North, who are aiding and abetting these people who are living on the Government, who come to our lines that they may get information for Mosby and his band of guerrillas, that they may, at the midnight hour, murder our pickets in cold blood. More anon."

Isaac Boulden, head waiter at the Howard House, died. He had worked previously at the Fountain Hotel while Jacob Johnson was proprietor. When Johnson took charge of the Howard House, Boulden accompanied him there.

The Post Office Department awarded the contract for carrying mail from Elkton to Chestertown to Joseph Wells of Elkton; from Elkton to Lewisville to Arthur J. Pitt of Lewisville, and from Chestertown to Easton to Wallace Woodford, formerly of Elkton.

By the end of April the double track of the P. W. & B. Railroad reached Newark and was expected to extend to Elkton within the next week.

But the big news was that the Great National Circus was heading toward Elkton. It was under the direction of Mrs. Chas. Warner, formerly Mrs. Dan. Rice.

The *Whig* observed that people liked to walk out of town on a spring evening toward the creek.

But some, more chivalrous than others, are not content with following up the old and weary mode of "footing it," but prefer going it on the equestrian style. While two of these young knights were taking their usual ride the other evening, and had reached the creek, where they halted to water their steeds, a horse, not remarkable for etiquette, which was running at large, approached the animal upon which one of the young riders was seated, who, not liking the familiarity of the stray animal manifested toward his own, started off at full speed—the loose horse following at his heels—and went in town as though he were pursued by a legion of rebs—crying out, "Stop that horse behind!—Stop that horse behind!"

We are happy to state that the young man received no injury, other than a severe fright; and that the pursuing animal was stopped before he had penetrated the town any distance, while the young man determined to abandon his prancing steed, and seek company with those of his more humble companions, who were witnesses of the scene—causing as much for them, as it did "fear and trembling" to the unfortunate.

From Fort Delaware, April 16, 1864, came a letter to the *Whig* in which the writer saw the shadow of nepotism in recent promotions.

> Messrs. Editors Baltimore American:
> ...Captain Koch, of Company I, a *brother-in-law* of Colonel Schley, has been promoted Major, over Captains Munmert and Ford, both of whom are his seniors in rank and equals in capability. Another promotion is that of Jenks, *another brother-in-law* of Colonel Schley, whom he has promoted to a Second Lieutenancy and assigned to Company I. This Jenks is a new recruit enlisted some time in February, and now promoted to command over men who are *soldiers* and have been doing active service for nearly three years, an act of injustice unparalleled by anything ever before perpetrated by Col. Schley since he has been connected with the regiment.
> J. Q.

STRAY

I hereby certify, that Josias Ramsay, farmer, of Cecil county, brought before me, the subscriber, one of the Justices of the Peace, in and for the said county, this 2nd day of May, in the year 1864, as a stray, trespassing upon his enclosures a RED MULY COW, with a white back, and a calf about two weeks old.
Given under my hand.
WM. TORBERT, J. P.
The owner of the above described Cow is requested to come forward, prove property, pay charges, and take her away.
JOSIAS RAMSAY

Much of the news had to do with taxes, appointment of assessors, and the sale of U.S. 10-40 bonds. T. B. Hopper of Chesapeake City was named U.S. Assistant Assessor for districts one through four; that is, for Cecilton, Chesapeake City, Elkton, and Fair Hill. E. E. Ewing held the same position in the remaining five districts: Brick Meeting House, Rising Sun, Mount Pleasant, Port Deposit, and North East. Governor Bradford appointed Richard McFarland Public for Cecil. Joseph G. Brown, son of Rev. Joseph T. Brown of Cherry Hill, was named assistant clerk in the office of Jas. C. McCullough, collector of the First Collection District of Maryland.

Butchers and manufacturers made their monthly returns of Internal Revenue for April by the 10th of May. Failure to have the returns in the hands of the assistant assessors on time resulted in a fine equal to 50 per cent of the tax. The principal assessor in the area, G. M. Russum, Esq., recently instructed the assistant assessors to follow the instructions to the letter, especially those regarding penalties.

Under an Act of Congress, March 8, 1864, Government 10-40 Bonds were issued. "They are exempt from taxation by or under any State or municipal authority....Their value is increased from one to three per cent, per annum, according to the rate of tax levies in various parts of the country."

Great National Circus
AND MODEL SHOW.
Under the direct management of
MRS. CHAS. WARNER,

formerly
MRS. DAN RICE
Will exhibit at HAVRE DE GRACE, Saturday, April 30th; ELKTON, Monday, May 2nd; Head of Sassafras, Tuesday, May 3rd; Chestertown, Wednesday, May 4th.
☞Admission 50 cents; Children 25 cts.
Performances Afternoon and Night, at 2 o'clock and 7½ P. M.

In 1862, Congress had passed an income tax law. Under the headline INTERNAL REVENUE, the *Whig* reported:

The following is the annual assessment for the year 1863. The assessment of licenses embraces by 8 months, from September, 1863, to May, 1864. The carriage and silver-plate assessments are for the year 1863, and the Income assessment for 1862.

Class A embraces all ad valorum assessments, among which are the Incomes. All incomes under $10,000 were taxed 3 per cent, and all over that amount 5 per cent.—Incomes derived from bonds of the United states are taxed only at the rate of 1½ per cent.

The tax derived from Incomes in Cecil on which 3 per cent was paid for the year 1862, was $3,892.44; and 5 per cent incomes, $2,659.20; and from United States Bonds, on which 1½ per cent was paid, $4.91; making a total from Incomes of $6,556.55. The amount received from licenses of various kinds was $3,244.89; and from Carriages, taxed one dollar each, $22.00; from two-horse carriages, which are taxed two dollars each, $108.00; on those valued at $600, and taxed five dollars each, $10; making a total for carriages in the county of $412.33. The whole amount of revenue from the annual assessment for 1863, which embraces the Incomes of 1862, is $10,213.88.

More and better Horses, Smaller and Finer Ponies, a greater number of Mules...

The annual assessment from 1863-4, which is now being made, will be much larger than the past years.

The amount of tax paid by Cecil county to the U.S. Government for the month of March was $1,588.97; the principal part of which is derived from manufactures. The tax from the manufacture of paper alone, for the month of March, was $681.42; from sheet iron $616.53; and from foundry products, composed principally of plow irons, $41.88; from butchering, $11.76. The balance was derived from miscellaneous articles of manufacture, and fractional licenses. The First Collection District of this State is composed of the eight Eastern Shore counties, and Cecil pays more tax into the U.S. Treasure, under the Internal Revenue Laws, than the other seven counties combined.

The monthly collection of taxes from several of the counties does not amount to the salary paid to the Assistant Assessor of those counties. Such districts are a losing business to the government. Where the monthly tax of a district is below the salary of the Assistant assessor, we think the government would consult its own interest by abolishing the office monthly, and only making an annual assessment in such districts, at which time the monthly taxes could almost all be gathered up.

A tragedy occurred in North East when Willie A. Jeffries ran across the street and was struck by a fish wagon. He died in the arms of his mother, Sophia Jeffries. A neighbor, Mr. Craig, dispatched a telegram to the boy's father, William J., of Company A, 8th Maryland Volunteers. The message never reached him because at the time the Battle of the Wilderness was raging in Virginia. Had the elder Jeffries received the notification, he would have been doubly distraught, for the message simply said: "Your child was killed by a wagon today. Come immediately." The Jeffries had three sons, both older than Willie, and the bereaved father would have had no way of knowing which child had died.

At any rate, Sophia sent him the letter, now owned by the Historical Society of Cecil County:

It is with a sad heart, I sit to write you these few lines to tell you I am not hardly able to stand it. Have had a hard time of it dear husband, I wish you could be at home before I lay my precious baby in the grave. I sent a telegraph dispatch to you, but I never got an answer from it. I am going to bury him Tuesday at two o'clock. I have got him in ice now waiting for you.

Mr. Craig has proved a friend to me; he say'd he won't see me want for anything. He went to the depot and telegraphed to you. I don't know what I will do; my poor baby gone and you away. Do try and get up if you can. It will almost kill me to lay him in the ground without you seeing him.

I must bring my letter to a close. May God bless and protect you. From your wife.

Sophia Jeffries.

William did not reply. More than likely, he never knew of the boy's death. Sophia buried her son in the Methodist cemetery. His marker read simply: Willie A., Son of William J. and Sara S. Jeffries. Died May 6, 1864. Aged 2 years, 6 months and 11 days.

The army in the meantime moved to Cold Harbor, where William Jeffries was killed and buried in an unmarked grave. For the second time within a month, Sophia lost a family member. The Council Chamber of North East published a tribute of respect in the *Whig* on June 18, 1864.

COUNCIL CHAMBER

Independent Council No 14, O. U. A. M.

Whereas, It has come to the knowledge of the Council that we are called on to mourn the loss of our late Brother Wm. J. Jeffries, Co. A, 8th Reg. Md. Vols., who was killed on the 30th of May, while fighting in defense of the Flag, the emblem of our Order. Therefore, be it,

Resolved, That we, the surviving members of this Council, do deeply sympathize with the family of our deceased Brother in their bereavement. By his death this Council has lost a worthy member, and each member a generous hearted brother.

Resolved, That we wear the usual badge of mourning for 30 days, as a token of respect to our deceased Brother, and that these resolutions be published in the county papers, and a copy be sent to the family of our deceased Brother.

W. P. F. WHARTON
JACOB GILBERT
I. N. BENJAMIN
D. M. RITTENHOUSE
JOHN H. GOODWIN,

North East, June 11, 1864

The notice in the *Whig* [5/16/64] stated that Sophia "was one of the nurses of our sick and wounded at Gettysburg, last Summer." Sophia, more so than most other women in Cecil, knew what her husband faced when he went into battle, for she had seen firsthand the ravages of war.

In the early days of the War, Ben Ricketts, alias Big Elk, wrote: "One of our sick [Wm. S. Harvey] of North East started in charge of his sister. She heard her brother was sick and came down alone; nearly a hundred mile of the route being by stage. I tell you old Whig that's what I call the right kind of a sister; I would not mind having a dozen such myself, *in case of accident you know.*" [See above, p. 90.] It is not certain whether Ricketts referred to Sophia or to her sister Mary. But in any case, somebody from the Harvey family appeared on the spot when another was in need.

> ...a better selection of Trained Animals; a larger Troupe of Performers, a more carefully arranged Programme....

Why did Sophia go to Gettysburg? Her husband's and brother George's regiment, the 8th Maryland, did not fight there. After suffering a contusion of the thigh at Fredericksburg in December 1862, her brother William reenlisted with Company K, 1st U.S. Artillery. This regiment did fight at Gettysburg, but no records indicate that William Harvey was wounded there. Perhaps he suffered from complication of the thigh wound. One can only speculate about Sophia's motivation in going to Gettysburg to nurse the sick.

William Jeffries' pension records reveal that Sophia, 29, was pregnant with another child when these sad events occurred. She applied for a pension based on the number of living children. After the baby was born, she applied for a change in status. Then she had to go to great lengths to prove to the Government that the child belonged to her husband. The letter to her husband referred to above was evidently written for her by someone else because she signed the statements with an X. Sophia died in North East in 1908 at the home of her granddaughter, Mrs. John Norman. [The paper mistakenly identified Mrs. Norman as Sophia's daughter. In 1883, her son Lewis drowned off Turkey Point, and Sophia raised his daughter Ida, who later married John Norman.]

"Cecil's Roll of Honor" in the May 21st issue of the *Whig* listed the following:
Wounded of the 6th Md. Regiment at Fredericksburg: Maj. Jos. C. Hill. Co. B—Thomas Bounce [sometimes spelled Bunce], John Campbell, Cor. John W. Dickinson, Wm. T. Davis, Marion Gillespie, C. C. McCullough. Co. E—Henry Vanhollen, John Carey, Wm. Moore, Jos. Carslow, Joseph Carter, Corp. B. W. Buckly, John Tarburtton, Jas. Edwards, George L. Price. Co. G—Sergt. J. T. Burkins, Sam'l Crothers, Jno. L. Crothers, John H. Drummond, Sergt. J. S. Smith.

Killed of Co. G—Lieut. D. G. Orr, Thomas Janney, _____ Temple.

Wounded of the 8th Maryland—Co. A—Geo. W. Harvey, C. W. Rigg, C. H. Norman, John Coleman, John W. Wilk, Geo. W. Yeoman, Corp. Wm. M. Simpers, David Murdock, Jas. Demon, Jacob M. Logan, Jas. T. Roach, Thos. P. Poe.

Killed—Co. A—Ambrose Gorell, Wm. McCall.

Missing—Co. A—Corps. John H. McCracken and Jas. D. Alexander.

Wounded—Wm. Sowers, Amos McNeal, John A. Steele, Co. C. 2nd Del., and Robert Short, 1st Del.

Wm. C. Alexander, of Co. B, 6th Md., before reported as killed, was not hurt.

Lightning killed William Morris, who lived near Head of Sassafras. In Chesapeake City, it struck the chimney of the pump house that supplied the canal with water. The storm, accompanied by heavy hail, also damaged H. H. Brady's stables and knocked out several telegraph poles.

The *Whig* explained why the draft became necessary in Cecil County:

> Although the first Congressional District had a surplus on its quota of upwards of 700, that surplus was not accredited to it as a District, but to the State at large. Cecil has supplied the state with many more troops than she has ever received credit for and her small deficit should, in justice, have been made up to her out of the surplus in the District to which she belongs....Captain Ireland recruited a full company in this county, which mustered in as Baltimoreans, and for that the county received no credit....We do not object to drafts, but we do object to being cheated in the manner above alluded to.

...and the evincement of a more correct Taste and Tone of Refinement...

There followed a list of sixty names by district of those who were drafted. The names of black draftees were designated by [n]. First District: Andrew Brown, Wm. Cunningham, Samuel D. Moore, W. T. Garnett [n]. John Flaner [n]. Benj. Anthony, Thos Griffin, Joshua Farrel [n], Dr. W. C. Perkins, Geo. S. Crawford, Samuel Milliken, Benj. Moore

Second District: W. Gilkey, James Lane, John Boyd, John McMan, Geo. W. Bradley [n]. James Richardson, L. Simmons, Jesse Hughs, Thos. Coats, Jacob Metz.

Third District: Dr. H. H. Mitchell, Benj. C. Biddle, Robert Scott, W. G. Gallagher, T. W. Scarborough, John Murdock, Henry Peale.

Fourth District: John Campbell, David H. Collins, David Sherer, Jas. S. Steel, J. T. Newland, Chris. Buffington, Chas. Shepherd, Jon. Richardson.

Fifth District: Robert G. Logan, Robert Spence, Chas. Cooper, Jos. S. Burns, Benj. Cochran, Wm. Arrants, George Chandler, Mitchell Holden, Jas. G. Thompson, Sam'l Myers, J. H. Woodrow.

Sixth District: Abraham G. Lincoln, Thos. J. Caldwell, C. C. McClair, John S. Green, James A. Riale, Gibbons Moore, Theo. Brickley, Jon. C. Bird, Wm. T. Kirk, George Gillespie.

Seventh District: Quota filled by volunteers.

Eighth District: Jos. W. Reynolds, Decator McNamee, Jas. Barrett, Reuben Alexander, Joseph Newland.

Ninth District: Joseph Brown, G. W. Janney, Jon. W. Nolan, Sam. L. Martindale, Elisha Lynch.

The new Odd Fellows' Hall was dedicated in Chesapeake City on Saturday, May 28, 1864. Following a 2 o'clock parade, there was a dedicatory service in the M. E. Church. Supper was served at 5 o'clock at reasonable charges, and the Citizens Brass Band provided music. Ladies were invited.

The paper mill at New Leeds changed hands. Theodore Megargee turned the operation over to B. F. Peterman and George F. Harlan.

Cecil Countian Lieut. John T. McCauley, Company H, Purnell Legion, was made Provost Marshal of Port Tobacco, Maryland. John Dunbar of Elkton, Sergeant in Company I, was promoted to Lieutenant in Company F, 5th Maryland Volunteers.

The *Whig* saw a need for houses, especially for mechanics. "Two classes of dwellings are wanted—those that will rent for $50 and $60, and those that will rent for $70 and $80 a year. Houses built properly to rent at these prices, will be readily taken, and will pay a good interest. Who will build a row, of ten or a dozen, of the kind of houses needed?"

Snow's Battery engaged in battle again in Virginia. On May 28, 1864, the *Whig* reported that Battery B suffered five casualties: Daniel Hamer, slightly in hip; Henry Mackinson, abdomen; W. Thompson, in leg. But the paper did not obtain the names of two other wounded soldiers. How unsettling it must be for those readers who had relatives in Battery B to read a casualty list that was acknowledged to be incomplete. Lieutenant Gerry now commanded the Battery, since Captain Snow commanded the Maryland Artillery. Battery B was with Siegel's army.

...Forty Performers: Equestrians, Gymnasts, Voltigeurs, Leapers, Dancers, Acrobats, Vocalists and Musicians.

[A marker presently identifies Gerry's house on Main Street in Port Deposit.]

Two articles by local historians relating to Snow's Battery follow. The first appeared in the *Bulletin of the Historical Society of Cecil County* [10/16/1961].

Last May Joe Ferguson and I, having a common interest in battles of the Civil war, made a tour of Shenandoah Valley, Virginia. Approaching the town of New Market, we talked about the battle that was fought here on May 15, 1864, between a federal army under General Franz Siegel and a Confederate army under General John C. Breckinridge.

We parked along the main street in the town, and Joe said, "Let's walk up the street a piece; there is something I want to show you.," I assumed it was a Confederate monument or something like that, and gladly went along. As we reached a yard in front of the Lutheran church I noticed a post, standing close to the pavement, with some object sticking out of its side. Getting nearer to it, I found the object was a 3-inch shell which had penetrated almost to the center of the post. This still did not mean too much to me until I looked up at a little framed sign above the shell, and then I had the surprise of our trip. The sign read, "This shell was fired by Snow's battery at the battle of New Market, May 15, 1864."

Battery "B," First Maryland Light Artillery, better known as "Snow's Battery" from its commander, Captain Alonzo Snow, was raised in Port Deposit in the summer of 1861. It enlisted 362 Cecil County men who served in the Union army for three years and made a conspicuous record for bravery The battery took part in the Peninsular campaign, and rendered distinguished service at Malvern Hill, at Antietam, and in the Shenandoah Valley.

In my boyhood days I knew some of the old veterans who belonged to this battery. One who I remember well was "Jake" McCardell, a sort of handyman, carpenter, and fence builder, who worked on my father's farm. Jake was a good workman, albeit addicted to too much "John Barleycorn" at times. My father told me that Jake had the reputation of being one of the best gunners in Snow's Battery. He said that on one occasion an officer sighted a group of Confederates at nearly a mile's distance, and ordered a shell to be fired in their direction. Jake McCardell sighted the gun, and the shell landed almost in the midst of the group and scattered them pellmell.

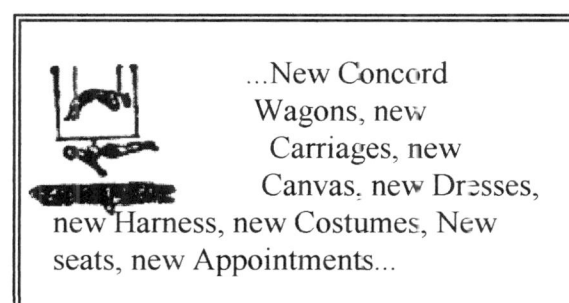

...New Concord Wagons, new Carriages, new Canvas, new Dresses, new Harness, new Costumes, New seats, new Appointments...

So, in my mind's eye, I can look back over the years and fancy it was Jake McCardell who sighted the gun and fired the shot that lodged in the post which stands along the street in New Market. Perhaps the group might have been General Breckinridge and his staff. Perhaps Jake, had he know that the general, a kindred spirit in his liking for "spiritus frumenti," was in the group, would not have sighted his gun too accurately for fear of shattering a flask of Kennedy bourbon which the General undoubtedly had on his person. Or if the Unionists had won, he might picked it up later as part of the "spoil of war."

Excerpts follow from Morton F. Taylor's article in *Uppershoreman*, October 1981.

...Jacob Tome, founder of Tome School, helped to organize [Snow's Battery] and supported it financially....Its officers, in addition to Capt. Snow, were Captain Lucius Gerry, First Lt. Theodore Vanneman, First Lt. James J. Kidd, Second Lt. John M. Bullock, Second Lt. Leonard Parker, Second Lt. William Trainor, and Second Lt. Enos T. Hall....

In the Battle of Antietam, the bloodiest days battle of the Civil War, Snow's battery took part as a member of the Artillery Section of the 2nd Division, 6th Corps, which Corps was commanded by Gen. William B. Franklin. On the day of the Battle, 1st Lt. Theodore Vanneman was in command and made the official report for the battery to Capt. Ayres, the artillery commander of the division. This report reads as follows: "Sept. 20, 1862—On the 17th, on orders of General Franklin, moved to the right and in front of Headquarters in a corn field, and ordered to shell woods in front, where an enemy battery stationed near a school house opened on us. We fired 300 rounds and with the help of other batteries silenced it. We suffered no losses. All the officers and men behaved with commendable bravery."

Today a monument to Battery B, erected by the State of Maryland, is located at this site on Cornfield Avenue at Antietam Battlefield. The woods where the enemy battery was stationed is known as "the Dunker Church wood" because it surrounds a little whitewashed church. The heaviest fire of the war took place around Dunker Church and as a result the little building suffered severe damage. After the war, Edward Gehr and Robert Craig, both members of the Battery, sent the Church a Bible.

In June 1864 Snow's Battery formed part of the forces under General Hunter, which took part in the expedition against Lynchburg, Virginia. The movement was not successful and Hunter was obliged to retreat via the Kanahaw Valley through the West Virginia mountains. His army suffered severe losses, and Snow's Battery lost a number of men by being taken prisoner. Nineteen of the Battery were captured on June 21 near Salem, Virginia, 50 miles west of Lynchburg. The following were held captive and most of them were sent to the infamous Andersonville Prison where a number of them died: Lt. James Kidd; Privates Mahlon Alexander, Henry H. Bond, John Churchman Brown, George N. Buckley, Robert Craig, Charles Griffin, John W. Gillespie, Samuel B. Gray, David J. Heckart, William J. Jackson, Wm. H. Jones, Wm. S. Jackson, Daniel A. Miller, Thos. P. Reed, Joseph Rice, John Simmers, Andrew J. Vancourt, James T. Wilson, Leopold Weistler.

Mrs. Chas. Warner, formerly Mrs. Dan Rice, will perform the far-famed Blind White Horse, Surrey, and her high-toned war charger, Champion.

Of these, two whom it has been possible to identify as having died while prisoners are John C. Brown and Thomas P. Reed, both having expired on August 22, 1864.

Following the war, reunions of Snow's Battery were held annually, beginning in 1887. There were usually held in Port Deposit or Perryville, but in 1894 the reunion was held in the GAR Hall in North East....A feature of that reunion was a parade carrying a flag which had a star knocked out in 1864 when the Battery fought against General Early's troops at Lynchburg.

In 1890 nearly every dwelling and store in Port had the national insignia floating in the breeze in honor of Battery B's reunion which was held in the Town Hall. In the afternoon the soldiers formed in procession with the Riverside Band in the lead, followed by a number of wounded comrades in carriages and marched through town....

Lt. W. F. A. Torbert of Elkton, formerly ADC to General French, was appointed Paymaster of the

Navy. Torbert enlisted in the summer of 1861 as second in command under Captain Ricketts, Company C, Big Elk Rangers, 2nd Delaware.

Joseph G. Brown, assistant clerk in the office of Internal Revenue, was run over by a hand car on the railroad. The accident occurred, said the *Whig*, when he used "his feet as setting poles, which threw him on the track, the car passing over his ankles."

In the same column, the editor remarks that the introduction of a female clerk in E. Brown's store was a practice that should be followed by other storekeepers.

On May 26, the first election was held under the act incorporating the town of Cecilton. Dr. Samuel V. Mace, Wm. T. Weldon, John Morris, Wm. H. Pearce, and Edward Semans were elected commissioners for the next year. Cecilton was no longer a village, but an incorporated town.

The Board of Examiners selected 4 men out of 68 drawn for service. 33 were commuted, 18 exempted on account of physical disability, and 13 did not appear. The provost marshal searched for them. Eligible men were encouraged to appear before the board and claim exemption, pay commutation, or go into the service; otherwise neighbors would answer the draft they unjustly evaded. But the exhortation was late, because some already skedaddled.

Capt. Thomas Patton, 91, of Port Deposit died in early June. He commanded a rifle company in the War of 1812.

J. S. Rossell added a distillery in the rear of his store for the concoction of various liquors but especially for blackberry wine. In lavishing praise upon that product, the *Whig* said: "Besides being an excellent drink it is a most effectual remedy for diarrhea, dysentery and that class of diseases."

Among the performers engaged are the celebrated Whitby Family, consisting of Mr. Harry Whitby, (formerly of Cooke's English Circus) who will introduce his beautiful performing Horses: Spot, Beauty, Constellation and Hawk Eye.

Two vehicular accidents shook up the people involved. John V. Reardon bought a colt at Bohemia Manor and drove it home with another horse. About five miles outside Elkton, the tongue detached from the carriage [Was it one that Reardon himself had manufactured?], and the horses ran out of control. Reardon's head was injured in the fall from the carriage, and the horses ran until the vehicle was destroyed. Fortunately a friend of Reardon's accompanied him on horseback. He took the injured man to Elkton, where he recovered after several days of delirium. Dr. Ellis, too, narrowly escaped injury when his horse, spooked by a train, kicked the carriage to smithereens.

Lt. Samuel P. Stewart, 61st Pennsylvania Volunteers, came home to Elkton on furlough after being wounded a second time.

As the 5th Maryland passed through Wilmington on its way from Fort Delaware to the front, a number of Cecil lads, "among whom was the comical Tom Tyson," temporarily excused themselves from service. The next day they arrived in Elkton and Chesapeake City, where they had a grand time until Provost Marshall Bennett threw a wet blanket over the proceedings, rounded them up, and directed them to their regiment. The *Whig* concluded: "It may also be well enough to state that the Colonel was really with his Regiment."

Under the category of Unlikely Combinations, a new barbershop opened at the eating and drinking saloon of Joseph Marrett.

McCauley wrote on June 14: "John W. Wood and John Robinson were captured by the rebels on the night of the 5th near Richmond, Va." The diarist mentioned Wood again on November 19: "John Wood captured in June in Florence, S.C.—was well but nearly naked—wished clothing and other articles sent to him." Two days later McCauley went to Baltimore to the Sanitary Commission to see if any items could be sent to the prisoner. The Commission replied that there was no certainty of anything reaching Wood while he was in rebel hands.

On June 18, 1864, the *Whig* told of Lincoln's appearance at the Sanitary Fair in Philadelphia.

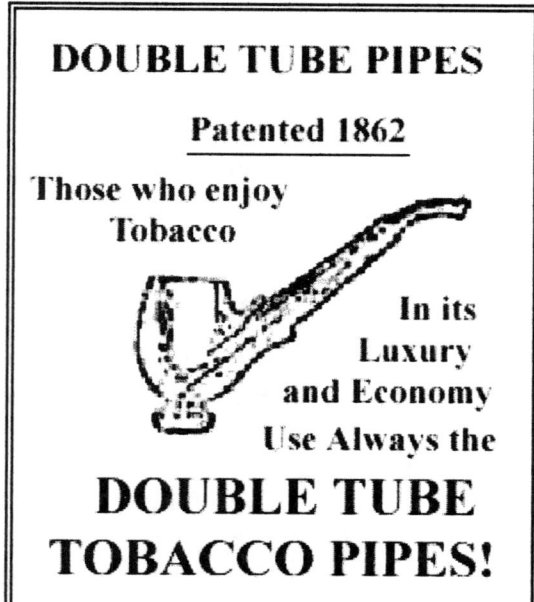

DOUBLE TUBE PIPES

Patented 1862

Those who enjoy Tobacco

In its Luxury and Economy Use Always the

DOUBLE TUBE TOBACCO PIPES!

The President of the United States visited the Sanitary Fair on Thursday last, and the ovation he met with is described by the Philadelphia papers as being one of the most cordial and enthusiastic.

A special train was provided by Mr. Felton, President of the P. W. & B. R. R. for Mr. Lincoln and suit, which went in advance of the regular morning mail train. The Presidential train passed Elkton with a shrill scream from the steam whistle about 10 o'clock, A.M., on Thursday, gaily decorated with flags.

Mrs. Lincoln brought from Washington and presented to the Fair a beautiful floral vase of Japanese manufacture, exquisitely fashioned. It is lacquered ware. It will be exhibited at the West Philadelphia table.

At the conclusion of the President's speech at the Fair he said: "My friends I did not know but that I might be called upon to say a few words before I got away from here; but I did not know it was coming just here. [Laughter] I have never been in the habit of making predictions in regard to the war, but I am almost tempted to make one. [Do it—do it!] If I were to hazard it, it is this: That Grant is this evening, with General Meade and General Hancock of Pennsylvania, and the brave officers and soldiers with him, in a position where he will never be dislodged until Richmond is taken. [Loud cheers.] I have but one single proposition further to put, and perhaps I can best put it in the form of an interrogatory. If I shall discover that General Grant, and the noble officers and men under him, can be greatly facilitated in their work by a sudden pouring forth of armed men to their assistance, will you give them to me? [Yes, and cheers.] Then, I say, stand ready, for I am watching for the chance. [Merriment and applause.] I thank you, gentlemen."

The *Whig* printed an account from the 2nd Delaware, which lost its colors on May 12.

Our Division was massed at daybreak on the 12th, and at daylight attention was given, forward march and we made the grand charge on the enemy's fortifications. Our Regiment covered the left flank, at double quick, for fear of the enemy attacking our flank; in case they did, we were ordered to face outwards and engage them, while the massed column kept on. We all moved on, however, but our Regiment having a jungle and a swamp to go through, we were stretched out considerably. The Johnny Rebs opened on us with shot, shell, grape, canister and bullets; but they were caught napping. Our colors were captured by the enemy, owing to the color bearer marching into a Rebel support. The color sergeant was captured and in the hands of the Rebels sometime, but was re-captured together with his captors. Our colors were also picked up by a Lieutenant of the 5th Michigan at the enemy's works. Many of our men were captured by being cut off, but were re-captured. Thousands of Rebels, cannon, caissons and small arms were captured. We give a list of the casualties in the company from this county:

Killed: Hugh C. Jones. Wounded: Lieut. Philip Johnson, arm; Amos E. McNeal, leg; John W. Murray, knee; Benj. Fernan, right hand; Joel Lacey, arm amputated; Thomas Miller, thigh.

Missing G. S. Bennett, Aquilla Mahan, Chas. Reed, George W. McNeal

Purnell Legion Infantry: Co. H.—Killed—Lewis K. Terry
Wounded: Wm. M. Thompson, Jesse S. Anderson, Samuel Hamilton, Wm. Robson, Oscar Slack, right leg off, Benjamin Wilson. Co. H. Wounded—Richard Martin, John Berry
Sixth Maryland—Company B: Killed—William Thompson. Wounded—Joshua N. Ash

A new two-cent piece came into circulation. An alloy of copper and tin, it resembled the $3 gold piece that was coined some years ago. On the obverse was a shield resting on arrows and surmounted with a scroll. In *God We Trust* appeared on the scroll above the year 1864. On the reverse the words *2 cents* appeared with a maize wreath. In an outer circle were inscribed the words *United States of America*.

A wounded soldier from Brick Meeting passed through Elkton on a train in mid-June. He threw out a paper with a message for the folks at home. "Wm. H. Robinson, Co. E., Purnell Legion wounded in the leg—going to Philadelphia."

Not many could jump from a train "under rapid headway" without doing damage to their physical person, but Joe Berry raised the feat to an art form. He successfully eluded captors eleven times by his ability to survive the jump unharmed. Berry was in such a hurry in his latest escape that he nearly knocked the conductor from the train, too. Perhaps because he was handcuffed this time, he did not meet with his usual success. The constable cornered and captured him in a patch of briers. He was charged with stealing dry goods from Andrew Kidd's store in Port Deposit and with taking money from J. J. Smith, proprietor of the Washington House. However, even the *Whig* grudgingly admired Berry's athletic prowess.

In that same issue appeared notification of the return of a wounded soldier.

> **A RARE OPENING**
> Wanted to rent the STOREHOUSE situated on the principal street in Chesapeake City, formerly occupied by J. Denning & Co. It is the oldest and amongst the best stands in the town. It having been occupied as a store upwards of twenty years. It has been lately rebuilt, and has all the conveniences requisite to business purposes. Apply to
> CHAS H. DENNING.

> Lieut. P. H. Ellis, of the 6th Pa. Cavalry, son of F. A. Ellis, Esq., of this town, was wounded in Sheridan's last raid, and is now at his home in Elkton. He was leading his men on foot, fighting as infantry, when he found he was alone, with the enemy in sight, his men having temporarily fallen back. The Lieut. threw himself on the ground for a while, but finding he would be captured if he remained longer, concluded to try and reach the Union lines by a run for them. Three vollies were fired at him, one grazing the spine, taking a downward course and lodging in the hip.
>
> The Lieut. threw himself in a gutter where he remained while a fight was carried on over him, our men eventually driving the enemy and taking possession of the ground. The ball is still in the wound, too deep at present to be extracted.

Elkton Academy closed, according to the *Whig*, when the legislature deprived it and West Nottingham Academy of funds. Trustees of Elkton Academy proposed to the School Commissioners that the building be handed over for use as a public high school. A recent law required that three public schools operate in the County, and one must be located in Elkton. "When the schools are again opened, we will learn whether the assessment of 20 cents on the hundred dollars will raise sufficient funds to give full effect to the Public School system of the county."

A correspondent from Company A, Fifth Maryland, wrote from camp before Petersburg on June 26, 1864. The *Whig* published the letter on July 2.

MR. EDITOR:—As most of your readers are aware, the 5th Maryland is at last really in front of the enemy. We reached fort Powhatan, South side James River, on afternoon 18th and bivouaced outside the Fort. Nineteenth, at daylight, were en route for City Point. Laid all night in the woods, and reached City Point; and finally by aid of steamer, Point of Rocks, Appomattox River, on evening of the 24th.

The Regiment was ordered to report the 21st to General Martindale, commanding 2nd Division, 18th Army Corps, and immediately assigned to the 1st Brigade—[Colonel Schley, by virtue of seniority commanding, and Lt. Col. March commanding Reg.]—Same night we were in front line of rifle pits, looking out for the "Johnnies," who were about 150 yards before us. And a little later, all hands were digging for dear life to have a better protection against morning from their sharpshooters.

We remained in the trenches until the night of the 23d, when we were ordered—all hands weary and worn with watching and work—to the rear for rest.—Think of *resting* just in front of our heaviest batteries and exposed night and day to the enemy's shells, answering their deep toned utterances.

The Regiment will probably go into the trenches to-night. Col. Schley has been relieved of the command of 1st Brigade, and ordered to report with his Regiment, to General Ames, commanding 3d Brigade, 2d Division.

The General is said to be an experienced officer, and the change meets the approbation of the regiment, as it thereby secures to it the personal services and experience of the Colonel.

The casualties thus far amount to 2 killed and seven wounded, which is regarded a small aggregate considering the strength of the Regiment. Companies A. and I. have occupied the same trench—A. has escaped entirely, while I. has lost three men, Orderly Sergt. Tuft and privates Bently and Opdyke, wounded. The loss of Sergt. Tuft is severely felt both by the officers and men of his Company and Regiment.

The writer had personal opportunity of observing his cool, calm courage hourly, and felt with others the moral influence of his soldierlike example in the performance of his duties in the trenches. Sitting some six feet from him when a mortar shell fell upon his leg and crushed it, there was no exclamation of agony as we generally hear—and when carried to the Surgeons, suffering intensely, he quietly remarked "I know it must come off, Doctor,

---

**MISS L. A. HUDSON,
FASHIONABLE
DRESS MAKER,**
RESPECTFULLY informs her friends and ladies generally, in the vicinity of Elkton, that she is prepared to FIT, make and braid anything in her line, with neatness and dispatch; also Stamping. Rooms at the late residence of Fredus Aldridge, Esq., 1st door below Mrs. Geo. Wells or 5th door above the meat and provision store of Joseph Wells, Esq., Elkton, Md.

be quick about it." Poor Tuft! It may in some degree cheer and comfort him to know that in the Regiment he holds, even in his humble position, the affection of every one. Such a man, Mr. Editor, is deserving of honors of gold.

There are nightly attacks on some portion of the lines, and duties are severe. A. and I. were complimented by a Gen. officer, on the night of the 23d. for their soldier-like "style."

Yours, Co. A.

The women of Elkton gave a supper for the returning Big Elk Rangers, who completed their three years' service. Of the 102 original enlistees, only 35 were mustered out in June 1864. The *Whig* [7/2/64] recalled the battles in which Company C participated and the soldiers who fell in each.

Their first battles were on the Peninsula, and their fame is mingled with names that cannot die; Gaines Mill, Peach Orchard, Savage Station, [where John Sowers fell, the first sacrifice by the Company to their country,] White Oak Swamp, Malvern Hill, Antietam—where Henry M. Bennett and Isaac Foreacre yielded up their lives in the cause of Liberty—Fredericksburg where William Kingston and Philip Johnson fell—Chancellorsville—where Lieut. Jordan was killed—Gettysburg—where Sergt. W. Davison and Corp. Samuel Biddle were killed—Mine Run, Auburn Hill, Wilderness, Po River, Spottsylvania, Toloptony Creek, Cold Harbor—where Hugh C. Jones was slain—and Petersburg, which closes the list of bloody fields so bravely trod by these now retiring veterans,—and where also their last sacrifice was made to the bloody Mars. Here William Sowers fell, two days before the company's time expired. His brother John was the first victim of the ensanguined strife. William passed through those three memorable years of blood and fire, and bore himself—how nobly his comrades in arms may tell—and died as the soldier hopes to die, with his face to the foe, midst 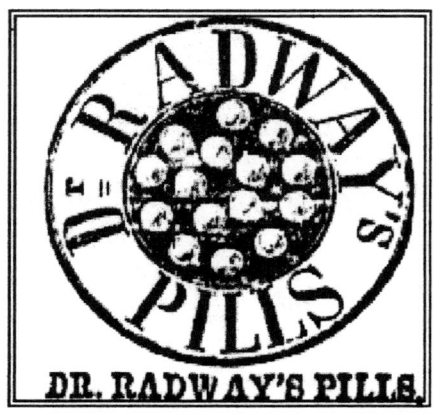 hurtling shot and shell. Of this band of braves, two perished by the stroke of disease—Thos. Jeffries and Robert McGowan. Twelve lives were yielded up in the service of their country, 35 were mustered out a few days since, and honorably discharged. The rest have been scattered by disease and wounds, leaving this remnant to receive the cordial welcome of "loved ones at home," which was tendered on the part of the ladies in a sumptuous supper, served up in Mr. Nicholas Hiss' lot under a tent pitched for the purpose.

The table was well provided with good substantial fare, and ornamented in the center with a handsome bouquet, the beauty of which was enhanced by miniature flags mingled with the flowers; and at either end of the well filled board, two large pound cakes were placed, one of them bearing the motto: "Presented by the Loyal Ladies of Elkton to Company C, 2d Del. Vols."

While the dessert was being served, which consisted of ice cream and cake, a choir of ladies and gentlemen sang "Home Again." The song, beautiful in itself, and so appropriate to the occasion, was received with touching effect.

After the supper was concluded, Jas. T. McCullough, W. J. Jones and H. R. Torbert, Esqs. delivered short and pathetic addresses of welcome to this little band of braves, seated round the festal board, while the quiet stars looked down, silent watches from heaven, upon them, as they have so often looked down upon the same brave spirits, as they slumbered round the camp fire, crouched watching on the solitary picket post, or stretched their weary limbs on the hoary battle plain. We remarked, as a significant feature of the times, that the slightest allusion to the name of Abraham Lincoln, was greeted by hearty cheers, from the soldier guests.

Remembering the old maxim, that "none but the brave deserve the fair," Mr. Torbert made a happy suggestion to all of them who were single men, now that they had so nobly sustained their country through three years' of fierce war, to choose from among those fair, who had from time to time, manifested so lively an interest in their welfare. The suggestion was received with a cheer from the guests and a blush and smile [approving] from the ladies.

After hearty cheers for General Grant, Abraham Lincoln, and their fair entertainers, this little remnant of the gallant Company of "Big Elk Rangers," of which there were less than twenty assembled, retired.

Three years ago they left their homes full of high hope, followed by the cheers and prayers of those who now extend to them a cordial welcome; yet mournful, when we look back over the well-fought fields they have so sternly trod, leaving a sacrifice of blood to hallow the ground, where shot and shell had thinned their ranks.

Major Hill of the 6th Md., who is at his home, in Elkton, suffering from a severe wound received in the Battle of the Wilderness, was invited as were all other soldiers in town. The Major was assigned the head of the table, and after the repast was concluded, was presented, by the ladies, with the center piece of one of the large cakes, with the compliments of the fair donors, which latter, we doubt not, were valued far above the gift. Captain Simpers, who was the last commander of the now disbanded Company, received from the same hands, the elegant bouquet which was woven by the fair fingers of Miss H. B. Altogether the entertainment was one of the most pleasant and best conducted, that we have ever had the pleasure of witnessing.

J. Tome renovated the banking room of the Cecil Bank. An Evans & Watson's Fire and Burglar Proof Safe, weighing five tons, was added. The walls were papered and the outer court tiled.

John E. Booth, son of Mr. J. Booth, died at Petersburg. He was with Company C. Purnell Legion.

The draft dragged on. The Board met again in June to supply the deficit of the first drawing. Out of 29 names drawn, 18 were commuted, 5 were unfit for service due to physical disability. One was in the Rebel army, 2 were said to be dead, and 3 did not show up at all. Eleven vacancies remained.

The *Whig* took exception to the commutation clause of the draft law. "It....defeats the primary object of that law, which is to raise men for the army, and that the only hope to make it effective was the repeals of the commutation clause, and thus require every drafted man not otherwise exempt to serve in the army or furnish a substitute."

Two more lawyers were admitted to the Elkton bar: Howard Ellis, son of F. A. Ellis, Esq., and W. Goldsborough, son of Rev. R. L. Goldsborough.

Capt. John Bennett of Elkton received a letter from his son Corp. Granville S. Bennett, Company C, 2nd Delaware Volunteers, who wrote that he was imprisoned by the rebels. Bennett reported that W. H. Founds, G. W. McNeal, Aquilla Mahan, and C. Reed, also of Company C, 2nd Delaware, were held with him. Also held were W. T. Forecacre [8th Md.] and James H. Stepter [6th Md.] slightly wounded. All were captured at the Battle of the Wilderness.

The *Whig* reported on Snow's Battery on July 23, 1864.

> In the encampment at Hanging Rock Ga, Va., on the 21st ult., this Battery lost the following in wounded and prisoners, besides losing four guns, five caissons and battery wagons; all of which occurred by not being properly supported by infantry.
>
> Wounded: John Powell, private
>
> Captured: one officer and twenty-four men: First Lieutenant James H. Kidd; John Russell, Wm. H. Jones, John C. Brown, P. T. Williams, I. T. Wilson, Wm. H. Lyle, Thomas P. Reed, Samuel B. Gray, Wm. Founds, Charles Griffin, A. J. Van Court, Wm. J. Jackson, W. S. Jackson, Robert Craig, M. P. Alexander, Joseph Rice, L. Wilson, D. I. Heckart, Samuel Miller, John H. Jones, John Simmers, John W. Gillespie, H. H. Bond and George N. Buckley. Some of the men were slightly wounded in the fight at Lynchburg, where they bore a very conspicuous part, the battery being charged upon several times, but the Rebs were driven back with canister.
>
> Yours & c., J.

Sgt John D. Tuft, 27, Company I, 5th Maryland, died at Fortress Monroe of complications from the leg amputation he suffered at Petersburg. His father was Wm. Tuft of the Fourth District.

[The Historical Society of Cecil County owns a fragment of the flag Tuft carried with him.]

In mid-July, rebel sympathizers occupied McCauley's thought according to three entrees in his diary. "Gunpowder Bridge partially destroyed by a company of rebel cavalry under Harry Gilmore," he wrote on July 11. "In Elkton the disloyalists are talking in groups and are evidently consulting."

On July 12, he added: "...excitement continues on account of rebel raid in Maryland—bell ringing and a company forming."

On the 15th, McCauley said: "It is reported that rebels have left Maryland [driving off 2,000 head of cattle and many horses].Sergeant James T. Lutton of Smith's Independent Cavalry is said to be recovering at a Salisbury, Md., hospital from a severe attack of typhoid fever."

The end of July signaled blackberry season in the county. Vendors came "from the barrens" into various towns early in the day to sell their wares.

Mr. Logan, postmaster at Charlestown, drew caustic remarks from the *Whig* when he allowed two con artists to use his home *and* the Post Office in their lottery scam.

> Quite a sensation was produced on Saturday evening last, by the arrest of two fancy looking gents calling themselves Johnson and Horn, who had been boarding at the house of Mr. Sam'l Logan, Post Master at Charlestown, in this county. They attempted to take "French leave" of their host, and leave him minus their board bill, by walking out in the evening, and taking the cars at North East. Mr. Logan pursued and had them arrested in the cars. The matter was about to be settled by the payment of the board bill, but W. J. Jones, Esq., late State's Attorney, happened to be present on the train, and ascertaining that the gentlemen in question had been operating rather mysteriously through the Charlestown post office in the bogus lottery policy business, demanded that the parties be detained by the sheriff, who, with his deputy, were at the time on the cars.
>
> A hearing was held before Justice Torbert, who committed the parties to jail for a further hearing on Monday morning.
>
> At the hearing on Monday morning, the evidence produced was insufficient to warrant the holding of the parties for Court, and they were liberated.
>
> An examination of the Charlestown post office books showed that from the 15th to the 17th last June 9, 1860 letters had been mailed by these parties to distant points, principally in the Western and Northwestern states. On inquiry, it appeared that so loose a system is pursued in postal matters at Charlestown, that those strange adventurers had free access to the mail bags, and conducted matters as they chose. Quite a number of circular letters, with a lottery policy enclosed, have been received by our citizens. An envelope directed to Fletcher & Co., New York, Box 3,743, was enclosed with each package. These circular letters gave a glowing account of a drawing that was to take place at Covington, Kentucky, the 30th of July, inviting the receiver to invest $10, and thus secure a fortune.
>
> This is the second lottery swindle that the Charlestown post office has been loaned to since Mr. Logan has been Post Master. These fellows might have been detected and sufficient proof procured against them to have convicted them had Mr. Logan lodged information of their doings immediately after the mailing of such heavy packages of letters.
>
> Reliable citizens of the neighborhood represent that these strangers had complete control of the mail and post office in Mr. Logan's absence, and sometimes refused to open the mail bags to receive letters that came to the office two hours before the mail was ready

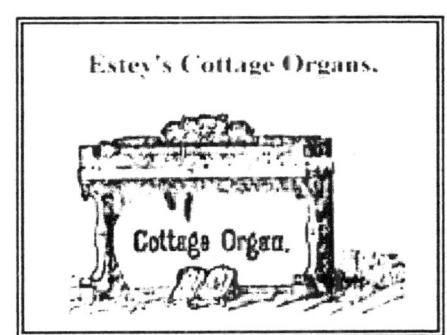

for delivery. A P. M. who allows the mail business to be conducted in so free and easy a manner is highly reprehensible.

The Hiss family, ardent supporters of Union soldiers, lost their 17-year-old son Thomas in a railroad accident. On July 30, 1864, the *Whig* described the scene.

> A train of empty freight cars going north, ran from the track at the "Blue Ball road," in town, about 7 o'clock. The switch-tender at the junction of the two main tracks discovered just as the train was approaching that he had lost his key, and was unable to adjust the track for running north. He went down the road a short distance with his flag, but he was either not seen by the engineer or the distance was too short in which to check the speed of the train. However, this would have made but little difference as the train would have run on another track; but some employee of the Company had early in the morning gone out with a hand car and opened one of the side switches a short distance above the main one, and neglected to close it again, and when coming to this the engine ran off and continued along the road for some ten or fifteen yards, when she stopped, the freight cars piling up in all conceivable positions behind, and displacing the track to some extent. Three or four of the front cars were badly broken, while the greater portion of the train remained on the track.
>
>
>
> **BUCKEYE REAPER & MOWER FOR 1864**
>
> By this mishap, Thomas Hiss, a brakesman on the train, eldest son of Mr. Nicholas Hiss, of this town, was instantly killed. He put down his own and another brake, and was running on the top of a car to put down a third one when the shock came, which threw him some distance in the air, and he fell on his head. He was quite young, about 17 years, and had been on the cars for about a year. He was devotedly attached to the business, having taken a great liking to it when very young. It is supposed he was the only brakesman on the train who was at his post when the alarm to brake was given. He was very careful and efficient, and a general favorite with the officers and employees of the Company. His remains were immediately taken to the residence of his father, a few hundred yards from the scene of the accident. With this exception, no one was injured on the train. The "wrecking train" came down from Wilmington, and in a short time the debris was cleared away, the track replaced, and trains passing over as usual.

West Nottingham and Elkton Academies closed, the *Whig* reported, when the Legislature cut off the $500-a-year donation. Miss Ada Pixley opened a "school for young ladies" at West Nottingham. The latter had to leave the South recently because she was born in the North. The editor wished her success with her venture and encouraged all Cecil Countians to lend the support that such an enterprise deserved.

But a letter arrived from Geo. K. Bechtel, Principal of West Nottingham, denying that the institution will close. There was such strong public support, he argued, that under no circumstances will the school be discontinued.

Shade trees died in Elkton, and the *Democrat* wondered if the new gas lines were responsible for their loss.

Thirty-seven black soldiers were recruited in Elkton during August, and five men sent substitutes. Only five more were needed to fill the quota. Some people, however, shirked their responsibility to contribute to the common fund. When so many volunteered and the quota filled rapidly, they invented excuses for not paying their share; they "lay the burden of getting clear of the draft on the shoulders, or rather the pockets, of their neighbors...those who have been striving with such commendable zeal to raise money sufficient to fill up the quota of the 3d district, are determined to let a draft supply the remainder, unless the shirks pay up their proportion, knowing those who have contributed liberally are competent to protect each other when the draft comes off."

"Efforts are making to rise money to give as bounty to volunteers—about 20 colored troops were ready to leave last night which required $5,000," wrote McCauley on August 10.

The *Whig* was disturbed that the 5th Maryland disintegrated as a military organization. "No better material ever shouldered a musket than the men of the 5th Md. Regiment, as the bloody field of Antietam attested, but commanded by an officer who skulked every battle, how could other than disgrace be the portion of the Regiment?"

From Weldon Railroad came an extract from a letter dated August 22, 1864 (*Whig* 8/27/64).

MERCANTILE
NEW STORE
IN
CHESAPEAKE CITY
J. M. REED
Has Just Opened with a Variety of
DRY GOODS,
CLOTHING
GROCERIES, &C.
TERMS
Positively Cash
OR ITS EQUIVALENT.

> We left our old camp on the 18th inst. and took possession of the Weldon Railroad. The 5th corps took the advance.—After we crossed the road, our Brigade [the Maryland Brigade] was sent to find the rebs, which we were not long in doing. We found them in about a half a mile. Our Brigade was in the front line. The rebs advanced on us and gave us an open fight for more than an hour, when we made them skedaddle.
>
> Our regiment [Purnell Legion] had 71 killed and wounded, and 14 missing. Seven were wounded in company H. George W. Porter was struck by thee balls—his wounds are dangerous. Clayton Zane was wounded in the shoulder and Thomas Green in the face, slightly.

Day before yesterday our regiment was sent on skirmish—the rebs drove us in, and brought on another fight when they got decently whipped. I wish they would attack us every day—nothing pleases us better.

We captured a whole brigade yesterday at one charge—prisoners were coming in all day.

In Company H there are but five men left. Lieut. McCauley is in command of the regiment, and Col. Graham of the Md. Brigade, in place of Col. Dushane, who was killed yesterday.

Gen. Warren gave the Md. Brigade great praise for their fight on the 18th. In yesterday's fight our regiment lost about 20 men and 2 officers. On the 18th we lost 4 officers—1 killed, 2 wounded and 1 missing.—Capt. Newton is missing, and is probably captured.

Isaac D. Davis, formerly of Company I, 5th Maryland, was commissioned Captain in the 118th Reg. U.S. Colored Troops.

In a card for Aetna Life Insurance of Hartford, Connecticut, readers learned that Dr. Charles M. Ellis was the agent for Cecil County. Drs. Ellis and Mitchell were the Company's medical examiners.

> HOTEL PROPERTY
> **At Private Sale,**
> THE HOTEL in the village of Brick Meeting House, known as the "Union Hotel," is offered at private sale by the subscriber. Apply to H. L. GUY, Carriage Manufacturer.
> Brick Meeting House, Cecil county, Md.
> P. S.—Also a SADDLE SHOP at the same place.

In August, the *Whig* pledged its support for the Lincoln-Johnson ticket in the coming election.

The *Whig* of September 9, 1864, noted that Henry R. Carter sold his Cherry Hill farm to I. D. Carter for $10,000. Henry was Lottie Carter Ricketts' uncle to whom her letters were addressed.

The drummer boy of the black recruits stationed near Elkton severely injured one finger of his left hand by the bursting of a gun.

The cornerstone of the Methodist Protestant Church in Chesapeake City was laid on September 7, 1864.

From Company H, Purnell Legion, came the sad news that George Porter of Cherry Hill and Hiram C. Zane of New Leeds died in a hospital in Bristol, Pennsylvania, from wounds received at Weldon Railroad.

McCauley, who worked closely with Zane's father, wrote on September 8, 1864: "Mr. Zane said his son Hiram died today at a hospital near Bristol, Pa., and he will bring on the body tomorrow." Subsequent notes indicated that the body was brought home in a pine coffin and buried at Cherry Hill.

In November, McCauley had the duty of delivering to the Terrell family a watch and $18 from their grandson, George W. Porter. When Porter was wounded at Weldon Road, he gave the items

UNDERTAKING

HAVING made a new and improved Hearse of the latest style, he is prepared to attend Funerals and furnish at the shortest notice Coffins of Rose-Wood, Mahogany, Walnut, or covered with cloth, and Metallic Burial Cases or Caskets, trimmed and finished in the newest and best styles with the finest materials. Silver Plates engraved with name, age and death furnished at short notice, when desired. Ice-Boxes for putting bodies in ice always ready. Having had a long experience in the business, he feels confidence in his ability to give entire satisfaction to all who may favor him with a call. All charges low, and no extra charge for attending funerals at any distance.

R. MARSHBANK

---

to Lt. McCauley to be delivered to his grandparents, who had reared him.

W. C. Rambo contracted to build two frame houses for Capt. Mike Really on the lot next to Maj. Hill's property in Elkton. Rudulph Bennett sold his storehouse in the west end of Elkton to W. H. Ricketts for $4,000.

Lieut. C. W. Palmer of Chesapeake City was appointed Deputy Provost Marshal for Cecil. He arrested Joseph Anderson of the same town as a deserter from Company A, 5th Maryland. Anderson escaped when his regiment was on its way to the front. "There are several more skulkers in this county who have received large bounties, that ought to be, and we hope will be, arrested and punished," the *Whig* observed.

Maj. J. C. Hill, formerly of the 6th Maryland, was promoted to Lieutenant Colonel of that regiment.

While black troops were in town, they were quartered in the fire house, and the engines moved outside. After the troops left, the engines remained out in the weather, much to the *Whig*'s chagrin.

Lt. P. H. Ellis, now an aide to General Torbert, wrote from Fisher's Hill on September 11, 1864: "The 1st Md., [reb] I learned, had been disbanded, and the members from Elkton, principally, have joined Harry Gilmor's command, who is now a Colonel. He is very badly wounded, and will, perhaps, never be able to take the field."

A Lincoln re-election meeting was considered a "very meager affair" in the view of the *Democrat*, but it reported that at a McClellan-Pendleton Club Meeting, 110 names were registered. Besides, a hickory pole and flags with the candidates' names graced the proceedings. Some degenerates, though, could not appreciate life's finer moments, for they hurled eggs at one another during a later meeting.

The *Democrat* commented further: "The supporters of Mr. Lincoln can no longer lay claim to this appellation. Mr. Lincoln has made the abolition of slavery the condition sine qua non of restoring the Union. Without slavery is abolished in every State, there can be no Union while Mr. Lincoln controls the administration. His party, therefore, have no right to call themselves hereafter 'Unconditional Unionists.'"

The death of Thomas Duling, 2nd Delaware, was noted in the *Democrat* on October 15, 1864. That same week the *Whig* outdid itself in disseminating useful information by publishing a long column under the creative headline: "Dead Horses and their Uses."

On the west banks of the Potomac, and about midway between the Long Bridge and Alexandria, stands what is called the bone factory of Messrs. Dawson & Hale. The establishment covers about half an acre of ground, and presents a conglomeration of old and new sheds of all sizes and at all angles. The firm owns one steamer and twelve barges, by means of which the carcasses are conveyed from Washington, Alexandria and Giesboro to their establishment.

The bodies, upon their arrival, are immediately divested of their hides, which, after being salted, are disposed of to the tanners. The hair of the manes and tails are washed and dried, and the larger part of the best quality exported to Europe, where it is manufactured into haircloth. The residue is disposed of in our own markets, and is used in various articles of commerce, but chiefly as curled hair.

After the hide is removed, the body is divided into small parts and conveyed to the tanks. These tanks are eleven in number, and capable of containing one hundred and forty bodies. Each tank has a steampipe connected with it, and these pipes are supplied with steam from a boiler of great capacity and power. The tanks are filled with flesh, and water is let into them from a Woodward pump, which answers well the double service of engine and pump. For nine hours the meat is steamed. At the end of that time the covers of the vats are removed, the oil is taken from the surface, and, after being cooled and strained, is put into barrels and sent to market. It is considered to be equal to any for lubricating purposes, except the finer fish oils. It is also used largely in soap making. The steaming process having been completed, the water is let out of the tanks, and the residuum of bones and other fibrous matter, thrown out upon a platform, where it undergoes a raking process, which separates the large hard bones from the small and softer ones. The hoofs are then selected, the shoes taken from them and sold as old iron; the shoeless hoofs are sold to the horn-comb makers, and other, in Philadelphia, where the parts suitable for combs are worked up, and the balance made into glue. When the large bones are separated and seasoned, they are ground into the fertilizer known as "bone dust."

The softer bones are taken, together with the pulp, and placed in sheds, where it lies for

---

FARM HANDS WANTED.

FOUR GOOD FARM HANDS WANTED to work from now to the 1st of December, to whom good wages will be paid.

Apply to   JAMES BENGE,
Kimbleville, Chester county, Pa.,
Fair Hill, Cecil county, Md.

a certain length of time under the action of sulfuric acid and other chemicals. It is then spread out in a dry atmosphere until all moisture evaporates, when it is ground to a coarse powder, and packed in barrels, or sacks ready for use.

By artificial means, this fertilizer can be prepared for market in thirty days, but it is not reckoned to produce so good an article as when prepared by the usual method, which makes an average time of four months. In quality, it ranks next to Peruvian guano, and readily commands from $60 to $65 per ton.

It will thus be seen that there is not a particle of the carcass of a horse wasted, everything being turned apparently to the best possible account. There are several of these establishments in the United States, but none that operates to such advantage.

At the beginning of this war the Government took the hides from the dead horses and buried their flayed bodies at Ball's Cross Roads and elsewhere, at a cost, it is said, or $50,000 a year. Now it receives from this firm $50,000 per annum to be allowed to take the animals off its hands. So in this little operation the country nets a saving annually of $100,000. Add to this the increase of capital accruing to the manufacturer and the farmer by the use of the materials obtained through the process above described, and it is not exaggeration to say this one establishment indirectly contributes to the wealth of the country in a single year $600,000.

The average number of bodies worked up per week for the last six months is three hundred and fifty.

DR. SCHENCK'S OWN CASE,
While laboring under Consumption and how his Pulmonic Syrup, Seaweed Tonic, and Mandrake Pills act on the system in Curing that Disease, and the
Great Success Attending It!!

The above is a correct likeness of Dr. Schenck, taken many years ago, after he had recovered from Consumption; by a course of his "SCHENCK'S PULMONIC SYRUP." The likeness, although it does not represent him anything like as bad as he was at the worst, yet it is in strong contrast with the hale and vigorous likeness of him at the present time. The contrast between these two portraits is so great that many would not believe them to be the same person. Yet there are hundreds of persons, in and around Philadelphia, who will recognize both portraits to be true representations When the first was taken he weighed 107 pounds; at the present time his weight is 200 pounds.

Two more young lawyers, Samuel Purnell and Reuben Haines were admitted to the Cecil Bar on the first day of court. The Democrats held a Grand Rally at Brick Meeting. At the October 22nd meeting of the Elkton Union Club, Thomas M. Coleman, Esq., former editor of the *Democrat*,

Dr. Schenck after being cured of consumption.

addressed the membership at the Court House. Immediately after, the Lincoln Invincible Torchlight Club urged its members to be present for the transaction of important business.

Tom Tyson, who took French leave from the Regiment for a few days last June, wrote a pro-Lincoln letter to the *Whig* [10/29/64] in which he mentioned how the prevailing sentiment in the military now favored Lincoln and would not vote for McClellan, whom they once so highly admired.

In late October, McCauley wrote that his son John of the Purnell Legion was mustered out of service. The father expressed his gratitude that the Lieutenant returned unharmed.

Frank Cummings, son of James Cummings of the 8th District, received a sword from the sergeants of his company in the 5th Pennsylvania Cavalry. The *Whig* quoted the *Philadelphia Press*: "On the Damascus blade is the motto 'Union and Liberty,' a patriotic arrangement of words to be put through a rebel traitor whenever an opportunity offers."

News of casualties in the 6th Maryland ran in the *Whig* [10/29/64]. It ended with a jab of "Damascus blade" at the Colonel.

Co. B—Wounded—Sergeant Thomas Duff, shoulder, slightly; Sergeant Joseph L. Mahan, left arm, slightly; Sergeant John W. McCullough, hip, severely; Privates—Amos H. Terry, hand, slightly. Missing—Daniel Emerson.

Co. E—Killed— Corporal William Luden, wounded. Wounded—Captain Henry Coggins, ankle, slightly; Sergeant George Tarburton, shoulder, slightly; Private George L. Price, foot, severely.

Co. G—Killed—Corporals Frederick McDunn, James F. Barrett. Wounded—Sergeant John R. Gallagher, leg, severely; Corporal Wesley Mendenhall, arm, severely; Private William T. Pierson, left arm amputated; Granville T. Morrison, arm, slightly.

Col. George R. Howard [formerly commander of that Reg.,] was *not* wounded, but probably will be by the men of that Regiment, on the 8th proximo.

What happens, pondered the *Whig*, when those who left the county to fight for the Confederacy become disillusioned and return home? Could those who lost relatives in the war be expected to welcome them back as returning heroes?

James Beers, Company B, 6th Maryland, died at De Camp General Hospital on David's Island. He was wounded at Petersburg.

Dr. B. J. Bing, dental surgeon, informed the public on November 11, 1864, that he would be in his office only on Saturdays for the next four months. While he attended medical lectures, his two assistants cared for patients. His ads were illustrated by a set of false teeth and his own poetry, distinguished chiefly by its length.

McCauley wrote of the death of Wm. T.[or L.?] Pierson, son of Peter P. Pierson: "He was a soldier in the 6th Maryland and was wounded with Sheridan in the Valley and removed to the hospital in Philadelphia where he died. He leaves a widow and three children."

A high school, under the direction of J. J. Tamanus, opened in the building once occupied by the Elkton Academy.

Notification appeared of the death of Sgt. Martin R. Reed, 40, Company E, 6th Maryland, who died September 19, 1864, at the Battle of Winchester.

A letter arrived from Fort Powell, Mobile Bay, Alabama.

EDITOR CECIL WHIG: —Sir—You will do me the kindness to publish the death of a young man by the name of Clarence G. Stanley, Co. B. 3d Md. Cavalry, who died at Fort Powell, Ala. September 23d, 1864.

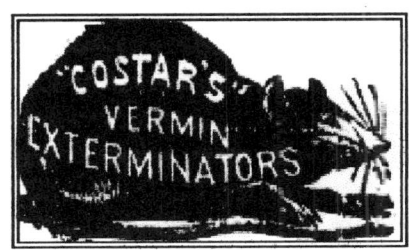

Unfortunately no one could tell the whereabouts of any of his friends. I remember hearing him say he had a sister living near Elkton, Md., is all the information I can get of any of his friends. He was born in S. Carolina; is buried on Little Dauphin Island, Mobile Bay.

By publishing the death of the young man, you will confer a great favor on his Captain.

JOHN S. PARKER
Captain Co. B.3d Md. Cavalry
Comm'd'g Fort Powell, Mobile Bay, Ala.

William T. Pierson, 31, son of Peter P. and Rebecca Pierson, died in early November from a wound received at the battle of Strausberg [*sic*] the previous month. His remains were brought from the U.S. Hospital, South and 24th Streets in Philadelphia for burial in Cherry Hill Cemetery.

A long ad appeared in the *Whig* [11/19/64] for Elkton High School, where Wm. H. Zimmerman was principal. It concluded with the directive: "Pupils entering the school at its commencement will bring with them such books as they may have on hand, until the books to be used are determined upon by the Board."

From the *Baltimore Clipper*, readers learned that William H. May was arrested in Baltimore by Government detectives and charged with having arrived there from behind enemy lines without reporting himself. He was interrogated before Colonel Woolley, and at the urging of his father, took the oath of allegiance. May was released on $5,000 bail.

The *Whig* ran a long article on Sherman's march through Georgia. It speculated where his new base of operations would be and listed the Confederate strongholds that now lay within his grasp.

On December 3, the same publication editorialized about the desirability of providing education for all citizens, regardless of color. The writer concluded: "We have demonstrated that fee labor is far preferable to slave labor and we know that intelligent free labor is far preferable to ignorant fee labor."

The railroad was often the scene of destruction in these years. A cow belonging to tanner Enos Reitzle was shot by soldiers on a passing train.

Vandals tampered with the railroad at Chestnut Hill, three miles north of Elkton. They built an obstruction so that a train traveling in either direction would be thrown off the track. The first train to encounter the obstacle was northbound, passing through Elkton at 7:40. The engine and three empty cars were thrown from the track. The engineer and brakesman were slightly injured, but the fireman was severely cut and scalded. Fortunately, the train was running slowly on the grade.

The following week the *Whig* reported that fireman Wm. Lindsay died of his wounds at the Felton House in Elkton. He had been under the care of Doctors Mitchell and Ellis. Lindsay was buried in Philadelphia.

> CANNED PEACHES, put up by Dr. H. H. Mitchell, for sale by
> ROSSELL AND HINES.

Normally marriages were noted very simply in the papers, but on December 3, the *Whig* gave the details of a wedding in a column that prefigured the society pages of later newspapers.

A WEDDING IN CHURCH.—Our town experienced one of those periodical excitements which set the fashionable world in a flutter and interest[ed] all ages, sects, and persuasions, in the rare occurrence of a Wedding in church, on Thursday evening last.

The happy couple were Mr. Wm. R. Nelson and Miss Mary A. Jones, both of Elkton. As the affair was to be attended with some ceremony and the bride very richly dressed, and no restrictions on witnessing the ceremony, the throng of curious spectators began to assemble in the yard of the M. E. church at 7 o'clock in the evening. The ceremony was to take place at 8½ o'clock and the doors of the church were not opened till eight.

By this time a dense crowd was assembled in front of the main entrance to the church, which reached back across the yard to the street, composed of all ages and sexes.—When at length the doors were opened the impatient masses that had been shivering in the frosty air, many of them for an hour and a half, made a rush for the building, and woe to crinoline and millinery that then ensued. The crush to this unsubstantial fabric of the sex was fearful, enlivened by the screams of some of the smaller specimens of humanity, who were threatened with the fate of being either crushed to death in the squeeze, or thrown down and having their lives trampled out by the multitude of feet passing irresistibly over them. Without any serious accident, however, the throng entered the church and were in a short time all comfortably seated.

At the appointed time, half-past eight, the bridal party arrived, and moved slowly up the aisle toward the altar, the target of a thousand eyes. The groomsman and bridesmaid were H. R. Torbert, Esq., and Miss Yhoe. The bridesmaid was dressed in a white Tarlton and her appearance elicited remarks of general admiration. The centre of attraction, however, was the bride, who was dressed in a magnificent white satin, with pointed bodice, large flowing sleeves, trimmed with lace, and a trail a yard in length rolled in pearly folds behind her satin slippered feet. Enveloped in an illusion veil, fastened to her hair with a bunch of orange blossoms, and leaning on the arm of the bride-groom elect, she moved solemnly up the aisle where the Rev. J. D. Curtis stood in readiness to unite for better, for worse.

The ceremony was performed with a ring, and when the moment arrived for the groom to place the golden circlet on the finger of the bride, her maid of honor raised the floating veil and presented the finger to receive the signet pledge. The solemn words "with this ring I do thee wed," a prayer and benediction were pronounced, and the twain were one flesh.

The bride now received the congratulations of her friends, while the church began to empty of its multitude. The bridal party retired to the home of the bride, where a reception was given to a party of select friends, and the next morning the happy couple left for Washington, on a bridal tour.

The Log Cabin schoolhouse, as it was popularly known, in the 8th District was vandalized in early December. The windows were smashed, the stove and desks broken or stolen.

Sgt. J. L. Mahan, Company B, 5th Maryland, was promoted to Adjutant with the rank of First Lieutenant in the same regiment.

Thomas H. Musgrove, who left the area three years ago to join the Confederacy, was arrested and imprisoned in Baltimore under suspicion of being a Rebel spy.

With the approach of Christmas, there was talk of upcoming parties and exhibitions. The county collected for a Christmas dinner for her soldiers in the field. And news of deaths in Battery B was published on December 10, 1864.

W. J. Founds, of Battery B, who was captured in Hunter's campaign in the Valley, is now sick at Jarvis Hospital. He reports the death of the following members of the Battery, from starvation and ill treatment by the Rebels

Herbert Bond died Oct. 3d at Savannah; W. H. Jones, Nov. 1st, at Millen; A. Jackson Vancourt, John C. Brown and another by the name of Jones from near Slate Ridge, Harford county, time and place of their death not given. Geo. Buckley was left at Andersonville, on the 7th of September, very ill, and has not been heard from since.

Blood! Blood! Blood!
Helbold's Extract Sarsaparilla.
SYPHILIS
This is an affection of the Blood, and attacks the Sexual Organs, Linings of the Nose, Ears, Throat, Windpipe and other Mucus Surfaces, making its appearance in the form of Ulcers. Helmbold's Extract Sarsaparilla purifies the Blood and removes all Scaly Eruptions of the Skin giving to the complexion a Clear and Healthy Color.

From a paroled prisoner, A. H. Snyder, of Co. C. 2d Del. Vols., who landed at Annapolis, on the 1st of December, we learn the following facts of some of our Cecil county boys, who are now in captivity or have died from hardships incident thereto, among the rebels. Including Mr. Snyder, there are seven; Martin V. Anderson, G. W. McNeal, J. H. Pigeon, and A. Mahan, are now in South Carolina. Chas. H. Reed and James Mahan died at Andersonville.

Maj. Ben Ricketts' sister Rachel married Dr. D. F. Ricketts, USN, at the bride's residence [Elk Vale] on Monday, December 12, 1864.

James and Ellen Hevalow lost 4 children in ten days; George K. in his 4th year; James in his 6th year; Martha R. in her 3d year; and Emma B. in her 7th year. The cause of death was not reported.

Two different tableaux were presented at the Court House on December 27 and 28, for the benefit of the poor of the town and the soldiers. The Christian Commission sponsored the events. The *Whig* encouraged all to attend. In addition to Oriental scenes and costumes, there were performances, "interspersed with ludicrous representation—the blind god leading in chains tottering, gray haired age, and blooming youth, with many other laughable scenes of a miscellaneous character, taking off the customs of the times, and the weaknesses of human nature." The stage was illuminated with gaslights supplied by a donation from Messrs. Warner, Miskey & Merrill, gas fitters of Philadelphia.

Lt. J. Kidd, Snow's Battery, recently released from a Rebel prison, told the *Whig* of atrocities he has endured.

...Lt. Kidd was confined in several Rebel prisons, or pens in the open field, where our prisoners are herded in the open air like cattle, their food consisting principally of corn meal, ground down like horse-feed, without sifting. The prisoners were moved from place to place, several times, when their treatment was somewhat varied, but always marked by barbarian cruelty. In Virginia they were treated with the most savage barbarity, and in South Carolina, with the most semblance of lenity.

Many died from cruelty, and some have been induced, to escape the horrors of a frightful death, by that loathsome disease, the scurvy, to join the Rebel cause.

While confined in South Carolina, a number of officers made their escape, by walking off when detailed to get wood. Their guards were the militia of the district, and many of them Union men, who were very careless about watching their charge.

Lieut. Morris, of the 5th Md., and Martin V. Anderson, of Co. C. 2d Del, also returned from a long captivity in rebeldom.

The year ended on a lighter note. A heavy snowfall was followed by slush, rain and drizzle. But then the wind shifted to the North, and a sudden freeze covered the roads with a sheet of ice. Then "sleigh bells made the welkin vocal with their merry chime."

INPECTINE
The Persian Fever Charm

For the prevention and cure of FEVER and AGUE and BILIOUS FEVERS. This wonderful remedy was brought to the knowledge of the present proprietors by a friend who had been a great traveler in Persia and the Holy Land.

While going down the river Euphrates, he experienced a SEVERE attack of FEVER and AGUE. On discovering his condition, one of the Boatmen took from his person and AMULET, saying, "Wear this and no Fever will touch you." Although incredulous as to its virtues, he complied and experienced immediate relief, and has since always found it an effectual protection from all malarious complaints.

On further investigation he found that the boatman attributed to it MIRACULOUS powers, and said that it could only be obtained from the Priest of the Sun. Sometime afterwards the gentleman in conversing with a Priest obtained from him the secret of its preparation and ascertained where the medicinal herbs were found, of which it was compounded. The wonderful virtues of this article have induced a full belief in the minds of the natives in the miraculous healing powers of the Priests.

Since his return to America, it has been tried with the happiest effect by several Ladies and Gentlemen of high character, who have given it the most unqualified praise. This remedy having been a specific in Persia for hundreds of years for the prevention and cure of Fever and Ague and Bilious Fever is now offered to the American people.

It will be sent by mail, prepaid, with full directions for use on receipt of one dollar.

Principal Depot and Manufactory, Main St., Richmond, Va. Branch office, Bank of Commerce, New York. Address JOHN WILCOX & CO.

6

Cecil County

1865

The *Whig* saw at least one bright spot in the severe weather that greeted the new year: the sleighing was superb, "and from the number of dashing sleighs and clashing, rattling, chiming bells, all who can manage to procure teams are enjoying the sport." The *Democrat* mentioned ice skating parties by moonlight.

William H. Eder, mail agent on the way line between Washington and Philadelphia, was promoted to head clerk on the railway post office car between Washington and Philadelphia. In April, he was credited with an invention that agents on the mail cars found useful. The *Whig* of April 29, 1865, wrote:

> It is a table about 8 feet by 8 feet. On this table are placed three half circle rows of boxes, each row rising above the other like steps. The divisions are movable, so that the boxes can be made to any desired size. By a half circular endenture in the table the depositor is able to reach any of the boxes without a change of position. When the matter is distributed and ready to be made up, a sliding board is pulled out which is used for folding the packages on, previous to their being put in their several pouches. At either side there is a drawer, one for paper, the other for twine. The advantages of this table are that it takes very little room, is readily changed from one place to another, and in assorting the letters for the different post offices, each letter is put in its proper place without the agent or clerk changing his position; whereas by the present system the mail matter has to be gone over several times, and in the "pidgeon box" arrangement, the distance from "A" to "Z" is some ten feet, which has to be walked over. This table will lessen the labor, while it will greatly expedite the assorting of the mail matter. It will prove a valuable article to the Post Office department, and will no doubt meet with favor at the hands of the Government. Mr. Heatzig, cabinet maker, furnished the first one of these tables this week, and it has been sent on to Washington.

Former Elkton resident P. C. Pearce bought Stockton House in New Castle, Delaware, from Mr. Broomfield for $7,500.

Capt. F. Layman of Chesapeake City sold a 4-year-old colt for $500. Jas. B. Marrett of Elkton owned the sire, Young Archy; Mr. W. Boulden owned the unnamed dam.

H. L. Guy of Brick Meeting house sold his carriage shop to Henry Hedley, who planned to continue the operation.

Martin V. B. Anderson, 21, died at his home in Cherry Hill. He enlisted in Company C, 2nd Delaware, in November 1861, but was captured in October 1863. "He remained in confinement in rebel prisons," said the *Whig*, "for fourteen months, and was released to return home, like too many victims of rebel barbarity and barbarism to die."

The Union, too, had its share of evildoers, according to the writer of the following letter in the same issue, January 7, 1865.

CAMP OF 6TH MD. VOLS.

Weldon Railroad, Va., Jan. 1st, 1865

MR. EDITOR.—Thinking a few lines from our regiment might prove interesting to some of your readers, I concluded to write the same, hoping that you may find room for them in the columns of your paper.

I shall not attempt to give you any news, but merely write a few facts in regard to the ungenerous manner in which we have been treated since rejoining the Army of the Potomac, about three weeks ago.

We have served more than two years in the army and have never before complained publicly. But now that we suffer almost daily from hunger, we think it quite time to say something. We do not wish to cast any part of the blame upon any of our Regimental or Company officers, for with them we have shared the dangers of the battle-field and quiet of the camp. Our connection with them for so long a period has served to bind our hearts together with the ties of lasting friendship. But we speak of those unprincipled miscreants who are robbing the soldiers of what justly belongs to them, and filling their pockets with their ill-gotten booty. These men in time of danger, are far in the rear. They have never heard the whistling of the bullet, the shrieks of the wounded, or the groans of the dying. Duty calls them not to

NEW LIQUOR STORE.
Brandies, Wines, Monongahela and Rye Whiskies.
AT WHOLESALE AND RETAIL.
Those dealing in our line are certain of procuring the best brands at the most reasonable rates, by calling on us at our NEW LIQUOR STORE, just opened on Main Street in "the Hollow"—Morgan's old stand.

HURRY & CO.

the front in time of battle,—neither do they suffer the hardships of the march.—To cold and hunger they are strangers, [at least since wearing the shoulderstraps of Captain and C. S.]

We well know that our Government allows its soldiers an abundance of rations, and when the regular ration is served, no soldier can eat his allowance. But during the last three weeks our rations have been so very scant, that we have suffered from hunger almost daily. A great many of the men wrote to their friends at home to send them by express boxes of edibles, some of which have been received although the receipts from the express agents have been forwarded to us by our friends and been received long ago. And now, sir, would you not call this ill treatment to men who have left home and friends to share the danger of the battle field and strike for that which every good man should be willing to battle for—*freedom and Liberty?*

In conclusion we would tender the thanks of the Sixth Maryland to those to whom we are indebted for an excellent Christmas dinner, which was received in due time; and we sincerely trust that when another Christmas day comes, our country shall be at peace and *Commissaries* and the *Confederacy* be numbered among the things of the past.

A ROWLANDSVILLE BOY

A note appeared under the ominous heading, U.S. INTERNAL REVENUE, reminding the people that the 5 per cent tax imposed upon their gains, profits, and incomes by the Joint Resolution of Congress, was due before the end of the month.

The *Democrat* pointed out that those who required the services of an auctioneer could reach Mr. Kidd at Corner Ketch or Nottingham.

The *Whig* said of Creswell's speech delivered in the House of Representatives: "It is a masterly argument in favor of abolishing slavery throughout the entire domain, by constitutional amendment, as provided for in that instrument.

"...It will be the regret of every true lover of his country, that the secession influence was *permitted* to dominate in this congressional district at the last fall election, by which means Mr. Creswell was not returned to Congress the next term."

Then the editor quoted the Cincinnati *Gazette:*

> ...Mr. Creswell, of Maryland, took the house by surprise with a speech in favor of the constitutional amendment prohibiting slavery, so able and even eloquent as to receive the closest attention during its delivery, loud manifestations of applause from members on the

---

HARE'S IMPROVED STONEWARE AIR-TIGHT PRESERVING JARS.—These Jars have been in use several years for preserving all kinds of Fruit in a fresh condition such as Cherries, Blackberries, Huckleberries, Peaches, Pears, Apples, Tomatoes, &c. For sale by

E. W. STAPLES.

floor, and at its close an eulogy from Thad. Stevens, in the opening remarks of the speech with which he followed it, more hearty and generous than the old veteran gives, except in the rarest cases. Mr. Creswell's anti-slavery utterances were of the most intensely radical character, and yet they gained weight from the fact, which he took care to emphasize, that he came of Maryland slaveholding ancestry.

A Mr. Robinson, "in a state of intoxication" stepped off a tug in the C & D Canal. Nobody missed him until his hat, which was more buoyant than its owner, was spotted on the water. According to the *Whig* [1/28/65], the body was found after a search.

Two notices regarding the Killingsworths of North East also appeared in that issue. A warehouse occupied by Killingsworth & Son was offered for rent.

John C. Killingsworth, son of O. P. Killingsworth, was appointed chief clerk of the quartermaster's department of General Sheridan's command, the Middle Military Division.

James Marrett, 54, mentioned above as the owner of a mare, died in Elkton.

The *Whig* corrected an error from the previous week in its reporting of the marriage of D. K. Price, 5th Maryland, and Mary E. Reynolds, both of North East.

On February 4, 1865, the *Whig* published a

> **WANTED.**
> **All the Buckwheat in Cecil County**
> At the highest market price, for which the cash will be paid, by the subscribers, at WOOLLENS' MILL, three miles east of Brick Meeting House, and two miles north of Blue Ball.
> WOOLEN & BROWN.
> Little Elk Mills, October 29, 1864

list of names with the following explanation: "It will be seen that only about 200 persons in this county have made returns of Income, all others claiming to fall below the $600 exempt by law from taxation. In order to ascertain the exact amount of Income of an individual, $600 must be added to the amounts published, that sum being deducted the Assessor, and the taxable amount only placed on the lists, a copy of which is here published."

J. J. McCullough's income, for example was $10,262 (plus $600), while W. H. Drummond's was $5 (plus $600).

Dr. J. H. Brown, a black phrenologist from Baltimore, lectured in Elkton for the benefit of the Elkton Colored Church.

Photographer B. E. Lodore sold "gem pictures" in his studio on Main Street. "These likenesses are very cheap and very pretty, a set composed of four, eight or twelve, being furnished for a dollar. As they increase in number, the cost of the likeness is, of course, decreased. The smallest size being adapted for setting in rings, breastpins, seals, &c."

A correspondent signed "Occasional" complained about Demon Rum.

A stranger, passing along one of our highways, not far from our village, a few days since, was struck with the appearance of two or three small tenements along the roadside. The signs for one were four dogs, and a pig leaning up against the fence in the sun; the others, fully represented by the canine race, without the swine. He stopped to inquire for a tavern, when the following conversation took place:

"We keep tavern."

"You do? What are your accommodations for travelers?"

"We don't keep no travelers."

"How do you keep tavern, then?"

"We sell whiskey."

"How do you get a license without having accommodations for man and beast?"

"We get restorant license."

"Where is your restaurant?"

"Up there, on that shelf."

"Six black bottles and a keg on the floor with a spiggot in it. Is that what you call a restaurant?"

"We don't care what you call it. We sell whiskey."

Passing along about three hundred yards further, he found three more houses of a corresponding kind. Taking another road toward Bay View, in a most secluded byroad, he came across a small house, not too large for a good chicken coop, he observed the symptoms of another such restaurant.

The proprietor of ebony hue, with an assistant, one of the sons of Erin, seemed to be doing considerable business.

Poor, down-trodden Maryland. No wonder she has not prospered, when the most abandoned creatures on earth can procure a license to deal out this, the worst of poison, in any community, by paying the paltry price of the boasted restaurant license. Don't need a single signature to his application for the privilege of poisoning the morals of a neighborhood.

Cannot our legislature, with the much boasted-of New Constitution, remedy this evil? Wonder if there is a state in the Union, now, with such a miserable license system. We will patiently wait to see.

CLERK WANTED.

A YOUNG MAN who has some experience in a country Store, can get a permanent situation, (if well recommended for honesty, sobriety and capacity,) by applying to

A. B. CARSON,
Port Deposit.

A Pennsylvania paper, the *Delaware County Republican*, wrote: "We were shown a few days since, an artificial jaw, with teeth attached, which had been made for a soldier who had been deprived of that useful appendage by a rebel musket ball, that carried away, in its course, a portion of the bones of the face. This artificial jaw is said by competent judges to be the most complete arrangement of the kind ever manufactured. It was made at the Pennsylvania College of Dental Surgery, by Dr. B. J. Bing of Elkton, Maryland."

At the end of the month, Dr. Bing went to Cuba to make a set of teeth for an unnamed "gentleman of renown, who, having heard of the doctor's professional skill, pays him liberally for the undertaking."

Under the headline, "What a Toad Did for a Soldier," the *Whig* ran a story [2/18/65] about a sleeping soldier whose leg wound was attracting flies. A toad hopped into the tent and "gobbled up the blue-bottles double quick. The moment [a fly] alighted within six inches of the spot, he [the toad] would square himself for the attack, his eye twinkling with excitement, and then with a flash of his tongue and a smack of his mouth, the unlucky insect would disappear."

When the soldier wakened, he was not overjoyed at the presence of an "ugly toad" so near him. But somebody pointed out the service the animal was rendering, and all present thanked him and nominated him for membership in the Sanitary Commission.

Both papers noted the death of John Rowan. The *Whig* wrote with just a hint of sarcasm.

KILLED.—John B. Rowan, who left this county in the fall of 1862, and joined the Rebel army, where he has served, since then, as an officer in an artillery company, was killed at the battle of Nashville, where Hood's army so narrowly escaped annihilation by Thomas. Of the little band of traitors, who left this county for their country's good, about that time, he is the only one, we believe, that has been killed. Rowan was killed by a piece of shell passing through his body.

The *Democrat* reported the death and concluded with a quotation from one of Rowan's friends: "He was the life of the camp, the star of the battalion, the pride of us all."

Married.

PRICE—REYNOLDS—At the residence of Mr. D. K. Price, on Bohemia Manor, on the evening of the 12th inst., by Rev. A. Wiggins, JAMES R. PRICE, of the 5th Md. Reg., and MARY E. REYNOLDS, both of North East.

[Owing to a little oversight, the above marriage was published wrong in *The Whig* of last week. The happy couple were united on the 12th inst., and by the Rev. Mr. Wiggins, and *not* on the 17th, and by the Rev. J. H. Jones, as published last week.]

Correction of Jan. 28, 1865

William Ritter saw Rowan fall and escorted his body to Elkton. Thirty-seven years later, the *Perryville Record* ran a column on October 14, 1902, under the headline, "Honor to Elkton Man."

The monument authorized by the State to the memory of the Soldiers of both armies who shared in the battles around Chattanooga, Tenn., erected at Orchard Knobb, near General Grant's headquarters, was dedicated on Thursday. The monument is a Corinthian column surmounted by the figure of a Union Color-bearer and cost $7,000. It commemorates especially the work of Maryland's Blue and Gray on the field of Chickamauga. There are two statues on buttresses at the base, one typifying a Confederate artilleryman watching the effect of a shot just fired and the other a Union infantry soldier standing at rest. On the plinch [sic] above the base are four inscribed tablets, one reads:

"Third Battery, Maryland Artillery, Confederate States of America, Capt. John B. Rowan, Lieut. William L. Ritter, Artillery Battalion, Stevenson's Division, Hardee's Corps, etc." The other reads

---

LOOK HERE.

THE undersigned is prepared to furnish or make to order CASTINGS for all the Plows in general use in the neighborhood. ODD CASTINGS for Stoves and Machinery. And having a good Blacksmith, is also prepared to do Horse-Showing and country smithing generally.

A good assortment of PLOWS & CASTINGS always on hand, at the Elkton Foundry, corner of Main and Bridge streets.

THOS. J. JONES.

"Third Maryland Veteran Volunteer Infantry, Col. Joseph M. Sundsburgh, First Brigade, First Division, Twelfth Corps, United States Army, etc."

Capt. John B. Rowan is buried in Elkton Presbyterian Cemetery. He was a brilliant young lawyer in Cecil in the years just previous to the war. With other Elktonians he wore the gray and fell at Nashville. Capt. William L. Ritter, his comrade-in-arms, married his widow, a daughter of the late Thomas A. Howard, of Elkton.

Someone left unattended a cauldron of scalding water on John Plummer's porch. His 18-month-old daughter tipped it over on herself and died within a few hours.

Notice was received that Mahlon H. West, Company D, 4th Maryland Regiment, son of W. T. West, died last August in Andersonville.

The *Whig* reported the examination of teachers on March 11, 1865.

On Tuesday last, the annual examination of teachers for the Public Schools of this county was held in the County Commissioners' and School Commissioners' rooms.—Both rooms were pretty well filled with aspirants to scholastic honors, composed largely of young ladies. There were 38 candidates, 37 of whom passed the examination and received certificates from the board of examiners. This Board is composed of three of the school commissioners, Messrs. F. A. Ellis, C. C. Brokaw, and Dr. S. B. Stubbs. The Doctor was absent on this occasion, the two former constituting the Board.

The following are the names of the successful candidates, with their post-office address, who received teachers' certificates:

John Galbraith, Susan Roe, Maria Devinney, Sallie A. Campbell, Elizabeth M. Hays, Laura V. Crouch, Marian S. Kershaw,—post office address, Elkton. John A. Rick, Ella C. Houck,—Chesapeake City. Lydia Field, Nathan L. Janney, Levinia A. Benjamin, Sallie H. Gamble, Jannie C. Trimble, Emma M. Russel, Bell R. Galbraith, Rachel E. Janney, Josephine E. Janney,—Bay View. Emma Wilson, Harriet A. Wilson,—Oxford, Chester county, Pa. Lizzie Ely,—Nottingham, Chester county, Pa. Annie E. Jenkins, Rock Springs. Martha E. Jackson, Emma J. Cregg, Emma J. McCall, Sarah F. McCall,—Principio Furnace. Carrie A. Griest,—Rising Sun. Edward P. Chandlee, Lizzie W. Morgan,—Cecilton. Ettie A. Kirk, Phoebe A. Moore, M. Augusta Brown,—B. M. House. Arthur A. Mackie,—Fair Hill. Edith S. Hanna,—Lisle, Lancaster co., Pa. Rebecca B. Moore,—Hickory Hill, Chester co., Pa. Maria Christie,—Rowlandsville. S. Sherer,—New London, Chester county, Pa.

> **Whiskers! Whiskers!**
> Do you want Whiskers or Moustaches? Our Grecian Compound will force them to grow on the smoothest face or chin, or hair on bald heads, in Six Weeks. Price, $1.00 — 3 packages for $2.00. Sent by mail anywhere, closely sealed, on receipt of price.
> Address   WARNER & CO.,
> Box 138, Brooklyn, N. Y.

Richard F. May, formerly of Elkton, was drafted in Indianapolis under the present call for 300,000 troops.

It appeared that in 1865, a correspondent, perhaps comparable to a free lance writer today, visited the towns of the county in turn and wrote a column of his observations. On March 11, he reported on Bay View. In his own mind, at least, he was qualified to judge the morals of the people in this life and to assign their places in the next.

> Bay View is a somewhat noted village, quite distinctly marked on a late map of Cecil County, located at the dividing line between the 5th and 9th Districts, about three miles from North East and two from Zion. Nearly everything indicates a want of progress and enterprise. The fencing around two lots in the center of "this great emporium" has disappeared, giving a wide range for swine and other animals. The Methodist Protestant parsonnage [a comfortable dwelling, recently erected] is not yet enclosed or painted. A commodious storehouse, finished years ago, has not yet been occupied, &c., &cc.
>
> The march of moral improvement seems to keep pace with significant surroundings. Some old professors, who have been going backward and forward, in and out, of "the

narrow way" for many years, unless they steer a straight course in the future, will not likely ever reach the "Celestial City."

A passing stranger would certainly regard this as a very loyal place. Two liberty poles attract the gaze, standing about one hundred yards apart, on a parallel line, due North and South—each however, occasionally displays "the good old flag," an emblem dear to every truly loyal American heart. "Long may it wave O'er the land of the free, and the home of the brave."

> **For Sale, Rent and Lease.**
> **For Sale, 2 Small Farms**
> NEAR PORT DEPOSIT;
> **FIVE NEAT DWELLINGS,**
> In the town of Port Deposit. Will be sold on good Terms. ALSO,
> Several Small Dwellings for Rent,
> and
> **BUILDING LOTS FOR LEASE**
> J. R. COULSON,
> Port Deposit.

The principal points of attraction to worldlings are Reed's Store and the "Bay View Inn," otherwise called the "Cave," owing to the fact that the bar is kept in the basement. At the former place men of leisure, idlers, pedagogues, political bores, whiskey tinctured gentry and hysterical old bachelors meet daily and nightly to discuss the great questions of the day—"The draft," "The assumptions of Lincoln," "The chances of the Southern Confederacy," and "The status of the negro." These discussions, however, are not likely to pass into history. Although a luminous periodical called the *Age* has shed a flood of light upon the latter question, our disputants have not yet fully determined whether negroes are men or monkeys! The proprietor of the establishment, although too good natured for the age and country in which he lives, has his soul occasionally vexed beyond the powers of endurance, and when his ire bursts forth "all must stand from under." The keeper of the "Cave" is a man of influence and business energy, and withal quite popular of the "ardent;" and though moralists may quarrel with and denounce the traffic, loyal citizens must "submit to the powers which be." In the pure days of the Republic he was but an old line Whig. His political whereabouts now, is hard to determine. May he become righteous before he dies. Another liquor establishment is kept in the southern precincts of the village. The owner is a good-looking bachelor of well developed physical proportions, and withal said to be quite popular with the ladies. Whether he will pass through life "solitary and alone," the future must determine....

Iron Hill Irish in the persons of Patrick Sullivan, Timothy O'Ruke, John O'Donnel, and Michael Quinlan landed in jail for their exploits and were held for a hearing before Justice Torbert. Sullivan was fined $1 and costs, but the others were held under a bail of $500 each. But let the *Whig* describe their antics in its own inimitable style:

On Sunday last, several natives of the Green Isle, hailing from the classic locality of Iron Hill, came down to renew their spiritual strength,—and succeeded to some extent,—but the supply on hand becoming exhausted, they proceeded to the Railroad Hotel, where they demanded a fresh supply, at the back door. They were told by a small boy—the only person in that part of the house—that they could not get any. They then passed through an entry to the door leading to the barroom. Here they commenced kicking the door down. While engaged in this very peaceable business, the barkeeper made his appearance, when a fight ensued, and the crowd becoming larger it was extended to the street. One of the Irishmen cut the barkeeper's head with a large knife, and one or two of the rioters were knocked down, and the claret made to flow pretty freely. During the fight clubs and stones were used in handsome style. Deputy Sheriff Janney made his appearance, and by the aid of several citizens, soon succeeded in arresting four of the rioters. The others escaped.

> **ALEX R. SHAW, M.D.,**
> **Homeopathist,**
> HAVING permanently located in Newark, Del., offers his professional services to the citizens of Newark and surrounding country. Office and residence on Main street, opposite Choat's Hotel.
> All calls in town and country promptly attended.

The *Democrat* added the following information to the story: "The four that were caught posted $500 bail each, to appear in the next Circuit Court to be held in April, when they will be duly punished by Judge Price, who hates whiskey generally and Sunday whiskey in particular."

In the Sixth District a new post office was established at what was called Vinegar Hill, Stony Batter, and Mount Pleasant Residents of the area decided to discard all the old names, and the new office was named Mt. Vista. James Trimble, who recently opened a store in the area, was post master. The office was to be "supplied tri-weekly by the Oxford and Port Deposit routes."

On March 18, 1865, the *Whig* reported irregularities in the enrollment process.

We announced in our last issue that 20 men had been mustered in to fill the quota of the 3d district. When the men were taken to Baltimore, however, they were tampered with by those sharks, the substitute brokers and their agents, till dissatisfaction was engendered among them and they refused to be sworn in. The government officers and substitute brokers appear to be in partnership for the sole purpose of cheating the government and the people. The exposures made by Detective Baker, recently, prove this fact pretty conclusively; but Presidential leniency encourages all such rascality, and of course it will continue to the end. The substitute brokers and their agents didn't make much, however, by their efforts on the squad of men who went from here last week, for in a few days they were back in Elkton, ready to go on another like expedition. So on Tuesday morning last six of the men were taken to Easton, where they were to be sworn in and then returned to Elkton to finish recruiting the quota of the district.

In justice to those who have taken an active and disinterested part in filling former, as well as the present quotas, we will state that they have come in for their full share of slander by the foul tongues of those who sit at home and give little when money is required, and do less in the way of personal exertions to have the quotas made up.

> **STRAYED**
>
> FROM the farm of the subscriber, about the 10th of June, a PALE-RED OX, with large horns. Any person returning, or giving information of said Ox will be reasonably rewarded.
>
> ELI COSGROVE

Melting ice sent the Susquehanna on an unparalleled spring rampage. The steam ferry-boat *Maryland* was carried down on the flats as it crossed with the Saturday morning train. Between Havre de Grace and Perryville, telegraph wires that crossed the river under the stream bed were swept away. The road between Perryville and Port Deposit was impassable, and lumber was washed from yards in the latter town. Streets and cellars were inundated there, too.

Upstream, John and David Shure lost several head of stock and a tobacco house with its contents of several thousand tons of tobacco. The rolling mill of the McCullough Iron Company and the flowering [flour?] mill of J. S. Christie & Co. were submerged but no serious damage ensued. From Harrisburg down, though, the freshet splintered bridges and crushed homes.

Dr. R. Wakeman and J. L. Ballance of Port Deposit patented a power machine for baling hay. The hay fed into it was cut into ¾-inch pieces. The pieces fell into a packer, where they were compressed into a solid mass. When a bale formed, it was tied with wire and rolled out. The bales weighed about 500 pounds and measured 4 feet by 2 feet by 2 feet.

The *Whig* praised Port Deposit when the town tore up "the old rip-rap stone pavements" and replaced it with "broad, square granite blocks."

Maj. E. F. M. Faehtz, 8th Md. Vols., was promoted to Lieutenant Colonel of that regiment. The *Whig* declared: "There isn't a better or braver soldier in the army, than Faehtz, and we are glad to hear of his promotion."

Dr. J. Dunott and his son, Dr. Thos. J. Dunott, packed up and left the county to open a drug store and continue their practice in Frederick City, Maryland.

Under the headline, "Tragedy in Mount Pleasant," the *Democrat* ran the heart-rending tale of Miss Gyp, who lately made her home with the family of H. E. R. Master. She loved not wisely, but too well, and became the mother of healthy offspring. When H. E. R. Master returned, he flew into a rage when confronted with the situation. Ignoring the pleas of his family and the cries of the distraught mother, he drowned it, but so far has escaped the county officers. "Until the commission of this inhuman act he was looked upon by his neighbors as a respectable, well-behaved man, and some now think him insane." Astute readers realized that the date of this story was *April 1*, 1865.

The *Whig* launched a two-fisted attack on Richard Miller, turnkey at the Elkton jail. The well there went from bad to worse. "The rain water has through the flood season of the present spring found the well a convenient reservoir; the filth of the yard has found it a convenient sewer; and numberless melancholy rats, a convenient place to commit suicide; If the jail well doesn't receive the attention of Miller or some other explorer of those aqueous lower regions speedily, we will not be surprised to find the prospectus of a new oil company published, based upon the strong indication of oil discovered in the waters of the jail well."

But the editor was not through with Miller yet. In the same column, he remarked: "...Mr. Richard Miller, who has held the position of Turnkey of the Elkton jail for some years past, but whose patriotism and big bounty induced him to go to Baltimore to enlist, a few weeks since, but who, when he got there, let 'troubles assail and dangers affright' to such an extent, that he beat a hasty retreat home, again fills the high and honorable position recently resigned by him."

SAML. T. ROMAN, M. D.,

HAVING permanently located at Mount Pleasant, 6th District of this county, offers his Professional services to the citizens of the surrounding country. Accessible at all hours, and all calls promptly attended to.

According to the *Whig* of April 8, 1865, Elkton had not yet recovered from the tendency to do things by fits and starts. Even the fall of Richmond did not motivate the town to rise from its torpor.

A "PHIZZLE."—A kind of attempt was made on Wednesday last, at Elkton, to get up a jubilee in honor of the victories at Richmond. But such a jubilee! An old cannon was procured at Wilmington, dragged round about the streets and fired off here and there. Pretty soon the gun went off from being heated by too rapid firing, or from carelessness in the man who held his thumb on the vent, or perhaps from both causes, while the gunner was ramming, wounding two of the men, one of them severely. The next feat in gunnery was to fire in the center of the town, breaking the Court House and Howard House windows. A torchlight procession was attempted, and such a procession! Some twenty or thirty, mostly yelling boys comprised this parade. A printed notice was sent round about sundown requesting the citizens to illuminate their house. Some who had illuminating fixtures on hand lighted up their dwellings quite handsomely; but the majority had no time to prepare. But the music! That was grand. The inevitable, irrepressible cow-bell-tin-horn-and-ash-bucket band got out their instruments, and the melody discoursed would have delighted the ears of a Chinaman....

Casualties from the 6th Maryland included the following:

Co. A.	Corporal Upon Decker, face;
Co. B.	Color Sergeant Robert Spence, neck severely; Lt. Thomas Duff, thigh bone fracture; Corporal James Gracey, left knee severely.
Co. C.	Killed: Orderly Sergeant Michael Halloren; Wounded: Corporal William R. Moore, left thigh, severely.
Co. F.	Corporal Christian Wagner, arm;
Co. G.	Private Robert D. Drummond, left leg, severely.
Co. H.	Private Lewis Gouker, neck.
Co. K.	Killed: Private Jesse Boulden. Wounded: Corporal Eli Baldwin, right arm severely; Private Robert C. Davidson, right arm and right thigh, severely.

The *Whig* observed [4/29/65]: "In both engagements of the 25th of March and the 2d of April the colors of this regiment were the first to float over the Rebel battlements."

Frank Cummings, 5th Pennsylvania Cavalry, was promoted to Commissary of Subsistence Volunteers with the rank of Captain.

Dr. B. J. Bing moved his dental office to two doors above the Presbyterian Church on the north side of the street.

When news of Lee's surrender reached the county, the bells in the Court House and churches rang out. People were employed to ring them from 7:00 a.m. until 6:00 p.m. In its typical hyphenated style, the *Whig* observed: "Everybody wore a smiling face,—even some of the quondam high-flying, never-conquer-the-South Secesh expressed gratification at the result."

Internal revenue agents of the 1860s did not enjoy a great deal of popularity. The *Whig* remarked, tongue-in-cheek, of course:

> Those Revenue officers of Uncle Sam, who are constantly poking their noses into everybody's dish, having served a notice on a spunky young lady, propounding a great many absurd questions, had it returned with the following answers annexed.
>
> Q—How much wheat did you harvest in 1864?

A—Half a bushel.
Q—How much corn?
A—Three pecks.
Q—How much oats?
A—One quart.
Q—How many bushels of potatoes?
A—One bag full.
Q—How much buckwheat?
A—Twenty cakes.
Q—State amount of poultry sold and consumed.
A—Scarce.

News of Lincoln's assassination reached Elkton at 6:30 a.m. on Saturday morning. People were shocked that such a horrid crime could take place in the capital. By Sunday evening the pulpit and altar of the M. E. Church were draped in black. When Rev. Mr. Kurtz led his congregation in prayer, some sobbed audibly. In the Episcopal Church, Rev. Mr. Mitchell prayed with his congregation.

Town Commissioners held a special meeting and recommended that all citizens display some badge of mourning from their houses for 30 days. On Wednesday, most businesses closed between 11:00 a.m. and 3:00 p.m., while the town bells tolled.

The *Democrat* reported: "The tragedy and consequences absorb all consideration. Business...is totally suspended; the city had put on the habitments [*sic*] of woe, and from every public building and many private dwellings the national flag waves in mourning."

From the County Commissioners' Minutes of April 18, 1865 : "The Commissioners adjourned over to Thursday next in view of the obsequies of Abraham Lincoln late President of the U.S. appointed to take place tomorrow, in Washington—ordering the Clerk to drape the Court House in mourning as a token of respect for the greatest martyr to Liberty the world ever saw."

In the intermittent silence, people heard the thunder of heavy guns from Fort Delaware.

On April 22, 1865, under the headline, "The Lesson," the *Whig* mourned the death of Abraham Lincoln.

Village Green Seminary

HOME SCHOOL FOR BOYS, begins September 4th.—Thorough course in English, Mathematics, Classics and Natural Sciences. Fine Library and Apparatus.—Surveying and Engineering taught. Boys of all ages received, and have the benefits of a home. The Principal aims at a moderate expense to supply to parents a good place for the education of their children. Number of Pupils limited. Send for a catalogue. Address

REV. J. HERVEY BARTON, A.M.,
Village Green Seminary,
Delaware county, Pa.

ABRAHAM LINCOLN is dead; but the Nation still lives. Struck down in the prime of his life and the midst of his usefulness by the hand of a dastardly assassin, his death will intensify the hatred of the American people for that accursed system, which delights in styling itself the "Peculiar Institution."—For that Slavery was the inciting cause of his assassination is as evident as that his death has sealed the fate of Slavery throughout the world.

The leaders of the rebellion may not have directly instigated the murder of President Lincoln; but the infamous cause they are fighting to establish begat and cherished the spirit that did it; and they are therefore responsible for the act—morally, if not legally. But while holding *them* to a strict accountability, let us ask ourselves if *we* are altogether guiltless.

Nations like individuals reap according to what they sow; and the seeds of Slavery that our fathers so carelessly sowed in the country's infancy, and that their children so carefully guarded through all the after years—even unto the ripening of a bloody harvest, are now yielding their legitimate fruits—Treason, Rebellion, Assassination!

Abraham Lincoln is sleeping in his bloody shroud—the victim of Slavery—a Martyr for Freedom and free institutions. Yet if we heed the axiomatic, but startling truth uttered by him eleven years ago: "The Union cannot permanently exist half slave and half free," he will not have died in vain. Each and all of us will in the immediate presence of the horrible crime that has filled our hearts with anguish, realize more fully that our chiefest duty now is the total extirpation of the Nation's giant curse—that prop and main-stay of the Rebellion—that sum of villainies—the iniquitous system of Slavery. Will we fail to perform the duty imposed on us by the murder of our patriot President.?

Now that the war was over, the P. W. & B. Railroad acquiesced to the wishes of local travelers by adding an "accommodation train" between Perryville and Philadelphia. It left Perryville at 7:30 a.m. and Elkton at 8:17 a.m. In Wilmington, it connected with the 9:30 a.m. train for Philadelphia. Visitors had about six hours to spend in the City of Brotherly Love before leaving on the 6:40 train for Wilmington and points south. The P. W. & B. no longer attached a passenger train to the through freight, as had been the practice during the War.

NOTICE
Farmers and Merchants

THE fast sailing Schooner AMERICAN EAGLE, CAPT. WM. REYNOLDS, will run regular as a Packet from Elkton Landing to Baltimore, carrying all kinds of Goods and Produce at a reasonable price.

The *Democrat* deplored local preference for dealing with strangers. "But let a 'Cheap John' come to town, and he can hardly get clerks enough to wait on the crowds that throng to his store. If they get cheated, so much the better, they will praise him the louder to keep people from knowing it."

On the train, the *Whig* editor ran into Cheap John Rowbotham, who looked as exuberant as ever. "His universal goaheaditive merchandizing genius has already established a store in Petersburg, where he is astonishing the played out secesh of the Old Dominion by a touch of that genuine Yankee skill which rivals the alchemist in the art of turning the baser metals to gold."

When S. M. Felton, Esq., retired from the P. W. & B. Railroad, his friends gave him an impressive gift: a two-foot model of the *Daniel Webster* locomotive made of silver and gold. The *Democrat* quoted the Philadelphia *North American*: "The steamchest, cylinder, dome & c. are of gold. The body of the locomotive is silver. The piece of work is a gem of the goldsmith's art. Its cost is about $2500."

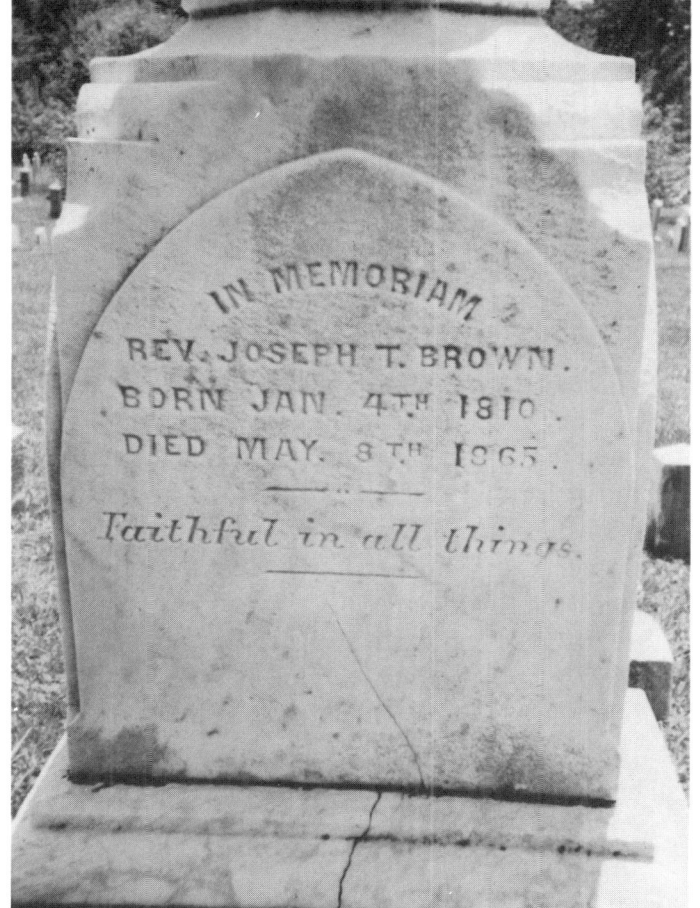

The *Democrat's* description of an accident that befell Moses Dean at McCullough Iron Works was both graphic and understated: "A portion of the hot iron struck Mr. Dean in the eye, closing the orifice and cooking the eye, and destroying the sight and giving the sufferer great pain."

Lt. Col. Joseph Hill was promoted to Colonel of the 6th Maryland, and Adj. Joseph L. Mahan was promoted to Captain of Company I of the same regiment. The 6th was presently camped at Danville, Virginia.

When T. Drennen lost over a dozen sheep, including a Cotswold ram, to a pack of dogs, the *Whig* recommended a dose of strychnine for "worthless curs."

Reverend Joseph T. Brown, 55, died at Cherry Hill. The Cherry Hill Council Chamber—Charles Peacock, Wm. C. Hasson, and Joseph Miller—formally mourned his passing in a note to the *Democrat*.

Elkton stores agreed to close at 8 o'clock every evening except Saturday. The Court House bell tolled at closing time.

The public was invited to the reopening of the M. E. Church in Elkton. Fire damaged the structure in January, and the repairs were completed.

All religious and literary societies were urged to contribute to a national monument to be built in Springfield, Illinois. Collections were taken up in public schools and in Sunday schools for that purpose.

Eli Pierson of Elk Neck fished up a double-barreled gun in his gilling net. It had been lost in March by a Philadelphian, who offered a $100 reward.

Rev. Stephen Cameron, formerly an Episcopalian minister in Elkton, and "special messenger of the Rebel raiders," according to the *Whig*, "joined the Roman Catholic Church in Quebec."

On June 3, 1865, the *Whig* editorialized in a column headed, "End of the War."

The last organized Rebel army having surrendered, the war is pronounced at an end—the great Rebellion crushed, and the Republic again restored to its more than former greatness and power. The Flag that has floated for four years at the head of our leading editorial column has this week been folded away, to be used in future, we hope, on no more war-like occasions than Fourth of July celebrations, or peaceful triumphs at the polls.

> **The Mason & Mamlin Cabinet Organs,** for different styles, adapted to sacred and secular music, for $80 to $600 each. THIRTY-FIVE GOLD or SILVER MEDALS, or other first premiums awarded them.

The *Whig* enlisted in this war with unwavering confidence in the integrity and intelligence of the people, and their determination and ability to vanquish every armed foe to the Republic. The result has shown that our confidence was not misplaced. As in the past so in the future we hope ever to be found on the side of popular government, and opposing that mawkish aristocracy whose origin, like the mushroom, may be traced to some dung-hill, and which owes to slavery the fostering influence that supported it.—Its decaying remains are still strewn round about through town and country, a stench in the nostrils of every truly patriotic and noble minded citizen. May it soon disappear along with other debris of the infamous rebellion.

The Comptroller of the Treasury reminded everyone engaged in oyster fishing within state waters to obtain the required license. Failure to do so resulted in a fine between $20 and $100.

A strawberry festival for the benefit of Rock Church was held in Biles' woods near Blue Ball Tavern on June 8.

E. W. Staples offered for sale mica lamp chimneys, which were less likely to break than glass. The lamp for sale in Staples' store could be lighted without removing the chimney.

Two county banks complied with requirements of the National Banking Law and were authorized to begin operations as Cecil National Bank of Port Deposit and Elkton National Bank.

The *Whig* [6/10/65] ran a curious column under the headline "SPORTING."

There was another trotting race on the Warwick course, on Wednesday last, between

William Boulden's mare and Samuel Gillespie's horse. The contest was very close, but the mare was declared the winner by a few feet. Gillespie's horse then trotted against A. Asbury Perkins' horse, of Elkton, for a wager of $25, and won. Another race for $50 a side will come off between the same horses on Wednesday afternoon next—Perkins being confident that "old rawbone" will win. There was a chicken fight, on Red Hill, on Tuesday between a couple of chanticleers—one of which belonged to James Fulton, of Elkton. There were several "rounds," when the fight was ended by Fulton's chicken killing his antagonist.

Horse-racing and cock-fighting are highly entertaining amusements, and their frequent occurrence lately in Cecil shows that a portion of the people, at least, are on the highway to respectability. Can't we have a "prize-fight" or two? There seems to be a good deal of partially developed "muscle" going about, and "fights is so interesting."

Oliver Wood of Baltimore started an early version of an employment agency in which he supplied farmers with good help for five dollars each. Employers paid expenses of travel and made their own bargain for wages.

Col. C. J. Hill, 6th Maryland, was home on furlough in early June. The Regiment, he said, was camped at Bailey's crossroads and would soon be mustered out.

Assistant Surgeon Reuben Tuft, 223d Pa. Vols., was also home on furlough.

Someone entered the M. E. Church and stole the 40 yards of black muslin used to symbolize the congregation's sadness at Lincoln's death.

When Reverend Kurtz preached a sermon directed to "The Fast Young Men," the *Whig* urged those to whom the description applied to attend. In fact, the paper went so far as to urge Reverend Kurtz to preach a similar sermon "for the benefit of our Fast Young Ladies."

Thomas E. Cropper of Cecil County was among 60 rebel prisoners below the rank of captain who were released from Fort Warren upon taking the oath of allegiance.

[Thomas Cropper appeared with different middle initials: *F.*, *E.*, and *S*. These may refer to one or several individuals.]

J. J. McCullough of McCullough Iron Co. bought a house from Henry L. Tatnall for $13,500. It was located in Wilmington on West Street between 9th and 10th Streets. McCullough intended to move from North East to his new residence in the fall.

The *Whig* [6/17/65] told how a lapse in communication added to the suffering of the Hyland family.

Wilmer Hyland, a son of Mr. Washington Hyland, of this county, a young man about twenty years of age, left his home on March last, with other young men of the neighborhood, and engaged as a hand on one of the Ericcson Line of steamboats between Baltimore and New-York. On Saturday night last, as the boat was passing through the Kingston lock, on the Delaware and Raritan Canal, Wilmer went upon the lock wall to take a line from the boat; while passing down the stone steps of the wall his foot slipped, and falling into the water between the stone wall of the lock and the side of the boat, no assistance could be afforded in time to save him. He was an expert swimmer, but as his body bore some evidence of external injuries it is presumed he was so disabled in the fall as to deprive him of the proper use of his limbs.

His body was afterwards recovered, put in ice and brought to Elkton by the early freight train on Monday morning, by one of his young companions, Mr. John Pennington, son of Mr. Azarias Pennington, of Elk Neck, and from thence removed to his father's residence that afternoon. The funeral took place on Tuesday last.

The afflicting intelligence did not reach his father and family until 1 o'clock P. M., on Monday, and then only through a young man who being in Elkton that morning hearing that the body was at the depot here, called at his father's house and informed him of his loss. There appears to have been most shameless neglect somewhere, as Mr. Pennington says he dispatched a telegram to his father, by way of North East, at 6 o'clock on Sunday morning, advising him that he would be at Elkton with the body early on Monday morning; but no such intelligence ever reached his father. It is seldom we have had occasion to chronicle so distressing an account.

Col. Barton H. Jenks and R. B. Goodyear, formerly of Philadelphia but now living in Cecil

County invented a loom for weaving mixed cassimeres. During the war, Jenks' factory in Bridesburg, Pennsylvania, turned out 200 Enfield rifles daily.

The *Whig* [6/24/65] reported the death of two soldiers with the same last name. Corporal William King, 22, of Company H, Pennsylvania Bucktail Regiment, died on January 12, 1865, while a prisoner of war at Salisbury, North Carolina.

Hiram King, 18, Company C, 7th Maryland, died in October 1864, while a prisoner of war at Florence, South Carolina.

When the Clerk's office was remodeled, workers found an old book of deeds, mortgages, and other writings from the years 1767 to 1772. It consisted of a thousand pages of heavy parchment and was once bound in fine velvet. The corners were protected by copper to prevent wear. A label on the side indicated that it was made in England for registering births, marriages and deaths in Saint Margaret, Westminster, before being brought to Maryland.

An ad ran in the *Whig* for disabled soldiers and others out of work to sell Frank Crosby's *Life and Public Service of Abraham Lincoln*. In another column, it was reported that John Galbraith and Levi Brown were the Cecil agents for the sale of the book. In this instance, the author's name was given as Crosly.

As the 6th Maryland mustered out, the *Whig* presented a review of their activities.

> The 6th Regiment Maryland Volunteers arrived in this city on Thursday, and proceeded to Camp Bradford, where they have since been paid off and discharged. This regiment, for the past two years, has never had any connections with the Maryland Brigade, but has always constituted a part of the Second Brigade, Third Division, of the old Sixth Corps, a corps which has never known defeat, and the only corps in the service which has passed through three successful campaigns in one year. This regiment has seen as much service and done as much hard fighting as any other regiment from the State. Its record is a brilliant one. No regiment now returning home has been more frequently under fire or employed in more difficult or important enterprises than the 6th Maryland. The following is a list of engagements in which this regiment bore a conspicuous part, and which have, by a special order from army headquarters, been inscribed upon their banners. 1863. Opequon, Winchester, Waping Heights, Brandy Station, Kelley's Ford and Mine Run. 1864. The memorable battles of the Wilderness, Spottsylvania, Laurel Hill, Po River, Ptolapotomy, Cold Harbor and Ream's Station; Sheridan's brilliant campaign in the Shenandoah Valley, where was fought the battles of Winchester, Flint Hill, Fisher's Hill

and Cedar Creek, the most decisive victories of the war. 1865.—The series of engagements in front of Petersburg and Sailor's Run, which resulted in the complete overthrow of the Rebel Confederacy and vindication of the Union arms. I would here state, as a joint compliment to the valor and conspicuous gallantry of this regiment that it was the first to enter the Rebel fortifications in front of Petersburg on the memorable morning of April 2d, which resulted in the downfall of that city and the city of Richmond. Sergeant John E. Buffington received a prize of $100 for gallant conduct, and for being one of the first to enter the rebel works at Petersburg.

The Phila. and Balt. Central Railroad Company.

THE Annual Meeting of the stockholders of said company will be held in the Hall in the Borough of Oxford, Chester county, Pa., on MONDAY, January 8th, 1866, at 12M., at which time and place an Election will be held for a President and twelve Directors to serve the ensuing year.

ROBERT HODGSON,
Secretary

The State of Maryland may well be proud of, and congratulate itself upon the efficient service this regiment has rendered the country.

The regiment returns home with about three hundred men.

The following is a list of its officers:—Lt. Col. J. C. Hill, commanding regiment; Major C. K. Prentiss; Surgeon, E. K. Foreman; Assistant Surgeon, Hugh A. Maughlin; Adjutant, J. L. Mahan; Quartermaster, J. H. C. Brewer.

Co. A. Capt. L. F. Byers, First Lieut. C. G. Fiechtner.
Co. B. Capt. J. R. Rouzer; First Lieutenant Thomas Duff.
Co. C. No officers.
Co. D. Capt. C. A. Danneth.
Co. E. Capt. E. S. Narvell. First Lieutenant F. K. Bryan.
Co. F. First Lieut. A. F. Rittenhouse.
Co. G. Capt. G. M. Eichlberger; First Lieut. Nelson McDowell.
Co. H. Capt. W. H. Abercrombie; First Lieut. A. F. Leeds.
Co. I. Capt. J. J. Bradshaw.
Co. K.[Capt.] J. G. Simpers; First Lieut. O. H. P. Mathias.

The Order of United American Mechanics held a Grand Celebration on the Fourth of July in William C. Hasson's woods near Cherry Hill. The program included John Perkins' reading of the Declaration of Independence and speeches by Rev. Thomas B. Miller and Hon. Philip S. White of Philadelphia; Wm. S. Oliver, Esq, and Franklin Supplee, Esq., of Baltimore; Rev. Joseph Miller of Cherry Hill; and James McCauley, Esq.

John M. Terrell provided dinner on the grounds; ice cream and cake were sold in prodigious amounts; and lest the four-footed celebrants be slighted, A. H. Saxton supplied horse feed.

The Chesapeake City Band played and there were seats for the ladies. The committee included Charles Peacock, Wm. C. Hasson, M. M. Whitcraft, James Spence, J. M. Terrell, and James Davis.

Capt. Vanneman's steamship *Alice* was chartered on the Fourth of July to make a trip from Port Deposit and Havre de Grace to Annapolis. Tickets were one dollar for a round trip.

Several local lads determined to take the boat from New Castle to celebrate the Fourth in Cape May. The early morning air whetted their appetites, and while they ordered breakfast in New Castle, the boat left without them. Undaunted, they made the best of the situation and decided to join the celebrations in Wilmington. The *Whig* described their journey home: "...it was nothing more than natural that weary nature should yield to the resistless power of sleep, and soon they were locked in the arms of Morpheus. They awoke at, or near Glasgow, to find their horse stopped in the road, and themselves minus their pocket-books. One of the same party was relieved of his spare change, also, after he reached home, by someone entering his room and rifling his pockets. One of the gentlemen who were robbed at Glasgow, will lose very heavily should he not recover his money."

THE SALEM LEG

UNDER the Patronage of the United States Government. Models of this superior leg may be seen at the Agency of the SALEM LEG COMPANY, No. 33 South SEVENTH Street, Philadelphia.
Call and see them, or send for a circular containing full information.

A correspondent in Frederick City, Maryland, described the winding down of the war (*Whig* 7/1/65).

June 28, 1865

DEAR EDITOR:—The long trains of army wagons and of cavalry passing peacefully through our mountain city remind us that the signs of war are rapidly being removed from us. The almost abandonment of the Quartermaster's department of this post, as Hospitals, and on Saturday morning the removal of the provost marshal and guard of some hundred men, give unmistakable evidence of the return of peace and quiet in our midst. They go to Harper's Ferry to join their brigade, and to be mustered out after a service of over three years. Many of them leaving their business and workshops at $60 and $100 per month, to serve their country in time of peril at $16, now have their hearts gladdened at the prospect of getting home to their families, and the beautiful country. Many were the sacrifices made by volunteers, when the country called for their services, and many are the hardships they have endured for their country's sake. We, who have remained at home, are under a heavy debt of gratitude to the soldiers who have served in the field.

Were it not for the 6th U.S. Cavalry being stationed near the city, we would soon be without the emblems of war. Col. Morris, commanding, shows signs of much service, having passed through the war with Mexico and four years of hard service just closed, commands profound respect for his bravery and gentlemanly deportment as an officer.—Capt. A. W. Evans, brother of Hon. Alex. Evans, of your town, we are told, commands a portion of the 6th U.S. Cavalry under Col. Morris.

Capt. Rutherford, who is now closing up his stewardship as Quartermaster of this post, has won the admiration of all persons having business in his department. He may truly be styled a model Quartermaster, looking carefully to the interests of the government, more than pecuniary aid or self agrandisement.

Capt. Wail, District Provost Martial [sic] of the Draft, is also preparing to wind up his department as fast as expedient. We know of no one having won the confidence and respect of the community more than the Captain.

These gentlemen have formed many agreeable associations in Frederick and vicinity, and the community part with them reluctantly; but glad that their services are no longer needed in their present capacities.

The farmers are actively engaged saving abundant crops of hay and wheat, which has been much retarded by the frequent rains during the past two weeks, some of which have been very heavy.

As we write many ambulances and horses, which look as though they had seen hard service and low diet, are passing to some point, no doubt to receive the stroke of the auctioneer's gavil, and then be transferred to civil life. Farmers are buying many bargains at these sales.

We are glad to receive our old friend, *The Cecil Whig*, on Saturday.

WESTWARD

Elkton lamplighter, Mr. Lowman, was busy in the first weeks of July cleaning the burners and glasses of the street lamps.

Miss Mary E. Brown was appointed postmistress at Cherry Hill to fill that post left vacant by the death of Rev. Joseph T. Brown.

The roving reporter conveyed his opinions of Pivot Bridge (*Whig* 7/8/65).

FOR SALE—Widwell's celebrated Bituminous Coal Oil Grease for Stages, Wagons, Carts, Carriages, Mill Gearing, &c.
WM. McCLELLAND, Jr.

MR. EDITOR:—As you have asked through the columns of your widely circulated journal for communications in reference to the doings in different sections of the county, I herewith furnish you a chapter on Pivot Bridge.

To those of your readers not familiar with its locality, I would state, it may be found on the Chesapeake and Delaware canal, one and a half miles from its western terminus, at which Chesapeake City is located, only a few hundred yards from the Delaware line. Formerly it was known by the name of "old Town," when it supported a tavern, and it is said had some notoriety for horse racing and cock fighting; occasionally, however, the fights were not confined to chickens. It was then the place for holding elections, had a post office, and the stage conveying the mail and passengers to the Peninsula passed through. But the population of Chesapeake City becoming more numerous, the post office was removed to that town, and the stage route changed accordingly. Old Town, at one period, is reported to have been enlivened by thriving business operations, and could boast of good mechanics of almost every description needed in a country place; there was a good store; a market for grain, &c. But in process of time—almost unaccountably—a very great change was wrought in the place. Mr. J. L. Clayton, who had been associated with its business operations some twenty years, retired from the same, and vacated his old residence; other changes and removals took place so that finally the wheels of business seemed to come to a standstill.

Thus it was in the fall of '63, Mr. Stephen B. Ford took hold and opened a store. In the following spring he commenced buying grain on commission, and shortly after built a wharf, where the steamer commerce stops to take in or land passengers and freight. He seems to possess the disposition to do more to revive trade, if he continues to receive corresponding patronage. But some say that he is "too honest" ever to get rich while others think that a rare failing in a merchant.

The farmers in this neighborhood who raise peaches have made arrangement with Mr. Garman to have them carried to Philadelphia for nine cents per basket. Mr. Garman furnishes two steamboats, making daily trips from Mr. Stephen B. Ford's wharf at Pivot Bridge and having several other stopping places along the canal. The crop is said to be much below an average one, but the fruit will be correspondingly larger.

Mr. C. Walters, on the farm of Mr. G. W. Bennett, near Pivot Bridge, has a field of wheat that shocks large enough to make 30 bushels to the acre.

OBSERVER

A new school law passed, which provided for a State Board of Education, to consist of the Governor, Lieutenant Governor, Speaker of the House of Delegates, and the State Superintendent. The latter had his office in Baltimore and visited each county annually. The State Board appointed school commissioners in each county.

COSTAR'S
CELEBRATED
BUCKTHORN SALVE

Cecil officially welcomed its soldiers home on Friday, July 28, 1865, with celebrations in Elkton. A soft rain the night before settled the dust, putting the roads in fine shape for marching and driving. J. S. Crawford, Esq, was the Chief Marshal.

Beginning at 8 o'clock in the morning, people passed through town on their way to the appointed grove. There were dearborns and wagons pulled by fine horses, rundown nags, and even army mules. Beck's Band arrived on the 10:10 train from Philadelphia; the Independent Council No. 13, O.U.A.M. arrived on the 11:11 train from North East. The returned soldiers and the councils marched to Landing Lane, where they met the steamboat from Port Deposit at noon.

The parade formed according to the marshal's plan at 12:30.
1. Band
2. Visiting Md. officers and officers without commands, clergy and speakers, mounted or in carriages.
3. Returned soldiers, Col. J. C. Hill in command
4. Order of U. A. Mechanics in order of their numbers, smallest number on the right.
5. I. O. Odd Fellows, in order of their numbers, smallest number on the right.
6. Citizens on foot.
7. Citizens mounted.
8. Citizens in carriages.

"The soldiers in the line," said the *Whig*, "wore the badge of the corps to which they belonged at the time of their discharge. In these the cross of the glorious old Sixth largely predominated, while the maltese cross of the Fifth and the trifoil of the second were sprinkled here and there. They made a fine appearance as they marched along with their steady 'tramp, tramp, tramp' and apparent careless air."

Because some participants did not know the arrangements, they were not in the proper place; even so, 200 soldiers marched up Main Street to Mill Lane, turned left, and entered the grove.

Reverend Wiggins offered a prayer of thanksgiving, and Hon. John A. J. Creswell welcomed the soldiers on behalf of the people. Colonel Bowerman and Major Simon were introduced, while Maj. E. F. M. Faehtz acknowledged the contributions of the women of the county.

> **ROWLEY'S**
> **Patent Excelsior Fruit Jars.**
> This Jar has been examined and tested by competent judges and pronounced by them the most simple and reliable Fruit Jar in market.

Several thousand people then enjoyed the dinner and ice cream afterward. Flags fluttered from the tables, as the Chesapeake City Band enlivened the occasion.

The *Whig* announced in the issue of August 5, 1865, that Dr. B. J. Bing was leaving town to be replaced by Dr. Edwin T. Darby.

President Johnson appointed Wm. J. Jones, Esq., of Elkton, United States Attorney General for the District of Maryland.

The *Whig* pointed out that a law requiring the registration of birth, marriages and deaths passed the Maryland Legislature in July. Eight marriage licenses were issued but only three marriages recorded. "The Clerk of the Circuit Court will be apt to stir some of the parties up whose duty it is to report such matters."

In mid-July the Methodist E. Church at North East reopened after its renovation.

E. A. Bastianelli frescoed the Clerk's and Register's offices in Elkton. The Railroad Company was in the process of engaging his services for the depot, and some residents, too, considered employing him in the decoration of their homes.

A wheat-laden vessel sank in Elk River near Isaac Z. Collings' farm. The schooner carried 2,500 bushels of grain, all of which was lost.

Word arrived that Major and Brevet Colonel Prentiss, 6th Maryland, died in Brooklyn on August 20 of wounds received at Petersburg in April.

In Cherry Hill, Charles Peacock and R. C. Carter dissolved their partnership by mutual consent. The former continued the mercantile business on his own account.

With all the celebrations and observations at the end of the war, there was no shortage of speeches across the nation. The *Whig* editor evidently heard enough to hold him over for a considerable time.

> **DR. J. H. JAMAR**
> Tenders his professional services to the citizens of **Port Deposit and vicinity.**
> ☞Office over the Drug Store of H. C. Nesbitt & Co.

A social Pic Nic will be held in the woods of Edward T. Mask, near Upper Principio, today, commencing at 12 o'clock.

The Charlestown M. E. Sabbath school will hold their annual celebration at Cool Spring, on Wednesday, Sept. 12, when addresses may be expected from neighboring ministers.

The Elkton and Westamwell Sunday Schools held their pic nic in McCullough's grove, on Thursday last. Both schools were fully represented, and the children, not being bored by any long and uninteresting harangues, were left to enjoy themselves in various plays and amusements incident to such occasions. The day was warm, but it was pleasant in the woods, and no one, we are sure, regrets going. May the children enjoy many more such pleasant seasons.

C. K. Palmer, portrait and miniature painter, moved his shop from North Street to another south of the Elkton depot. The *Whig* editor admitted that he knew very little about this quiet artists. However, he was pleasantly surprised when he saw the quality of Palmer's work. He just finished a portrait of a well known local citizen, and everyone—including the subject—admitted the likeness was striking.

E. F. M. Faehtz, recently of the 8th Maryland, was breveted Colonel for meritorious service during the war.

Mr. Broad, a submarine diver working on the construction of a bridge over the Susquehanna, suffocated in his diving suit when an air pump malfunctioned.

On September 23, 1865, the *Whig* announced the coming of G. F. Bailey & Co.'s Metropolitan and Quadruple Combination. It consisted of James Melville & Co.'s Grand Circus, Herr Driesbach's Extensive Menagerie and Sand's Nathans & Co.'s Performing Elephant and Giant Hippopotamus.

The *Whig* carried a notice under the heading, "Public Schools of Cecil County."

For the purpose of meeting inquiries coming from various quarters it is deemed proper in this manner to give notice to all parties interested that the Tuition Fee of one dollar per quarter is no longer required, the schools being free to all white youth of the county, between the ages of six and nineteen years. A charge of Fifty cents per quarter is required of each pupil for the Books and Stationery furnished by the Board, and this must be paid invariably in advance; unless the parents of the child are unable to pay, of which the Commissioner of the district must be the judge.

We deem it proper also to call special attention to the 4th section of chapter 2nd of the School Law,—title School House,—which reads thus:

"SEC. 4. If any person shall willfully injure any School House, or the buildings and fences connected therewith, or disfigure the same with paint or otherwise, or make thereon any obscene words, figures or devices, or paste thereon any figures or devices, he shall on conviction thereof in the Circuit Count of the county where the offense was committed, or in the Criminal Court of Baltimore, if the offense be committed in the city of Baltimore, be punished by fine not exceeding fifty dollars, or by imprisonment in the County Jail not exceeding thirty days, or both, in the discretion of the court. The fine shall be paid one-half to the informer and one-half to the School House fund for the school district."

Teachers will please see that the section is read in each school, and due notice of its provisions given to the pupils.

F. A. Ellis
President

WM. TORBERT, Secretary

Morris Cummings and F. E. Bradbury dissolved their partnership, but Cummings continued to operate the bakery at the old stand in the Hollow.

Captain Reynolds made regular runs with the schooner *American Eagle* as a packet from Elk Landing to Baltimore. The ship carried all kinds of goods and produce.

In the October 7 issue, the *Whig* ran an extensive list of qualified voters in the various districts.

Mitchell & Stump sold their mill property east of Elkton to Col. J. C. Hill and E. A. Alexander for $20,000.

I. D. Davis merited a column in the *Whig* when he was promoted to Lieutenant Colonel.

As every locality in our country can boast of some distinguished son, whose talents have been brought forth during the enormous struggle from which we have just emerged, Cecil county lays claim to the brave patriotic officer, soldier and gentleman who heads this article.

Col. Davis enlisted as a private in Co. I., 5th Md. Vols., October 15th, 1861, and served as a private until Dec. 10, 1861, when he was promoted to the responsible position of Color Sergeant. In April, 1862, he was promoted Commissary sergeant, which position he filled with credit to himself and to the satisfaction of those in authority over him, until May, 1864, when he made application for a commissioning a colored regiment, and after passing a rigid examination, was found capable of commanding a company, and received a commission as captain in June 1864.

The reason of the Col. taking this step was the deceitful manner in which he was served by the commanding officer of the regiment, who had repeatedly promised faithfully to recommend him for the office of quartermaster of the regiment, but afterwards ascertained that he had been guilty of gross duplicity in his case, as well as that of others, he having as faithfully promised several First and Second Lieutenants the same position.

Col. Davis joined his regiment in Kentucky July, 1864, and assisted in organizing the same, which was afterwards known as the 118th W S. C. Troops. While in command of his company in Kentucky, he made several successful scouts, he having broken up, captured and dispersed several gangs of guerrillas who infested that region. In October, 1864, Captain Davis was ordered in front of Richmond with his regiment, and, after his arrival, was immediately detailed for the responsible position of Brigade Commissary;

A STILL GREATER TUMBLE!

DOWN!

DOWN!

DOWN!

PRINTS, 12½ cents.
MUSLINS, 12 cents.
SUGAR, 12 cents.

STEPHEN B. FOARD,
At Pivot Bridge, Md.

which position he filled until January, 1865, when he rejoined his company, and then with his regiment, was ordered for duty to Brownsville, Texas; at which place he has lately secured a commission a Lieut. Colonel of the same regiment. This position was tendered to him by his superior officers unanimously; his superior military capacities shining conspicuously. Like many of our best and bravest officers, he learned to command by first learning to obey.

Jealousy alone was the cause of his not receiving the same appointment in his original regiment, the 5th Maryland, his military talents being far superior to most of the officers of the regiment.

His numerous friends in Cecil county will be pleased to hear of his well-merited promotion; and may he soon secure a more exalted position, which he justly deserves.

T. F. G.

The accommodation train between Perryville and Wilmington no longer accommodated. It was withdrawn and replaced by the measure employed during the war—a passenger car attached to a freight train.

A shoplifter was observed in Elkton as she slipped shoes into a covered basket in two different stores. The clerks removed the stolen items when *her* back was turned, and she had the good sense not to create a disturbance.

In November, W. Wesley Janney took the oath of office, replacing Sheriff Price. The latter took up residence in Mrs. Smith's Railroad Hotel.

Samuel J. Price and his sons went gunning in Elk Neck. They were surprised when their dogs flushed out a 12-pound wildcat. Cornered, the cat put up a valiant fight and almost escaped before Price shot it.

The steel bell in Elkton Presbyterian Church, which was made in England and installed in the steeple at a cost of $500, was cracked and rendered useless. The ladies of the congregation held a pre-Christmas fair to raise the necessary funds to replace it.

S. M. Felton, whose retirement from the P. W. & B. Railroad was noted above, was elected president of the Delaware Railroad Company.

The *Whig* recorded the death of Major Benjamin Ricketts:

Major Ben Ricketts died of consumption, at his residence, Ricketts' Mills, on Sunday

---

CHRISTMAS GOODS.

PHOTOGRAPH ALBUMS, Children's Presentation Books, Picture Books, fine assortment of Perfumery, and Pocket Knives, suitable for Christmas Presents.

Also, a fine assortment of Fresh Confectionery, such as Candy Toys, fine Candies, plain Candies, Raisins, Figs, Currants, Citron, &c., just received and for sale by

E. J. MOORE,
Druggist and Apothecary,
Port Deposit, Md.

evening last. He was a brother of the late P. C. Ricketts, Esq., the founder of the *Cecil Whig*, and for twenty years editor of that paper.

Major Ricketts, early in the rebellion, raised a company of volunteers which were known as the "Big Elk Rangers," and as there were some obstacles in the way of his company entering a Maryland regiment, they joined the Second Delaware. He served as captain of his company under McClellan, through the terrible Peninsula campaign. The deceased, after this campaign, was promoted to the rank of Major, and in the sanguinary battle of Fredericksburg, fought by Burnside, was dangerously wounded, by the bursting of a shell. The major was conveyed home from this field of carnage on a litter. He never fully recovered from the effects of this wound and his previous hard campaigning, but continued in feeble health to the time of his death.

With soldiers still suffering and dying from their wounds, it was difficult for Cecil Countians to put the war behind them. But they tried. Events such as the Presbyterian Church fair allowed participants to celebrate somewhat the way they did before the war. But the clock never turned back.

Perhaps the prayer below, found in the pocket of a dead Confederate soldier, expressed the thoughts of combatants on both sides of the Civil War.

> I asked for health,
> that I might do greater things;
> I was given infirmity that I might do better things....
> I asked for riches, that I might be happy;
> I was given poverty, that I might be wise....
> I asked for power,
> that I might have the praise of men;
> I was given weakness,
> that I might feel the need of God....
> I asked for all things, that I might enjoy life;
> I was given life,
> that I might enjoy all things....
> I got nothing I asked for,
> but everything I hoped for.
> Almost despite myself, my unspoken prayers were answered.
> I am among all men most richly blessed.

Appendix A

Letters

Ben and Lottie Ricketts

These letters are owned by the Historical Society of Cecil County. They were written by Ben and Lottie Carter Ricketts to her uncle, Henry Carter. Ben and Lottie were married in November 1860, when he came home to vote in the election. Apparently, after Ben returned to camp, Henry escorted Lottie to her new "home" in the log cabin at Camp Wilkes, Drummondtown, Virginia.

> Camp Wilkes
> Drummondtown, Va.
> Dec. 5, 1861
> Sunday Night

Dear Henry,

Well here we are, Lottie and I. I wish you could have staid with us until this time. Then you could have seen how comfortably we are fixed. I hope you are safe at home by this time; for I know if you are, you are better satisfied than you would be any other *place—even down at Drummondtown*.

We are both very well. Lottie tells me to write that she is happy and contented; and not to be at all uneasy about her. She says she very seldom coughs any; but feels very well. She has been laughing all the evening about one thing or another.

A box was sent to one of the colored servants named Meyers; and in a mistake it was opened by one of my men of the same name. A crowd was standing around looking what he had from home; and the poor fellow came to two daguerrotypes. And upon opening them he found they were pictures of black women. The men all yelled with laughter at the poor fellow who just then found out his mistake. But he was too late. The joke was against him.

Henry we are really comfortable and happy. I love my dear little wife very much and you may rest assured I will take care of her. Mrs. Col. Wharton and Mrs. Colonel Baily have both been to see her and they will both be very kind to her. She will not be without friends, Henry; if she is away from home. She sends her love to Mother and to you. She will write you a long letter very soon. She, [and I too] are both anxious to hear from home. Please let us hear from you as soon as you can. Hoping you are well, I am truly yours, Ben.

Lottie sends her love to Lydia and Lottie; and wants them to write very soon.

Dear Uncle—I want a coal oil lamp. Will you please ask Aunt Janie to get me one, and please take the things I told Lottie to give you down to Aunt Janie and let her wrap them up with the lamp, and please have them put up as small as possible, I think perhaps she could put them in a little paper box, or just as you both think best. Mr. Torbert expects to leave here tonight for home, and will remain in Phila. A few days. Do not say anything about it for I guess he wants to surprise them at home. You can find out when he gets home, and if you will have the things wrapped up as small as you can

The Ricketts' homestead on the Big Elk

and give them to him he will bring them down to me. Do not tell him I wrote to you. Just tell him it is something you want to send to me. Candles are very high here, 40 cts. Per pound I will write to Janie about the lamp, and you can give the notes to her. Perhaps you had better tell Torbert to be careful of the box. Have it as small as you can. I read your dear good letter and will answer it soon. Do write often to me. Don't wait for me to write. You know I have so little to write about that would interest you. I expect Torbert will be up to see you, but do not depend on that. See him and give him the things in haste. Love to all from Bennie and I—Lottie.

[In Ben's handwriting]

Mr. Torbert will not be home, but Mr. Smith, son of John S. Will and please get the lamp and the butter and leave them with Janie and Mr. Smith or Mr. Mcneal will call and get them. Attend to it as soon as you get this letter, they leave this morning. I need the lamp very much, I can get the oil here. They have but 12 days furlough, so you will have but little time to get the things.

Mr. Henry Carter
Present

Camp Wilkes, Va.
January 7, 1862

Dear Uncle Henry,

It is now after night; and a dark disagreeable night it is. My dear little wife and I are alone in our little log-cabin; and I know of nothing else I would rather do than write you a letter. *So here goes.*

I have a lot of things to tell you or to ask you from Lottie. Tell Lottie P. That she is very much obliged to her for taking such good care of the flowers. Ask Mother if she has any scrapple now. Have you killed your beef yet? Tell Charlotte to broil a piece of toast a piece of bread and send it down for breakfast. A lot of boxes came down last week for the men and everything in them that would spoil was spoiled. Lottie says she would like to kiss you; and she expects that when she does see you, she will kiss you to pieces. Lottie looks much better than when she came. I really think she has been very happy since she came here.

Lottie has not yet received her mustard spoon from Aunt Janie. Do you know anything about it? We are both looking very anxiously for a letter from you. Lottie wants to know if you have had much company since she left. She wants to know how old Tag and Nero are getting along? Lottie says she so often thinks about the night you were so cold down here. She says she is afraid you will think her careless, and she almost cries every time she thinks about it. How are the roads now Henry? Especially the stony hill near Jackson's gate, near Mr. Brown's. That used to be a very bad hill sometimes when I used to drive along that road. I wish you would tell me when you write. Lottie wants to know if Lottie Parker ever

Camp Scene: Reenactment Photograph

touches the R string. Lottie says you will understand it. How is Robert Spence getting along? Does he still go to see Kate Brown? Lottie says have you paid any Quarterage since she left? Col. Wharton and his wife are both away and have been for more than two weeks. Lottie says tell Charlotte that we have cold-slaw almost every day: and it is *splen*, too. Lottie makes it. We sent you a letter by Henry Mullin the other day. He has gone up home. We have had a great deal of wet weather here; raining every day or two. Where is Mrs. Raymond? Lottie sends her love to her.

When you write tell us the news from around your neighborhood. *Anybody married? Anybody dead? Anybody born? Anybody courting?* And for goodness sake tell us what people say about Lottie and Ben Ricketts. Give my love to dear old grandmother, Lydia and Lottie. Tell Day I hope he is well, and doing well. Tell him I would give five dollars for a good old fashioned walk with him. Tell little Harry I still have the picture of the cannon he gave me.

Appendix A: Letters

How is Dr. Bob getting along now?

Well Henry, I guess I will stop writing now; it is after tattoo. Good night.

Lottie received a letter from Lottie P. Today. I tell you what it is Henry. She was glad to receive them. My Oh! You ought to have been here tonight and heard the music. One of the men had a violin and one a flute; they played about 25 or 30 different tunes. Some of them old as the hills. Dixie; Rory O'Moore; Gay and Happy; Over the River to Charley; Arkansas Traveler; and lots of such tunes. Lottie says she hopes everything you sent by Smith will come safe; She will answer your letter soon and tell you how everything comes in the box, whether all right or not. I send you a copy of our paper. Well, Henry, I hope you will soon write again. My but we are glad to receive your letters. Lottie and I send our love to Mother and you. I hope you are well.

Very truly yours,
Ben Ricketts

I played on the Jews-harp *tonight*. I *did*.

On January 1, 1864, Robert Spence married Kate Brown. She was the daughter of Rev. Joseph Brown of Cherry Hill, chaplain of the 6th Maryland. A reunion of the Regiment was held in North East on September 11, 1886. Colorbearer Robert Spence, who planted the first flag on the Confederate works at Petersburg, was applauded at the reunion.

Drummondtown, Va.
Jan. 18, 1862

My Dear Uncle,

Just see what a large sheet of paper I have commenced on. I told Bennie I was afraid I would not be able to fill it. He said never mind he could. Well, Henry, you cannot imagine how glad I was, and how surprised, to get a letter from you yesterday. I shed tears over it and Bennie was not far from it. I tell you we thought you cared for us or you would not have written. I told Bennie I always thought you loved me, but now I know it. Please do write again sometime. It does me such good to get a letter from you and Bennie enjoyed it as much as I did. I sat on his knee and read it to him. Henry, Bennie loves you very much. He says you have always been so good to him, we were talking about you a few days ago [as we often do] and he said, "Lottie if we ever go to housekeeping and Henry is not married, I want him to live with us." He asked me to make something right nice for you and he would send it, but indeed I did not know what to make.

Home of Henry Carter near the Little Elk

Well, we are getting along very well. I do wish you could see us. Why the house does not look like the same, since we got fixed. Bennie has got a great many little things for me, which add much to my comfort, and indeed Henry he is *very kind* to me. I hope I do not forget my dear friends at home, indeed *I love you all more than I ever did*, and would like to see you. You said in your letter you were glad to hear we were happy together. When I read that to Benny, he said, "I believe that Lottie."

I thought a great deal about you after you left. I was afraid you would have to stay in Balt. over Sunday and I knew you were very anxious to get home. You must have been very tired. I know you miss me very much, try to be happy. Lottie will be kind to you and do all she can for you. God bless you my dear Uncle. You have been very kind to me, and I know you will be rewarded. It is now 7 o'clock PM and I am alone. Benny has gone to "Military School." He will not be gone long. Col. Wharton called this afternoon. I was alone and we had a very pleasant chat. My, Henry, but he is a nice man. I like him better every time I see him. Mr. Vaneman and Lt. Kidd took tea with us. We had *fried oysters*. Mr. V. Told me to give his kind regards to you. Henry, he told us he was a *class leader*. You very soon found your way to "Elk Vale" after your return home. You did not say how long you stayed. I want you to tell me the particulars. After this, Bennie had a letter from Rache and she said you had been to see them, and they were very glad to see you. What do you think we have? A paper published here now called the *"Regimental Flag."* I tell you it is quite interesting. A man came to the door this morning and said "Capt., have a paper today." I was glad to hear it. It seemed like living. If the 2nd Del Reg. stays here a little while longer, I think the people will begin to wake up, for they certainly have been sleeping for the last 50 years.

My oh Henry, if you were here now, you would hear fiddling done. Some one across the street is [as you used to say] making it fairly ache. We had quite a severe battle here on Tuesday. I would give you a description of it but Bennie is going to send you a paper which will give you a full account. Another good thing, we will soon have a telegraph to Drummondtown. Tell Lottie she must not think hard of me for not writing to her. I consider them a part of our own family, and of course when I write home expect them to read all the letters. I will write to Lottie the next time. Tell dear Mother I read her kind letters and not to be uneasy about me. If I get sick Bennie will bring me home, if it is possible for me to get there. I do hope she may be well. Tell her to try and be happy, not to trouble herself about anything. I wrote her a letter last week. Hope she got it. Henry before you commence writing to me again I want you to get a supply of paper for I like long letters. Henry, do write often. It will be an advantage to you and happiness to me. *Tell Lottie I have got my best friend sure*, and tell her I never receive any letters more acceptable than hers.

My oh but Bennie did laugh when Lottie said you were trying to write to me but couldn't concentrate your views. Last Sunday was a delightful day here. Bennie and I took a walk in the morning. I enjoyed it very much. Did not suffer any from difficulty of breathing. This level county suits me. You know I am not very expert at running uphill. I feel very well and have an excellent appetite. I hope you are all well at home. Give my love to dear Mother, and all inquiring friends. Did you get the box from Ferris? Has Saxton paid you? Did you have money enough to take you home? Mrs. Wharton was in to see me yesterday. I like her very much. And Mrs. Bailey is a dear little woman. I guess I will have to stop or Bennie will not get to write much. Do not forget me when you go to "class meeting." Give my love to Charlotte. So goodbye. Your affectionate, Lottie.

Sunday morning

Well my dear friend Henry; when Lottie commenced she said she would leave me plenty of room on this sheet to write you a long letter. But I see she has lengthened hers out pretty well and only left me a page which I will try to fill with something. But I cannot "concentrate my views" this morning. Well Henry I tell you what it is; if you only knew how glad we were to get your letter you would write often. It has been read over and over again and I suppose we will read it over again a number of times more. Henry, you say you wish the war was over. Well I wish so too. And I wish we were settled down somewhere near each other so we could see each other often.

Well I am going to write plainly to you now. We are comfortable and have a great many little conveniences that you would not think of. My dear little Lottie is I know much better than she has been since I knew her. And I tell you what it is; I fully believe that she is happy and contented. You know I could soon tell if she was not really happy. Of course she often expresses a wish that she could see you all. But that is natural, you know. I try to be kind to her. And I mean with the help of the good Lord to make a kind husband. She is kind to me, Henry; and she loves me.

Appendix A: Letters

We often have our friends to call and see us. I tell you what it is, Henry. It is not every officer that I invite in to see us. But only a few. And they are those with whom I am glad to associate with. We have some one into tea occasionally, which is very pleasant. Lottie is sitting on my knee and she won't get up. What shall I do?

Monday Noon
January 20, 1861

Well I did not get quite done when I finished, so I will commence again. Some of my men will be up on a furlough sometime soon, and we want some *butter* sent down. Will you please engage for twenty [20] pounds from Maria Drummond, or if she has not, get it from Sallie Valentine. It is almost impossible to get good butter down here.

You will please pay for it and we will pay you. When some of my men go up I will get them to get it. Put it up as you think best. Lottie just received a package containing her shoes and paper, also a letter from Aunt Janie. The man will let you know when he goes home. I will send you a letter by him.

Tell Aunt Janie if she has anything to send for my men, send nothing but underclothes, and delicacies for the sick. Do not send any quilts or pillows. We have too many now.

Tell Aunt Janie to send Lottie's mustard spoon in a letter. It will not get lost. I'll tell you all about the flag in my next letter. I received a letter from Mrs. Hiss about it and Lottie says tell Mother that she thinks she will get her fill of chicken now, as she has chicken almost every day. Tell Aunt Janie that we have Regimental Hospital now. Just alongside our camp; and if anything is sent to the sick of my Co. they and they only will get it. Henry, Lottie wants you to send her in the same box with the butter a rolling pin and a potato smasher, such as you have at home, and wants you to make them, if you can. Our love to all at home and hoping you are all well.

I am truly yours,
Ben R.

Written around the margin of the page:
If you cannot get the butter where I named, you might try at Jackson's near my mothers, if not too much trouble.

Ben has titled this page Number 2. Possibly it was included with the page above. Chronologically, it must come before Lottie's letter of February 1, because by then she mentions having received the provisions that he is still waiting for in the following:

I am going to build a new and a larger kitchen this week. I guess you think we need a larger one. There is a court martial to meet this week on Wednesday. I am one of the members. We will meet at 11 a.m. and adjourn at 3 p.m. There are a number of cases on hand I believe; I suppose the court will last a week or two.

There are three officers from our Reg. Col. Baily, Maj. Andrews and myself. The rest of the officers are from the different Regiments of the Brigade. Henry you need not be surprised if we are kept here the most of next summer; that is if the war continues so long. [which I do not believe]. But we will be home in the spring; or before that time if Lottie wants to go.

There are but few of our men sick. Have you seen Simpers? Mrs. Hiss sent me another box and it cost $5.00 from Salisbury here. And the box & contents were not worth more than $2.50 or $3.00, I believe. Guess that sort of sending will not pay. We have not been paid as yet but will this week.

We sent last Friday to Baltimore for some provisions. I do not know when we will get them. Soon I hope.

Well Henry I want you by all means to write to us soon again. It pleases Lottie so; and to tell you the truth it pleases me too. Mrs. and Mr. Aldred have not come out to camp yet; and do not expect to. I guess their Co. will be sent back. Now Henry be sure and give my love to dear old grandmother; tell her I would be very glad to see her; and expect to before many months. Remember me to Day, and all my friend who may inquire after us; and do not forget Elize Spence whatever you do. Tell her Lottie has not cried to go home yet; but that she has almost made up her mind to "live and die in Dixie." Well that is so long as I may stay here.

Reenactment

Now goodbye Henry.

Do write to us soon. Lottie says goodbye and a kiss to you and Mother, Lydia, & Lottie. Write to us soon and believe me Henry to be very truly your friend,

Ben

Camp Wilkes
Jan. 22, 1862

Dear Henry,

Lottie and I want you to send us [$20] dollars in Delaware Notes. Send four notes of five dollars each. Lottie says you know where her money is at. Send it as soon as you can. We are nearly out and the paymaster has not yet come. Lottie and I send love to you and mother. Hoping you and she are well as we are. We remain yours very affectionately

Lottie and Ben

♦ Appendix A: Letters ♦

Camp Wilkes Feb. 1, 1862
Saturday Night My Dear Uncle,

Well here we are Bennie and I together, sitting by a good warm stove, and oh my but I do wish you were with us for a few hours at least. I do want to see you right bad. We are getting along very well, and I think my health is very much better. Mrs. Baily and I feel quite at home together. She is in here or I there every day. We go out walking whenever it is fit to walk. She is a very nice woman Henry. I know you would like her. She and the Col. dined with us today. I will tell you what we had for dinner: roasted ducks and chicken, potatoes, and cold slaw, for desert green peaches, the sutler gave me a can and they were the nicest I ever ate. How kind you are to write to me so often, please write to me at least once a week, and I will try to do the same. Keep me posted in all that is going on. You told me to consign your first letter to the TP. You do beat all. I tell you what it is. I studied over it, and at last came to the conclusion you meant the *ten plate stove*. When Bennie came in I told him, and he guessed it right away. He says he has studied the "Ency" and indeed I think he has. He reminds me of you every day. He told me to tell you the K joined, and the T was but a few steps from the LC. He said you would understand it, you had studied the "Ency." when you write tell me if you did. I am sorry to hear your ox is sick. Hope he will soon get well. Also hope that you will have snow to enable you to accomplish what you so much desire, but recollect Henry, *making calls* and *going sleigh riding* is very dangerous. *Be careful.* I am afraid Robert Spence will get himself into trouble, but I suppose he knows his own business. I don't wonder Mrs. R. is furious. I don't think that will ever be my situation. You ask what has become of Vandivere. He is with Co. M. About 20 miles from here at a little vilage [sic] called *Horntown*. Oh my Henry do you ever think of Pongoteague? I'll bet you are going to make me a rolling pin and a potato masher. How kind you are. I know they will be nice, and you may rest assured when I leave I would never leave them here. Why Henry I would not live in this country if they would give me the best farm in the state. I hope Day's children have got well. Give my love to Harry and tell him I would like to see him. Tell him I hope he is a strong Union boy.

I read your letter with the $20 enclosed yesterday. When it came we had $2.60 in the house. You are afraid we are spending too much these hard times. Well Henry we have not got anything that we could possibly do without. Bennie had loaned considerable, and you have no idea how expensive it is living down here. I will give you an idea. We pay 60 cts. per pair for chicken., 25 cts. per lb. For coffee, 15 cents for brown sugar, and 20 for white, 40 cts. per pound for candles and 30 cts. for butter and firkin butter at that, and glad to get it. Saxon owes me $3.53. You can give him a receipt if he pays you. I read Lottie's letter and glad indeed to hear from her. Hope she will write often. I have never heard a word from Lou since I came down here, except what Lottie wrote me. You know I wrote to her before I left home, and have written since I came here, and Henry I don't think I will ever write to them again if they don't write to me.

Henry I am going to send you $100 and I would be glad indeed if you could get Day to take it and give me gold for it, and if he cannot, ask him to please give me Delaware notes. He is always paying out money, and I want to lay it away, and I don't have much faith in treasury notes. At least I do not want to lay that kind of money away. Please attend to it for me, and put it with the rest. I wish you could get the 20 dollars back you give in exchange for notes you sent me. I will leave it all to you, and know you will do the best you can. I don't want anyone else to know anything about our affairs but you. Tell me how you succeed when you write. I am sorry to hear Mother has not been so well. I would like very much to see her and often do in imagination, and Charlotte too. I hope her throat has got well. Tell her the yeast cake is splendid. I use if for buckwheat cakes. We buy our bread. My Henry but Levi is a good old fellow and he is as kind to me as he can be. He reminds me of Charlotte. I wonder if Johnny would like to see me, Henry. Billy and the carriage will get a good rest now. Won't they? Henry, you say I will be welcome home, come when I may. God bless you. I believe that. Won't I be glad to see you and I have so much to tell you that I cannot write about. Tell me what you paid for the butter. We got our things from Balto. This week, *ham, candles, coffee, sugar, tea, pepper, and sausage.* We have to pay 15 cts. per lb. for sausage down here, and not good either.

Tell Lottie I am glad to hear she is so fat, and still able to laugh. Tell her I guess I can laugh some too. Levi concluded not to lay on the shelf. He has torn it down. Bennie was going to build a larger kitchen, but I think he had better not. It will be more expense and it is so uncertain about our staying her any length of time. Henry tell us all the flying reports I think Uncle William is carrying a bold stroke, poor fellow. I don't know what will become of him. It is after 10 o'clock and I must stop and wash Bennie. Who washes you now. I wish I could. Bennie joins me in love to dear Mother, Lydia and Lottie, and all our friends. Do not forget me, and write often. Goodbye,

> Your affectionate niece,
> Lottie Ricketts

> Camp Wilkes Feb. 1st 1862
> Drummondtown, Virginia

My dear Uncle Henry,

My dear little wife received your kind letter yesterday. My oh, but we were glad to hear from you, and to hear that you are so well. Why Henry what is the matter with you, you must be getting fat; as you say you would hardly believe how well Lottie looks. She and I are both getting heavier. I will be so happy if I take her up home again looking a great deal better than she was when she left home. I tell you what it is. I have my own fun plaguing her. I told her the other day at the dinner table, that I was getting uneasy about her. I said I was afraid she was hurting herself by eating so much. But without joking she has a most excellent appetite and I am very glad of it.

Sunday Night—Well I thought I would have written a very long letter this time but I really have not time. I will however write soon again.

Henry Mullin is going home tomorrow morning. Lottie is busy writing. We were paid off a day or two ago. I am officer of the day and have been busy. A good many of the men are out from camp without leave. Henry we want you to write to us often. You would not believe how glad we are to hear from you. Remember me to Day and Dr. Give my love to dear old Mother. My oh! But I would be glad to see her. I do not know when we will leave here. Not until next spring I expect. When you write tell us all the news.

I hope you are well and enjoying yourself very much. How many squirrels and partridges did you kill this season? How is your O. Has he got well? Lottie and I are studying the Ency. Tell her if you understand what she says about the K and P being near the L. C. Well goodbye Henry. I will write you a long letter soon.

Very truly and affectionately yours,
Ben Ricketts

[Undated letter that may have been included with Ben's letter of 2/1/62. He says that Lottie is writing a letter, and she asks for a dress to be used if they stay until March.]

Henry, I would like to have a thinner dress, if I stay here until March. The dresses I have with me will be too heavy. It is so much warmer here than there. We have not had one right cold day yet. I have not seen the least bit of ice yet. Mr. Mullin is going up and will bring it down to me. Ask Lottie to look in the large chest in the garret and get my *barege dress* I got last summer, and do you unlock my bureau drawer. I think the one next to the bottom and she will find the little cape like the dress. If it is not there, tell her to look in the other drawers, but I think it is in the one I spoke of. She need not look in the drawer where the money is. I know it is not there. Henry do not let anyone have my key but yourself. Wrap the dress and cape up as small as you can and give them to Mr. Mullin, directed to me. How is Silas and Mary and the children? Give my love to them.

Lottie wants to know if I have had to spat Bennie with a shingle. Tell her not yet, but indeed I think he is right happy. I will ask him. He says he has deserved it many a time, but I spared him. You might send me two pr. of stockings. You will find them in the little drawer next to the entry. I will send you the money the first opportunity I have, and get gold. If you go to Elk Vale, tell me all about it. This is Sunday night. I can see you lying on the sofa. How I would like to step in. I know you miss me but never mind. I hope we will all meet again under more favorable circumstances.

Goodbye,
Lottie

Camp Wilkes, Va.
Feb. 24, 1862
Monday Afternoon

My Dear Uncle,

It is now about time for me to write you another letter. It seems to be a great satisfaction to you to hear from me, and I am sure it is a pleasure for me to do anything I can for you. I don't know what I would give to see you just now. I wish this cruel war was over, so that we could be situated where we could enjoy the society of our friends. What do people in general think of the war? Do they think there is any prospect of a settlement?

We have a great deal of wet weather here. Today it is clear and blowing a perfect hurricane. The old cabin fairly shakes. I read your kind letter. My oh Henry don't talk about breaking up housekeeping. It makes me feel sad. I know while you have a home I have one, and rest assured if ever I have a home to call my own, you have a home too. *So says my dear husband too.*

I hope Charlotte will soon be well and then with Lottie's assistance you can get along very well, I think. Don't break up housekeeping while Mother lives, anyhow. She would never be satisfied anywhere else. I hope her health is better. So you have been to see Sallie, and she had a great deal to say. Well, Henry, let her talk and all the rest put together. I don't know as they can do me any harm. I wish them all well. Thanks to kind Providence I have a husband that [as you say] I believe will take care of me. I know he will try at least. I suppose it is a terrible thing I didn't go out to Lou's before I came down here. Well I expect I would go and have done as much for Lou as some others.

I wish you could send me some scrapple. I tell you I could enjoy it now. I would like to see old Nero wag his tail. I expect he has forgotten me. I am sorry to hear of Sarah Lynch's misfortune. I am glad you paid my quarterage. I know you will take care of the money. Bennie and I dined at Col. Baily's today. I don't know when the Reg. will leave here. One day they are going right off. The next they are going to remain here all summer. Col. Wharton is putting an addition to his house [a bedroom for his daughter]. He does not know when we will leave here more than we do. Mrs. Baily has just come into tell me she and Col. are going to Wilmington and to leave her keys with me. They will return on Saturday. Everything is done here in a hurry. They knew nothing of it this morning. Bennie and I are going to take a ride tomorrow. We get oysters now quite often. I stewed some for Bennie last night. They were "splen." we did wish you could help us eat them.

Bennie was officer of the day and had to be up until midnight. Tell me if you need the money I sent. Lottie says you often talk of not sending your letters after you write them. Now I hope you will never do that. If you knew how I appreciate them, I think you would feel paid for your trouble. I have never heard from Lou yet. Bennie wrote to Mrs. * asking him [should be *her*?] to write and let me know how she was. I am glad to hear your health is so good. Hope it may continue. We are both well as usual. We had *Lieut. Todd* to dine with us last week. Poor fellow, he is no better. I guess he will have to resign. What do you think of the little paper, *The Regimental Flag*?

Henry don't you intend to go to E V any more? My but I would like to talk to you about it. Tell Lottie I will answer her kind letter. Bennie joins me in much love to you, Mother and Lottie. When you write tell me all the news. I read the Balt. Sun today from Aunt Janie. I have nothing more to write about so I guess I will stop. Give my love to all inquiring friends, not forgetting little Harry.

Your ever affectionate niece,
Lottie

The letter above ends the correspondence between the Ricketts and Henry Carter. Ben wrote the following after Lottie's death, when he expresses his deep sense of loss to his clergyman, Joseph Brown of Cherry Hill.

♦ Appendix A: Letters ♦

Washington, D.C.
January 5, 1864

My dear Mr. Brown,

Ever since I came back to this city, I have been thinking of writing to you. And tonight I will try and write you a few lines.

I am now boarding at No. 470 Seventh Street and an excellent boarding house it is. I have not commenced work at my new office yet; but am still during the great part of the day at the Ordnance Office. I go up there because I have to pass away the time somehow; and I get tired of staying in my room all day and night too. But I expect with a few days to go to work in my new situation. So if you come here before you hear from me again call either at 470 Seventh Street or Room 45 Ordnance Office war department. It is nearly opposite the War Buildings.

The weather is very cold here now. It snowed nearly all day yesterday, and tonight it is clear and cold. The streets are very slippery, and walking is almost dangerous. There is nothing new here of any account in fact the city looks rather dull to me.

Well Mr. Brown I wish I was ready to leave this world; I think I now want to go. I am very sad and low now. I never knew before what it was to have sorrow and trouble. But I know now. May the good Lord help me to try and live a better man, and try to live so that I will when I die go where my darling Lottie has gone. She was a frail, delicate little mortal, but I loved her almost as well as I loved my life I think. I do not know how well I loved her; but I loved her as well as I knew how. Poor dear child. I tried to be good and kind to her while the good Lord let us be together; and I am glad now that I was. My Oh! but she did love me; just as true and as sincerely as ever a man was loved. I miss her company, I miss her kindness, I miss her love; and I miss the blessed influence her life and example had over me. God help me to try and live a purer, holier life; and live for heaven. I fell very bad indeed, and I scarcely know sometimes what I shall do.

I hope you are getting much better, and that you will soon be well. Write to me and please direct your letter to Room 45 Ord. Off. War Dept.

Remember me to all the family. I hope they are well. I feel so sad and lonely that I cannot write to you as I could wish.

Yours very truly,
Ben Ricketts

Another letter found in the Historical Society of Cecil County:

Elkton, MD. R. D. 5

My Dear Mrs. Patterson,

I am returning the letters you so kindly let us read. How sad it was for my Uncle Ben to lose his wife he loved so well. After the war, his health was so impaired he could not engage in business, and that was an added trial. We could have learned much more from my father, but he felt his loss greatly and did not talk to his children much about it. Only one of my father's sisters outlived him, and she never seemed to us to know anything about it. I have the watch and wedding rings. We also have Uncle Ben's sword, which he left to my father, but we always had to hide it to keep it out of the children's reach. However it is safe here in the house somewhere. I trust you and your husband will come to see us sometime and if we can give you any further information will be glad to do so.

Yours very sincerely,
Margaret Ricketts

Columbus Washington Wilson of Port Deposit served in Company G, 6th Maryland.

Battlefield   Hanover Co. Va.
June 8, 1864

Dear Bud,
I have a few minutes of leisure time and I thought I would write you a few lines if you don't think a nough of me to write.

Bud, I am nearly plaid out for we have been on the go for over 2 months night and day and it is trying for a man but it is getting a great deal easery on us but they keep us knocking away at the joneys and also grant is at his Vicksburg plan for digging them out of there holes. We have dug nearly all Virginia up we dig nights and days we fight. We are within a couple hundred yards of the rebels breastwork and we can see them anytime.

Bud we crost over the rapodan on the fourth of May and on the fifth we were in a fight. We went in about five o'clock in the evening and fought till nine at night and the next morning was renewed and fought all day and the next also wich was the seventh of the month and our loss was nearly two hundred, I believe and we have been fighting for the balance of the time and are now still fighting. We could now [not?] get much sleep. But I don't know when I did not here a cannon or a gun for they are going all the time and the bullets are flying thick over our heads but none has struck me down. Glad I have come out safe so far.

Bud we are within eight miles of Richmond. Can you see the **** that was the matter with **** leg her boot woden fit her. Bud I would like for you to send me the baltimore american till I could see the news. I would be a blige to you. I will end my best respect to all and please exept the same from your true friend.

CWW
Columbus Wilson Esq. son of old man Wilson

Write soon and give the partikulers
Directions, Columbus Washington Wilson, Co. G, 6th Md. Vols. 6 A. C. Via Washington, D. C.

♦ Appendix A: Letters ♦

Camp Brandy Station
December 25

Friend Bud,

I received your letter in dieu time and I was very glad to hear from you, and I also hope these few lines may find you and all the rest well and enjoying good health.

Bud this is what they call Christmas but it is no more Christmas with me.

I have seen the time I could see some gay old times on that day but it is plaid out for a while. But I hope I may see them times again in part I hope you will enjoy yourself and enjoy my part too.

Bud your father started from this camp on last Wednesday morning for hope. I hop he reached his plantation safe. Bud I want you to send me a Christmas present for there is nothing like that down here. All we can get is hard tack and slip gut until you get as fat as a pig for me. I am so fat it makes me pore to carry it. My wait is 175 pounds clear of cakes and such like.

Bud if I was home on this day I would hert myself I know for I would eat and drink all of old Christy Baker's winter supplies and I know he would not have any lager beer left for the bummers around him. I know I would eat Phillip's Bakery out.

Bud, they are giving furloughs in the Regm. now and I hope I will get one stray one as it passes by and don't you be surprised if you see a long legged man jump off the port steamer and walk up toward the street and jump upon the curbstone like someone from the city. I must close. Give my best respect to all and please exept the same from me.

CSS Private in Co. G 6th Md.
2 Brigade 3 division, 3 corps
Army of the Potomac

The following letter was written to Dr. Charles Tilden Sempers of North East, surgeon in the Sixth Maryland.

Elkton, Maryland
June 23, 1864

My dear Doctor,

I received your letter with a great deal of pleasure.

The Sixth Maryland is very dear to us, especially since the evidence of their heroic devotion which the last few months have furnished.

Major Hill is better now, but for a while was very ill. Some portion of his clothing was forced into his wound and did not come out with the ball, and caused great swelling and inflammation, until it finally worked out. He is able to get out a little on crutches now.

You ask about the opinion here in regard to the Army of the Potomac among the rebel sympathizers. Just what it always has been, viz., that it never has and never will gain a victory over Lee. Of course with them "the wish is father to the thought." Their incredulity is part of the deep seated hatred of everything which looks to the maintenance of democratic institutions. They want Grant to fail and Lee to succeed because they know that sooner or later these states must be united under one government, and they desire that government to be the one which southern aristocrats have commenced to build but which, if ever finished, will be finished into the most complete tyranny ever devised by man.

But there is no loyal man today who does not feel that the Army of the Potomac is the nation's hope and that it is the noblest army that ever trod the earth.

There is very little news of a local character. The nomination of Mr. Lincoln is well received and would be very enthusiastically hailed but for the more important war program. Speeches would doubtless be the order of the day but for the fact that we feel that the best speeches and the most effective are those from Grant's guns.

The convention goes slowly but I think not less surely to its great work of making Maryland a free state. I am not pleased with the slowness of the convention.

I would be very glad if, after casualty in any of the Cecil companies, you would inform me of the fact and state who are killed, who wounded and the character of their wounds, as most of the relatives come to my office for news.

Tell our boys that we are all very proud of them. The Cecil company of the second Delaware is expected daily, and our ladies are preparing a good welcome for them.

Truly yours,
W. J. Jones

Dr. Sempers wrote the following to his wife. The photographs he mentions can be seen in the Historical Society of Cecil County. Captain Beaver married Emma Alice Browne, a Cecil County poetess, in 1864.

Head Qrs., 6th Md. Vols.
February 22nd, 1864

My Dear Wife,

Yours of the 9th has been received, also that of the 17th. When you next write, send me three more of the photographs in the letter as I desire to give them in exchange for some of the officers of our regiment. I have inclosed two photographs, one of Colonel Horn and the other of Capt. Beaver of our regiment.

I wrote a letter to W. J. Jones, one of our representatives in the Legislature, relative to Maryland soldiers being sent home to vote at the election in April next. To my surprise I saw an extract from it in the next CECIL WHIG purporting to have been from a citizen of Cecil who had been six months in Libby Prison. I saw it copied in the Baltimore American and also in the Washington Chronicle, a notoriety that I did not dream for the letter when I penned it. If you should feel enough curiosity to see it, you will find it in the CECIL WHIG of last Saturday, February 13th

It is snowing and blowing here, but our hut is warm and comfortable. I pity the poor fellows who have picket duty to perform such weather as this. How I fervently pray for this war to be ended. There seems to be little use in indulging in such thoughts as there will be no peace until the rebellion is crushed, which apparently is in a fair way to that consummation. I should rejoice if that could take place tomorrow. We will hope for the best, perform our duty, and leave the issue in the hands of the Great Disposer of human events.

Write me soon. You will please take care of the photographs of the officers sent as I wish to preserve them. I expect to get more and wish them to be kept together.

C. T. Sempers

Dr. Sempers and Reverend Joseph Brown of Cherry Hill were Libby Prison inmates. While there, Sempers loaned $4.25 to the chaplain, who proposed a plan of settlement in the letter below.

Dear Doctor:

I wrote on the 9th to the Colonel and Major stating that it was my wish that you would buy my horse. I shall not be able to resume my duty in the Regiment owing to my present condition of health, and unless I could get a position in some of our hospitals when I recover my health, I shall have to retire altogether.

I therefore offer you my horse for what I gave for him, namely 60 Dols. He is a good horse. I gave him a fair trial on the 7 days' march on the Rapidan, and John Hagey told me that no horse in the regiment stood the march and retreat from Winchester better than he did. I refer you to Hagey who takes care of him.

By the time this reaches you I will owe Hagey 10 Dols. for taking care of him. If you should buy the horse I want you to pay Hagey the 10 Dols. I also owe you $4.25 contracted in Libby Prison which will make $14.25 to be deducted from the price of the horse. He is certainly worth twice the amount I ask for him if I had him at home. The saddle you can have for nothing.

I hope, dear doctor, you will do the best you can for me and let me hear from you on receipt of this. I am still confined to my room. Give my love to all the officers and men.

Yours as ever,
Jos. T. Brown

Colonel Joseph C. Hill of Elkton described the participation of the 6th Maryland in the battles preceding Lee's surrender. Robert C. Davis, one of the four reported wounded, died of those wounds on April 19, 1865. He is buried at Leeds.

My dear Friend:

Your kind and welcome note of the 21st, came to hand last evening, and I hasten to comply with your request.

So please find enclosed a copy of your discharge. Well, old friend, I and the Old Sixth have seen some hard times since you left us, in the way of marches and hard fighting; but I am proud to say that the Old Sixth has made herself a good name, not only in the brigade and division but in the corps. There is none stands higher in the estimation than the Little Six, as we are called.

♦ Appendix A: Letters ♦

In the charge on April second, in front of Petersburg, the colors of this regiment were the first to be planted on the Rebel works. But our loss was heavy in the officers; in all I lost six officers wounded, four men killed and nineteen wounded. Major C. K. Prentiss was badly wounded but he will recover. Captain Ocker, I understand cannot live and Lieut. Angel has died of his wounds. There are very few of the old officers left in the regiment.

We had a hard fight on the 6th of April at Sailors Run, but our loss in that fight was light; we lost only four men wounded. For my own part, I had the misfortune of being captured in that fight, but I had the good fortune of getting away from them and in rather a singular way.

It happened in this way. After being captured I was hurried to the rear, where I found five field officers and some two hundred men in reserve of their main line. By the time they got me back our cavalry was in their rear, and they found they would all be captured. They said they didn't want to be captured by our cavalry, and if I would take them out they would surrender to me; so I ordered them to throw down their arms, which they did, and I marched over two hundred prisoners out. So you see, I did right well for one man.

But Doc., it would have done you good to have been with us at the surrender of Lee's Army! Such an excitement I never saw and never expect to see again. All was joy and gladness, and little did we think that our joy would so soon be turned to sadness. It was but a few days until the sad news reached us that this hell-begotten rebellion had culminated in the murder of our beloved President; every soldier felt that he had lost his best friend, and if the rebels do not think so, they ought to; for as you say, I think they will not find the milk of human kindness flow so freely from Andy Johnson as from our late President.

Dr. E. K. Foreman wishes to be remembered to you, as do all the officers and men of the regiment. We expect to move back along the railroad in a day or two; our division is to guard it from this point to Burkesville.

I am well and hope this may find you the same.

I am very respectfully your obedient servant,
J. C. Hill

James Touchstone was quartermaster with the 6th Maryland.

Camp near Culpepper, Va
Jany. 12th 1864

My Dear Son

I ought to have written a letter yesterday, but my time was occupied until it was too late.

I am happy to be able to say that I and "Pips" are well.—Haze is enjoying himself exceedingly. He was a little sick yesterday (Sunday) with headache—caused, I think by drinking some cider made of dried apples and eating too much. I put him to bed with a hot brick to his feet and he was well enough to eat his supper. This morning he is allright and is full of fun. He as been sitting by me all day *Making* out *Requisitions*. You would be surprised how expert he is at it. He can fill up a blank better than some of the officers. Mother need have no fear of him learning anything bad here. He is always with me. Indeed, situated as we are here, he is much better with me than he would be at home. He spends part of his time in reading books which I got him at Washington.—One called "Swiss Family Robinson" and one called "Pollocks Course of Time." I think he will do better here than he would if he were even going to school at home unless I were there to look after him.

I am getting up my accounts and want to have all straightened by the 1st of March, when you may expect me home. The time will soon roll round as we are now nearly in the middle of January. I have said that I was well but perhaps I should qualify the word "well," a little. I have a cold in my head. With this exception, I am all right.

I do not know what I am going to do for a pair of boots for Haze. His are entirely too small. I wonder why Mother had them. They will never do him any good. If I had the ones I left at home, he could wear them out in knocking about.

I wouldn't care if Mother would send me a box by express. I should like to have some good butter in it.—a chicken or two—a few biscuits and a few mince pies. If a pair of good *large* boots can be got for Haze, perhaps Mr. Orr would bring them when he comes back. I think he will be home some time next week.

Kiss "Mom" and the "pets" for me and give my love to all—I suppose you are at school remember what *you promised me about school.* Write soon.

Your affect. Father
J. Touchstone

Around the margin:
I hope you have sold the horse. If not, see Geo. Owens and perhaps he can sell him for you.

Appendix B

Cecil Confederates

According to the records at the Historical Society compiled by Nelson H. McCall, the following are the Cecil soldiers who joined the Confederacy. The names are from Daniel D. Hartzler's *Maryland in the Confederacy*.

A. B. Alexander, Pvt., Co. C, 2nd AR Infantry, CSA

N. E. Alexander, 1st Maryland

John Archer, Capt., Asst. A., Gen. C. S. Winder's staff

Alexander Briscoe, Elkton, sailor, CSA

Henry Briscoe, Pvt., Co. H. 1st Maryland Infantry, CSA

Charles Bryan, Pvt., Chesapeake City, 1st Maryland Cavalry, CSA

George W. Buckingham, Elk Landing, 1st Virginia Cavalry, [Sgt]

James Thomas Bussey, Capt., 2nd Maryland Infantry, CSA

Enoch Cantwell, claimed forced enlistment

Giles Buchner Cooke, Maj., Asst. Adj. and IG., Gen. R. E. Lee's staff

Thomas E. Cropper, Pvt., Co. B, 1st Maryland Cavalry, CSA

Appendix B: Cecil Confederates

John W. Dunning, Pvt., Chesapeake City, Co. D., 43rd Virginia Cavalry [Mosby's]
  Used treasonable language. Tried to evade military duty by leaving county. Confined to Fort McHenry

Harvey S. Ewing, Pvt., Co. D, 1st Maryland Cavalry, CSA

Stephen H. Ford, Master, Navy, on CSS *Indian Chief*

John Gilpin, Elkton, Corp., 1st Maryland Cavalry, CSA

Elias Glenn, Pvt., 1st Maryland Cavalry, CSA
  Was seen by Doctor Ellis when he was in Richmond (*Democrat* 8/2/62)

J. Sewell Glenn. Captured Winchester, Va. 1863

William Oliver Green, Pvt., Co. B, 2nd Virginia Infantry

John Hasson, Charlestown, Lt., 1st Maryland Cavalry, CSA
  Son of James; accidentally shot through hand (*Democrat* 3/1/56)

Ed. Langley, Sgt 3rd Maryland Artillery

Mansfield Lovell, Maj. Gen., Dept. of New Orleans

William Whann Mackall, Brig. Gen. Bragg's Chief of Staff

Nicholas P. Manley, Pvt. Co. B, 9th Virginia Infantry

James A. May [Elkton]

William H. May, Corp., 1st Maryland Light Artillery. CSA
  Was seen by Doctor Ellis when he was in Richmond (*Democrat* 8/2/62)

William R. McCullough, Sgt. Maj., 2nd Maryland Infantry, CSA

Charles McMahon [Elkton]

H. D. Miller, Pvt., 1st Maryland Light Artillery, CSA

William P. Minor, Pvt. 20th Virginia Heavy Artillery

♦ Appendix B: Cecil Confederates ♦

William Moffet, Pvt., Lucas' 15th Heavy Artillery [S.C.]

Thomas H. Musgrove, Pvt., 1st Maryland Light Artillery

William Thompson Patton, Port Deposit, Lt., 3rd Maryland Light Artillery. CSA

John B. Rowan, Elkton, Capt., 3rd Maryland Light Artillery
    4/25/57 married Sarah Howard, daughter of Thomas Howard
    12/7/67 Sarah married Ritter, who had escorted Rowan's body to Elkton
    6/25/92 *Democrat* death of Sarah Rowan Ritter

John L. Vallindingham, Pvt., Co. B. 1st Maryland Cavalry CSA

David G. White, Port Deposit, Lt. Col., [resigned from West Point]
Notes supplied by E. A. Howard in the Historical Society files, dated 4/24/1964, state:

> Col. David G. White, who died at West River, Maryland, on April 13, 1889, was a native of Port Deposit, where he was born in 1840. When he was 17 years old his father sent him to Delaware College to complete his education, but in 1858 he went as a cadet to the Military academy at West Point.
> When the Civil War broke out in 1861 he, along with a number of other Southern cadets, resigned and joined the Confederate army. He attracted the attention of General William J. Hardee by his gallantry and was given a position on his staff with the rank of captain. He rose rapidly through the ranks of major and lieutenant-colonel to colonel.
> At the battle of Missionary Ridge on November 25, 1863, Col. White was chosen by General Hardee, who was holding the Confederate right, to capture the "Glass House" just below the tunnel where Federal sharpshooters were ensconced and picking off Confederate officers. At the head of 300 soldiers he dashed down the steep slope and soon reduced the house to ashes. Col. White at that time was 23 years of age. General Cleburne said of him that he was "the personification of a soldier." When the war ended he was suffering from a severe wound which he received while in command of a cavalry brigade.
> When the Khedive of Egypt re-organized his army with the aid of American officers Col. White was offered a commission, which he accepted and did valuable work for the Khedive. He commanded an expedition into Palestine and led a column into Abyssinia. After his return from Egypt and until his death he had been engaged in the coal and lumber business at West River.
> Col White was the second son of Captain David White who in the 1850s was a familiar character and resident of Port Deposit. He owned and controlled a line of small steamers which ran between Port Deposit and Havre de Grace, and he also operated a line of packets to Baltimore.

♦ Appendix B: Cecil Confederates ♦

A small gravestone in North East Cemetery bears this inscription:
Major David C. White
C. S. A.
Died Aug. 11, 1889
A tribute by Wingate Post
No. 9, G. A. R.
July 4, 1898

This appears to be inaccurate because the account of Col. White's death is reported in the *Cecil Democrat* of April 20, 1889, p. 3.

An item from Port Deposit published in the *Democrat* of March 22, 1873, reports that Edwin C. White, son of Capt. David White, formerly of that place, was buried in the North East cemetery on March 20, 1873.

Stephen Frick Cameron was an ordained minister, who seems to have deserted his wife, Mary Stites Cameron, and their three children to become a chaplain in the First Maryland, CSA. According to his testimony at the trial of John H. Surratt in 1867, he was born in Philadelphia, the son of a Catholic mother and a Protestant father. The family moved to Cecil County, and Stephen considered himself a Catholic up until he was about ten years of age. Then, under his father's direction, he attended the Episcopal Church. On June 24, 1853, he married Mary A. Stites, daughter of Henry S. Stites, who owned a mill east of Elkton.

Cameron studied for the ministry at the General Theological Seminary in New York. Their eldest son Clarence was born in New York *circa* 1856, presumably while Stephen was studying there. On April 17, 1858, a notice of the reorganization of Trinity Church's vestry appeared in the *Democrat*: "Vestry—S. S. Maffitt, George Earle, S. B. Foard, John Partridge, W. Ward Henderson, Capt. James Hughes, T. H. B. Hollingsworth, R. G. Reese. Wardens—Roger Hurry, S. F. Cameron. Register—R. G. Reese." In May or June of 1861, Cameron was ordained.

He first crossed to the South on June 24; his commission was dated July 24, 1861. At some point, he was caught crossing the Potomac. He carried only religious books with him and was confined to Carroll Prison in Washington for 3 months. He then joined Morgan's Guerillas as chaplain. Whatever his clerical duties might have been, he also was a courier between Richmond and Confederates in Canada.

On February 18, 1865, the *Democrat* carried the following:

> The St. Alban's Raiders—We notice that Rev. Stephen F. Cameron, formerly of this town, was a messenger between Richmond and Montreal, bearing documents to be used as testimony in this case. A dispatch from Montreal dated Feb. 14, says: "Cameron, the

messenger from Richmond, formerly Morgan's chaplain, arrived this afternoon, with documents proving the belligerency of the raiders. He left Richmond the 4th inst. and was delayed by ice in the Potomac. Two others of his company were drowned."

On August 16, 1865, the same paper noted:

Died. Near this town, on Saturday evening last, John S., son of Stephen F. and Mary Cameron, aged about six months.

This child would, then, have been born about February 1865. Yet, Cameron claimed under oath that he had not seen Mary since "about 1863."

Cameron reverted to Catholicism on May 1, 1865, at a ceremony before the Vicar General at Quebec. In November, he traveled to Liverpool, where he wrote a few articles for the *Liverpool Post*, and the *Daily Courier* about the rebel ship *Shenandoah*. At this time, he saw John Surratt in London. Cameron visited France, before returning to Canada, where he lived with a priest at St. Michel Bellechasse, about 15 miles from Quebec.

In 1867, Cameron returned to the U.S. from Canada about six weeks before John Surratt's trial began. The *Democrat* reported comic relief in the courtroom.

"Cecil County" Wanted. The Washington *Star* of July 25th, says: On Wednesday, in the Surratt case, a large number of Cecil county witnesses were called for the defense to testify to the character of Stephen F. Cameron. After several of them had been examined, Mr. Merrick, one of the prisoner's counsel, called a witness who did not answer, and wishing to have some witnesses on the stand at once, asked the bailiff to call Cecil county. The bailiff, thinking some witness of that name was wanted, immediately shouted "Cecil County!" and the other bailiffs about the room called out hastily for "Mr. County!" While this was going on the witness previously called came forward to answer to his name, and was conducted by the bailiff to the stand. One of the counsel asked "Who's this?" to which the bailiff answered, "That's him. Cecil County—the man you wanted," amid a loudish titter in which the prisoner, counsel, judges and jury participated.

If the town had been ripped on a horizontal line between North and South during the war, it was torn on the diagonal when Cecil Countians testified for or against Cameron. Strong Union supporters [*e.g.* Dr. Ellis], whom one would expect to testify against him, appeared for the defense, while some [*e.g.* John V. Reardon] who had harbored anti-war sentiments supported the prosecution. The *Whig* wrote on July 27, 1867:

CAMERON.—The latest excitement in Elkton is the Cameron excitement. Readers of *The Whig* have, during the rebellion, seen occasional notices of an excentric [*sic*], miscellaneous genius by the name of Stephen F. Cameron. His name got into the history of the rebellion by his being a kind of spy and runner for the rebels. He was captured in one of his expeditions during the war and confined in the Old Capitol Prison at Washington. After being there awhile, he was considered of so little importance that his escape was winked at.

Cameron has recently appeared on the stage again, as a witness in the Surratt trial, called by the defense to impeach the evidence of Dr. McMillan. Last week the prosecution summoned several witnesses from Elkton to testify to Cameron's character for truth and reliability. The witnesses called in order by the prosecution were Jos. Wells, Jas. S. Crawford, James T. McCullough, John Torbert, Jos. L. Mahan, John V. Reardon, and Frank Titus, all residents of Elkton and intimate acquaintances of Cameron, while he resided here. The burden of their testimony was that he was an erratic, crack-brained fellow, whose reputation was bad, and whom they would not believe on oath. The defense, to show what a universal genius this Cameron was, summoned another batch of witnesses from Elkton, who were examined in the matter of Cameron's reputation as a man of truth, reliability and good character, on Wednesday last.

Rev. Stephen F. Cameron
from John F. Headley's *Confederate Operations in Canada and New York*

The witnesses from Elkton called by the defense were Geo. R. Howard, Daniel Bratton, Eli Cosgrove, John Partridge, R. G. Reese, W. G. Purnell, Thos. Drennan, John Hogg, Hon. Hiram McCullough, Dr. C. M. Ellis, Joseph R. Brown, Aaron G. Tuite, Joseph P. Cantwell, David Scott, John M. Miller, James B. Groome, S. B. Foard, Reuben D. Jamar, and Perry Litzenberg.—These witnesses all knew Cameron intimately, they testified, who had an excellent character for veracity and truth. Several made it a point to testify that they moved in Cameron's circle, which "circle" has become quite a by-word since, among Elktonians.

The "general reputation" of the excentric Stephen has apparently risen very rapidly within a few days with some of our citizens. Cameron's status before the Surratt trial was fixed by all parties to be a kind of cross betwixt a knave and a fool. This perhaps explains the seeming difference of opinion between the honorable gentlemen called to the stand. Those who testified to his reputation being bad and his word not reliable, contemplated him in the character of a *knave*, and those who considered his reputation good and could believe him an oath, doubtless viewed Stephen as a fool, it being a proverb that fools speak the truth. On no other theory can we reconcile such conflicting testimony on the part of honorable witnesses, who all know the man so well.

The man who runs off and forsakes an amiable wife and family of interesting children, for no other reason than that he is too lazy, worthless and good for nothing to exert himself to support them, leaving them to the care of others; who apostatizes from a protestant minister to a catholic priest; who under false pretense of aiding the Union cause procured a pass over the railroads of the country, in '61, from the Secretary of War, and used it to practice the business of a rebel spy, has no claim whatever, to good character, or reputation for truth. All of these crimes is Stephen F. Cameron guilty of, and the crowd of witnesses named above who testified to his good character, knowing these things of Cameron are guilty of aiming a mortal stab at piety and the most sacred Christian virtues. Not one of all those witnesses who testified to Cameron's "good character," has the least confidence in him as a minister, as a husband, or as a man.—A man destitute of all the virtues which adorn these positions in life, cannot possess a good reputation.

Mary Cameron sued for divorce, according to the *Whig* of September 7, 1867, on the grounds that her husband had abandoned her. Her father, General Henry S. Stites, died at his residence near Elkton in March 1870. The General was for 12 years a Judge of Orphan's Court. Under the old militia system, he attained the rank of Brigadier General. Mary inherited the mill and apparently operated it, for she was listed in a local atlas as a farmer and miller. She died in 1907 at the home of her son Clarence in Philadelphia.

Stephen F. Cameron was in the process of writing *History of the Confederate Secret Service*. He mentioned this venture in the Surratt trial. An unsigned manuscript attributed to him is in the archives of the The Museum of the Confederacy in Richmond, Virginia.

During the trial, when Cameron was asked directly if he was a curate, he replied, "No sir. They sometimes admit laymen to their association when they are of a respectable character." It may be that he did not become a Catholic priest as the *Whig* suggested. A search recently conducted by the Archdiocese of Quebec did not reveal his name in the archives. No one knows when or where he died.

Appendix C

Military and Pension Records of other Cecil County Soldiers

In addition to those of Maj. Benjamin Ricketts, the military and pension records of several other soldiers were requested from the National Archives in Washington, D.C. The information gleaned from those records and from the two local Cecil County papers follows.

Henry M. Bennett, Company C, 2nd Delaware
September 17, 1862. He was shot in the neck and died at Antietam.
May 19, 1873. His mother, Ellen Jane Bennett, applied for a pension because she had no means of support. She was the widow of Henry P. Bennett, a butcher.
  Amos E. McNeal, H. H. Bennett, and Chas. J. Smith signed sworn statements to the effect that they were in the service with Henry M. Bennett and knew that he sent money home for the support of his parents "each and every payday." Palmer C. Strickland anad W. L. Purnell swore to similar statements.
December 18, 1878. Ellen Jane Bennett died and her son-in-law, W. L. Purnell, swore that he was her legal representative and had borne the expenses of her last sickness and funeral.

Isaac Foreacre, Company C, 2nd Delaware
September 17, 1862. He was wounded in the thigh at Antietam.
September 30, 1862. He died from that wound. His mother, Sarah Foreacre of North East, applied for a pension. Her husband was disabled by diseases that Dr. Buckley named as valvular disease of the heart, paralysis of the left arm and leg, and hemiplegia. The post master said that in his early life, Daniel Foreacre "drank too much. Now temperate."
  George Lottman and William T. Leinch [Linch?] swore before John Torbert, Deputy Clerk of the Circuit Court for Cecil County, that they witnessed Sarah Foreacre make her mark on the statement.
  Merchants Richard L. Thomas and L. W. Thomas declared that before enlisting in Co. C. 2nd Delaware, Isaac Foreacre supplied his parents with provisions and clothing from his wages. They further stated that he purchased such good at their store.
May 28, 1867. Sarah was admitted to a pension of $8 per month, commencing on 30th September, 1862.
December 4, 1884. She was dropped from the roll on, for "failure to claim pension."

♦ Appendix C: Military and Pension Records of other Cecil County Soldiers ♦

George Hardy, Company C, 2nd Delaware

March 14, 1863. Hardy requested a 10-day leave to visit his family, noting that he had not had a leave of absence for over a year.

March 31, 1863. Lieut. J. R. Horner of the 10th NJ Vols., on duty at the V & O Railroad Depot in Washington, DC, swore: "That Lieut. George W. Hardy Co. C. 2nd Del. Did attempt to desert, he being dressed in citizen's clothes when arrested, at the B & O R. R. Depot, denying that he was in the US service, and said that he was a clerk in Wilmington, Del. But upon being taken into custody he produced an expired leave of absence proving him to be a deserter."

He was court-martialed but the verdict of the trial was never made known. At Gettysburg, his commander wrote [7/22/63] on his behalf: "Lieut. Hardy was placed temporarily on duty previous to the battle of Gettysburg; his conduct upon that occasion was such as to entitle him to every consideration...."

Col. Wm. P. Baily wrote [7/19/63] that Hardy also rendered effective service at Chancellorsville and at Gettysburg when his captain was wounded. Baily recommended that Hardy be relieved from arrest and returned to duty.

Dec. 12, 1863, Hardy requested a 10-day leave to visit his family in Elkton.

March 16, 1864, Hardy requested of Charles J. Smith permission to be absent for 24 hours to accompany his wife to Washington. Request granted.

Hardy was by trade a carriage painter. On his return from service, he worked for Reardon and later for Witworth. Finally, he was employed for Dean and Kendall in Wilmington at the same type of work. Hardy was unable to keep a job because he could not keep his mind on his work. "His mind seemed to be weak and he was unfit for the discharge of his duties." He died at the Government Insane Asylum near Washington.

Their children included Ella, born Nov. 20, 1861 and died Jan. 13, 1872; George, born Dec. 22, 1864; Samuel, born October 14, 1867; John, born May 10, 1870.

His widow, Sarah J. Hardy, 34, of Wilmington, Delaware [place of birth, Cecil County], married James R. Baxter, 44, of Chester County, Pennsylvania, on October 16, 1875, Reverend Joseph Welch, pastor of Madison Street Methodist Episcopal Church in Chester, Pennsylvania, officiating.

William Harvey, Company C, 2nd Delaware

He was the brother of Sophia Jeffries and the brother-in-law of William Jeffries. The family lived in North East. When he was sick in Cambridge, Maryland, his sister, possibly Sophia, made the 100-mile journey by stage to meet him and take him home. Captain Ricketts wrote and reminded him to obtain a physician's certificate because his furlough was about to expire.

August and September, 1862. On detached service with ambulance duty.

December 14, 1862. Wounded in the thigh at Battle of Fredericksburg. Treated at Stanton Hospital in Washington, D.C., for contusion of left thigh.

December 26, 1862. "Deserted" and reenlisted with Company K, 1st U.S. Artillery. Here he gave his occupation as shoemaker.

June 12, 1864. Discharged at White Oak Church, Virginia.

March 7, 1868. Wm. Harvey, laborer, 25, married Josephine Smith, age 16 years. Their children include Josephine Baily [b. March 14, 1873], Elizabeth [b. September 20, 1878], Bessie [b. February 6, 1883], Milton [b. February 17 or 18, 1885], Samuel P. [b. February 28, 1886], Charles [b. April 4, 1887].

March 9, 1878. Charges of desertion were removed.

October 8, 1879. Dr. Napoleon Morrison of Wilmington, Delaware, attested to the fact that he prescribed medicine for Harvey's rheumatism and dyspepsia.

October 9, 1879. Samuel Boyer, 42, and John McGlory, 46, both of North East, swore they were privates in Co. C., 2nd Delaware, and that William S. Harvey was in the hospital at Drummondtown, Virginia, during the winter of 1862, sick with rheumatism and dyspepsia.

January 30, 1891. Wm. S. Harvey appeared before a Justice of the Peace in North East and applied for an invalid pension, stating he was unable to earn a living by reason of "dyspepsia, rheumatism, consumption, hemorrhages and disease of the liver, kidneys and general debility."

Nov. 20, 1893. Reapplied for a pension.

William Beatty and Lewis W. Thomas, druggists, swore that they furnished him frequently with medicine on prescription from a physician. Before he went into service, Harvey was healthy, but upon his return he was afflicted with rheumatism and dyspepsia.

June 23, 1899. William Harvey died of pulmonary tuberculosis and was buried at North East Methodist Cemetery.

July 1, 1899. Josephine applied for a widow's pension.

Josephine died in Atlantic City, New Jersey, on May 7, 1934.

There is a curious ambiguity about Josephine's maiden name. When William filled out a form on May 4, 1898, he gave his wife's maiden name as Josephine Elizabeth Helinger. The copy of the Marriage Record shows her as Josephine Smith.

Ephraim Jordan, Company C, 2nd Delaware

He was promoted to Lieutenant when Richards resigned. Jordan was shot through the lungs while on picket duty at Chancellorsville on May 2, 1863. He died at Sandy Hook Hospital near Harpers Ferry. His mother, Elizabeth Jordan, lived at Cherry Hill. She had married her husband, also named Ephraim Jordan, on April 22, 1834, in Marcus Hook, Pennsylvania.

Mrs. Jordan received news of her son's death in following letter.

> 1st Division 2nd Corps Hospital
> Near Potomac Creek, Va.
> May 6th 1863
> Sir:
>
> Your son Lieut Ephraim Jordan was brought to this Hospital about 3 o'clock on Monday morning mortally wounded having been shot through the lungs by a sharpshooter while on picket duty. He died about seven o'clock the same morning. I tried to have him

embalmed and sent on to your residence but I could not find an embalmer nor could I have him sent to you. I have had him buried as decently as possible and have marked his grave by a headboard.

I have his pocketbook which contained Eighty five dollars [$85.00] also two rings and a gold watch which I will keep untill I receive orders from you.

Permit me to console with you in the heavy affliction which it has pleased the Almighty to place on you.

> Very Respectfully
> Your Ob'd Serv't
> Philip M. Plunkett
> Asst. Srg. 2nd Del. Vols.
> In charge 1st Div Hospitals

November 27, 1865. Robert C. Carter and Joseph Miller testified that "since the death of her husband she has no other person to look to who is able to assist her and that prior to the death of her son Ephraim N. Jordan she always received from him a portion of his wages. In fact he was a more reliable provider for her for several years before his death than her husband and [now] that he is gone she is left without anyone to aid her in raising a large family of young children."

July 26, 1866. Joseph Miller again testified, this time with James H. McCullough, that "the father was a drinking man and abandoned the support of his family about the year 1859 and did not provide for their wants thereafter — that he finally joined the Army and died on or about December 10, 1863."

To prove that her son supported her, Elizabeth submitted the following letter.

> My dear kind Mother   Camp Hancock   Feb. 23, 1863
> I sit down to let you know that I am well and harty and hop you are injoinge the Same kind blessinge. I received your kind letter to day wen I read it I fealt Sory to here that the familey is to be broken up, and Irwin is the first to go. I do not like it but I recond it cant be helped but wen I get able I will take him my selfe and Send him to Scol my Selfe he is to Smart to be kep down at worke wen he aught to be goinge to scool like I was. I to day mite have bean at Sumpinge beter if I had onley went to Scool wen I had a chance. but I will See that he git more Scoolinge my Selfe. I have onley 15 munth more to stay in the sirves then I will be able to take him my Selfe if I live thou it wich I hop I will fore more then one thinge. Well mother I Send you $140 dolers by Cap John G. Simpers if you need it you can use it fore your Self and the Childern. Lieut E. M. Jordan
> let me know how father is geting a longe by this time **** all the children —I got a letter from Aunt Beck and one Janey Gooman [?] to day. Know more but anser Sune and let me here from you and ho bought the old house
> Know more but I Still remain you Sun   Lieut E M Jordan

♦ Appendix C: Military and Pension Records of other Cecil County Soldiers ♦

The 1860 Census listed the Jordan family in the Fourth District as follows:

Name	Age	Sex	Profession	Birth
Ephraim Jourdan	49	M	Paper Maker	Pa.
Elizabeth	46	F		Del.
Mary	26	F		Md.
John	24	M	Paper Maker	"
Joseph	22	M	Paper Maker	"
William	20	M	"	"
Ephraim	17	M		
Irwin	10	M		
Elizabeth	8	F		
Victor	7	M		
Herocinthy??	6	F		
Louis	2	M		

Lieutenant Jordan's body laid to rest in St. John's Cemetery. His inscription reads:
"He was in all the battles of the Peninsular campaign and at the battle of Antietam, in the absence of his Captain, he had entire charge of his company. He led them nobly forward, his voice heard above the din of battle cheering his men. He fell a sacrifice to his country at the battle of Chancellorsville May 3, 1863, age 19 years 10 months, and 20 days."

December 11, 1894. Elizabeth died.

William Henry Kingston, Company C, 2nd Delaware
May 4, 1834. His father, John L. Kingston of Elkton, and Eliza Avis Kingston were married in Philadelphia, Pa., by Rev. Jos. H. Kennard.
December 13, 1862. He was severely wounded at Fredericksburg.
January 5, 1863. He died at Douglas Hospital, Washington, DC., from the accidental discharge of a comrade's weapon.
August 8, 1873. His father, George Kingston, died.
November 19, 1889. Eliza died of angina pectoris and was buried in Fernwood cemetery.
December 19, 1889. Samuel, Emma, and Annie Kingston applied for a pension for siblings, who were under sixteen years of age at the time of his death and who were dependent upon him.

Name	Birthdate
George W.	February 22, 1848
Samuel	August 7, 1850
Annie	April 29, 1853
Emma	December 21, 1855
Theodore	March 26, 1860—September 4, 1889

The family submitted the following letter to prove dependence upon their brother.

♦ Appendix C: Military and Pension Records of other Cecil County Soldiers ♦

October 28, 1862
Bolivar Heights
Near harpers ferry

Dear Father and Mother
I received your letter and was glad to here from you all I wrote a letter to you and had mailed it the same night that I received your letter we have been payed off. I have sent $20 dollars I sent it by a man that was down here to see some of the boys he belong in Elkton I sent it by him to Victor Bennett that keeps that brick store as you go into Elkton where the butcher shop is the money is there by this time And you can go there and get it And as soon as you get the money write and let me no something about [it.]
I also sent my likeness to the same place when you go there ask for both the money and the likeness the other letter I wrote it was about the money but the mail was robbed about the time I sent the other letter and I thought I had better write Again And tell you about the money. And likeness there is some prospect of us Staying here the winter. And if we do I will try And get home to See you all I would like to see you all very much I will now bring my letter to a close no more at present
    From your Affection Son Wm. Kingston

July 5, 1862. Letter from Headquarters Bank of James River

Dear father and mother brothers and sisters—
I now take this opportunity of writting these few lines to you to let you know that I am well at present hopping these few lines will find you all the same. I received your letter and was glad to hear from you all I have not been in no regular engagement—yet —but I have been where the shells come over among us pretty ****. We were supporting a battery of *** Oak Swamp and the rebels atacked us there with there Artilery And they killed and wounded a great many mules. And killed and wounded some of our men but —our batery Silenced them towards night we had no muskettery *** fighting there for we tore their bridges up and they couldent get across I received two *** yesterday on the fourth of July one from you and the other from Mary Jane we are very bad of for officers we have not a officer in our company fit for duty. I think they have got the bullet *** we have got—A officer of Company D. To take charge of our company all of our field officers have been sick. Colonel Lieutenant Col. And Major.
We have had some very heavy marching to do sense we have been down here I sent ten dollars home but I dont [know] whether you have received it or not just let me know in the next letter it was sent by our Co ***his brother was to diliver the money our company sent a good bit home that way some of the boys that there parents ***the money and some say that they have not peter shannon is down here with us now And he sends his love to you and Alf sends his also I believe I have [told?] you all at present so I will bring my letter to a close. From your affectionate Sone Wm. Henry Kingston

April 4, 1889, Eliza applied for a pension and testified that her son died on or about the 13th of December, 1862, of a wound to the thigh, incurred at the Battle of Fredericksburg. He was carried from the field by his comrades John Alfred Steele [Is this the Alf mentioned above, who sent his love to all at home?] and William Sewell. The Declaration for an Original Pension of a Father or Mother was signed by John A. Steele, Henderson Scott and Eliza Kingston.

December 19, 1889. A Proof of Dependence form states that the family farm was sold in 1864 to defray the cost of the John Kingston's last sickness and burial. The father had been an invalid. William "was the main support of the family; brothers and sisters; working on, and managing the farm before his enlistment and sending home his earning while in the army-service."

Aquilla Mahan, Company C, 2nd Delaware

Boatman by trade.

July 3, 1863. Slightly wounded at Gettysburg. Hospitalized in Wilmington, Delaware.

5/12/64. Captured at Spottsylvania. Confined to Andersonville Prison. Saw his brother starve to death. Enlisted in the 10th Tennessee CSA.

December 28, 1864. Recaptured by Union at Egypt Station. Confined to Alton, Illinois, Military Prison.

April 14, 1865. Reenlisted in 5th US Vol. Inf.

January **, 1887. Wrote the following letter to Mr. Black.

> Sir I was talking with Senator Hires [?] a few days ago and he said I was marked with desertion from the second delaware Volunteers I enlisted on the 22 day of May 1861 on or about the 10 day of May 1864 I was wounded and left lying by the side of the road and can produce officers who were in command of the regiment at that time and who can certify to the fact I enlisted for 3 years or unless sooner discharged when my term of enlistment expired I was a prisoner of war after serveing a long while in andersonville prison I was shipped to Florence prison where in a dying condition I was influenced to go *** by men that were older and wiser than I and who are now liveing it was understood among us that I was ** in order to get hospital attendance and when I became all [well?] I was to make my escape any way I could to the union lines how can you bring up desertion or disloyalty against me if there was any desertion it would be on the part of the regiment for leaving me in a helpless condition lying by the side of the road for the rebels to capture how can the government bring up such a charge against me after being in the army 3 years and being wounded 3 different times and lying in a Southern prison so long and what is more the agony of seeing a dear Brother starved to death and me powerless to render him any assistance in that horrible andersonville prison The scene of it has never left my mind nor never can be effaced my left side and leg has been effected ever since I was wounded at gettysberg and this winter the rheumatism has taken such a hold of me that when I do work I have to work in agony after going through so much it is so bad to be received in such a light. Respectfully Aquilla S. Mahan

♦ Appendix C: Military and Pension Records of other Cecil County Soldiers ♦

January 6, 1887. His wife also addressed a letter to Mr. Black.
April 4, 1888. Applied for a pension
April 13, 1890. Applied for a pension from Salem, New Jersey. Letter follows.

Dear Sir,
    I see that in the case of 2 applicants for pensions you have rendered a decision that defines the status of prisoners of war who having enlisted in rebel service to escape imprisonment and returned to their comrades are not barred against getting a pension. This bar has been against me for a number of years. I never had but this one thing against me, and now it is lifted. I think there will be no trouble in my getting a pension If you would please look up my claim I would be very thankful. I have suffered more or less since the war from wounds recieved at Getty's-burg, and am in poor health with a large family dependent on me, a pension would be of great benefit. I was in the Company C. 2nd Delaware volunteers. I served 3 yrs. Faithfully. I was about 7 or 8 months in prison. If I don't deserve a pension I don't know who does. The number of my claim is 436008.
                Yours Respectfully
                Aquilla S. Mahan
                Salem New Jersey 49 West Broadway

Annie Mahan wrote to support her husband's claim on January 6, 1887.

Mr. Black or to whom it may concern. I am the wife of Aquilla S. Mahan I have seen all of the written and witnessed statements that we have receved relateing to his plea for pension, and I cant see how it is that you can bring up such a charge against him he being nothing but a boy and being ignorant and uneducated at that after serveing honorably his 3 years out and undergoing Such hardships after his time had expired to my way of thinking the charge is a fraud my husband is a poor miserable sickly war wasted piece of humanity getting more so if possible each and every year he has got a wounded leg that has broken out several times since the war and this winter the rheumatism has taken hold of him in his wounded leg that he is incapable of working a good deal of the time I would like you to give this matter attention as it is if the government would respond to his assistance I shall have the man to maintain in a very short time it is simply outrageous for the claim to lay there year after year nothing being done with it in the face of so much testimony and proof of the man being a brave and loyal soldier the man is not only a wreck in body but in mind also having been out of his mind 2 times since the war and when in that condition he is constantly going over those seens in those horrible Southern prisons years ago The last time he became better in mind he loss his situation that he had held some years on account of his mind being shattered it is a serious drawback to him in getting work when able to do it doctor Sharp was the doctor I employed to attend him when he was out of his mind now you have my story only one of thousands quite like it and for the sake of my 4

♦ Appendix C: Military and Pension Records of other Cecil County Soldiers ♦

children I hope you will give the case all the attention it merits please answer this Very Respectfully Mrs. Annie Mahan. Salem N Jersey

Doctor Edward S. Sharp, M.D., of Salem County, New Jersey, testified as follows:

This is to certify that Aquilla S. Mahan late of Company C. 2nd Delaware Infantry first consulted me in 1874 suffering from varicosity of **** *** veins of left leg caused by shell wound at the battle of Gettysburg and has at intervals been treated by me since that time until the present date, as well as for asthma, hemorrhoids and *** **** from all of which he is still suffering to such a degree as to incapacitate him from manual labor and as he is dependent upon such work for support of himself and family he is in danger unless relief is obtained of becoming an object of charity, especially as his intellectual faculties are obviously impaired from his sufferings, and he cannot secure employment from that cause.

Washington rejected the appeal.

> Department of the Interior. March 3, 1891. Washington. The Commissioner of Pensions. Sir:-
> I return herewith the papers in the claim for pension No. 436,008, of Aquilla Mahan, who was a member of Co. "C". 2nd, Del. Vols.
> The case was considered by the Department on appeal, January 28th 1891, and was on that date returned to your Office for a supplemental report from the records of the War Department.
> The claim was rejected December 10th, 1883, on the ground of disloyalty pursuant to the provisions of section 4716 Revised Statutes, from which action the appeal was taken.
> It appeared from the original report from the War Department that he enlisted May 31st 1861, for three years, and was reported present for duty until wounded at Gettysburg, Pa., July 2nd 1863, from which date he was reported absent, in hospital until December 31st, 1863. He was reported present from then until May 12th, 1864, when he was captured at Spottsylvania, Va., and while a prisoner of war at Andersonville, Ba., he enlisted in the Rebel army; recaptured by the U. S. Forces at Egypt Station, Miss., Dec. 28th, 1864; confined as a prisoner of war at Alton, Illinois Military Prison, and enlisted in the 5th U. S. Infantry, April 14th, 1865. The report did not show that he was ever discharged from that organization.
> The supplemental report shows, however, that he deserted June 16th, 1866, from Fort Reno, D. T., which is the last trace of him shown by the records. It is also stated in said report that the 5th Infantry was composed of rebels — men who were held by the United states forces as prisoners of war. The claimant clearly has no pensionable status, not only because he was never finally discharged from service, but he is barred by the provisions of Section 4716 of the Revised Statutes.

He appears to have been a good union soldier, having served for nearly three year, and received a wound in battle. But this is offset by his subsequent unsavory record.

He took up arms against his government, and when recaptured, his old comrades in arms evidently believed in his disloyalty, for instead of restoring him to his proper place in his command, he was enlisted in an organization composed of disloyal soldiers.

The rejection of the claim is affirmed.

    Very respectfully,
      Cyrus Buss[e]y Assistant Secretary.

George McNeal, Company C, 2nd Delaware

November 1861. On duty as co. cook
June 19, 1861. Enlisted for 3 years at Elkton, Md. Age 19 yrs.
December 13, 1862. Wounded slightly at Fredericksburg
February 18, 1868. Notation. This man while a prisoner of war at Andersonville Georgia enlisted in the 10th Tenn. CS [rebel] Infty. Was captured in arms against the United States at Egypt Station, Miss., Dec. 28th 1864 was confined at Alton Ills. January 23 1865 and enlisted in the 5th US Volunteers April 14, 1865.

Thomas Dougherty Reardon, Company C, 2nd Delaware

Reardon was 5 feet, 10 inches tall, with blue eyes and brown hair. By trade he was a coach maker.
October 11, 1858. Thomas D. Reardon married Helen Amanda Poulson in the Protestant Episcopal Church by Samuel Durborow

Circa 1863 Emma Louisa born.[She was 16 months old when her mother died.]
Circa 1864. Helen Amanda Poulson Reardon died. [Two years before her husband's death.]
July 16, 1864. Reardon apprenticed his daughter to Thomas and Eleanor Williamson. See document below. Williamson states that this took place when Reardon was home for his wife's funeral.

THIS INDENTURE Witnesseth that Emma Louisa Reardon of the township of Londongrove in the County of Chester and State of Pennsylvania by and with the advice and consent of *** said Father Thomas D. Reardon testified by his signing as witness hereto, hath bound and put herself, and by these presents doth bind and put herself Apprentice to Thomas H. and Eleanor Williamson of the township of Londongrove County of Chester and State of Pennsylvania.

  After the manner of an Apprentice, to dwell with and serve the said Thos H. And Eleanor Williamson from the day of the date hereof, for and during and until the full end and term of 15 years 8 [months ?] thence ensuing. During all which term the said Apprentice her said Master faithfully shall serve, and that honestly and obediently in all things, as a dutiful Apprentice ought to do. And the said Thomas H. And Eleanor Williamson shall teach or cause to be taught and instructed, the said Apprentice, in the Art,

trade, and Mystery of a Housewife and shall give his said Apprentice Three months Schooling in Each and Every year of said term of servitude and shall and will find and provide for the said Apprentice, sufficient meat, drink, apparel, washing, and lodging, during the said term; and at the expiration thereof shall and will give his said Apprentice a sufficiency of clothing suitable for such an apprentice and shall keep and provide for said apprentice as long as she lives with them the same as if she was their own child and have adopted her as their own daughter and will provide for her as such.
SEALED AND DELIVERED
IN THE PRESENCE OF

	Her mark
Amos Lamborn	Emma X Louis Reardon
Melchor Shop	T. D. Reardon
Josephine Poulson	Thomas H. Williamson
	Eleanor Williamson

September 29, 1865. Reardon died.

August 19, 1905. Thomas H. Williamson in a General Affidavit swore:

I knew claimants parent before they were married the mother from infancy, the father several years prior to marriage and have a personal knowledge that neither of them were married prior to their marriage to each other. Soldier was sound and in good health prior to and at time of enlistment, the mother died while soldier was in war he came home on a furlough to funeral of wife I was at funeral and I saw her dead in coffin, claimant lived with soldier to the date of her death as he was at funeral, I know that the claimant is the child of soldier and his wife, for at the funeral he made arrangements for me to take his child the claimant and keep her which we did so I am sure that he is there child and deserving of and entitled to a minors pension being 3 2/3 years old when soldier died.

January 16, 1908: In a statement notarized by J. Foster Meck of Blair County, Pa., E. Louisa Reardon Linton wrote:

My father, Thos. D. Reardon, died Sept. 29, 1865, aged thirty three years and three months. This record was taken from the stone which marks his grave in the old cemetery at New London Pres. Church, New London, Chester Co. Pa. And is undoubtedly correct. The stone was placed by my aunt Isabella Apsley, who was my father's only sister. Both she and her husband, W. W. Apsley, have been dead for many years. I know of no one now who could give the names of the physician who attended my father in his last illness.
After the close of the war, after arranging with Thos. H. Williamson and his wife to take care of me and in the event of his death to keep me as their own child, he returned to Washington, D. C. to try to begin life anew. He was greatly broken in health. When Father

Williamson remembers, My mother had died two years before, when I was but sixteen months old. The same stone referred to bears the date of her death also.

None of his family were with him during his last illness. His brothers were notified of his death. Two brothers, Rev. James D. Reardon of Lock Haven Pa. And John V. Reardon, of Elkton, went to Washington and brought him to New London for burial. Both these brothers have been dead several years. My Aunt, Mrs. James D. Reardon is living in Loch Haven, Pa. She wrote a letter staring the above facts, which letter is in the hands of Hon. Tho. K. Stubbs of Oxford, Chester Co., Pa. In this letter she also states what was always understood to be the cause of his [my father's] death. Bowel trouble, the result of disease contracted while in the service.

      Submitted January 16th 1908
       by E. Louisa Reardon Linton
        1717 13th St. Altoona, Pa.

      Office of THEODORE K. STUBBS
        ATTORNEY-AT-LAW
    Oxford, Pa. December 25, 1908

Mrs. L. R. Linton
 Madam.

I think your plan to get your congressman to pass a Special Pension Bill for you, a good one. They asked me to prove cause of soldier's death by Physician. Dec. 11 1908 they asked me for evidence of immediate cause of soldiers death stating your swore Jany 21, 1908, "I always understood cause of death to be bowel trouble but am unable to furnish evidence to prove this as a matter of fact." As I am President of our Borough council I certainly shall take pleasure in presenting your husband's name if we need any engineering done. Your Congressman will present a bill like the sample I enclose granting a pension to you the daughter of a soldier.

I can find a soldier who knew your father, but knows nothing of his sickness, he must have been sick in service, as he was transferred to "Invalid Corps."

I thought the enclosed check for expenses had been cashed but return it, for a new one; in preference to running it through bank. It is unfortunate for us that the death Record by Washington, D. C. Board of Health only dates back to 1866.

I think that you will get through all right yet.

Wishing you a Merry Christmas and a Happy New Year,
          I remain,
          Very Truly,
          Theodore K. Stubbs

♦ Appendix C: Military and Pension Records of other Cecil County Soldiers ♦

December 26, 1908. Letter from Louise Linton.

My understanding of the enclosed paper is that my father objected to having me adopted in a legal way—as he wanted me to have my own family name. At the same time he wanted Thos. H. And Eleanor Williamson to have the undisputed right to claim me as their own child because he did not want any of his own family to get possession of me. There had been some bitter feeling in the family about his going off to war as a volunteer. One of my Uncle's visited my father once during the war while he was ill in a hospital in Washington and he was coldly received by the sick soldier—because this Uncle was a Democrat —and opposed to the war. It may be the illness referred to in a diary of my mother's in which she writes of news being brought her of my father being ill with typhoid fever. When I read of her hardships during that time —of the anxiety—and fear—the struggle of a young and delicate woman with a young child—and the care of her invalid father—of financial losses due to her husband's absence, then of her physical breakdown and death—leaving me only sixteen months old, I can but feel that there is nothing the Government can do however much—that can compensate me for the loss of father, mother, both—in infancy—so that even the memory of them is not mine. They lost everything they had for they were young people just starting in life.

Thos. H. and Eleanor J. Williamson, always loved and cherished me as their daughter. I always called them father and mother. They were people who worked hard, but always provided me a good home. Father Williamson is now eighty-four years old —on his next birthday which will be Jan. 9, 1909.

He has been alone in the world since the death of his cherished wife. For eighteen years he has had his home with my husband and me and our children.

        Louise Linton
        Maiden name E. Louisa Reardon

I meant to state that the fact of my father providing for my future in this way would seem to mean that he either expected to be killed — or was serving in an invalid corps and knew that his health was impaired and that he had not long to live.

Dec. 18, 1915. Louise Linton wrote from Altoona, Pa.

To the Honorable
    The Commissioner of Pensions,
        Washington, D. C.
Dear Sir: -

My father, Thomas D. Reardon, who was a soldier in Company "C", Second Delaware Infantry, in the civil war, died on September 29, 1865, shortly after the close of the War, when the writer hereof was three years old, or thereabouts. I have always believed that I was entitled to a pension, as a soldier's orphan. I made application under Minor Original,

833,764, but have understood that since the rejection of that application, notwithstanding that the same was rejected, I am entitled to the pension allowed to soldier's orphans, from the date of the death of my father, until I arrived at the age of sixteen years.

Will you please send me an Application Blank, so that I can apply for what I believe to be due me as a soldier's orphan, under the General Law.

I am

Respectfully yours,
Louise R. Linton

William Sands, Company C, 2nd Delaware

Sands was 5 feet, 10½ inches, tall, with light complexion, gray eyes, and brown hair. By trade, he was a coach painter.

Born in Philadelphia. The family Bible shows that in his family, Emily was born December 18, 1829; Joseph, June 11, 1832; Wm., August 27, 1833; Emma, October 29, 1836; Matilda, March 19, 1939; Benjamin, September 11, 1841; John, January 1, 1844; Clara, June 23, 1848; Catherine Elizabeth, 1852;

May 27, 1861. At 26 years of age, he enlisted in Co. C., 2nd Delaware, in Wilmington.

June 10, 1861. Appointed sergeant.

August 1861. Detailed for band.

February 9, 1863. Certificate of Disability stated he was convalescent since his enlistment.

February 16, 1863. Discharged. Address is Westville, Gloucester County, NJ.

June 5, 1866. Married Lizzie A. Nield at the Methodist Church in Gloucester, NJ, Ceremony performed by Rev. Molton.

After he left the service, Sands lived in Wilmington, Delaware, for one year; Gloucester City, NJ, for 2 years; Alba, Pennsylvania for 4 years; Gloucester City, New Jersey, 4 years; Rome, Georgia, 1 year; Cartersville, Ga., 7 years; Orlando Florida 11 years, and returned to Gloucester City about 1896.

March 4, 1907. At 73 years of age he filled out a Declaration for Pension form.

May 25, 1912. Under the Acto of May 11, 1912, he filled out another Declaration for Pension form. On this one he signed his name with an X. Witnesses were J. S. Nield and Rena Sands.

June 13, 1915. Sands filled out a form the Pension Office sent him requesting information about his own children. He appears to have written the responses himself. The handwriting is shaky, the dates confused. It appears, though, that by this time his wife had died. The children's names were Rena, Jessie, John, Casie?, Edith, and another whose name is indecipherable.

Finally, at some point, Sands received a pension of $50 per month, which continued until his death.

Dec. 7, 1921. Wm. Sands died.

♦ Appendix C: Military and Pension Records of other Cecil County Soldiers♦

John G. Simpers, Company C, 2nd Delaware
June 19, 1861. Mustered into service.
February 22, 1863. Simpers requested 10-day leave to visit family in Cecil Co.
March 10, 1863. Records contained a pass.

> Captain Jno. G. Simpers Co. "C" 2nd Del Vols will report forthwith for duty to Lieut. Col McKelvey, Com. of Convalescent Camp near Long Bridge Va.
> <u>Guards will pass.</u>
> By command of Brig. Gen. Martindale
> (Military Governor of District of Washington)
> Signed   Henry C. Lockwood

July 3, 1863. Wounded in ride side and hip at Battle of Gettysburg. Simpers was in the "front line of skirmishers...at or near Round Top."
July 9, 1863. Letter from Simpers in Wilmington, Delaware.

> L. Thomas
> Adjt. Genl U. S. A.
> Sir:
>   I have the honor to report my arrival in this town, and to inform you that this will be my Post Office address
> I am Sir Your Obedient
> John G. Simpers
> Captain
> 2nd Reg. Del. Vols.

January 27, 1864. Simpers wrote to Charles J. Smith, Lieut and Adjt., to request a 10-day leave to visit his home.
June 19, 1864. Discharged
Commissioned for one year as Capt. Co. K. 6 Md. Vol.
June 30, 1865. Discharged
February 22, 1879. Married Alice Coale by Rev. Wells at Oxford, Pa.
April 6, 1895. James T. Kelly, 52, came before deputy clerk R. D. Bowland and declared that Simpers was wounded at Gettysburg. The facts were known to him by reason of "my being wounded myself at the time and members of my company relating to me at Field Hospital all that were wounded and that capt. John G. Simpers was among the number."
May 3, 1898. Lived at Colora, Md. Applied for a pension. Justice of the Peace N. A. Nickle. Witnesses: J. H. Hartenstine, Custer R. Brown, and Ernest Rowland.
August 18, 1907. John G. Simpers died.

♦ Appendix C: Military and Pension Records of other Cecil County Soldiers♦

John W. Sowers, Company C, 2nd Delaware
October 11, 1861. Enrolled at Elkton, Maryland, and mustered in in Wilmington, Delaware, for 3 years.
June 16, 1862. Died of sunstroke near Fair Oaks, Virginia.

William H. Sowers, Company C, 2nd Delaware
May 31, 1861. Enrolled at 21 years of age.
June 19, 1861. Mustered in.
September 17, 1862. Antietam. Wounded in the hand.
January 1863. Appointed corporal.
July 2, 1863. Gettysburg. Wounded, slight.
October 13, 1863. Hospitalized in Wilmington, Delaware.
June 16, 1864. Petersburg. Killed in action.

> The records of the Sowers brothers are sparse, indeed. But the *Whig* points out that John was the first of Company C to die, and William was the last.

Samuel Cook Stretch, Company C, 2nd Delaware
Born in Wilmington, Delaware, he was a potter by trade. Stretch was 5 feet, 6 inches tall, with light complexion, blue eyes and brown hair.
October 12, 1854. Married Elizabeth T. Leslie at the 10th Presbyterian Church in Philadelphia by Dr. H. A. Bondman [or Bordman].
June 19, 1861. When he was 27 years old, he was mustered in at Elkton, Maryland.
July 1862. Absent on detached service as hospital clerk.
August to December 1862. Absent, sick in hospital.
November and December 1862. Attached to hospital as cook and entitled to extra pay.
September 17, 1862. Wounded slightly in foot at Antietam.
May 3, 1863. Captured at Chancellorsville, Va.
May 9, 1863. Confined at Richmond, Va.
May 15, 1863. Paroled at City Point, Va.
May 22, 1863. Sent to Washington, DC.
May 29, 1863. Presented at Camp Convalescent, Va.
July 24, 1863. Presented at Camp Convalescent, Va.
November 1863. Special Orders #106. The following named enlisted men will report at these Hdqs at 5½ o'clock P. M. today for fatigue duty, fully equipped and without ****
        Samuel C. Stretch, private 2nd Del. Vols.
        By order Col. Baxter[?]
        Chas. Hatch
November and December 1863. 4 months back pay due—3 mos. and 7 days as 2nd class member of band.

March 1864. Absent with leave.

June 19, 1864. Co. C., Second Delaware, mustered out.

April 15, 1865. Enlisted in Co. K., 215 Pa. Inf..

July 31, 1865. Honorably discharged from Company K. 215th Pennsylvania.

June 14, 1883. Died.

June 18, 1883. Buried.

July 15, 1890. Widow filed for pension.

June 27, 1890. Josephine Elvilson, 61, of 2182 N. 13th Street, Philadelphia, and Mrs. Anna W. Wilson, 62, of the same address, swore to Mrs. Stretch's identity and situation. Mrs. Wilson was a witness at the wedding of Mr. and Mrs. Stretch.

November 12, 1890. William H. Worrall, Kennett Square undertaker, swore that he prepared Samuel Stretch's body for burial and that he was buried in Union Hill Cemetery outside Kennett Square.

September 24, 1891. Elizabeth submitted a statement in which she swore she was destitute, dependent upon the charity of neighbors for fuel and food. She had the care of an epileptic daughter who was in no degree able to contribute to her own support. Notarized by Wm. Polk.

November 12, 1890. John W. Binnex, 56, of Kennett Square, and John M. McGowan, 54, also of Kennett Square, testified to the truth of Mrs. Stretch's situation.

September 18, 1891. On a letterhead of the *Kennett Advance*, the editor, William W. Polk, wrote to the government on behalf of Stretch's widow:

Dear Sir: there is living in this town Elizabeth Stretch, widow of Samuel stretch, a Union soldier **** to being absolutely destitute. She has the care of an imbecile daughter. More than a year ago she made application for pension through Mr. Wray, a Philadelphia attorney. ... a year ago all the evidence asked for by the government was forwarded which included proof of soldier's service, time of his death, time of marriage and of dependence, and she was assured by her attorney that her case was clearly established. [In similar cases]... the pension [was] long ago granted. Can anything be done in the case of this woman or must she go to the almshouse?
        Respectfully, William W. Polk

1899. Dropped from rolls. Failure to claim pension.

William F. A. Torbert, Company C, 2nd Delaware

July 19, 1861. Commissioned Lieutenant by Governor of Delaware.

July 14, 1862. Special Orders. No. 64. Torbert was appointed Aide de Camp to Brig. Gen. French.

August 5, 1862. Torbert asked for a leave of absence "to go to Philadelphia Pa. For the purpose of recovering my health."

September 5, 1862. At Camp Confidence, Dr. G. Grant certified that Torbert was "suffering from incomplete fistula in ano that he has been suffering from the same for two months..."

September 26, 1862. Dr. Mitchell of Elkton wrote: "I do hereby certify that I have operated upon this officer for Fistula in Ano, and that in consequence thereof he is in my opinion unfit for duty.

I further declare my belief that he will not be able to resume his duties in a less period than fifteen days from the expiration of his present leave Oct. 1, to prevent permanent disability." Notarized by Wm. Torbert.

September 27, 1862. Document notarized by Wm. Ricketts, clerk of the circuit court of Cecil Co.

September 29, 1862. Letter from Torbert at his home in Elkton. He states: "The cut that was made in the operation is not entirely healed yet. I hope to be well enough to join you next week."

October 16, 1862. Letter from Wm. H. Pancoast stating that Torbert "has just undergone a surgical operation and will not be fit for duty in less than 15 days from date, as he is still under treatment."

October 31, 1862. Same as above.

Nov. 15, 1862. Letter from 1030 Chestnut St., Philadelphia, Pa.

I hereby certify that Lieut. W. F. A. Torbert Aide de Camp to Gen. French, is yet under treatment and will not be fit for Aug. In a less period than ten days.

Respectfully,
Wm. H. Pancoast, M. D.
Act. Assist. Surgeon
U. S. A.

November 25, 1862. Letter similar to one above.

December 4, 1862. Same.

December 12, 1862. Same.

September 1, 1863. Torbert, on detached service on General French's staff is relieved of duty as adjutant and reassigned to Co. K., Second Delaware, as 1st Lieut. Vice Chas. J. Smith appointed adjutant.

February 1, 1863. Dr. D. McLachlin certified that Torbert was unfit for military duty because he was suffering from acute tonsilitis and inflammation of ****.

August 24, 1863. Letter from Headquarters, Third Army Corps

Captain,

I would most respectfully apply for three (3) days leave of absence to visit Baltimore Md. for the purpose of turning over some important public and private papers to Maj. Wharton, 9th U. S. Infty., with whom I served as Adjutant when he was Colonel of Vols.

Respectfully,
Your Obt servant
W. F. A. Torbert
Lt ADC

October 7, 1863. Letterhead Third Army Corps.

Special Orders, No. 173.   [Extract]

2. Lieut. W. F. A. Torbert A. D. C. Is hereby detailed to inspect the arms of the 99th Penna Vols. And will make a report in compliance with General Orders no. 74. Hd. Qrs. Army of the Potomac dated August 3, 1863.

December 21, 1863. Torbert requested 10 days' leave to "visit Philada on business."

May 16, 1864. Elkton, Md. Torbert wrote to Secretary of War Stanton tendering his resignation from Co. K., 2nd Delaware, "for the purpose of accepting an appointment as Acting Ass't Pay Master in the Navy...."

May 20, 1864. Discharged.

March 28, 1864. Letterhead Head-Quarters Third Army Corps.

> General T. Williams   Asst Adjt General   Army of the Potomac
> General
>
> By directive of Genl French I remained to see everything closed up at these Head Quarters. Will you be kind enough to give me an order which will enable me to leave the army. I turned over all that was necessary for the 2d Corps to Col Walker AAG yesterday.
> Respectfully, Your obt servant,   W. F. A. Torbert   Lt. & ADC

May 20, 1864. Special Orders, No. 182.

> 1st Lieutenant W. F. A. Torbert, 2d Delaware Volunteers, having tendered his resignation, is hereby honorably discharged the service of the United States, he having been appointed Acting Assistant Paymaster, U. S. Navy.

George Turner, Company C, 2nd Delaware

May 31, 1861. Enlisted at age 34. Served as assistant wagonmaster, brigade teamster, and forage master.

June 1864. Married Mary T. Cantwell in M. E. Church in Elkton by Rev. J. D. Curtis.

June 19, 1864. Discharged at City Point, Va.

April 12, 1890. At 67 years of age, he applied for a pension on the grounds that he suffered from varicose veins and heart disease. George A. Blake and J. Polk Racine, who wrote *Recollections of a Veteran*, signed an affidavit verifying Turner's identity.

January 8, 1891. George Blake swore on a Neighbors' Affidavit form:

> That he became acquainted with the said George Turner in the year 1872. He did not know the claimant before his enlistment....he had no disability and his physical condition was good, he being apparently sound and strong and his physical condition did not then prevent him from doing manual labor or interfere with his occupation of a teamster. He was a teamster when I first knew him and he is now. There has been a continuous decline in his physical condition for the lst four or five years. While his mental condition is as good as ever his physical condition has declined fully ¾. His capacity for following his usual occupation is quite limited, he being obliged to decline all heavy work and do only light **** as he cannot lift heavy things. I know these facts from my own knowledge.

April 14, 1894. Dr. John H. Jamar supplied additional evidence of Turner's physical problems and certified that his disability was in no way due "to vicious habits."

Appendix D

"Cheap John" Rowbotham

Everybody called him Cheap John, and he promoted himself as "the poor man's friend." John S. Rowbotham was born in England circa 1820. He became an auctioneer, married Eliza [or Elizabeth] six years his junior, and migrated to the United States. [Not necessarily in that order.]

By 1860, the family was living in Wilmington, Delaware. A relative, Caroline Rowbotham, was a member of their household. There was a 10-year-old daughter who had been born in Pennsylvania; 9-year-old Mary E. was born in Maryland; and 4-year-old John H., in Pennsylvania.

Cheap John established a store on Fourth Street, and then at 412 King Street in Wilmington. While the King Street store was being remodeled, he took his business to Newark, Delaware, where he operated from DeHaven's Hotel. The *Delaware Republican* reported that his way of doing business was novel, and that he was sure to attract a crowd.

He sold household items, wearing apparel, and just about everything else. He'd sell goods for others on consignment. One ad in the *Republican* suggests that he operated a 19th-century pawnshop as well: "If you want to leave your goods for a time—at the highest advance—and redeem them afterwards, go to the store of Cheap John."

On Christmas Day for several years, he gave away a thousand loaves of bread to the poor of Wilmington. The bread was baked by Matthew McCulley on the northeast corner of 6th and Spruce. One black man said, "God bless you, massa." John replied, "He already has or I should not have been able to make you happy today."

It is not clear when John came to Elkton. His ad first appeared in the *Whig* at the end of 1860, but with his first appearance, he was talking of closing and going to Newark. His store was located "on Main Street, opposite McClelland's Store, in what was lately known as Mahan's Flour Store, ELKTON, Md."

On January 5, 1861, Cheap John responds to "a number of citizens," who ask him not on any account to leave Elkton. His response follows:

> At the solicitation of a large number of citizens of the town of Elkton and vicinity, I will condescend to stay here for a limited time longer. As I am the Poor Man's Friend, I shall stay to accommodate the poor, and prove that to the satisfaction of all. I shall continue to have a Fresh Supply of Goods every day. I have now a very fine new lot of CLOTHING just came down.   Yours respectfully,
>
>   CHEAP JOHN

Appendix D: "Cheap John" Rowbotham

During the spring of 1861, Rowbotham returned to England to settle an estate, but he reappeared in late June after eleven weeks. That fall the *Republican* noted that "Cheap John did not take out an auctioneer's license this year, but he continues to keep the store, and it continues to keep him...."

The following year, Rowbotham offered to supply coal oil for Elkton's street lamps if the town authorities would install them. He found another merchant willing to donate a dozen posts. "Come," urged *The Cecil Whig*, "let us have the street lamps, now that the fire engines are in good order and are not to be any more expense."

Cheap John joined Enoch Crouch in hiring Jacob Rambo to build a "large ice cream saloon and refectory" at the east end of Elkton on Crouch's lot. The 20-foot by 35-foot structure featured an octagonal pavilion for picnics and cotillion parties. Visitors could enjoy the bowling green and other recreational facilities. While Crouch's establishment was mentioned afterward, Cheap John's connection there seems to have been severed when he eventually closed his general store.

Rowbotham was mentioned in the proceedings of Orphans' Court when he sent a free black man, John Manluff, with a wagon load of goods from his store in Wilmington to the Elkton branch. Deputy Sheriff E. W. Janney arrested Manluff because he did not obtain permission to leave Delaware and enter Maryland. The unfortunate driver, whose only crime was doing his day's work, was fined $20 and costs.

In 1863, Cheap John pulled out of Elkton, selling his store to Robert C. Levis and Thomas Merrit. He then based his grocery and dry goods operation entirely in Wilmington.

In a diary, James McCauley of Leeds mentions his departure: "Cheap John is preparing to leve [*sic*] town where he has been for a year past puffing himself as the poor man's friend. I bought a carpenter's level."

Rowbotham faded from view until a fracas involving Maryland men outside his Wilmington store would have reminded Cecil Countians of their old friend. "Another ball struck an iron awning post and glanced through one of the splendid plate glass windows of the famous Cheap John. We believe they succeeded in arresting nearly all of them. Whiskey as usual, was the cause of the whole disturbance. The only person seriously hurt was a small jackass in cheap John's window, which we believe lost its tail."

The Cecil Democrat cast a jaundiced eye upon Rowbotham, due in part no doubt to their political differences. In deploring Maryland's preference for dealing with strangers, the paper noted in 1865, two years after he had pulled out of Elkton: "But let a 'Cheap John' come to town, and he can hardly get clerks enough to wait on the crowds that throng to his store. If they get cheated, so much the better, they will praise him the louder to keep people from knowing it."

The *Whig* was friendlier and reported seeing Rowbotham on a train bound for another new store in the spring of 1865. "His universal goaheaditive merchandising genius has already established a store in Petersburg, where he is astonishing the played out secesh of the Old Dominion by a touch of that genuine Yankee skill which rivals the alchemist in the art of turning baser metals to gold."

Now John and his family disappeared. Perhaps further research will pick up his trail in Wilmington or in the South. In his own time, though, he grabbed readers' attention by his outlandish advertisements in local papers.

At the end of 1861, Cheap John ran an ad that is read from bottom to top of each column, starting at the lower right and reading the columns right to left.

MACHINE POETRY
by Cheap John

John's style	Him smile	Evermore	Other store
To get into	It often makes	Now and	Than any
Know	A way	Will both	Goods
Try all they	In such	Always	And fresher
The rest	His goods	Too and	Sells more
To see	John gets	And cheaper	Cheap John

In 1862, the column-long promotion takes the form of "A New Catechism." The answer to each question is CHEAP JOHN. Who was the first man that had the nerve to put goods down to their right prices? Who was the first man to sell molasses at 7, 8, and 10 cents per quart? Who was the first man to cut the ladies' gaiters down from $1.75 to $1.25, and men's long boots from $8.00 to $1.75.

Periodically, the questions in the "catechism" change, but the answers remain the same. By the end of the year, John addressed an advertisement...

To All Whom It May Concern
BE IT KNOWN
That I have associated with me MR. JOHN HART of Lancaster, Penna., for the purpose of enhancing the business heretofore carried on by me.

If one JOHN can do for the people what I have done, certainly TWO can do a great deal more.

The business now at CHEAP JOHN's will be conducted on a vigorous scale.

The name of JOHN should be revered above all others. Take for example John Smith, the notorious; CHEAP JOHN, the victorious; John Vanhaser, the glorious; Rev. John Chambers, the precarious; John McDonough, the spontorious; John M. Clayton, the senatorious; John B. Gough, the great ex-whiskeytorious, [no allusions to Cheap John], John Brown, the gallowerious; John Keyser, the Marshallorious, John Bell, the traitorious; John B. Breckinridge, the cowardorious, and John B. Floyd, the thiefarious, and so on to the end of the chapter.
We intend to petition the Governor to have all male children born in Maryland in the month of December named John in honor of the great event above named.   Yours, CHEAP JOHN & CO.
   Mackerel 6 cts. Per lb.; by Bbl. $9.00; Half-Barrel, $4.50; Fourth-Barrel, $2.75.

♦ Appendix D: "Cheap John" Rowbotham ♦

Cheap John must have had time on his hands in 1862, for he wrote another long ad for the *Democrat* in August in which he takes a few pot shots at competitors.

> If you should by chance at anytime drop into Elkton enroute for Cheap Goods and not exactly know where the place is to get such goods, just walk cautiously along the main street, and if you should come to a store, look in and if the proprietor is sitting ready a paper, be shure [*sic*] that is not Cheap John's. Go on further still, and if you should happen to look in and see the clerks playing checkers, and signs on the outside called Cheap New Cash Store and all that sort of stuff, you would be very much estray to take that for Cheap John's. Go on again quietly and still further, and if you should see about one-half of a store hanging outside the building exposed to the weather, and if you should see some half-dozen dogs come in turns and measure the height of the boots, buckets and oil cloths, and then pass on to another store of the same kind, it would be madness to think that was Cheap John's. Now change your course and walk cautiously back, and if you should see a respectable and substantial larger brick building, with the door in the center, and two large bulk windows each side, no goods nor signs hanging outside at all, walk in. If the first thing you see is a large lot of 62 cent Floor Oil Cloth marked 45 cents a yard, and Stair Oil Cloth 13 cts. Look to the right, and if you see two pretty young ladies with each a yardstick in their hands, and a smile on their countenance, as busy as they can be measuring of 8, 10, and 12 cents calicoes, or 6-¼ Berages, 12 cent Delaines, Brocades, Mohairs, Valentias, Alpacas, or showing the cheapest Ladies Hose and Sun-Umbrellas in the State, begin to feel a little easy; then cast your eyes over on the other side, and if you see about four male clerks weighing up 8, 9, and 10 cent Sugar or Apples at 7 cts. Or if you see a great rush in the cellar with jugs of all denominations for Syrup and Molasses at 40 cts. per gallon, Sugarhouse at 25 cts. And from 40 to 100 people in the store and everything looks pleasant and tidy, you can then make up your mind that you are in no less a place than the headquarters of the great original Cheap John's, the poor man's friend, who deal right with everybody, and will never deviate from that purpose.

The next week the editor of the *Democrat* added in a note that "business is business and Cheap John is doing it up brown at his headquarters for cheap goods in Elkton. Cheap John's store is the general rendezvous for the poor, who want to buy cheap and the most for their money."

Was he a charlatan or a philanthropist? Whatever motivated Cheap John Rowbotham may never be known. But he held Cecil County's attention, however briefly, in the mid-nineteenth century.

BIBLIOGRAPHY

Headley, John W. *Confederate Operations in Canada and New York*. New York: The Neale Publishing Company, 1906.

Manakee, Harold R. *Maryland in the Civil War*. Baltimore, Maryland: Maryland Historical Society, 1961.

Mitchell, Reid. *Civil War Soldiers: Their Expectations and Their Experiences*. New York: Simon & Schuster, 1989.

Portrait and Biographical Record of Harford and Cecil Counties Maryland. New York & Chicago: Chapman Publishing Co., 1897.

Racine, J. Polk. *Recollections of a Veteran or Five Years in Dixie*. Elkton, Maryland: The Appeal Printing Office, 1894.

Scharff, J. Thomas. *History of Delaware, 1609-1888*. Philadelphia, Pa.: L. J. Richards & Co., 1888.

Trial of John H. Surratt in the Criminal Court for the District of Columbia. Washington: Government Printing Office, 1867.

Wheeler, Richard. *Witness to Gettysburg*. New York: Meridian, 1987.

Newspapers and Periodicals

Bulletin of the Historical Society of Cecil County

Uppershoreman

The Cecil Democrat

The Cecil Whig

The Perryville Record

Index

Antietam, 136–40, 143, 145
Arelia, Margaret, 214
Army
    artillery, 64
    branches of, 64
    Cecil's quota, 130
    insignia, 63–64
    pay, 66
    weapons, 64–66

Barr, Capt. J. J., 119
Bay View, 257
Benjamin, George W., 173–75
Bennett, Henry, M., 143, 306
Bennett, John, 143
Big Elk, letters, 44, 47, 48, 50, 53, 58, 61, 66, 82, 86, 90, 93, 97, 103, 107, 108, 117, 145, 148, 150, 156, 157, 160
Bonds, Government, 221
Brown, Rev. Joseph T., 116, 168, 208, 296

Cameron, Stephen F., 266, 302–5
Cecil Guards, 29, 31, 46
Cheap John, 4, 84, 102, 159, 213, 265, 325–28
Churches, 81–82
C. J., letters, 169, 175, 179, 200–202
Coin, two-cent, 231
Crazy Delawares, 160
Creswell, J. A. J., 54
Cummings, J. Frank, 60, 68, 69

Davis, I. D., 277
Dentists, 92
Draft dodgers, 135
Dysart's Tavern, 18–19

Eastern Shore Regiment, pay, 73
Elkton Academy, 12–13, 232, 238
Elkton Public School Program, 112–13
Ellis, Dr. Charles Manley, 35, 120–21, 128, 169
Emancipation Proclamation, 166

Faehtz, Capt. E. F. M., 62, 103, 172, 260, 276
Farmington Lyceum, 30
Flags, significance of, 57
Ford, Samuel, 173–75, 202–4
Foreacre, Isaac, 306
Fort Delaware, 145, 220, 197–98
Frenchtown Railroad, 10–11

Gettysburg, 196

Habeas corpus, 52
Hardy, George, 307
Harvey, Wm., 307
Hill, Joseph C., 297
Holly Hall, 11–12
Horse racing, 110, 267
Horses, dead, 242–43
Hospital fire, 187
Howard Guard, 108
Howard House, 152

J. G., letter, 98, 100
Jail, Elkton, 43–44
Jeffries, Wm., 222–24
    Sophia Harvey, 222–24
Jordan, Ephraim, 308–10

Kingston, William Henry, 310–12

Index

Lincoln, assassination, 263–64; 1860 election, 23–24, 25
Lists,
  draftees, 225
  teachers, 257
  traders, 124
  union supporters, 28

Mackall, Wm. Whann, 46
Maffitt Zouaves, 55
Mahan, Aquilla, 312–15
Maryland, 5th Reg. Vols., 98, 102, 139, 147, 163, 182, 213, 232, 239
Maryland, 6th Reg. Vols., 132, 153, 210, 216, 219, 244, 251, 262, 269, 297
McGuire, Andrew, 38
McIntire, Henry, 119, 166–68
McNeal, George, 315
Mills, 9–10
Mitchell, Dr. H. H., 152
Mitchell, Rev. Mr., 74
Money, counterfeit, 38
Moving Day, 177
Mule School, 76–80; auction 106

Ottley [Ottley], Robert, 145, 152

Physicians, 92
Pivot Bridge, 272–73
Plank road, 15–17
Prize fighting, 202
Purnell's Legion, 133, 140

Reardon, Thomas Dougherty, 315–19
Red tape, 177
Ricketts, Capt. Benjamin, 40, 73, 121–22, 140–43, 160, 162, 188, 278–79, letters, 280–93. *See* also Big Elk.
Ricketts, Charlotte Carter, 73, 205. *See* letters, 280–93.

Roman, Joseph R., 168
Rowan, John, 56, 198, 255–56
Rowbotham. *See* "Cheap John"

Sands, Wm., 319
Schools, 134, 256, 276
Sempers, Dr. C. T., 295–96
Simpers, John, G., 320
Slavery, 19–23
Slaves, 25, 33, 171
Smith, Charles J., 138–39, 189–95
Snow's, [Alonzo] Battery, 56, 128, 144, 181, 212, 226–28, 248
Soldiers, pay, 37, 66
  black, 212, 217, 239, 240
  daily schedule, 50
Sowers [Souers], John W., 321
  Wm. C. 202, 321
Stretch, Samuel Cook, 321–22
Susquehanna, 15, 197

Tax, assessment, 221
  internal revenue, 252, 253, 262
Tilghman, Tench, 67–68
Torbert, W. F. A., 127
Touchstone, James, 131, 133, 153–56, 298
Turner, George, 324

Wedding, 246–47
West Nottingham Academy, 232, 238
Wilson, Columbus Washington, 293–94
Wilson, John B., 182–84

975.2 GAR POR
Garrett, Jerre.
  Muffled drums and mustard spoons : Cecil County, Maryland, 1860-1865